NO INDIVIDUAL HEROES:

Ouray Mountain Rescue Team

D1602432

Karen Mollica Risch

For Mary & Ken –
Enjoy!

Karen Mollica Risch

WESTERN REFLECTIONS PUBLISHING COMPANY®

Lake City, Colorado

ISBN 978-1-937851-45-3
Library of Congress Control Number: 2018954339

Printed in the United States of America

Cover and book design by Laurie Goralka Design

Western Reflections Publishing Company®
P. O. Box 1149
951 N. Highway 149
Lake City, Colorado 81235
www.westernreflectionspublishing.com
(970) 944-0110

Contents

*To those who respond in the darkest nights, the hottest
days, monsoon and blizzard –*

O brave new world that hath such people in't!
Shakespeare, **The Tempest**

Foreword

"THE TEAM MEMBERS OF OURAY MOUNTAIN RESCUE (OMRT) are in a unique position to make positive things happen in difficult situations, and we do." Such is the spot-on insight of long-time team member Sam Rushing.

And "unique" serves as the operative word here, as all aspects of this rescue work accomplished over more than four decades demonstrate elements of singularity.

Unique can start with the wonderfully rugged and beautiful terrain – steep stuff that invites many mishaps – found within the confines of Ouray County. Next we have a group of thirty-or-so dedicated, trained, generous volunteers (and over ten times as many involved over the forty-four years) ready to drop whatever's going on in their regular lives to respond for people in peril. Sure, there are rescue organizations most anywhere there are big mountains. But how many can claim a handful of members who own and / or teach in a Ouray-based, world-renowned outfit called "Rigging for Rescue"?

Then we count the amazing support of an appreciative Ouray County community. When the rescue team outgrew its one-truck-plus-closet garage bay in the ambulance barn at City Hall and launched an ambitious fundraising project to build a new rescue facility, community members responded with necessary six-figure support. For a decade now, the two-story barn on the edge of the Uncompahgre Gorge has served the team, and thus local outdoor adventurers, well.

My first association with the team was as a newspaper editor. I had acquired the *Ouray County Plaindealer* and *Ridgway Sun* in 1995 and quickly realized that, man, reporting news of what goes on here amid these tall mountains was, well, unique and often extreme.

I grew up and newspapered in the Sangre de Cristo foothills of New Mexico, where terrain was non-technical and rescue involved, maybe once a decade, a sheriff's posse search. Ouray, as reflected in the newspaper story assignments, was a whole 'nother world. Such as the Saturday afternoon when I was reading on the south porch of my Fourth Avenue home next to the Presbyterian Church. All of a sudden I heard a horrific screech and crash. I looked up to see a huge plume of dust emanating from the lookout hairpin above town … a brakeless semi off the edge, two people trapped on the hillside. Who you gonna call? Mountain Rescue, of course.

I'm convinced the *Plaindealer*'s subscription level has historically far exceeded its home city's population because 1. People love our unique little town (with many summer residents), and 2. because the news content reflected the unique mountain lifestyle and incidents requiring Rescue Team callout.

Ouray being a small town, my ace reporter was dating the then OMRT captain. Suffice it to say she had a pretty reliable source of rescue news, and her reports were thorough, popular and often dramatic. Meanwhile, I got to know the local glass blower, the aforementioned Sam Rushing, and got hooked on some of his first-hand team action accounts. Some four years after my Ouray relocation, I was a team trainee.

On the squad at that time was a couple who had retired from Colorado's Front Range and built their dream home on lower Ninth Avenue. Bob Risch, though, was no newcomer, but a Ouray native. Karen was training the team's first-ever rescue dog, the lovable lab Lyra, whose nose would help in searches and avalanche scenarios.

The low-key Risches and other team veterans quickly demonstrated to the newbie that any mission was all about outcome. Egos had no place in the equation. Sure, some teammate had to rappel down into the "hole" to a fallen ice climber, but that choice centered solely on the best outcome, and not whose turn it was to be in the newspaper photo.

I also came to rapidly understand that team emergency responses that end up in the headlines constitute just part of overall activity. Behind every sensational story lie countless hours of training, fundraising, refreshing equipment, balancing checkbooks, selling T-shirts, performing community outreach, keeping team vehicles ready, barn septic tank maintenance, and on and on.

As you read the stories Karen Risch has exhaustively researched and excellently compiled, themes of motivation will emerge among the past and current team members. These volunteers have given their time, expertise, energy and personal expense to meet a vital community safety need. Or probably better put at the most basic level – "a fellow human being needs help. I have the ability to provide it, and I do."

Over these years, skills, techniques and protocols have advanced to where the Ouray Mountain Rescue Team can rightly be considered a world-class organization. This book helps recognize the tremendous "get-er-done" origin of those amazing folks back in the 70s who didn't enjoy the options of high-tech gear and modern rope work.

Through its history, OMRT has exhibited the constant as an organization of volunteers who expect nothing in return other the satisfaction of knowing they are a part of a team in a unique position to help people, serve the public and save lives.

Truly unique. Enjoy the stories and be safe out there.

David Mullings

Beginnings

J.J. GIBBONS was a Catholic priest stationed in Ouray from 1888 to 1892. In a short book of sketches, *In the San Juan*, Father Gibbons relates some of the events that happened during his tenure. One of those stories was the unfortunate tale of the miner Billy Maher who had a small cabin and mine high in Governor Basin at an elevation of over 12,000 feet.

One morning in late February Billy went to retrieve several sticks of dynamite he had been thawing in the warming oven of his stove. The sticks, including one in his hand, exploded, destroying the cabin and blowing the stove through the roof. Billy was blown across the room under a bunk where he lay seriously injured, blind and almost totally deaf. His partner, who had been washing dishes, was shocked by the blast but otherwise not seriously wounded. Once he determined that Billy was still alive, he promptly set off to find assistance, which would be available at a larger mine – the Terrible – located less than a mile away. Unfortunately, the trip to the Terrible required thrashing through several feet of snow without the benefit of skis or snowshoes, which – though available – he did not know how to use. He finally reached the boarding house of the Terrible, thoroughly soaked and completely exhausted, seven and a half hours later.

A rescue team of four miners prepared the equipment necessary to retrieve Billy and bring him back, first to the Terrible boarding house, and then to transport him to a lower elevation. On the way to Billy's cabin the rescuers stopped by another nearby operating mine, the Virginius, to arrange for a backup team to assist in the later transport. Four Virginius miners agreed to meet the first team at the Terrible boarding house several hours later and continue the downhill transport from there.

The first group struggled up towards Billy's cabin as dusk and an increasing snowstorm steadily enveloped them. They eventually located him, huddled with his dog in a splintered bunk, but still alive. They wrapped him as best they could and fabricated a makeshift sled to transport him back downhill. The snowstorm continued to increase in intensity and the trip was exhausting to the point that it was uncertain if it could be completed. At one point, when the team was crossing a low point before beginning a steep climb to the mine, the thunderous roar of an unseen but nearby avalanche startled them.

When the exhausted rescuers finally reached the mine, they were dismayed to discover that the promised reserve team from the Virginius had not arrived. They were thus left with no option other than to continue the transport toward Ouray on their own, which they proceeded to do.

When the rescuers returned to the Terrible the afternoon of the following day they encountered a Virginius miner and began berating him for the failure of the promised support team to appear. On being informed that the four-person team had in fact left for the Terrible at dusk the evening before, it became immediately obvious that a second, even more tragic, disaster had occurred. Confirmation came on reaching the avalanche path where, first a hat, and then a protruding hand were seen on the surface. Three of the four would-be rescuers had died immediately in the dense snowpack but one trapped miner had apparently survived for several hours, before freezing to death, unseen and unheard in the darkness. Billy, meanwhile, having seemingly lost the will to live in blindness, died within a few days at the Ouray Miners' Hospital.

Billy Maher's story is but one of hundreds, if not thousands, of disasters and rescues that occurred in the first hundred years of the San Juan mining era. The thousands of miners, working either large mines or smaller prospects, were in constant danger from both their hazardous occupation and unforgiving environments. However, when the inevitable accidents or other tragedies befell them, other occupants of the alpine zone were generally not far away. The miners and their eventual families knew and swiftly executed their responsibilities to care for each other.

One hundred years later, in the 1970s when mining had largely ended in the San Juans, a differently motivated and less communally protected population began invading the mountains. They would require a different type of rescue-support system. What follows is the story of that Ouray Mountain Rescue Team.

Bob Risch

Preface

IN THE MAGNIFICENT MOUNTAINS of southwestern Colorado, adventurers and travelers all too often underestimate or ignore the laws of physics. This book features some of the more unusual and riveting of these events. If they are lucky, people survive their all-too-human encounters with the forces of gravity – falling rock or ice, cascading snow, gushing water.

In the past, fellow miners, travelers, friends and neighbors pulled the unfortunate from avalanches and rockfall. Today, they often owe their transformed lives to small, enduring cadres of men and women like the Ouray Mountain Rescue Team, formed in 1974. Where possible, their encounters with Nature are told from multiple viewpoints, for in a complicated and death-defying rescue, no one person sees everything. Both victims and rescuers have amazing tales to tell, many of them now one to four decades old. Sometimes the victims are unlucky and the natural world prevails, in spite of heroic human effort and efficient machines.

This is also a history of the team, how and why it was born, the unending schemes for funding and equipment, the personalities and perseverance of its members. From 1974 through 2018, 353 men and women have trained and served. Two have thirty years of service, two have twenty-five, nine have twenty, and thirty-six have served ten years or more. They come from diverse walks of life: artists, teachers, doctors, lawyers, engineers, business people, outdoor guides, students and military veterans. Some were teenagers, some fifty years older. Many have finely honed outdoor skills, have hiked and summited the mountain ranges of the world, explored caves and waterways, skied powder and glaciers, worked aboard ships, run marathons. Others joined and became skillful navigating the harsh and beautiful world of the outdoors. Still others offered their talents in documentation, artistic creation and commerce.

New members soon anticipate frequent callouts near the end of the day, sometimes at night if the need is urgent, and it often is. A tired climber stumbles descending Mt. Sneffels, an ice pillar gives way, a Jeep spins off an icy mountain road, an ATV or motorbike misses a curve, hikers are overdue, ordinary people vanish. In the remote backcountry of Ouray County, it's not unusual for hours to pass before help arrives. The victim's companions may have to downclimb a mountain and hike to a trailhead before driving a steep dirt track for help. No one may have witnessed an accident until a snowplow driver sees tracks leading off a highway's edge in the night.

Rescues proceed in moonlight and snowstorms, on hot summer afternoons on high trails, in shadowed gorges with falling ice. Dinner cools on the stove, a business closes, a party is disrupted by the call for help. Rescuers keep their seasonally adjusted packs, gear and boots in their cars, ready to respond: winter, spring, summer, fall. Year round training – on ice and snow, in water and gorges, on trails and jeep roads – helps to anticipate these calls. Anyone who can walk, ride, drive, ski, snowshoe or climb may also need rescuing.

"Anyone, anytime, anywhere" – the team motto – is unusually accurate. Strings of rescues, including three in a day or five in a week, do happen. Then, the twenty-five or so members are stretched thin and reserve members respond. Often, the larger community helps too. Firemen, miners, ranchers, county and city employees and citizens donate muscle power, coffee and food; they transport victims in their trucks when ambulances break down. In unusually large and specialized rescues, other counties send their teams and law enforcement to help. Assistance may come from large military bases on Colorado's Front Range or elite military training units in the form of helicopters or from statewide rescue organizations. OMRT is not only formed from the larger community, it relies upon other citizens and specialists as well. It represents the best of human endeavor and aspiration translated into action.

Karen Mollica Risch

Acknowledgements

The record keepers:
Plaindealer editors Joyce Jorgenson, who chronicled the beginning; Guy and Marcia Wood, David Mullings, Alan Todd and Beecher Threat, who enhanced the record; and forty-four years of dedicated reporters.

Secretaries, mission writers, archivists, photographers, cartoonists.

The men and women of OMRT who shared memories, even the terrible ones. The librarians of Durango, Montrose, the Western History Collection of the Denver Public Library, the American Alpine Club. The Ouray County Coroners.

The inspired and the passionate:
Kurt and Lynn Kircher, Rick Trujillo, Mike Hamrick, Doug Walker, Elwood Gregory, Laszlo Kubinyi, George Pasek, Charlie Ricker, Jerry Wakefield, Dr. Dave and June Bachman, Mary Hoeksema, Otto Scheidegger, Rick and Peggy Lyon, Pete Smith, Jerry Roberts, Bill MacTiernan, Bill Dwelley, Bill Whitt, Randy Gerke, Sam Rushing, Steve Lance, Tim Eihausen, Dr. Dave Sherwood, Mike and Joanie Gibbs, Sean and Jenny Hart, David Mullings, Mark and Colette Miller, Erin Eddy, Jeff and Nicole Skoloda, Don Carlton, Kevin Koprek, Matt Hepp, Mike MacLeod, Tricia Eischied, Kim Miller, Tim Pasek, Ruth Stewart, Tom Kavanaugh.

The transcribers:
Rebecca Irey, Chris Tetrault, Lynn Kircher, Debra Braden.

Those who lived to tell about it:
Art Porter, Earl Ellis, Betty Leavengood, Dan Bender, Joe and Linda Sullivan, Gary Ryan.

The lawmen / women:
Jerry Wakefield, Dominic Mattivi, Jr., Sue Kurtz, Eric Berg, Warren
Waterman, Tom Gilmore, Rick Rowan.

Readers and critics:
Bob Risch, who lived some of these events; Nancy Mollica Ihnat,
persistent and appreciative; Amy Risch, Ralph Risch, Trina Mollica
Alexander, Chuck Mollica, Mark Mollica; Jerry Roberts, David
Mullings, Rick Trujillo, Bill MacTiernan, Bill Whitt, Sam Rushing,
Jenny Hart, Jeff Skoloda, Debra Braden.

Publishers and editors: P. David & Jan Smith, Western Reflections
Publishing.

The proceeds from these stories will be donated to OMRT.

CHAPTER ONE

1974-1977
"Some of us could've gotten killed"

TOM MOUREY DID NOT INTEND to spend the night of June 16, 1974, on Mt. Sneffels. He and three companions began their descent of the Snake Couloir in a high sun that warmed their bodies. Suddenly, an ice chunk loosened and his body accelerated, tumbling 1,500 feet down the narrow rocky chute into rocks jutting out of the snow. His wife Donna and friends descended the treacherous route, found him alive but sprawled in pain on Blaine Basin's prominent snowfield. The women stayed while Robert Just ran three miles to the trailhead, drove to a ranch and reported the three-hour old accident.

Ouray County Sheriff Art Dougherty immediately called Army Medical Air Service Transport (MAST) and Sky Choppers, a helicopter outfit in Durango. Pilot "Spike" Kinghorne, was fighting a fire at Mesa Verde. Diverted to the icy heights of Ouray County, he hovered over the basin that evening, but could get no closer than 500 yards to Mourey, had no long line to pick up a litter, and knew that if he landed at 12,500 feet, he might not lift off again.

Sheriff Dougherty alerted local mountaineer Kurt Kircher at 7 p.m. He drove to the 9,400-foot trailhead at Willow Swamp with Police Chief Keith Kelley. Kinghorne dropped them into the basin, where they planned to carry Mourey 500 yards to a spot where the helicopter could land but decided it was too dangerous. Kinghorne flew in a slab from a picnic bench so they could stabilize Mourey. Montrose Deputy Sheriff Warren Waterman arrived with a backboard and blankets and Kinghorne dropped them into the basin at dusk.

Chief Kelley, wearing only boots, jeans and a light jacket, sat in the snow in twenty-degree temperatures, holding Mourey to prevent his

Mt. Sneffels, 14,150', June 1974: Avalanche tracks are visible in the upper center of Blaine Basin's massive snowfield. The Snake Couloir extends upward to the right.

Photo by Rick Trujillo

slipping farther downhill. Mourey was conscious, but back, head and internal injuries made every movement agonizing. He was in such terrific pain that Kircher said they gave him Demerol to get him through the night. Several lawmen spent the night at Willow Swamp near the trailhead with a mobile radio, but couldn't communicate with them until Monday when Kinghorne flew in a compatible device.

Monday morning, a powerful Huey jet helicopter from Ft. Carson in Colorado Springs flew into Montrose. Pilot Philip Prather and crew stripped every unnecessary item – including doors and seats – for a high-altitude rescue and took off with minimum fuel. The Huey at full power reached the accident site at its "altitude ceiling." In the cool air, Kinghorne landed his small chopper in Blaine Basin and radioed weather information to the Huey. Deputy Waterman listened from the trailhead. "It really stuck in my mind ... the radio traffic between the two chopper pilots." He realized how "essential that was to have someone on the ground who understood" what the other needed. Prather radioed Kinghorne, asked if he had Mourey's family.

"I've got the wife here with me."

"I want them to understand that when I pick him up, if I start to go down, I'm cutting him loose. There's never been a rescue made from this altitude before and I don't know what's going to happen. I will not endanger three people's lives for one."

"Let's go ahead with it."

Kinghorne's transmission of wind speed and direction gave the military pilot crucial information as he orbited and lowered a long line and hook uphill from the patient. Wearing a big glove on his hand to protect himself from the electrically charged cable, Kircher caught the line as it went by at twenty to forty miles per hour, ran downhill and hooked it to the litter. The Huey flew over the watchers at Willow Swamp, heading toward Montrose Memorial Hospital (MMH) twenty miles away. It landed in the parking lot with just minutes of fuel left. Mission commander Capt. John Tragis told Sheriff Dougherty that he thought this was the first successful helicopter rescue ever made from 12,500 feet.

Medical help came none too soon. "It was the kind of thing that they make movies about, but you don't quite believe it," said Doug Walker, who was with the base ground crew. "They said he had minutes to live." After X-rays in Montrose, the Army helicopter flew Mourey to St. Anthony's Hospital in Denver for surgery. Later, he transferred to the paraplegic rehabilitation program at Craig Hospital in Englewood. The Montrose Search and Rescue (SAR) veteran would never walk again. There was "no bitterness," he told Walker. "These aren't the cards I would've dealt myself, but it's what I got and I'm going to do the best I can with it."

◆ ◆ ◆

Just eight days later, four teenagers were "horsing around" unroped on Sneffels' north side after ascending from the south. At 2 p.m., fifty feet below the summit, Michael Bolger, fifteen, slipped while chopping footholds in the ice. After watching his friend roll and bounce 1,800 feet down a snow chute, Jonathon Koehler, eighteen, climbed to the summit, hurried down the southeast side – the

Michael Bolger's body rested within 300 yards of where Thomas Mourey lay eight days earlier. One unshod foot is visible.

Photo by Rick Trujillo

standard climbing route – and found the Camp Bird Mine. Lee Richardson, the mine watchman's wife, reported the accident at 4. Steven Bolger, eighteen, and Emmet Gray, seventeen, descended the chute to Michael Bolger. A Colorado Fish and Game plane appeared and pilot Gordon Saville, using a loudspeaker, asked about the fallen boy's condition. The teens lay down in the snow to indicate a fatality.

◆ ◆ ◆

Kircher, fifty-six, Walker, twenty-nine, Rick Trujillo, twenty-six, and Mike Hamrick, twenty-nine, hiked into Blaine Basin, built a fire at timberline and huddled around it. "It was getting late," said Trujillo, "so we decided to camp (bivouac) at tree line and retrieve the body the next day." They had "no provisions for camping because we expected it to be a rapid recovery.... This was the era of survival kits and Doug had a space blanket along, which we used to reflect heat from the camp fire...." The next morning they passed "a fully laced, empty boot" before they found the body, 300 yards from where Mourey had landed. The boy's neck was broken, most of his clothes and boots missing. They bagged and lowered his slender body over slick snow to the trail and transferred it to Chief Kelley's horse.

Sheriff Dougherty said the young man's death was probably instantaneous. He was indignant that the teens said they used the climbing book, *Guide to the Colorado Mountains,* and thought that Mt. Sneffels was an easy climb. The southeast route, accessed from Yankee Boy Basin, is a fairly easy route with some scrambling required, but the boys were on a technical summit route, with little climbing experience and no gear except ice axes.

◆ ◆ ◆

Earlier that month, a false alarm on the Chief Ouray Trail east of town sent Kircher and Walker, who thought someone was in trouble because of mirror flashes from Cascade Mountain, hiking an hour uphill. They found a woman and four children signaling relatives in town. "That is when it really all started," said Kircher. "We decided we ... better do something about it." The Sneffels' recoveries proved Ouray needed an official mountaineering response, marking a departure from the past. For ninety-eight years, miners, firemen, Sheriff's Posse, other agencies and volunteers rescued unfortunate workers and travelers from mine accidents, canyons and avalanches. But this was before backcountry use in Colorado exploded in the late 60s and early 70s and many new recreationalists found themselves in dangerous situations.

Colorado had two rescue teams, both on the Front Range. "The Colorado mountains had been discovered," said Trujillo, "and people started going to the mountains not knowing much ... and getting themselves in trouble." Rocky Mountain Rescue Group (RMR) in Boulder, founded in 1947, one of the oldest in the country, and Summit County Rescue Group in Breckenridge, incorporated in 1973, were 300 miles, multiple high passes and seven car hours away. Kircher, Walker, Hamrick, Trujillo, Chief Kelley, Sheriff Dougherty and Deputy Jim McGuire met June 19 to create Ouray Mountain Rescue Squad. Thirty-five years later, Hamrick spoke with pride as he recalled his participation. He wrote Bill Gardner, the twenty-six-year-old founder of the Silverton Wilderness School, asking for advice. Gardner, "a skier and mountaineer," was also Silverton's Chief of Police. He responded:

I share your serious concern that we establish some kind of responsible mountain rescue organization for the San Juan Mountains.... More and more people, particularly inexperienced people, are starting to hike and climb in our mountains. Here in Silverton, there is no trained rescue organization.... Sheriff [Virgil] Mason relies on skilled to semi-skilled volunteers to effect rescues. Fortunately, as in Ouray, there are a handful.

Two weeks later, the death of Frances "Frankie" Licht, twenty-six, an experienced climber, Gardner's partner and co-founder of the Silverton Wilderness School, underscored the need. Licht and students were descending Trinity Peak south of Silverton when she slipped on a wet rock at 13,000 feet while "making a transition from rock to snow." Silverton was four wilderness hours away. Gardner believed that if there had been a rapid-response mountain rescue group in Silverton she might have had a slight chance of getting medical aid before she died.

◆ ◆ ◆

Eighteen rescues in five months, some quite complicated, created great interest in Ouray. In August, *Ouray County Plaindealer* editor Joyce Jorgensen wrote:

For a few weeks there, the mountain rescue people and the police were beginning to feel that, with or without chocks or nuts, the mountains were becoming chock full of nuts – what with one rescue after another, some more serious than others, as climbers overestimated their abilities and otherwise went unprepared for trouble.

One incident involved the Uncompahgre Gorge near Engineer Pass turnoff on US 550. After its right front tire blew, a speeding car left the highway and ended up 400 feet down. The man was alive when Emergency Medical Technicians (EMTs) Kircher and Walker reached him, but died despite their efforts. Unfortunately, as they labored 100 feet below the highway, crowd control was nonexistent and they were "pelted with rocks," said Walker. "Some of us could've gotten killed." In hindsight, he thought, "maybe it was the fault of Mountain Rescue that we should have said none of us will go down unless one of us is up top doing crowd control."

◆ ◆ ◆

One beautiful day late that summer, Bill Hopkins, Kircher, Hamrick and Walker met on the Courthouse steps. Kircher wanted to form a non-profit to purchase equipment since rescuers had nothing but personal gear. Eventually, ten men created a rescue team. Patsie Hamrick took minutes, Kircher and Mike Hamrick created By-laws and an Accident Report and Kircher suggested the name Ouray Mountain Rescue Team (OMRT). Attorney Phil Icke filed for state incorporation. Kircher's rescue log began the continuing practice of discussing callouts at meetings. They made a team list of names, phone numbers and qualifications. Chief Kelley loaned them a five-watt CB radio, to be used by the first one out on a rescue, and Sheriff Dougherty shared a thank you note, from the parents of the boys climbing with Michael Bolger.

A first donation, $10, came from Jack Fors of Chicago, rescued August 1 from a cliff three-quarters of a mile up Twin Peaks Trail. Tired and unable to finish, Fors was stranded until Hamrick and Bob Larson climbed above him with ropes, which allowed him to complete the climb. Chief Kelley's description of Fors looking exactly like "a cat hanging on a screen door," appeared in the *Plaindealer*. Hamrick protested this frank evocation of his situation in a letter to the editor. He said it was hard to believe that Chief Kelley was quoted correctly. Editor Jorgenson responded, partly tongue in cheek:

> *we resent the statement that the* Plaindealer *was in error and the implication that our reporter makes up quotations from anyone at all, at any time, ever. Our account was part of the police report for the week and entirely accurate, including Chief Kelley's statement, which was only descriptive of the physical situation of the climber.*

In September, Idarado Mine manager John Petty offered OMRT heavy equipment as needed, a promise soon redeemed. LaVern and Wanda Lou Kingery, returning late from a fishing trip, rolled their 1961 Jeep 325 feet off Engineer Pass Road. They were thrown out, seriously injured, and lay in the dark canyon until a Basque sheep-herder found them early in the morning. The sheepherder rode his horse four and a half miles to US 550, then waited an hour until Jeep tour operator Fran Kuboske came along. Luckily, a passenger spoke Spanish. At 9 a.m. the Idarado miners showed up in Four Wheel Drive (4WD) trucks with litters. They drove the couple to the highway and a waiting ambulance. Rescued none too soon, suffering from exposure, they were in shock, with broken bones, bruises and lacerations. The Jeep was totaled.

◆ ◆ ◆

OMRT focused on rescue, knowledge and safety. Hamrick scheduled EMT training and Kircher got stickers, which allowed red lights on vehicles doing emergency calls. They practiced vertical evacuation with RMR in Silverton. Enthusiastic supporters donated $225 and they opened a bank account with the captain and lieutenant as signatories. Kircher tried to reimburse Chief Kelley for the CB, but he eventually wanted it back, so OMRT bought a second radio. Kircher also forged a good relationship with Sheriff Dougherty, found out that his department was entitled to two Motorola radios from Law Enforcement Alliance of America (LEAA), and made sure he got those.

In November he wrote up the first twenty-one rescues for the *Plaindealer*. Unfortunately, the story fueled complaints at the next meeting, refreshingly summarized by Patsie Hamrick:

> *Several people had their feelings hurt … if every member wrote a news release, they would all handle it differently. The question remained as to what would be the best approach, with the most likely being to write what everyone wants to hear, stepping on no one's toes, and giving everyone in the county credit for doing something.*

◆ ◆ ◆

In 1975 Idarado modified the City's Stokes litter and attorney Rich Tisdel researched a liability policy for the team. They bought basic equipment: A 600-foot spool of 7 / 16 Goldline (a nylon climbing rope), a Kelty pack, pulleys, carabiners and lights. Rice Lumber donated orange vests and Colorado Fish and Game two boxes of rockets. They practiced burying a dummy and a live victim, Walker, with a bloody bone concealed in his pants leg above the Box Canyon Motel in snow laced with catsup. Benda Walker, with daughters Cinnamon and Ivy, watched from a rock. She wrote a letter to the editor: Eighteen OMRT members "quickly found the 'victim' and started administering first aid.... Very quickly the men had the surviving victim in the litter and on the way down the hill. The whole thing looked so real, some people stopped to ask if there had been an accident." She spoke for many members' families: "Altho I personally have many anxious moments when they are on an actual rescue, I'm thankful and proud of the work the OMRT is trying to do. I think it is something the whole community can be proud of."

They learned first aid with a Resusci-Annie manikin, did scree evacuation east of US 550 and the old town dump, practiced technical climbing, river crossing, survival, orienteering, communications and signaling. They met in the stone jail room in the basement of city hall. "That was our space and we had very limited equipment," said Laszlo Kubinyi, a man who enjoyed spending "his adult life crawling in caves."

In June a hiker was stuck on cliffs 700 feet above Lake Lenore. Lt. Hamrick, Chris Candee and John May belayed him to safety from the Pony Express Mine. In August, two Silverton men drove off Red Mountain Pass, landing 300 feet down. One walked out; the other required evacuation. At the Blowout north of Ouray, a miner broke his leg in two places and walked out part way with help from his crew and OMRT. Another rescue four days later – of a man who fell

OURAY DAYS, June 1975: Mike Hamrick and Kurt Kircher simulate vertical rescue at City Hall, lowering the Stokes litter to Doug Walker, the victim. This event raised a welcome $135.
Photo by Lynn Kircher

seventy feet down Cascade Cliff and lived – closed out a relatively quiet summer.

◆ ◆ ◆

Walker suggested that only those who attended trainings and meetings should be part of OMRT, a practice followed to this day. Members included EMTs, High Altitude Evacuation, Communicationsmen, Low Altitude Evacuation and Aircraft. "Not OMRT Members" were four female RNs and two Support persons – one man and six women. Members originally thought Sheriff Dougherty would accept Chief Kelley as captain since he was a law enforcement officer who knew the backcountry. The Chief was very pro-OMRT, whereas the Sheriff was somewhat skeptical of newcomers, said Hamrick, especially those with long hair. The Sheriff figured his Posse could go anywhere and rescue people. Walker, who was suspect because of his mustache, said they "probably had better relationships with the Posse than we did with the Sheriff."

Diplomatic, peripatetic Kircher, a veteran familiar with the chain of command, became captain that December. He did chores every morning at his Box Canyon Motel. Afterwards "he'd make this circuit" through town said Hamrick. He would visit the Sheriff, "go down to Joyce's and have coffee and come back up by the Post Office. He had a whole bunch of friends." Hamrick had short hair because of his Bureau of Reclamation job. He and Trujillo, "a really spiffy, military type," also communicated well with the Sheriff. They told jokes and stories about Sheriff Mason: One time, Hamrick said, the educated, articulate, 300 lb. Sheriff, after avalanche training, stepped onto the hood and then the roof of his police car and the car "goes woof." He "thanked everybody for coming," talked about people who had died. "He was just a character."

◆ ◆ ◆

OMRT was down to $20 in January 1976, after paying for insurance, supplies and repairs. Gilbert and Viola Martinez offered to do a Mexican Dinner, said Hamrick. Gilbert was a gung-ho member, a man of all trades and they both were huge team supporters. Viola, the best restaurant cook in town, said: "We're going to put together this Mexican Dinner to benefit the rescue team." She put members to work: "We were kitchen help, prep cooks." They shredded cheese, chopped lettuce and sliced tomatoes; printed tickets, found donors, wrote an article for the paper, made posters and table decorations;

contacted churches for announcements. The dinner sold out, not a scrap of food remained at the end of the evening. Everyone knew Viola Martinez and that "anything that Viola was head of was going to be good to eat." OMRT made $503 – $372 from the dinner, the rest from donations. They bought new ropes and radios.

As they prepared for Mountain Rescue Association (MRA) certification, they needed at least twenty-five members, five qualified for mountain rescue (EMTs) and travel capability (high altitude) and twenty support persons for communications, transportation and victim assistance. Capt. Kircher wrote, "This is the backbone of the Rescue Team ... we are short six members." Some previous support personnel, including several women, made the membership list.

◆ ◆ ◆

1976 was an equal opportunity year for being lost, stranded, injured or killed in the backcountry. Three June callouts included a hiker who fell into Canyon Creek, dislocating his shoulder. A week later, four members responded at 5 p.m. to Owl Creek Pass. A man had driven his pickup off the road. He was put on life support, given first aid for fractures and abrasions and hauled 150 feet to the road. Five days later, a lost boy showed up just as they prepared to search.

July got really busy. Walker didn't get home for two days during a hot, sunny Fourth of July weekend. Hell's Angels invaded Ouray, a street party enveloped Main Street and a bomb threat was made for the Courthouse and bank. *Plaindealer* editor Jorgensen wrote that Telluride "blew their celebration out of proportion years ago, with national advertising and saturation advertising in Colorado. When they got bigger than they could stand, they shut down. It would have been nicer if they had simply let it lie there, instead of pointing the way over here."

In the first of five holiday rescues, Walker responded on Saturday to Box Cañon parking lot for a young girl who had fallen 220 feet into the Uncompahgre Gorge. Her younger brother reportedly threw her shoe over the 6X6 wire fence separating the lot from the gorge. She went under the fence to retrieve it, tumbled down the upper scree slope and fell off the lower cliff. Walker asked a visiting doctor in the parking lot if he'd ever climbed before. He hadn't, but was willing to have Walker take him down. They rappelled the scree slope and cliff band. "And amazingly, she didn't look hurt ... there was no blood." But when the doctor did a reflex test on the bottom of her foot, her toes curled up – "a very bad neurological sign." She was transported to Grand Junction where she died a few days later. Walker attended her in the ambulance and took it hard. A father of two young girls, he said, "That particular one really hit.... I was very strict with my kids ... (about) riding bikes in the street and things like that."

That evening, a 1955 Willys Jeep overturned on Portland Road when its driver lost control, traveling 117 feet off road and ejecting both occupants. The men, with internal injuries, fractures and abrasions, were put on life support before being evacuated by 4WD and ambulance. On July 4, two boys were stranded on Ouray's west cliffs above the 4J Trailer Court, but got down before rescuers arrived. That evening, a young man drove 200 feet over the Ruby Cliffs on US 550 south of Ouray and died instantly. His passenger was thrown clear of the wreck and survived with a cut-off tongue, respiratory problems and abrasions. Bystanders helped with the scree evacuation. Capping off the disastrous weekend was a Monday report of a body lying below Box Canyon Falls near the hot water pipeline for the Hot Springs Pool. A young man had apparently "hiked in and just done the drugs," said Walker. He survived.

On July 11, a six-man team found two lost men above the Chief Ouray Mine at 2:30 a.m. Three days later, a Jeep rollover in remote Silver Basin injured four people. They were given first aid and evacuated by 4WD vehicle. On July 22, another pair of lost hikers were discovered on an Amphitheater cliff and belayed to safety. In August, OMRT responded to a CB radio call for an overturned Jeep north of Ouray, investigated and determined it was a hoax.

Jim Fife, Trujillo, Rick Blackford, Kubinyi, Lt. Hamrick, Elwood Gregory, his son Doug Gregory, and Capt. Kircher aced interrogation, line search, scree evacuation and vertical evacuation during the MRA evaluation by RMR. Late that afternoon, however, the real world intruded: a pair of hikers – George Weiss, thirty, and Emma Schliess, twenty-seven, of St. Louis, Missouri – left town Thursday morning, intending to hike the Bear Creek Trail to American Flats and return on the Horsethief Trail Friday afternoon. They were overdue.

Eight OMRT and RMR members searched at 5 a.m. A Civil Air Patrol (CAP) plane flew across the area, but gusting winds and rough weather forced it to fly too high to see anything. Trujillo climbed to the top of the Amphitheater after someone reported flashing lights, but found nothing. They scoured American Flats, Difficulty and Wildhorse drainages and Horsethief and Bear Creek trails. The hikers, after wandering awhile, found Bear Creek Trail and walked out.

In late August, as two men searched for two boys and a dog reported stranded in Sneffels Creek Canyon above the Camp Bird Mine, the subjects walked out. It was the 14th callout since June. There would be six more by late December. In September, an older man drove off Red Mountain Pass above the Idarado Mine eleven miles south of Ouray. His wife survived the 200-foot plunge, though neither wore seatbelts. When rescuers arrived, the state trooper on the road and the county sheriff's representative on the scree slope were arguing over who had jurisdiction. The highway was state territory, but the car and occupants had fallen onto county land.

Meanwhile, the car was "smoking and ready to blow up," said Kubinyi. He and a partner descended with a stretcher, found the driver hunched over the steering wheel and his wife lying in shock next to him. They asked for help. Just as the woman opened her eyes, the sheriff's representative responded, "What's the hurry? That son of a *** is already dead!" Six rescuers and some bystanders evacuated both victims up the slope. Kubinyi was disgusted: "These two guys, instead of doing something productive, they're arguing who's in charge."

◆ ◆ ◆

A memorable rescue for Walker and Trujillo involved a hunter with a heart attack in the Big Blue (now Uncompahgre) Wilderness. A Citizens Band (CB) radio call at 11:30 p.m. on October 15 to Sheriff Dougherty reported the camp was in Wetterhorn Basin, "but their description of the terrain didn't match the area." At 12:50 a.m., the OMRT men drove for an hour to West Fork trailhead in the Big Blue Wilderness. Under a nearly full moon they hiked several miles over West Fork Pass. Finding nothing in Wetterhorn Basin, they decided to check Oben Creek and hiked over an unnamed 12,874-foot peak west of the pass.

At 7 a.m. they picked their way through a small forest in an old avalanche path at 11,300 feet on the Cow Creek Trail, found the hunter, who appeared stable, and requested a helicopter since the campsite was relatively flat. Unfortunately, said Trujillo, there was no suitable Landing Zone (LZ) since the trees had regrown thickly, were short and looked like "dog fur," – slang for trees of the same age, short, narrow in diameter and thickly spaced like a dog's coat. The hunters had no axe, so Walker used his wire saw on a six-inch tree, but the sapling was gummy and the saw stuck. Something needed to happen fast, with a helicopter coming. A hunter retrieved a rifle and standing next to a tree, felled it with two shots. Others joined in. Another hunter sat down "and went 'p-choo, p-choo, p-choo, p-choo, p-choo' and just worked his way bullet after bullet after bullet," said Walker, cutting down a much larger tree. In a few minutes they had an LZ.

A MAST helicopter flew into the narrow canyon at 10:30. Crewmembers were "hanging out each side of the helicopter with headsets on," said Walker, telling the pilot how much clearance he had. Because of the remote area, the rescuers gave instructions to the State Patrol dispatcher in Montrose on a hand radio and he relayed them to the pilot on a military frequency. The chopper landed, they loaded the man and the pilot apologized for not being able to fly them out. "I would love to be able to take you guys with me, but we just don't have the lift capacity."

After a fresh pot of coffee, the remaining hunters struck camp. At that point, some men from nearby camps, rifles ready, arrived and asked what happened. The camp men merrily explained the situation, but it wasn't particularly humorous to the newcomers. "You guys sure know how to ruin a great hunting area!" Whatever deer or elk had been in the surrounding forest had departed for parts unknown during the fusillade that felled the trees.

As Walker and Trujillo prepared to hike out, the Texas hunters, thankful for their help, insisted they ride horses. "Against his better judgment," Trujillo, who had never ridden before, got on the horse. "He looked like Ichabod Crane," said Walker, "couldn't find his stride or balance with the horse, and apparently he was squeezing his knees together on the saddle to try to stay in place." When they reached the bottom of the trail, his legs buckled under him as he dismounted and he "fell right underneath the horse." Walker helped him up. Trujillo said it was the last time he ever rode a horse. He didn't know anything about them, the beast tried to rub him off at every tree, and he was so sore he had to rest half an hour before he could walk again.

In late October, members hiked past Twin Peaks to pick up a human skeleton, found by a hunter. Sheriff Dougherty said it appeared to be that of a young woman, who "may have recently had brain surgery. There were several circular cut marks on the skull, which had not completely healed." The remains of her backpack suggested she had been there since summer 1975. In December a truck overturned at the Ironton switchbacks. The driver had a fractured leg, but no other help was available, so OMRT transported the man. A drunk driver went off US 550 on New Year's Eve at Tuffy's Corner, an accident-prone curve named for the local undertaker, just north of town. The driver said two hitchhikers rode with him, but a river search found nothing. Rescuers "thought the driver was not telling the truth" and ended the search.

◆ ◆ ◆

In January 1977, OMRT became one of forty elite MRA units in the country, one of seven in Colorado. Capt. Kircher seized the opportunity and wrote to the Board of County Commissioners (BOCC). The team was "in urgent need," of two radio packsets for communication with the State Patrol and other agencies, numerous rescues had cost $1,000, lack of a county 4WD emergency vehicle and the limitations of CB radios threatened their effectiveness. He noted that the MRA certification, which allowed them to respond to disasters like airplane crashes or other major emergencies, was an asset to the county. "Any help you can give us is most appreciated!"

Nothing happened, but the City of Ouray and Chamber of Commerce donated $200 each, so they bought more CBs, batteries and MRA patches. By April they were down to $36.11. Another Mexican Dinner brought in $600 and paid for helmets, six copies of *Mountain Search and Rescue Techniques* and sixteen more rescues. In October the BOCC finally met with Kircher and requested a list. He had one: "10 watt Motorola VHF radio, 2 portable spotlights with quartz-iodide bulbs, 6 headlights, rope, batteries, 2 jumar ascenders."

◆ ◆ ◆

1977 was a tumultuous year, with intense rescues on a scale they hadn't experienced before. On the night of April 25, an injured pilot walked into Sleeping Indian Ranch after his plane crashed in Owl Creek valley. Three hours later, Kircher and Rick Blackford rested on a fence by a corral. Patty Blackford, the EMT on the ambulance that night, said, "They were just sitting there talking, shining their flashlights around, because there were other guys out and about, searching. And a second guy comes walking up and Rick shines his flashlight in his face." Six members evacuated the passenger, who had head injuries. The next day, they raised two motorcyclists who had been thrown 100 feet over a cliff onto a scree slope eleven miles south of Ouray on Red Mountain Pass. In April they fought a forest fire on Camp Bird Road and rescued someone hit by rockfall. It was the first of several rescue clusters.

The first June callout began with an argument in a bar the warm evening of June 15. Afterwards, three people headed south to Durango in Colleen Dugan's car. At Bear Creek Overlook, she ordered the driver, Richard Lawrence Yule, twenty-three, and Carl Aring, twenty-five, to stop and get out. The twenty-four-year-old said goodbye, "just floored the car and went straight," said Walker. The road curved sharply left; "a four-foot-high chain link fence" guarded Bear Creek Falls to the right. Her car rolled "down a slight embankment and became airborne."

After "the car hit the cliff on the far side, " said Walker, the two men returned to town. Police Officer Corky Kesner took their call at 9:50 and alerted the State Patrol. Undersheriff Frank Merling hurried to the scene. Before they alerted the authorities, however, the young men had gone back to the bar and announced: "Colleen just drove off the cliff."

The Sheriff's Department called an ambulance and wrecker and turned their attention to unruly spectators who would not cooperate or stay away from the edge. James Costello, thirty, from Ouray, and former resident Jim Kelly asked the Undersheriff for a flashlight. With others, they searched the canyon. Officer Kesner went down to search for the wreck, which landed on its top in Bear Creek. Dr. Richard Heidorn, monitoring radio traffic on his way to the accident, realized that OMRT should be there, "so he relayed a request for Doug Walker and Kurt Kircher." Benda Walker took the call at 10:50 and alerted OMRT, which "assembled at City Hall to get their gear and went to Bear Creek. As they were going into the canyon, they met a group carrying Dugan's body out." Deputy Coroner Walker said, "They never should have, but they moved the body."

Kelly reported he had lost contact with Costello, so Walker, Fife and Carl Kircher (Kurt's son) descended the scree slope north of the falls. In mist and wind, they crossed Bear Creek "well below the falls, climbed toward the falls along the steep north bank, and crossed the Creek once more to the south side just below the falls." They found Costello's body with massive head and chest injuries and the rescue became "a lower priority recovery." Apparently, he had slipped trying to cross a draw on the south side of the bridge, fell down a chute and landed 227 feet below. A tow truck from Al's Service Station lowered a litter on the sheer north side. Walker crossed the stream to get it.

Under "extremely dangerous, wet and dark conditions," both Fife and Carl Kircher, who were dressed lightly in the sixty-degree night, were becoming hypothermic. Even Walker, in a waterproof orange and white EMT jacket, chilled as he worked in the steady mist blowing off the waterfall. Tying a bowline to secure the litter to a tow hook became a slow motion chore for a man who could normally "do it one-handed ... without looking.... At this point, there was some discussion about postponing the recovery until daylight," he said, "but we proceeded in the dark." They loaded the body into the litter, secured it and crossed the creek once again to attach it to the tow truck line. It was out of the canyon by 2 a.m.

Then came the questions. "'Are you okay? Are you okay?'" Walker realized that "apparently I must've been slurring words or something because of the cold" and Dr. Heidorn and others worried. The three rescuers hiked and climbed back down the creek, meeting other members "who had come to help us back up the scree slope. We really appreciated that." Dr. Heidorn and Capt. Kircher later complained to officials about terrible crowd control. Spectators crowded the edge, kicked rocks on those working under the cliffs, and tripped on and drove over ropes. The doctor asked three times for crowd control. Capt. Kircher said it was "extremely dangerous, to try to rescue anyone from anything, and others could also have wound up dead."

◆ ◆ ◆

Rescuers plucked an eleven-year-old boy from sandstone cliffs above Rotary Park on June 26 as Sheriff Dougherty, Deputy Merling and Police Officer Allen Hudson kept spectators from climbing up, even as a large crowd formed and people parked at the edge of the highway. This time, people cooperated when asked to move their cars. The next emergency personnel weren't so lucky. Fourteen-year-old Mark Trujillo of Ouray fell to the bottom of the falls at the old power company dam south of town when a knot in a rope he rigged gave way. His companion Joe Condotti, Jr. climbed down, found him conscious but seriously injured and ran for help. Officer Hudson and EMTs Donna Sim, Kathy Workman and Dennis Lunday responded. While they worked, onlookers started down from above, kicking rocks loose. Trujillo was hit before they could shield his body. Workman and Sim were pinned against the cliff. A softball-sized rock fell toward them, but fortunately bounced and slowed just before hitting Sim, who yelled at them. Sheriff Dougherty ran over to stop them, which she credited with probably saving their lives. "It was only luck that Sim was the only one injured by the falling rock, and that her injuries were minor," said Walker.

Before that day was over, a seventeen-year-old boy was trapped 300 yards west of Cascade Falls. Larson and Carl Kircher climbed the cliffs and brought him down. That week's *Plaindealer* covered the back-to-back rescues and featured Walker's heartfelt plea: "Well-meaning people are endangering themselves (one was killed last week), the victims, and the organized rescuers ... please join the OMRT. We can teach you to become an organized, efficient and safe rescuer instead of a danger to yourself and others."

Five days later, Bradford Walters, twenty-five, of Grand Junction, limped two and a half miles from the Dallas / Corbett trailhead to Ouray. He got to the trailhead at 8 p.m. and realized his keys were in his pack, miles above him. His knee was dislocated, but a companion, Barbara Muir, was seriously injured. She had fallen thirty to forty feet into Corbett Creek Canyon near timberline while downclimbing a cliff and had severe hip and leg pain. They were backpacking "when they took a wrong turn ... ran out of water and were trying to get some from a stream."

It was a weekend, so rescuers weren't necessarily home. Elwood Gregory was watching *Silver Streak* with his wife Rosanna at the local theater. They "came in and got me out of the movie and we headed up Corbett Creek." Twelve men left town at 10 p.m., hiked the Dallas to the Corbett loop and an old hunt camp. The trail became really fuzzy, said Kubinyi. The oak brush hillside was combed with old mining and deer trails, but they knew that an injured person needed help. Yelling into the night, they searched the steep hillside and creek bottom, moved cautiously in the darkness, and tried to avoid the really dangerous places where the deep oak brush opened abruptly at the edges of vertical cliffs. Struggling through snagging, waist high brush, Kubinyi carried a Thomas splint, four feet long. On loan from the medical clinic, it cost a couple hundred dollars and, somewhere in that dark night, he lost the splint.

At 2:30 a.m., they slept in place. At dawn, Gregory and Walker stood on a little promontory, gazed down at a beautiful, big waterfall and smelled smoke. Gordon Saville's CAP plane flew over. His passenger, Montrose Sheriff Tom Gilmore, was amazed that the hikers reached such a remote spot. Using the loudspeaker, Saville asked the men to lie down if they were searchers. They did and he announced that they were the closest ones to the missing party, a half-mile up the canyon. When they reached two women camped on a scree slope below the mountain wall, one was stoking a smoky fire. Muir lay wrapped in an insulated vest. The men provided relief for her painful dislocated hip by pulling on her leg while hooking her under the arms to provide traction. Dr. Heidorn came and gave her painkillers. The Posse arrived, a helicopter landed on a knoll a mile away and OMRT and the Posse took a litter downhill. They dragged the litter out of the canyon, uphill to the chopper. Later, Capt. Kircher said that they could not have managed that without the Posse's help. The rescue finally ended at 2 p.m.

The lost Thomas splint became a liability. It belonged to the medical clinic; Dr. Heidorn said the team could replace it for $200. Capt. Kircher negotiated, to no avail. The following summer, he asked Kubinyi if he could go look for it. Kubinyi's neighbors had a teenage visitor and asked him to take the young man hiking. On a nice Sunday he and the boy hiked the trail to Corbett Canyon. He tried to remember where they had crawled around and found himself in "this really nasty place" on a fifty-degree scree slope with

In January 1975 OMRT adopted the design but had no money for team patches. The set up charge was $300 and the minimum order was seventy-five at $3 each. Instead, they bought plastic copies of the logo to use on helmets. Years later, Bill MacTiernan said the logo "nailed the idea of the area."
Photo courtesy Tricia Eischied

*Capt. Kircher, left, and Rick Trujillo, right, wear white Bell Labs helmets
bearing the red and white team logo, which still identifies members. In
October 1974, Greg Genuit submitted the red and white design with the
image of Mt. Sneffels and a red cross. He had been an illustrator/graphics
designer for Lockheed Aircraft Corporation. Designing "the original patch
... was easy for me," he said. Lt. Hamrick crafted the finished emblem, with
a "three-dimensional surface," of different thread colors: white, dark and
light grey and red. He sent it to an embroidery company in North Carolina.
They designed the lettering in a circle.*

Photo by Doug Walker
Courtesy Rick Trujillo

a vertical drop off. "I look down and I'm looking at this Thomas splint." The contraption's webbing was eaten away by animals, but the frame was intact. Dr. Heidorn was so relieved to get it back that the clinic replaced the webbing.

OMRT answered fifteen callouts in 1977, including the mother of all of them, for a lost hunter in the "difficult area east of Mt. Baldy." In July Doug Walker, "Mr. Magician," who figured out and fixed everything, resigned, burned out with rescue work, and moved to Missouri. Capt. Kircher resigned effective July 31. Fife and Trujillo met with Kurt and Lynn Kircher and offered to do things in Ouray if he stayed through year's end. He agreed.

CHAPTER TWO

A Vanished Hunter

ON A COOL FALL SUNDAY, November 6, 1977, in "low hanging clouds and fog," Steve and Janice Okeson hunted in heavy timber northeast of Baldy Ridge. At one point they split up and agreed to meet. She did not come. Her husband looked for her, but all tracks had disappeared in new-fallen snow. She "was no stranger to that country," said Rick Trujillo, was warmly dressed in red parka, blue stocking cap and snowmobile boots, and carried a rifle, orange day-pack and CB radio. That afternoon Steve Okeson scoured the rough hillside and called, but her CB was silent. Worst of all, at one point he thought he saw boot tracks, but they ended near an abandoned trail on the northeast side of the ridge. Below lay Winchester Gulch, a nearly impassable world of grey rock pinnacles and waterfalls drop-ping hundreds of feet to Cow Creek.

The day before, the couple had driven 200 miles from Aspen Village to Thistle Park northeast of Ouray and backpacked into the family hunt camp on Baldy Ridge above the Okeson Trail at 10,500 feet. Steve, twenty-six, and Janice, twenty-one, had hunted together for years. She grew up in Delta and he was from Ouray. The short day ended. Desperation drove him down the snowy ridges to find Trujillo, a good friend, former classmate, OMRT founding member, mountain runner and climber of Mt. McKinley. Trujillo was his first choice to find her. In deepening snow, they searched through the early night. At 2-3 a.m. they returned to town and notified Sheriff Art Dougherty. He ordered a formal search, calling out OMRT and the Posse.

◆ ◆ ◆

Sheriff Dougherty contacted Sheriff Tom Gilmore, an outdoor man who enjoyed being in the midst of the action. On Monday, Sheriff

Gilmore, Deputies Rick Rowan and Warren Waterman, and thirty to forty Montrose Posse members assembled in the cold dawn, laid out their maps on the hoods of pickups at the Ridgway Fairgrounds and planned their operation. Sheriff Gilmore led the Posse to the ridge on horseback and they searched in snow that ranged from knee to belly deep. They rode 2,000 feet downhill in heavy downed timber east of Baldy to where Courthouse and Red Creeks flow into Cow Creek. Some areas were impassable, but Sheriff Gilmore said they did find one oddity: at the head of a cliff in Winchester Gulch, a six-inch mountain willow limb had been broken off.

The search took another direction on Tuesday. Ouray Posse member Bill Hotchkiss, cousin to Police Chief Keith Kelley, along with Ron Slafter and Hotchkiss's German Shepherd, drove up Cow Creek with Sheriff Dougherty. The Sheriff dropped them upstream of Red Creek, 2,600 feet below and east of Baldy Ridge. As they climbed the slopes and draws near Winchester Gulch, they found what they thought was a woman's track. Hotchkiss and Slafter stayed overnight near the top of Cobbs Gulch Trail at the Neilson camp. The next day, in clear weather, on their way down alongside Winchester Gulch, Hotchkiss lost his backpack when it slid down "where they didn't want to go." The strenuous trip, through two feet of snow, was otherwise uneventful and unproductive.

SAR K-9 teams – three handlers, bloodhounds Yeager and Tig and a German Shepherd – arrived Thursday from the Front Range. A chopper ferried Training Officer Jim Fife, a twenty-nine-year-old civil engineer and the SAR K-9 teams to Baldy. Fife was assigned to them because they were unfamiliar with the area. Two Hueys from Ft. Carson Army base brought other searchers. A confusing welter of tracks hindered the K-9s, but the dogs did reveal something crucial: they all lost her trail at the same spot. Tugging on their lines, they begged to explore Winchester Gulch, but Fife said they were told not to venture into that treacherous terrain.

◆ ◆ ◆

On the first clear morning after the snowstorm, Lt. Hamrick and Laszlo Kubinyi snowshoed a Jeep road to the trailhead. At 8 a.m. they waded through heavy snow up Shortcut Trail to Baldy Ridge, but all the knolls looked alike. Hamrick wondered, "Where in the world would we start?" After noon they warmed themselves at a big campfire some hunters had made. "We were so cold," said Hamrick. Kubinyi had a hunch that they should be looking on the steep eastern side of Baldy, so they tromped on through heavy timber, fighting their way through the inevitable downfall. On the east side, they found only elk tracks. Late in the day, Hamrick said, "Let's go home, this is no fun." With nothing to show for the day's effort, they descended the four and a half mile Cutler Creek Trail and drove home. They returned to their jobs, rested a few days and rejoined the search, flying in a Huey up the Left Fork drainage to an LZ partway up the Okeson Trail. They were annoyed to have to descend to the same point later, but Hamrick said they later realized that the pilots were avoiding downdrafts from Baldy into Cow Creek.

◆ ◆ ◆

Ridgway volunteered its town hall for mission control and immediately the walls were papered with maps and lists. Heavy snow, fog and temperatures below zero bedeviled searchers through Tuesday; the brutal conditions made their work seem more urgent. Sheriff Gilmore estimated the wind chill was twenty to thirty below zero. Silverton SAR, Gunnison Sheriff's Posse, Colorado Courtesy Patrol, CAP, Colorado Rescue Dogs and the Red Cross searched. Local residents assisted with searching, vehicles, food, coffee and cider.

The next weekend, over a hundred people came to help. The Hueys flew dogs and even psychics to Baldy for sixty hours, depositing searchers on the ridge in just fifteen minutes. Otherwise, getting to Baldy from Ridgway meant driving eight miles south on US 550 and four miles east to the trailhead using 4WD vehicles. From there, it was two and a half miles and 1,200 feet of muddy, snowy uphill hiking to Janice Okeson's last seen point. CAP pilots donated time and planes as weather permitted. Psychics contacted authorities and some independently pinpointed the same area. One psychic, dressed in the missing woman's clothing, was flown over Winchester Gulch and "'got chills' and a strong reaction over one of the deep ravines."

◆ ◆ ◆

On Saturday, El Paso SAR from Colorado Springs set up an impressive communications system in a large trailer at Ridgway basecamp. Backcountry communications jumped dramatically since their equipment could reach over the mountain ridges into Cow Creek. Thirteen Colorado rescue teams – from the Front Range to the western slope – were in the field. A youth rescue team from Arapahoe and another from Vail searched by day and bunked at Ridgway High

School at night. On the second Monday, two Arapahoe Rescue teens and three Evergreen youths, along with an adult rescuer, rappelled down snowy Winchester Gulch, but found nothing. Rick Blackford and Rick Trujillo rappelled the same area, looking for any clues.

The best estimates were that 7,000 rough acres [about ten plus square miles] had been searched by the end of that long weekend. On Saturday "about 106 people were involved in the search ... about 120 on Sunday. On Monday only about twenty ... highly trained in search and rescue," including Capt. Kircher and Tom Whelan, remained. As they left for the Front Range, Colorado Search and Rescue Board (CSRB) executives – J. Hunter Holloway of Arapahoe Rescue Patrol and Harry Ledyard of Evergreen's Alpine Rescue Team – praised Kircher's work. "You're lucky to have him in this area." CSRB was critical to the extended search, coordinating rescuers and doing field plotting. They got a second Huey and a fuel truck, giving searchers more time.

Finally, hopes for a live recovery were gone. Sheriff Dougherty called off the search and said it was impossible to estimate the cost

Rick Blackford rappels Winchester Gulch the April after Janice Okeson's disappearance. He and Rick Trujillo engaged in a "futile effort" to find her.

Photo by Rick Trujillo

for such a complex SAR operation. Had Ouray County received a bill, it would have been for several hundred thousand dollars. Over nine days SAR groups from as far as 300 mountainous miles away had logged more than 5,000 man-hours.

During the winter and spring, Trujillo, Steve (who quit his job to look for his wife) and brother Neil Okeson searched repeatedly. One time, Trujillo said he and Steve Okeson found themselves disoriented, the first and only time Trujillo – who knew the country well – could recall that happening. They radioed camp, a shot was fired and then they knew which way to go. On one memorable day, April 17, 1978, they drove a road wet with new snow to Thistle Park and headed uphill on foot through oak brush to the helicopter LZ. The weather alternated between strong wind, sun and snow. After lunch they put on skis, continued upward and emerged above the Okeson camp. "At that time," said Trujillo, " there was a rudimentary but well used trail from the main trail on (east) Baldy down Winchester Gulch." It had "a hazardous narrow bench above a vertical cliff that had to be crossed by anyone using this route." Janice Okeson knew of this trail. She "might have gotten lost in the thick upper forest on the Cow Creek side of the mountain, and ... maybe tried to find it and descend to the creek."

They explored down to Bergman's meadow on the north side and through deep snow to the cliffs but found nothing. Returning to the ridge, they skied downhill to the truck. The six-hour journey made them realize that the "snow is still too deep to do any serious searching and [Steve Okeson] was able to relax somewhat." They looked again on June 10 to no avail.

OMRT, Sheriff Gilmore, the Ouray, Montrose and Delta Posses and a helicopter mounted a last massive, systematic search for Janice Okeson on July 8-9, 1978. They found nothing, but friends and neighbors continued to search. Ridgway's mayor, Lloyd "Swede" Neilson, rode in a helicopter over the Baldy / Cow Creek area during the initial search and owned a hunt camp on the ridge near Winchester Gulch. "I think I know where she is," he told his wife, Joellean. He had dreamed of her in the Cow Creek drainage.

They waited for the snow to melt and Cow Creek to be fordable with his 4WD truck. Because it had been a big snow year, that wasn't until mid-July. Lloyd Neilson knew the country well, having been born in Telluride and raised in Ridgway. Cow Creek was really running and they had to be careful fording the stream in the truck. As they started hiking, they saw to the west three little gullies descending from the ridge. He chose the one that still had running water. As they rested part way up, Joellean noticed beautiful blooming flowers and stooped to drink some of the crystalline water. He said she shouldn't have done that:

> *"You're drinking water off a dead body."*
> *She thought he was joking. They climbed upward and eventually sat on a hollowed out graveled ledge at the top of the gully. Abruptly, he said, "Here she is" and walked over to a small washed patch in the gravel. Part of a body and a belt were visible. Joellean Neilson walked over and asked how he knew she was there.*
> *"I smelled it," he said.*
> *Her first instinct was to dig Janice Okeson out since it bothered her that she was suffocating.*
> *He quieted her, "Don't disturb it ... we have to go get the cops."*

Joellean Neilson remembered drinking the water and wondered if she was poisoned, but her husband said she would be fine. Thirty-five years later, she marveled that she had never seen anything like that. The young woman must have fallen on her head and her body was well preserved, frozen all winter. It was a beautiful place to die, she said, and she seemed so peaceful lying on her side.

Fifteen rescuers assembled by Sheriff Dougherty to bring Janice Okeson's body down the cliff and out the canyon did find her orange daypack, but her rifle and CB radio were never located, perhaps covered by the same gravel that concealed most of her body in the heavy spring runoff.

CHAPTER THREE

1978-1982
"These hills in their darker moments do not forgive."

OMRT'S REPUTATION FOR EXCELLENCE was confirmed with the MRA certification and in 1978 twenty-nine-year-old mountain runner and climber Rick Trujillo became the last founding member elected captain. A beeper now streamlined callouts – one man wore it for forty-eight hours and passed it on. Kurt Kircher proposed buying an FM radio packset for backcountry communication with the State Patrol and helicopters with $1,600 in donations. They raised $350 from a third Mexican Dinner. Diners vicariously climbed Mt. McKinley as Trujillo showed slides from his May 1977 expedition. They ascended the Kahiltna glacier and West Buttress, summited, and made an historic northern descent to the Muldrow glacier.

Felix Pfaeffle, Tom and Marilyn Whelan, and Kurt and Lynn Kircher suggested publishing a cookbook. Pfaeffle, a former magazine art director and Kurt Kircher's friend, and Mike Hamrick asked *Plaindealer* subscribers for recipes. Cooks from the United States and abroad responded. The 112-page *Ouray Cooking* with 270 recipes cost $636 for 500 copies; it sold for $3.50 plus 50 cents postage. Trujillo wrote about the strangeness of a rescue team selling cookbooks in the forward. Rescues cost money, but "We do not charge for our services." Marilyn Whelan was "responsible for getting it going;" Kurt Kircher filled orders.

They needed a vehicle. The Kirchers found a green WWII ambulance for $75; members scooped up the best parts littering a Delta scrapyard. First Presbyterian Church pastor and mountaineer George Pasek, joined OMRT and worked on the "Orange Beast."

Mountain Rescue Fund-Raising Dinner April 20

Seven members advertised the Mexican Dinner. "From left, front: Kurt Kircher, Bob Zimmer, Mike Hamrick, Rick Trujillo. In rear, standing: Elwood Gregory, John Tjossem and Doug Walker. Other active members of the 1977 team, not shown here, were Jim Fife, Rick Blackford, Laszlo Kubinyi, John Kropuenske, Robert Larson, Carl Kircher, Gilbert Martinez, Don Camerron, Lynn Kircher, Patty Blackford, Jeannie Fife and Rosanna Gregory."

Photo courtesy *Ouray County Plaindealer*

We spent a number of hours with wrenches ©Coke, hacksaws, screwdrivers, and ever bigger hammers ... stripping a lot of steel military weight and converting to 12V. Then we drove it down to Ridgway, parked it in front of Don Sim's place and with a lot of laughter "spray" painted it. Notice the "orange peel" effect in various places ... we mounted a Red E-Light and drove it ... at 35 MPH. Someone, again probably Kurt, found some budget civilian tires and it would make 37 MPH!

On one operation up in the Amphitheater, I drove it up with red light flashing ... and people passing! After the patient was packaged and transported, we loaded up our gear ready to return in triumph! Climbed up in the cab, stepped on the brake pedal and ... nothing, nada, zip ... clear to the floorboard with a resounding metallic "clank": NO BRAKES. Now, folks, there was not a wrecker in the county big enough to tow that hulk back down the hill. So after a few moments of discussion, I cranked it up and drove it back DOWN in a low, low, lower gear!

One winter night a drunk driver slammed into the Beast. Pasek, awakened by the loud bang, investigated. Not even a chip of orange paint was gone, but the small car's left front fender was "just crushed." A young driver misjudged the corner. Today, the Beast remains a team mascot, parked near the rescue barn. But for almost two decades, it was an indispensable vehicle, ferrying – slowly, with copious amounts of stinky exhaust – rescuers and equipment to Yankee Boy Basin, Red Mountain, Imogene, Dexter Creek, and beyond.

◆ ◆ ◆

Ouray Medical Center became the rescue base at Dr. Bob Maisel's invitation, replacing the Box Canyon Motel. 1978's nine callouts were grim: five body recoveries, a serious motorcycle crash, an injured teenager and a jeep accident. A nightmare scenario unfolded in February when an immense East Riverside slide, five miles south of Ouray on US 550, buried a rotary plow and its driver. On June 27 a thirty-two -year-old Illinois motorcyclist suffered multiple fractures and head injuries after he "failed to negotiate a sharp left turn" three and a half miles south on US 550. Seven minutes after the report, two rescuers descended 100 vertical feet into the Uncompahgre Gorge to stabilize the semi-conscious man. OMRT set up a scree

Fourth of July Parade, 1978: Kurt Kircher rides the Orange Beast, his wife Lynn hangs onto the right side and Brad Rhees stands on the passenger side bumper. All are wearing OMRT's first T-shirt.

Photo by Anna Kircher; Courtesy Lynn Kircher

evacuation, attached a rope and pulley system to the rear of a tow vehicle and drove slowly down the road, raising the litter, victim and attendants. Within an hour, the man was in the ambulance.

Five days later, a one-year-old boy disappeared from the KOA campground four miles north of town. After a two-hour search, his small body was found in a shallow, fast-moving irrigation ditch. On August 15, a seventeen-year-old boy taking pictures from a precarious perch above Cascade Creek's third set of falls, fell and rolled fifty feet into a rock-strewn basin. Pasek said he drove the Beast partway up the road to where he, Jim Fife, Roger Sherman and Elwood Gregory could climb the cliffs to reach the boy. Fife and Sherman scrambled up to check his status. Pasek hoisted the big, Kelty-framed medical pack, Gregory took the rope, and they "started hoofing," using the rope to belay in precarious spots along the way. It was a brutal evacuation; then, as Pasek was about to descend, he felt a tugging on his harness. It was Sherman – a good climber who worked as a carpenter rebuilding houses before he later moved on to medical school. He was "Just checking" Pasek's knot. Altogether, it took four-and-a-half hours to reach the boy, stabilize him on a stretcher and lift him down with ropes and pulleys.

A week later, a Jeep accident at 'Oh! Point' atop Engineer Mountain called out OMRT, EMTs and a BLM helicopter to evacuate several injured passengers. In September Walt Gorrod was prospecting around the Barstow Mine and found a dead man sitting beside Commodore Creek, "boots off and a survival blanket around the shoulders." The body sat a mile and a half from Imogene Pass and a mile from US 550. William Richard Adler, twenty-nine, of Redlands, California, had been missing since November 1977. His car was found abandoned in Marshall Basin on the Telluride side of the ridge. San Miguel Sheriff Fred Ellerd said that Adler was given a ride to Imogene Pass and not seen thereafter. The "frozen body of Lea McClain, forty-eight, was found by a search dog" from Silverton on December 8. Fourteen people from the Sheriff's Office and OMRT searched for two miserable days in a snowstorm. George Pastor and SAR K-9 Leo were summoned from Silverton; Leo found Lea's snow-covered body in twenty-two minutes, curled up under a cedar tree less than 100 yards from her home.

◆ ◆ ◆

Capt. Trujillo resigned in October, forced to move from his beloved native place to make a living. A mine geologist, he stayed ten months after the Camp Bird Mine closed in January. For years, when he was home between mining jobs that took him around the United States and South America, he volunteered with OMRT. A new executive board – Capt. Pasek, Lt. Tom Whelan, Equipment Officer Mike Hamrick and Dr. Maisel – met to reorganize. The next two years saw fewer callouts, though two were among the most intense and complicated in team history.

In August 1979, a bloody woman walked out of a side road near the top of Imogene Pass, was refused help at a camp and "convinced them to give her a ride to the next campsite," wrote OMRT member Tom Sylvester. After a 9 p.m. callout, rescuers and EMTs searched with flashlights until 1 a.m., found another woman with a broken neck and the driver, with a nearly severed foot, wedged in a small pickup.

Jan Smith had just sat down to nurse her infant son when this "most dramatic call" of her EMT career came. Patsie Hamrick, who also had an infant, took over maternal duties. During the bumpy ride to the ambulance at Camp Bird, Smith held the woman's neck in tension in the back of a pickup. She escaped paralysis; the man's foot was surgically fused.

Four hikers were lost near Engineer Pass on August 17 in terrible weather, with only one poncho. Two hiked out, met a driver going to Lake City and some campers, but no one helped. The report said four people were injured on Bear Creek Trail. At midnight two rescue parties deployed: one hiked Bear Creek from US 550 and one descended the trail. Laszlo Kubinyi said they wore team helmets and orange jackets and carried new radios. At dawn, hiking across American Flats at 12,400 feet, snarling Basque dogs woke them fast. Yelling into the radio, he said they might need rescuing after the dogs were through. The herder appeared and gave them hot chocolate.

The second group picked up one hiker and found another on the Pass. They were "led on by one of the victims by searchlight" and bivouacked at 12,600 feet in light drizzle, snow, hail, fog and thirty degree temperatures. Just before 8 a.m., a Hinsdale Deputy spotted the missing hikers. In low visibility, on the confusing highlands of American Flats, they were disoriented by ninety degrees, initially heading toward wilderness.

Pasek wrote of the hikers' good fortune: "Overall, the party was terribly ill-equipped to travel in these mountains: no matches, no compass, no map, no extra clothing, which these hills in their darker moments do not forgive ... they are extremely lucky folks." He admitted that he was "probably growling" as he wrote. The captain, worried about searchers sent into a storm, realized that "the life of no victim is worth the life of a rescuer." The survivors knew how lucky they were. Jim and Sally Smyth of Ouray wrote: "It is extremely comforting to know that so many dedicated people are prepared to drop everything and participate in a search."

Five days later, USFS regional coordinator Ray Loffholm had a heart attack on Bear Creek Trail. Unfamiliar with the area, he was hobbled by knee injuries. Five rescuers hiked four miles in pitch-black darkness to the Yellow Jacket Mine, arriving at daybreak. A Lama helicopter came from a government agency. Pasek watched as it flew up the narrow canyon: "Jim Fife built a fire to give them some smoke so they could see which way the wind was blowing. I remember Jim standing there and getting blown all over the place by the helicopter coming in ... he was hanging on to his parka." A three-page letter and a check expressed Loffholm's gratitude. He had been "startled to see you and your four associates – Jim Fife, Jim Boots, John Radcliffe and Dave Houtz – appear out of nowhere to give me some help."

On Labor Day, a 1975 Chevrolet Nova missed the "Oh shit" descending radius corner north of Bear Creek Falls and plunged 400 feet down a big talus slope. The pager sounded, Capt. Pasek ran two blocks downhill and jumped on the ambulance as it went past. Three miles later, he jumped out in helmet and harness, ran over to the edge amid onlookers, looked down and saw remnants of a car. Jumping into scree, he ran past a continuous debris field – the hood, the trunk, the battery, cassettes, clothing:

> *I'm looking for a guy, get down to the bottom, car is right side up.... I look in and in the passenger seat there is a human being! It looked like he was breathing.*
> *"Can you hear me?"*
> *He opened his eyes and looked at me and said, "Yeah."*

Other rescuers arrived but they couldn't get the door open. Finally, "one of the big Radcliff boys came down" and broke the seat back. They maneuvered the victim onto a backboard and slid him out the empty back window. The litter and 500 feet of Goldline came down.

The Orange Beast, parked at road's edge, and a Jeep with a sling and pulley were rigged for a low angle raise. Rescuers watched as the Jeep drove slowly up the road but the litter, with sixty-one-year-old Kurt Kircher and Capt. Pasek holding the uphill end and others on both sides, didn't move. Finally, the Goldline, with a ten percent stretch factor, reached its limit and contracted. They ran uphill, trying to avoid bumping the patient against the rocks. At the top, Bob Larson put out his hand and retrieved the litter. The forty-year-old captain "tumbled onto the road on hands and knees and just put my forehead on the road. I was spent, totally spent." The twenty-two-year-old victim was cited for driving under the influence and careless driving.

◆ ◆ ◆

In 1980, Capt. Pasek was named Elks Citizen of the Year for community service. Ouray's 1980 Fourth of July celebration was disastrous as Ouray filled with drunken revelers the night of the Fourth; the Fire Department hosed them down and OMRT helped control them. By then, however, rescuers had already put in a full afternoon and evening. The more serious of the day's two Jeep accidents, at 4:40 p.m., was for a GMC that went off Camp Bird Road (CR 361) just below the Drinking Cup. The driver lost control on the gravelly dirt road and his truck slid sixty-nine feet before it went off to the right, rolling three times and ejecting all five occupants. It rested on its wheels in rocks 200 feet below the road. A fourteen-year-old Ridgway boy was killed, his sister and two others injured. The driver fractured his left leg. A rollover in the annual flare parade, just south of town on US 550, occurred at dusk. The Jeep pickup crossed the center line, ran off the left shoulder and rolled, resting on its top forty-four feet down. The driver's back was broken, but his wife jumped out of the Jeep before it went over and escaped injury.

Ouray hunter Steve Martinez was rescued from a steep cliff at Angel Creek on Camp Bird Road on October 26. His brother-in-law Bob McClaren fell and thought he was gone. He saw light and grabbed a tree, but his rifle lay in pieces 600 feet down. Martinez decided that he wasn't going down while McClaren realized that he had fallen to just the right place to hike out. When Pasek and Doug Gregory arrived and climbed to the top, they inadvertently knocked rocks down and Martinez yelled at them. The captain made his way down, grabbed the hunter's rifle and they climbed out. Martinez hunts elsewhere these days. There "was nothing there anyway." It's the kind of place, he said, where "you need a pan and saltshaker" since you can't pack a carcass out. "You have to cut it up, bone it, and leave the pieces for the coyotes."

◆ ◆ ◆

"A spectacular rescue ... on top of Mt. Sneffels" during Labor Day weekend had serious communication problems, so OMRT ordered an RCA $3,640.77 mobile communications system. The first female captain Linda Hash, 1981-1982, organized and promoted the team. She gave demonstrations of rescue equipment and spoke on backcountry survival to school assemblies, distributing a brochure, "Be A Wilderness Survivor," which covered fatigue, falls, dehydration and hypothermia. OMRT rescued three lost hikers, an overdue jeep party, a fallen climber and stranded hunters from June to October 1981. On a unique callout in November, Capt. Hash, Lt. Tom Hash, Mary Hoeksema and Pasek responded to a poaching incident.

For Hoeksema, a gifted climber and painter who moved to Ouray from the Front Range and joined in 1980, the unusual retrieval was memorable. She knew there was no body involved; they "were just supposed to go down and look for elk bits." She and Pasek scrambled into Canyon Creek and found a leg. She walked toward Box Canyon Falls and found "a whole elk carcass ... and it was skinned!" She hauled it a ways, then went back to tell the others she found a carcass "with a bullet hole!" Pasek brought down an orange plastic rescue sled and "We start hauling that puppy up that hill," said Hoeksema, "and we just ruined that sled ... but we got it up there!" Laughing while they carried out this unusual mission, they hauled the discarded, headless elk from "a place that was inaccessible except by technical climbers." Charlie Ricker, OMRT's radio wizard, managed to keep everyone communicating.

On October 12, a 5 p.m. callout abruptly ended Charlie and Elaine Ricker's 24th anniversary plans. An Oklahoma father and son on a hunting trip were stuck on a cliff 150 feet above Cow Creek. Rick, thirty-four, and Ricky Warren, fourteen, climbed up Cutler Creek, crossed Baldy Ridge and descended until they could go no further. They spotted four Texas families camping within yelling distance of Cow Creek and alerted them with rifle fire.

As Hoeksema drove her 4WD Subaru up Cow Creek, Sheriff Dougherty spotted her and persuaded her to join him. "You'll never find it," he told her. They "bopped along" in his 4WD cruiser; he gave her apples, sandwiches and a giant radio, which she stuffed into her pack, already laden with gear. As night fell rescuers spotted the stranded hunters' big fire from the creek bed. At Pasek's insistence, Hoeksema, OMRT's first technical woman and a self described "climbing fiend" familiar with night ascents, led up the dirty, junky cliff with teen member Jeff Swanson following. They fixed a line so others could follow. Globs of rock broke off at a touch, so they climbed southward, emerging above a slimy, dark cliff . They had a full moon but heavy cloud cover prevented seeing much. Eventually, they found the hunters hunkered down in the cliffs. Hoeksema unloaded the Sheriff's sandwiches and apples from her heavy pack to the relief of famished hunters and rescuers, then loaned gear for the night. "I always carried a hat," she said, "a climber's sleeping bag and a bivouac bag, so I gave somebody the hat and somebody else the sleeping bag, somebody else the bivy bag…. George and I had our feet in my pack, trying to keep our feet warm." It was a long, drizzly night.

In the morning, she said they could lower the hunters on the fixed line. Pasek said they had pulled it up the night before because they needed the rope. That left two options: hike up and out several miles the way the hunters had come in or rappel the cliff to Cow Creek. They decided to rappel. The boy, snug in a team harness, went first, but the father refused. Pasek said he couldn't persuade him, but Hoeksema, "with a woman's touch, talked him into it."

More responders had arrived in the Orange Beast the night before and found the Texans in "the most marvelous camp … like it came from a big circus," said June Bachman. "They had a wood burning stove in the middle, chairs and tables all around, they had a tent for sleeping, they had a refrigerator." The hunters in those luxurious accommodations treated the rescuers, now off the cliff, to breakfast. "Everyone was happy," said Hoeksema. "No one was hurt."

◆ ◆ ◆

That summer, fifteen-year-old Brian Johnson, the *Plaindealer* editor's son, told his Mom that he and a friend were taking an afternoon hike on Twin Peaks Trail. Later, she discovered that his friend hadn't gone. Johnson had no gear for an all-night stay. Capt. Linda Hash and Pasek decided a night search was warranted. Pasek followed footprints all the way to Twin Peaks, where he lost the tracks. He radioed Sheriff Dougherty that he would stay the night. The Sheriff said there were "coffee and donuts down here." Lt. Tom Hash and Swanson searched Oak Creek Trail; Alvin Klein and Doug Gregory searched Silvershield. They slept out, too.

Johnson, thinking he'd back by dark, started down around 8:30 but lost the trail in the dim, dense forest. He climbed to the Silvershield Trail, built a pine bough shelter and slept. At 6 a.m., he walked into the arms of Charlie Ricker, who had spent the night at the trailhead. Ricker relayed the news. Pasek radioed: "Will you look at that kid's shoes and tell me what the tread looks like?" It matched the prints on Twin Peaks. Editor Joyce Jorgenson was eloquent:

> *There are times when words just aren't enough.*
> *What can I say that is sufficient about our Mountain Rescue*

Team? We know they have finely-honed skills, are beautifully coordinated, and know their business.... Words work at a distance.

But it's when one is on the receiving end of their help as nightmare sets in and the world narrows down to just one thing: the safety of a loved one, that you really understand how skilled, how well they work, how giving this service is. Then gratitude becomes inexpressible and "thank you" is too puny and too easy to say. But I am grateful and I do say "thank you!" to all the rescue team members who "did something" when it was thought that Brian could be lying hurt, or worse, on that mountain last Thursday night.

◆ ◆ ◆

In mid-July, the driver of a rental Jeep in rugged Poughkeepsie Gulch southeast of Ouray had to back down in a tough place. The passenger, a twenty-two-year-old woman, got out, the Jeep slipped sideways in snow on shale, hit a bare spot and flipped one and a half times, killing her. The nineteen-year-old driver suffered a fractured pelvis. Capt. Linda Hash drove the injured driver in her Jeep to the ambulance. Lt. Tom Hash packaged the body and took it to Montrose in his Jeep.

Six days later, a tourist from Austin, Texas, was knocked unconscious when her horse stumbled and threw her near the Bridge of Heaven, four miles up the Horsethief Trail. The 4 p.m. callout yielded but eight rescuers, who discovered that the 300-pound woman had to be carried down. "She was scared to death," said Capt. Hash, "would not get on the horse." They really didn't want her to walk: "She probably would have had a heart attack."

Sixteen years later, the rescue remained vivid for June Bachman. The effort stretched the small team to their limits: "My arms grew carrying [her] down the trail," said Bachman. "We'd carry her for about fifty feet and take a break ... it seemed like a hundred miles." Earl Bashaw said they did "only a couple of switchbacks at a time" on the narrow trail before resting. Capt. Hash realized that they needed more help and hiked down to Undersheriff Wakefield, manning the base at the Bachelor/Syracuse Mine. "We can't bring her down ... just call out anybody who can," she said. It was Friday afternoon and Ouray was filled with tourists, but "Jerry Wakefield went to town, hit all the bars," said Bachman. "All the guys from the bars showed up to help us carry her down." Finally, they had enough people to rotate the litter carry.

The ambulance waited, but when Dr. Maisel examined her, he found nothing wrong. "I chastised the person who rented her the horse," said Capt. Hash. "We were from the Wild, Wild West back in the day," said Lt. Hash. After that, OMRT bought a wheel for the litter.

Dr. Dave Bachman was working in Telluride during that rescue, but his turn came the next night. Two experienced hikers, Joel Huelscamp and Randy Berry from Craig, Colorado, crossed a snow bank on Blaine Peak on the way to Sneffels. Huelscamp slid, his crampons snagged on rock and his ankle snapped. They struggled back to camp, Berry made a fire and hiked out.

Otto Scheidegger, Earl and Sue Bashaw, Doug and Elwood Gregory, Rick Blackford, Dr. Bachman and two friends, Jerry and Debbie Hinman, hiked three miles into the basin in darkness. Three rocky, wet crossings of Wilson Creek were a challenge but they finally reached Huelscamp at 3 a.m. The doctor left the injured man's boot on to stabilize the ankle, said Earl Bashaw. Then he fed him tea and bouillon all night. It was impossible to bring the injured man out by foot, so they decided on a helicopter evacuation. The 12,000-foot elevation was too high for the St. Mary's helicopter in Grand Junction, so Sheriff Dougherty requested a Chinook military chopper for 7:30 a.m. It arrived at 9:45. The wary pilot barely hovered "over the orange cross marker the rescuers had laid down" on the slope, said Bashaw. They loaded the patient and were out by 11:30, but the Hinmans may have had enough of Ouray wilderness, said June Bachman. They never visited again.

In mid-October, Dr. Bachman answered a heart attack call from the Little Chef in Ridgway. Charlie Ricker drove the ambulance, his wife Elaine was EMT; they stopped to pick up the doctor. When they joined Undersheriff Wakefield, however, they learned the man was in a San Miguel County hunt camp two and a half miles up Alder Creek Trail, off Last Dollar Road.

Charlie Ricker drove in as far as possible, but had to stop part way up the rough road. A good Samaritan offered the doctor a ride on the back of his motorcycle, which got him within three-fourths of a mile. While hiking into the 10,500-foot camp "in crippling weather," the captain said he wore only his office clothes – slacks, leather sports coat and Wolverines. Hunters cut trees to move the six-foot, six-inch Texan onto a blanket. The Flight for Life pilot surveyed the scene and "realized that although he could land, he would have difficulty taking off." He dropped an oxygen bottle and left to wait on the highway. Vietnam veteran Burt Metcalf, in a Bell 44, flew the man out. The team stood by in case the hunter had to be carried out.

Later that month, two Pennsylvania hunters, staying at the Hashes' Timber Ridge Motel and unfamiliar with the area, "just totally got lost" after hiking the Horsethief Trail past the Bridge of Heaven toward American Flats. Elwood Gregory drove four rescuers at night up the rough road. Stan Laidlaw and Earl Bashaw hiked five hours across American Flats and down Bear Creek to US 550 looking for the men. In heavy snow and "zero visibility," they tied themselves together and used compasses to pick up the Bear Creek Trail. Bashaw "had never seen it snow that hard." Mary Hoeksema and her brother Ron Hoeksema, fit runners in peak condition, searched from Engineer Pass to Horsethief, using map and compass to navigate the confusing terrain. It was snowing as they set out with emergency bivy sacs, food and water. "If we ran," she said, "we thought we could do it in three hours ... there was a storm coming in." The terrain sloped down, except for Cascade Pass.

Hours later, they were nearly done for and needed to "get outta here now or we're going to get in trouble." They called into the storm one last time. A gun fired in the direction of the Horsethief/Difficulty junction, downhill from the pass, deeper in the wilderness. They looked at each other. "Do we really want to find these guys?" she said. "Shall we just say we didn't hear that?" They did the right thing and headed for the hunters. At 6:15, they found two lost, tired, dehydrated men, shivering near a fire, at the junction.

"Do you have any water?" one asked.
"Yeah, just take a sip," she replied.

The thirsty men drank all their water. They hiked over the Bridge of Heaven, relaying their find and position through Montrose Dispatch. The team met them in the trees above Dexter Creek.

Lt. Hash had given the hunters their instructions, said Mary Hoeksema: "It's all downhill ... you can't miss the trail." The men, undaunted by the experience, returned with other companions for several years. "One of them that led the group ... he'd take us out to the Bon Ton and buy us all dinner," Lt. Hash said. Having customers at the motel "that time of the year" was welcome, too.

◆ ◆ ◆

Cascade and Portland Creeks flooded Ouray for two days in July 1981 and for four in August 1982. The floods rivaled the worst in Ouray's history.

> *The war began Friday afternoon around three p.m. with three loud cracks, sharper and more earthbound than the sound of thunder, as the first of innumerable large boulders and logs pounded down Cascade Flume.... The boulders, and logs, some of them as hefty as telephone poles, rode a torrent of roiling brown water that hurtled down the flume with a rumbling like a freight train.*

Both flume underpasses plugged up at Main Street. Heaps of debris mounted on the road as repeated attempts to clear the channels underneath failed. Work crews piled debris to the north and south of the underpasses and channeled floodwaters over the road and back into the flumes on the downhill, western side. Smaller bridges were shredded or swept away whole. In a town of 684 people, twelve businesses and civic establishments were damaged, thirty residences and yards took on water and mud, small sheds floated into neighboring yards, and a cement mixer disappeared under mountains of debris. City, county and state road crews, law enforcement agencies, EMTs and private citizens "manned shovels and heavy equipment." OMRT monitored the flood, said Capt. Hash. "Telling them they were in danger ... here comes Portland, get out of the way." Portland Flume ran five-six feet tall, filled with rocks, boulders, huge trees, said Lt. Hash, who monitored Portland Bridge above town.

The second night of rain and flood saw two vehicles buried. Felix Pfaeffle's closed Subaru station wagon was dug out with no interior damage and he drove it away. An open blue station wagon parked at the Bon Ton was not so lucky – it filled with muck and water. Capt. Hash watched as floodwater moved it a block downhill to the bank. The third day, OMRT ferried twelve elderly residents to shelter at the school. By the end of the fourth day the flooding eased, though it rained another two days. No one was injured or killed. The city's buildings, infrastructure and the heavily damaged Portland Bridge were rebuilt.

◆ ◆ ◆

In August OMRT aced MRA recertification, conducted by Alpine Rescue from Jefferson County on the Front Range and Mountain

Rescue of Aspen. A scree evacuation at the Ruby Walls utilized thirteen members, including Undersheriff Wakefield, Capt. Hash and three men who would become captain: Tom Hash, Dr. David Bachman and Otto Scheidegger. June Bachman reorganized and reprinted the cookbook, with a new section on preparing and serving wild game. In what would become a fine advertisement for Ouray, Coors came to town to shoot pictures of ice climbing for the company's 1983 calendar. Mary Hoeksema teamed up with Peter White, the English climber who assisted in the 1980 Sneffels rescue.

Coors photographer Terry McElhenny took six hundred shots of Hoeksema and White on the natural ice of a cliff in the Uncompahgre Gorge near Camp Bird Road. In the photo on the March 1983 calendar page, Hoeksema leads the climb. The burgeoning sport of ice climbing would change both the team and Ouray.

CHAPTER FOUR

A Father Of Three

THE HAYDEN SURVEY ARRIVED at Red Mountain Pass in the course of their topographical work in 1874. Franklin Rhoda described "the box-cañon" of the Uncompahgre as "barring all egress." Eight years later Otto Mears, the legendary pathfinder of the San Juans, began a toll road from Ouray through the gorge, across Ironton Park and over Red Mountain Pass, turning a trail into a wagon road in 1883. "It wasn't until 1919 that the wagon trail became suitable for the automobile and was still questionable." In 1921, it was widened to one lane with pullouts for passing. How it acquired the nickname Million Dollar Highway is uncertain – perhaps from the money needed to reconstruct it, perhaps from the gold ore in its dirt road base. Not until 1939 could Colorado's Department of Transportation (CDOT) keep it open year round. It is still the "most avalanche prone segment of highway open in the winter in the United States." Thirty-eight avalanche paths threaten the twenty-three-miles between Silverton and Ouray. East Riverside, on Mt. Abram's west side, is the most dangerous. It begins in a seventy-five-acre catchment basin 3,200 feet above the road and runs for a mile, narrowing and steepening as it approaches US 550. In 1908 "miner Elias Fritz was swept away while pulling a freight sled with two horses and his dog under the path," the first known victim in a place where "the highway takes the full brunt of the sliding snow. There is no runout zone – the snow fills the Uncompahgre Gorge."

◆ ◆ ◆

On the second day of a large spring storm, Sunday, March 3, 1963, Rev. Marvin Hudson, accompanied by daughters Amelia and Pauline, headed from Ouray to Silverton to conduct church services,

43

US 550, the Million Dollar Highway, curves dramatically as it leaves Ironton, heading north through the canyon of the Uncompahgre to Ouray. East Riverside's paths dump onto the road where it disappears along Mt. Abram, to the right. The large patch of snow in the canyon below the mountain is from slides during winter 2015-2016.

Photo by Mike Boruta

"despite phone calls asking him not to come." He passed avalanche warning signs and three snowplows clearing debris. Snowplow driver Leo Janes had just cleared one lane through six feet of snow left on the road by an early morning East Riverside slide. The plows had backed up in order to widen the single track when Rev. Hudson drove by. His car spun out forty feet before he reached "the main chute of the East Riverside.... He jacked up the car and put a chain on the left rear wheel.... The girls remained in the car. J[anes] then started ahead in his highway truck to pull Rev. H[udson] back down the road." East Riverside ran again, filling the air with fine, dense snow, "making breathing almost impossible." The minister's broken body was found in a week, his mangled, torn vehicle two weeks later, six hundred feet from where it stopped. Six eggs and a jar of cream resided unbroken on the back shelf of the car. A flashlight with bulb and batteries, every inch packed tight with snow, was in the glove box. Eighty-eight days later, relatives who had been checking the massive slide area found the last daughter's battered body twenty feet downstream from the car. The slide was a climax event, filled the creek with snow thirty to sixty feet deep and extended downstream for six hundred and fifty feet. Seven years later, same month, almost the same day, March 2, 1970, East Riverside struck again. Highway maintenance worker Robert Miller's watch stopped at 11:56 a.m. Rescuers plowed three trenches in the snow, found his lunch pail and thermos at the second level, his glasses and body at the third. Avalanche mitigation began in 1956 when the National Guard provided CDOT with a first artillery piece, a 75mm pack howitzer; Mike Friedman and Telluride Helitrax, a heli-ski operation, began heli-bombing in 1986.

◆ ◆ ◆

Nearly eight years later on February 10, 1978, East Riverside had run once and US 550 was blocked by "a minor slide," eight feet of snow. State Highway Department boss Blaine Thompson called Terry Kishbaugh in "because of the lousy conditions," even though it was his day off. At 10:40, they worked back to back to clear the slide. Kishbaugh's rotary plow chewed into the mountain of snow, then he moved aside for his companion in the bulldozer to move what had been loosened. Kishbaugh's plow was chewing snow and spitting it out for the dozer to move when East Riverside ran again. Multiple runs are a common occurrence with East Riverside. This particular incident was indelibly imprinted in Thompson's memory.

I was in a state truck on the Silverton side of Riverside and he came up from Ouray and made a couple of passes.... I was parked under the cliff watching him. Terry comes by again and holds one finger up to let me know he would make one more pass. Just as he starts under East Riverside, she runs again, for the second time. Big! His plow is blown away ... almost hits me as it goes by. I step out in the hopes of seeing something. Another surge of the slide caused a blast that tore off my hardhat and glasses. The snow drifted down around me and I couldn't see anything....

When the powder cloud cleared, the snow lay thirty feet deep in the canyon. There was no sign of either Kishbaugh or the plow. Thompson radioed the state patrol dispatcher in Montrose. The Ouray Sheriff and Emergency Services were notified and called OMRT for help. Bill Hopkins responded after Chief Kelley came by his motel.

"Hey, we got a problem on the Pass. Terry Kishbaugh's snowplow has been knocked over." And we went up there on the Riverside and we had the avalanche poles ... fifteen of us down there trying to put our avalanche poles in the avalanche snow and that stuff was incredible – it was concrete, you couldn't penetrate it an inch.

At 11:10 a.m. two of the first responders, wearing Skadis (the first effective avalanche safety beacons), made a hasty search of several large cracks which had appeared in the hard-packed snow, hoping for a signal from the beacon that Terry carried with him in the plow.

The search turned up nothing. So Hopkins, nine other rescuers and five more volunteers probed on six-foot centers, hoping to find Kishbaugh's plow. The overcast sky degenerated into a blizzard-like storm with strong winds and temperatures in the 20s and 30s. Avalanche debris extended forty yards east to west and 120 yards north and south, filling the river canyon to a depth of forty to fifty feet at the center. Patty Blackford, twenty-five, tried to push her pole into the massive slide without much success. "That's when I got to become the lookout," she said, assigned to watch the West Riverside slide, situated slightly to the south across the canyon. It had not run, but everyone knew that if it did, the runout zone could extend across the canyon to the road where they worked. Most of the searchers did not wear Skadis.

When San Juan County Rescue (SJCR) arrived at noon, the search area was cleared so that George Pastor's K-9 could work. "The dog showed interest," wrote Capt. Rick Trujillo, "near large cracks and hand trenching and probing was begun." At 12:20 nothing had been found, the storm's intensity decreased and visibility improved. Everyone evacuated so CDOT could shoot East Riverside's avalanche paths with the howitzer, but nothing ran. A lookout was posted again at 2 p.m. and searchers and dog returned to the snowfield.

A call went out to Montrose for metal detectors and Deputy Sheriff Warren Waterman delivered them. When he later went down to retrieve something from the CDOT barn just outside Ouray, he saw Terry Kishbaugh's father John Kishbaugh, part of the Montrose Sheriff's Posse, standing silently at the avalanche gate across the road. Deputy Waterman got out to talk and the man asked if he could ride up with him since "they won't let me come up there." At the avalanche scene, they stood silently at the edge of the road, watching the rescue work.

Chris George, proprietor of the St. Paul Lodge on the south side of the pass, skied several miles down to the site with two helpers, with fourteen-foot probes and shovels. George remembered Thompson standing there, a shocked survivor: "Damn it, damn it, damn it." George said they "probed and then our hands would get hot and the probes were made of metal. What would happen as the probes would go back down, they would melt some snow and that would freeze to the probe, and then the probe would freeze in the hole." It took two or three of them to unstick the probes. The USFS brought smaller diameter, hollow probes, which made the exhausting, dangerous work somewhat easier. The rescuers nervously checked the other, lesser East and West Riverside avalanche chutes as they struggled with the dense snow in the canyon.

SJCR directed fine probing with thirty searchers on a line parallel to the avalanche fall line and perpendicular to the creek. The line began at the center of the debris, moving in two passes to the upper and lower edges. Terry Kishbaugh's dog was brought to the scene and showed interest in the same area as the K-9. The searchers hand trenched that spot, but by 3:30 fine probing found nothing. Hopkins said they "gave up, we can't find anyone and this is dangerous." He had been "to avalanche school in Silverton and they were talking about how oftentimes an avalanche will run twice and I looked up at that chute.... I couldn't move fast enough if that thing rolled." Many years later, Jerry Roberts also noted the futility of finding anyone alive in such a massive slide: "Of course you're going to dig, but it was a little spooky because it was before the days of helicopters being used for [avalanche] mediation. There was no guarantee that something else wasn't going to come down." Heavy equipment, including bulldozers, began digging after the searchers retreated to the road. At that point, many people left for the warmth and safety of their homes. As the sky darkened at 5:30 p.m., only twenty remained.

The Denver office ordered highway personnel back to Ouray, but CDOT's bulldozers worked through the night, driven by family members and friends. "Bob Miller from Idarado Mine offered use of a geophysical magnetometer." It arrived at 10 p.m. and its operator examined the whole slide area in fifty minutes, identifying one major anomaly. "Due to unfamiliarity with the instrument," Trujillo wrote that the operator was unsure "of the significance. After a telephone call to the manufacturer, uncertainty was dispelled and by 01:00 Saturday the most promising area was located and an estimated depth was given (30 ft.)." The bulldozer concentrated "near the center of the creek, approximately 30 ft. below the road and 150 yds. north (downstream) of the truck's last seen location." Fragments of the plow emerged by 7 a.m. Saturday, ending the dozer's work. The weather turned colder, but still searchers labored in blizzard conditions to find the twenty-eight-year-old father of three in the snow-filled canyon. Then a backhoe struck a hard mass. At 7:30 it punctured the right front tire of Terry Kishbaugh's plow, "lying upside down, sitting tilted on its tail." They decided to "bulldoze the snow rather than backhoe further or hand dig to the cab. Because of the truck's position relative to the high center of the avalanche debris, enormous amounts of snow had to be moved to allow the bulldozers to operate and the truck was uncovered extremely slowly."

As they sat in the warmth of Deputy Waterman's patrol car, Terry Kishbaugh's father, tears running down his face, said,

> *"Warren, there ain't no way."*
> *"John, we can't give up," replied the deputy.*

At 3:30 that afternoon, West Riverside ran "in a fine cloud" and buried the creek "under as much as twenty ft. of snow, 400 ft. south of the East Riverside avalanche." The slide didn't reach the road, was "moderate in size and accompanied with a large dust cloud," wrote Trujillo. "Most rescuers and observers at the site saw or heard it run. There were no injuries, though some people were somewhat shaken."

"They found his big rig," said Hopkins, but "he wasn't there." Rescuers reached the empty, crushed cab at 5 p.m. The driver's door was gone and they realized he must have been blown out immediately. They dug around the plow for another hour, but found nothing and "agreed it was best to wait for the spring thaw to uncover the body," wrote Trujillo. Ironically, OMRT had scheduled avalanche practice that day, which was superseded by this real time, complicated search. Sixty-seven people searched for Terry Kishbaugh over thirty-three hours in constant storm and occasional blizzard conditions. The initial thirty-degree temperature fell below twenty before they were through.

◆ ◆ ◆

As early as 1908, "pleas started for some sort of tunnel or shed" to protect travelers from Red Mountain Pass avalanches. In 1970, State Highway Engineer Charles Shumate told the *Montrose Daily Press* that a "plan for a tunnel at the Riverside site, costing approximately $1 million, has been in the files ... for 'three to four years,' but that funding had not been available." The lack of money and questions about "the feasibility of a snow shed" in that terrain prevented it from being built. Intense local lobbying of the governor and legislature began shortly after Terry Kishbaugh was buried. Trujillo spoke for both rescuers and the Ouray community in an April 1978 letter to Gov. Richard Lamm. The time had come to tame "the killer slide."

> *As a group committed to search and rescue operations, we feel it is our duty to bring your attention to an extremely hazardous condition ... five miles south of Ouray. The East and West Riverside slides empty into the narrow canyon and present blind slide paths to the highway ... at their impact and runout area. This highway is the major north-south route in this area.... The hazard presented ... is extreme.*
>
> *In the past fifteen years ... five people have died in the white death of East Riverside.... The most recent victim was a snowplow operator ... caught on February 10, 1978.*
>
> *Ouray Mountain Rescue Team responded ... and searched with more than sixty people from other organizations under the very real*

danger of additional avalanches. The thirty-three-hour mission proved futile and the victim's body has yet to be recovered.

◆ ◆ ◆

Thompson's hat and glasses were never found: "It tears a guy up to lose a fellow worker like that." Roberts, who skied daily through May, said he routinely went by the slide debris to probe for Terry Kishbaugh. He didn't find him, but in late May John and Fred Castle, two of Kishbaugh's brothers-in-law who helped check the fences daily, found the body "in the first of two fences across the creek, 150 feet below where the plow had been found," 300 feet downstream of where he worked. OMRT helped retrieve the body. Dr. Maisel's examination "determined that Kishbaugh's death had been instantaneous as a result of head injuries."

A petition drive collected over 400 signatures. It went to Denver with sixteen people from OMRT and SJCR, Ouray School, three counties' commissioners, Chambers of Commerce, Club 20, Ouray and Ridgway City Councils, and Ouray and San Juan Sheriffs' Departments. On May 1, 1978, they met with Gov. Richard Lamm and CDOT officials. The governor listened and declared "a study be conducted as soon as possible to determine whether a shed or a tunnel was best...." It recommended a 1,200-foot shed to shield travelers from both Riverside slides. The "outrageous price tag stalled construction for years, until [Ouray County Commissioner Howard] Williams pointed out that a 100-foot shed would cover sixty percent of the slides, and a 200-foot shed would cover ninety percent ... 'right in the killer slot.'" A 184-foot snowshed was finished in November 1985. The 685-foot north extension and a 450-foot south extension were to be built when funds were available. At the dedication, Rev. William Doll of St. Daniels Catholic Church in Ouray said, "Never again need hundreds of rescuers search right in the slide zone, risk their lives to save buried victims or recover frozen bodies ... no more monuments to the dead should have to be erected...." "Everybody kind of thought we solved the problem," said Roberts, but the snowshed only protected those under the worst of East Riverside's chutes. Fourteen years later, in 1999, CDOT told the county that it was "prohibitively expensive" to lengthen the snowshed.

◆ ◆ ◆

On March 4, 1992, a monster storm etched "the latest chapter in the violent history of the Riverside slide," wrote historian Marvin

Gregory. Multiple avalanches, including East and West Riverside, ran along both sides of the road. Three Grand Junction men coming home that night made it over the pass and through the snowshed around midnight. A few minutes later, the first slide hit their truck "and almost swept us from the road." Ben Martinez, Arnuelfo Muela and Jose Renus tried but failed to free the pickup, sitting precariously on the road's edge. They waited, thinking someone else might come along. Two hours later, Martinez said, they thought they would have a better chance of surviving if they began walking. "By the time we left, the truck was almost buried by the slides." The State Patrol found them just outside Ouray, walking through a dangerous storm dressed in light jackets, cowboy boots, tennis shoes, jeans and T-shirts. The fortunate threesome spent the night at City Hall under warm blankets. Martinez's wife drove 100 miles from Grand Junction to get them. "I'm not really worried about the pick-up," he told the *Plaindealer.* "I know we are lucky to be here now." Meanwhile, the intense first blast of the storm had dropped three feet of heavy, wet snow which "landed on an unstable base ... melted and bound together during warm weather." The new snow released "almost immediately, causing numerous avalanches ... the road between Silverton and Ouray" was blocked by gates at 1:30 a.m. March 5.

◆ ◆ ◆

Foreman Don Castle finished the swing shift, Eddie Imel came from Ridgway for the graveyard and the pass was closed. With District Supervisor Bob Feldman they swept the road from Ouray to the pass. They found Ridgway resident Barb Taylor driving her pickup. She followed them to the snowshed where another CDOT man, Phil Spindel, waited. Imel radioed a new employee, Danny Jaramillo, thirty-six, who was driving a snowblower north of the snowshed. Imel said he was coming out, ran fifty yards to the machine, "scooted Jaramillo over and took over operating the snowblower." Castle watched as he did a "rammer-jammer," pushing the machine hard so that snow blew faster into the canyon. Then it "threw a chain ... and they were stuck." The men got out and "it ran bigger ... everything turns white and there is a lot of noise. We all were wearing the avalanche beacons of course but we thought maybe they got swept off into the canyon ... as soon as it settled down, I put mine on receive." Spindel's "eardrums pounded as the avalanche came down. Looking out, "he could see only the back three lights of the plow barely above the snow. 'Then it was silent ... probably everything was blown out by the slide. It was eerie.'"

They radioed dispatch to initiate a rescue. Castle, the twenty-six-year-old nephew of Terry Kishbaugh, grabbed a shovel and hurried into the storm, but stuff was still running, so he was forced back to the shed. He tried a second time, wading in chest deep snow to the heavy pile where the plow had been. He dug for them. "The wind's blowing and you're trying to listen to the beacon ... it's like concrete trying to dig.... I stayed out there for probably 20 minutes, seemed like hours, to the point I just couldn't dig anymore. I was just wore out." He waded back to the shed. As he rested, he thought about his wife: "I couldn't go back out." East Riverside ran again within minutes, closing the north end. The south side was partially blocked.

Snowplow operator David Dunn attempted to "reach the accident scene from the north, but was stopped just past the Engineer Pass turnout when Mother Cline ran and covered the hood of his vehicle. He escaped.... Six slides ran across the road between Ouray and the snowshed." While searching for Dunn, Undersheriff John Radcliff drove his Blazer through a small slide and saw a snow-covered form, said Sheriff Jerry Wakefield. He saw a "flashlight bouncing along and all of the sudden [Dunn] turns and goes the other way as hard as he can go. John can't figure out what it is ... sees another snow slide ... slams on the brakes and gets stopped.... They load up and high-tail back toward town."

◆ ◆ ◆

OMRT responded at 4:30 a.m. as the steady, heavy snowfall and extreme danger continued. The officers and Sheriff Wakefield debated whether anyone could even get up to the tunnel and bring those inside to Ouray. Lt. Randy Gerke said that the team was in a "transition period ... when you start thinking of the safety of the rescuers."

Capt. Michael Foxx called Jerry Roberts and asked him to scout the road on a snowmobile. Bill Dwelley, Lt. Gerke, Mike Briscoe and Ken Miller rode in the power company's snowcat to see if it was possible to get to the snowshed. "That snowcat was just a metal box on the back and we were in there with our gear ... and Mike is smoking like a train," said Dwelley. About to protest, he caught himself: "God, but if it's your last smoke, Mike."

The rest of the team waited impatiently at the closed gate above town. "These guys were ready to go skiing," recalled Foxx, "do anything to get up there." Roberts skied up to the rock face of Mother Cline slide where eight feet of debris now blocked all passage. He turned around and shook his head "No" to the others. "You can't get people in there." Finally, to everyone's relief, they all returned safely, having only gotten as far as Bear Creek. The once hopeful rescue party delivered bleak news. "Man, there's avalanches running that don't even have names yet," said Roberts. "With that much snow, what are you going to do when you get there? How are you going to get anybody out of that?" Confronted with the extreme risk to rescuers and too much snow to even be able to get to the search site, let alone try to get anybody out of the canyon, Sheriff Wakefield and Capt. Foxx reluctantly ruled out any rescue attempt from Ouray. The Sheriff "caught a lot of flack for that ... [but] we would have had more casualties ... it's stuff that's not talked about a lot, but you always consider the safety of the rescuers," Foxx said.

◆ ◆ ◆

San Juan Mountain Search and Rescue (SJMSAR), George Pastor and his K-9 finally managed to get to the top of Red Mountain, but could go "no further because of avalanche danger. Snow was still falling and visibility was poor." At that point, Gary King, the senior CDOT maintenance worker stationed in Silverton, decided to risk a trip to the snowshed in a rotary snowblower, mostly out of concern for what might happen to those in the snowshed, said Castle. The canyon was already filled with snow and West Riverside could still pack the snowshed from the south. Plow driver Brad Perkins and Sheriff Greg Leithauser drove behind the snowblower. At the top of the pass the procession of vehicles slowed down as the snowblower and plow labored to clear slide debris in what was to them unfamiliar territory. Snow lay two and a half feet deep on the road winding down from the pass, across Ironton and down through the intense, avalanche laden switchbacks to the snowshed. Sheriff Leithauser said afterwards that it was "horrendous, with slides coming down ahead of us and slides coming down behind us." The snow blocking the south snowshed entrance was "200 feet long and as much as ten feet high."

For eight hours, the four trapped inside the snowshed ran the machines to keep warm. When King got there, they were relieved to be going to Silverton, even though it was the wrong way from home. "We almost got wiped out going back – from Guadalupe [a notorious pair of avalanche paths east and west of the highway] right before you get to Crystal Lake," said Castle, who was driving Taylor's truck. He returned home that night, going the long way through Durango to Cortez, Lizard Head Pass, Telluride and Ridgway. The pickup he had left at his house in Ouray had three feet of snow standing on its top.

◆ ◆ ◆

In "an air pocket below the plow," Imel and Jaramillo dug upward. Imel had the pliers he had carried around the plow to work on the rear driver's side tire, but he wasn't dressed for such an ordeal, wearing a light jacket, "cowboy boots and cotton blue jeans." Jaramillo followed his boss out of the plow with a big 6 D-cell flashlight, both men in violation of "protocol that had been built up after all those avalanche paths, after those other plow drivers have been killed," said Roberts. "You stayed in your truck and made a phone call. You communicated that way."

Jaramillo used his flashlight as a pick, said Castle. The two men dug desperately through rock hard snow, but after fifteen hours of labor in darkness and cold, thirty-eight-year-old Imel succumbed. They "talked during the entire ordeal, and Jaramillo struggled to keep his partner alive.... Imel began showing signs of hypothermia.... Finally Jaramillo had to attempt to save himself." After his boss died, Jaramillo dug to "the hood of the buried plow and smashed the front window to retrieve a K-Mart shovel." He dug himself out, "creating an eight-foot wormhole." His insulated jumpsuit kept him warm and allowed him to wriggle upward. He emerged 200 feet from the snow shed at 9 p.m. He had been buried for eighteen hours.

Spindel's plow, stuck in the snow blocking the north entrance to the shed, still had fuel and a working radio. Jaramillo ran the engine for warmth and called Montrose Dispatch. The person on duty "thought somebody was just pranking them," said Gerke. Jaramillo finally convinced them he was alive. "His first request was to contact his wife and children in Ouray. Then he complained that his cigarettes were wet and asked the Silverton crew to bring a fresh pack up." Sheriff Wakefield "didn't believe in reincarnation ... but when they called me ... I swear that's how I got all my white hair ... right then."

♦ ♦ ♦

Jaramillo's rescue crew brought the desired cigarettes from Silverton. Snowplow drivers Gary King and Kathy Daniels cleared the way and Sheriff Leithauser and SJMSAR Guy Lewis tucked in behind them. The snow finally stopped just as they arrived at midnight. Jaramillo's "clothes were wringing wet ... he was suffering from shock, hypothermia, and carbon monoxide poisoning, yet he was able to relay his experiences to his rescuers." They lowered Lewis "into the narrow hole that Jaramillo had hacked to climb out, and retrieved Imel's body ... the motor of the rotary plow was still running, and diesel smoke made the rescue difficult." From Silverton, Jaramillo went by ambulance to Mercy Medical Center in Durango.

When CDOT workers were able to clear the road from Ouray on Saturday, March 7, they spotted the abandoned pickup of the Grand Junction men lying on its side halfway down the canyon, its descent from the road halted by a tree. They wondered if someone might need rescue but found no one in the truck. Jaramillo joined his family in Ouray on Sunday, March 8. Another storm hit the pass the same day and "simply buried two days worth of clearing." Imel's funeral was Tuesday, March 10 at First Baptist Church in Ouray; the road crews did not work that day. He left a wife and three children. Roberts interviewed Jaramillo a month after it happened. He "had that survivor's remorse," said Roberts. "Why did I survive and Eddie didn't?" He soon moved away from the area.

Red Mountain Pass reopened Wednesday, March 11, at 1 p.m., almost a week after the initial gate closures. The partial snowshed saved four lives, but as Roberts said in a classic piece of understatement, "When the repeat happened with Eddie Imel, after the snowshed was built, that was a bit depressing." Others were furious. *"IT DIDN'T HAVE TO HAPPEN"* Ouray historian Marvin Gregory wrote.

> *The latest chapter in the violent history of the Riverside slide is now, irrevocable, history.... If, as we were allowed to believe, when that segment of snow shed was built in 1985, it had been followed up with the other two segments in the two succeeding years, traffic could have emerged from either end of the tunnel into a safe area.*

Out of the outraged public meetings today's solution emerged. A series of SNOTEL remote weather recording sites continually monitor the weather of the pass and areas along US 550. Observers based in Silverton ski to those sites daily to assess snow conditions. Roberts said the forecasters have a "stellar record of no avalanche deaths since the program began in 1993." They "watch the weather, watch the storms come in, forecast how big the storm is going to be, studying the geostationary satellites, radar, vorticity maps and weather models ... out all night long, measuring storm boards every hour for precipitation rates, seeing how heavy the snow was...." They would "close the road in the middle of the night, if it was bad enough. Other times we'd wait until the next day, where we could really see what was going on."

◆ ◆ ◆

Castle worked eight more years and enjoyed the job. He drove his wife Tammy up to see the spectacular sunrises and sunsets one Christmas morning, sitting in the plow with coffee. But he has never forgotten the helpless feeling of not being able to keep searching; Jaramillo said that he could hear Imel digging in the snow. Castle always felt "a little edgy around February and March ... and I was real protective ... of the crew and how we operated things." But, working on the pass was "like playing cards. Too many chances and it will get you."

CHAPTER FIVE

The Mountain Shook

ON THE EVENING OF AUGUST 31, 1980, Art Porter experienced both a beautiful sunset and Mt. Sneffels bathed in moonlight. The thirty-six-year-old engineer had climbed 6,000-meter peaks in Bolivia two years before and directed Colorado Mountain Club's (CMC) Pikes Peak mountaineering school. He had climbed Sneffels on a standard snow route but lusted for a mountaineer's test piece: straight up the brooding, intricate rock of the North Buttress, claimed by Dr. Henry L. McClintock of the San Juan Mountaineers and his teenage children Mary and Frank in 1933. CMC member and strong rock climber Brent Dubach agreed to accompany him.

The day before, they drove six hours from Colorado Springs to Ouray and stayed at the St. Elmo Hotel. At 2:30 a.m. they got up and drove an hour to Blaine Basin trailhead. They were hiking by 4:30, anticipating a long climb, but they also knew the "sybaritic delights of a soft bed, a hot shower, and a great meal" at the hotel awaited them at the end of the day. They might not descend by the same route, either because of a late hour or unsafe snow conditions and instead descend the standard route and hitch a ride into Ouray.

By 8:30, the massive snowfield stretched beneath them as they moved onto the first rock pitch (a section of rock that cannot be climbed safely without protection). Dubach went first. They moved deep into the mountain's shadow and tall, thin, red-haired Porter's hands became thoroughly chilled as he belayed Dubach in the thin air of 12,650 feet. The North Buttress was a nasty climb from the beginning, said Porter, with unstable, near vertical rock in places. He was leading the second pitch when he felt a huge block of rock break beneath his foot. The mountain shook and huge clouds of dust boiled up as he fought for balance. Neither man was hurt.

Porter kept moving but the rock became so rotten he couldn't set pitons – they just peeled off the rock. At noon they reached the top of the second pitch. The climb eased but the rock worsened. They stowed the rope in order to move more rapidly, while watching their footing. There would be no recovery if they stumbled here. The mountain fell sheer 1,500 feet below them.

At 2:30 p.m. they were lost on the complex north face, west of the summit, off route on a serrated ridge. On an exposed pitch of extremely rotten rock, they roped up. Porter climbed the first pinnacle and realized the summit was close. Dubach joined him, and after a short descent into a loose rock notch, he led up another pinnacle. It was now impossible to touch anything that didn't break. Porter joined him and studied the options: they could climb the steep ridge or ascend rotten rock in the icy couloir below them. Porter decided

Art Porter and Brent Dubach climbed Mt. Sneffels' north face, ascended the central icy snowfield above Blaine Basin and climbed the dark rock wall (the North Buttress) to the serrated ridgeline above the Snake Couloir. The arrow points to the spot where Porter fell into the icy couloir.

Photo by Karen Risch

to traverse ledges running alongside the ridge, halfway above the couloir, proceeding carefully around a bulging rock.

A huge, four to five foot high block of rock fractured, carrying him down to the ice and rock of the couloir in a pendulum fall. He slid against the ridge for twenty to thirty feet. Part of his rope hooked on a rock outcrop and Dubach held him without relying on the belay. It was now 4:30. Dubach tied Porter off, securing the rope around a pinnacle. Then he rappelled off the ridge just below him to avoid showering him with rocks. He climbed to Porter and turned him on his back to assess his injuries. They were relatively minor, though he would not leave the mountain under his own power. His helmet had saved his head, the pile jacket and Gore-Tex outer jacket that he wore against the cold prevented serious injury to his torso, but he had a shattered ankle and two broken, lacerated fingers, one on each hand. Dubach helped him to a broad ledge, wrapped his bleeding, torn fingers to sound ones with gauze and put their spare longjohns, wind pants and rain jacket on him. Porter lay in pain, facing an exposed night on the mountain.

◆ ◆ ◆

Dubach left Porter their uneaten lunches, a quart of water, a Mylar emergency blanket and Millarmitts for protection against the cold. He had never climbed Sneffels on the standard route from Yankee Boy Basin and had no clear map for the route. At 6 p.m. Porter watched him move carefully up the broken rock and ice of the couloir. The time seemed interminable, though Dubach thought he made good progress. An hour and 300 vertical feet later, he waved from the top. Porter waved back. In fading light, Dubach picked his way down the southeast couloir to the saddle – Lavender Col – and then descended 800 feet on a steep scree slope to the approach trail. He saw lights in Yankee Boy Basin where Mountain Rescue men Richard Flemming and Gary Williams, from Albuquerque, New Mexico, were camped. They drove him to Ouray and notified Sheriff Art Dougherty, who called out OMRT. Fortunately, it would be a relatively warm night where Porter lay, with little wind and temperatures only slightly below freezing, though ice crystals formed in his water bottle by morning.

◆ ◆ ◆

After a 10 p.m. briefing, Capt. George Pasek and Medical Officer Jim Fife departed for Yankee Boy Basin and a night ascent of the standard route. A fatigued Dubach stayed in town, fearing that he would slow them down. He described Porter's location and assumed they would spot him from the summit. Dubach slept till 4:30 a.m., re-climbed Sneffels with the Albuquerque men and reached the summit by 8 a.m.

Pasek and Fife experienced a very different mountain as they negotiated the southeast couloir with headlamps casting a small pool of light, surrounded by high rock walls and darkness. A waning moon crept west as gale force winds swept the mountain and the temperature plunged. A second rescue team – Roger Sherman, James Burwick and sixteen-year-old Doug Gregory, who carried 500 feet of Goldline – arrived at 3:45 with powerful quartz iodide search lamps. Even with these, which lasted only thirty to forty minutes, they couldn't find Porter, given the adverse conditions on the mountain. By 5:15, the wind chill was minus ten. They hunkered down, Pasek said, scraping together whatever rocks they could find for a rough wind barrier.

◆ ◆ ◆

Porter lay below the summit, sheltered from the wind. Cold penetrated his clothing, his sleeplessness aggravated by a full bladder since his injured hands couldn't undo his pants. The pain in his swollen ankle was terrific, but he managed to loosen his bootlaces. At 2:30 a.m., he heard men's voices and saw lights on the summit. He blew repeatedly on his whistle and shone his headlamp, but the wind roared so hard the rescuers never heard him and didn't see his light. He assumed they were just waiting for sunrise.

At 6:30, Fife said he and Pasek went to pee over the lee side of the mountain. Porter's shout startled them and they sprang to action. Gregory had the yeoman's job of keeping the 500 feet of Goldline untangled as Pasek and Sherman lowered Fife and Burwick. They took warm clothes and a stove to make Porter a hot drink, gave him first aid, and carefully packed him in a litter. At 7:15, Englishman Peter White, one of Pasek's climbing partners, on a solo ascent of the Snake, came upon them and stayed to help. During the night a third team of rescuers hauled equipment to Lavender Col. Elwood Gregory, Tom Hash, Felix Pfaeffle and David Smith bivouacked there and made the summit by 8:30. Elwood said his pack included heavy coils of rope (courtesy of Hash) making for an especially tough trip and a surprise when he looked inside.

A Chinook helicopter from Fort Carson got there at 9:40. Sheriff Dougherty sent Charlie Ricker a military frequency radio for communications with the pilot, who landed at Yankee Boy rescue base. Callout coordinator Linda Hash and Kathy and John Dalton routed rescuers up the mountain.

The pilot didn't have enough clearance to lift Porter out of the couloir, so Pasek and Fife devised an alternate plan: They would raise Porter from the Snake to a larger fifteen by twenty-five foot scree shelf at 14,005 feet, just below the summit, hoping that the pilot could pick him off the mountain. Pasek said the pilot had fuel for only one attempt at that altitude. This complex operation, though, needed more people. He drafted Rich Tisdel, nearing the summit with his family, to help and sent Sherman, Doug Gregory, Flemming, and Terry Morris, one of four men from Silverton, down the north side to set up a "Z 3:1" pulley system. This allowed for a directional change in the rope to haul Porter 150 feet up and across the face of the mountain.

A twin rotor Chinook helicopter from Fort Carson in Colorado Springs hauls the litter and injured mountaineer Art Porter from near the summit of Mt. Sneffels.

Photo by Richard Tisdel
Courtesy Ben Tisdel

At 1:20 p.m. the captain summoned the Chinook. The pilot lowered the winch cable and hook, discharged static electricity against the rock. White provided a safety belay for Fife and four men sat on White. The line swung out over the 1,500-foot face. In the hundred-mile-an-hour downdraft from the chopper's twin rotors, Fife made a heroic leap to catch the hook. At 3:30, the litter – with Porter strapped in and blindfolded against the prop wash – spun, swung wildly, and rose slowly toward the aircraft. The litter disappeared into the chopper, the doors closed, the pilot opened his window and stuck out his thumb. Wild yelling, cheers and tears erupted from the mountain. In the safety of the bird, an attendant gave a grateful Porter a quart bottle to empty his bladder. By 6 p.m. OMRT was off the mountain.

The helicopter flew Porter to Penrose Hospital in Colorado Springs. His ankle eventually healed, but even years later, prolonged running or skiing left him barely able to walk. His broken right hand finger still doesn't bend and the healed left one is cold sensitive. Never again could he even go for a run without carrying ibuprofen. Shortly after the accident, he described OMRT's sterling performance: "The rescue was a textbook example of near-perfect planning, organization and execution." Fife doubted the *Plaindealer*'s description of the heroics. He maintained the rescue was just a bunch of hard work and they weren't the superheroes they were made out to be.

CHAPTER SIX

1983-87
"As unforgiving as they are beautiful"

WHEN TOM HASH SUCCEEDED HIS WIFE Linda as captain with Dr. Dave Bachman, his lieutenant, for 1983-1984, he installed a V-8 360 engine in the Orange Beast, replacing a "little military 4-cylinder." To David Koch, who kept it running, the "Orange Beast was as life threatening as any aspect" of a rescue.... It's amazing it ran." It was "friggin' top-heavy ... there were times I thought, 'I'm going to roll this sucker with half the team in the back.'" Tod Bacigalupi got the idea to put the VISA sticker on it, where it resides today. He joked that when they got a victim out, they would ask for a credit card. Then, "ka-ching, ka-ching, ka-ching" they would ring it up.

◆ ◆ ◆

On Saturday July 9, 1983, *Durango Herald* reporter Chip Hines, thirty-six, told his wife Carrie he'd be back that afternoon after climbing Mt. Sneffels. At 5:30 p.m. she alerted Sheriff Art Dougherty, who found his car parked below Yankee Boy Basin. Capt. Hash, Otto Scheidegger, Rick Lyon and Paul Lugen drove the Beast to Yankee Boy, setting up base camp as night fell. Jack Munson and James Burwick, who owned Uncompahgre Mountain Guides, also responded. Outlaw Restaurant owner Paul Klein sent up sandwiches and coffee.

They searched until midnight. Burwick, thinking that Hines might be injured, ran to "the summit, screamed hellos," but found no sign of him or a register signature. He slept poorly on Lavender Col in lightning, hail and snow. They all woke bone-weary since the callout had come only a couple hours after a strenuous training session. At 5 a.m. Dr. and June Bachman and Training Coordinator Tom Whelan started for base, but the rocky road ripped out their transmission. A tired rescuer drove down to pick them up. Communications Officer Charlie Ricker and Undersheriff Jerry Wakefield brought up OMRT's new Pieps. Though it was early July, the peaks surrounding the basin sported hanging cornices from late, heavy spring snow.

Burwick checked out Sneffels' steeper routes and Dr. and June Bachman, Capt. Hash, Scheidegger and Lugen searched other approaches. Lyon walked the slopes under the jagged ridgeline of Kismet to the east. They found nothing. Sheriff Dougherty called pilot Gordon Saville who, with Montrose Sheriff Tom Gilmore as spotter, flew over the tight, jagged terrain, but couldn't get low enough to see anything. Then the Bachmans and Capt. Hash cleared an LZ at Wright's Lake for helicopter pilot Burt Metcalf, who swooped in wearing his trademark aviator glasses and cowboy boots. He picked up Burwick and they flew around the mountain.

Carrie Hines and a friend arrived to bleak news: There was no sign of Chip. A rescuer talked about 13,694-foot Gilpin Peak and its semicircular ridge, prominent to the south. She interjected, "That's not Gilpin, that's Sneffels." They told her it was indeed Gilpin. She replied, "My husband thinks that is Sneffels." Scheidegger, scanning with binoculars, realized they might have been looking at the missing man below Gilpin, perhaps mistaking him for a dark rock in the snow. Metcalf flew along the rugged northeast face and spotted a body 1,000 feet below the corniced ridge. He picked up Dr. Bachman and Capt. Hash. It was too dangerous to land, so he stuck a runner in the snow and told them to jump.

Lt. Bachman pronounced Chip Hines dead of massive head injuries. Burwick said he had gone "off the face of Gilpin and slid a long way down the snowfield and hit the only rock around." Perched on the steep slope above them lay his pack. His hands were abraded, said Scheidegger, as if he had grasped at the rock ridges for help. They loaded the stiff body into the helicopter net. Burwick, upset that Carrie Hines would see the corpse flown out, didn't want her "to have a vision of this scene in ... mind forever." June Bachman, who broke the news to her, said, "It was a pretty clear picture" when they heard that a man had been found and was being brought back on the runner of the helicopter.

Scheidegger and a teammate watched as Metcalf flew:

to this knoll we're on and dumps the body and throws the black bag out and says, "Okay, get him in the bag and get him down the mountain."

Sunset on Gilpin Peak, June 18, 2017, as OMRT searches for a missing climber, the third in twenty-four years to die on the peak.

Photo by Clint Estes

It was my first real life dead person ... he split his head open ... was lying in the snow for two days so he was very well preserved ... he looked almost alive. I just stood there for a few minutes and thought about things. I didn't want to rush putting him into the body bag.

For Scheidegger, a hunter, the intense moment was like when he kills an elk – he said a little prayer. Nobody knew what happened. Did this man stand on a rock outcropping and it gave way? Was there a possibility of foul play? He remembered climbers leaving nearby Stony Peak as they arrived. This was an accident that didn't have to happen. In contrast to its sharply chiseled north face, "the back side of Sneffels doesn't look like much," he said. A topographic map and compass would have led Chip Hines to Sneffels. Journalist Roger Anderson summed up the tragedy: "The San Juans, for all their seeming benign majesty, can be as unforgiving as they are beautiful."

◆ ◆ ◆

Five months later, on a starkly memorable Valentine's Day, 1984, Dr. Bachman, four team members, Undersheriff Wakefield, Deputy Sheriff Rick Lyon and State Patrolman Randy Jones were called out in the middle of the night. Miners coming home from Silverton reported a vehicle burning at the bottom of a 200-foot embankment near Bear Creek tunnel. Seven responders found a grim scenario. It was Dr. Bachman's first case as Coroner: "There was a car off the road, pinned, and we got up there and Randy Jones and I got down ... this torso was in the car, the arms and legs were burnt off ... the body just totally burnt."

Bacigalupi, Mary Hoeksema, Koch and Pete Smith said this was one of their most gruesome experiences. For Koch it was a first body recovery. It was "the roughest ... the hardest one to get through for me." They descended to a flat area twenty feet from the river. In the car, facing backward in the front seat was a grotesque, charred body – "her extremities were gone," said Koch, her eyes and mouth wide open, as if in a horrific scream. Bacigalupi noticed that she "had her hands raised like she had been told to stick'em up, but at the time I thought it was the horror of her knowing she couldn't get out of a burning car that she had driven off the road, carrying extra gas for the trip over the mountains."

Koch and Dr. Bachman saw a baby carrier in the front seat and toys scattered around. The Ouray County Social Services caseworker "wanted to make sure there was not a kid here." They searched, but found no child. "We were thinking she went over in the car and the thing exploded," said Hoeksema, "and she was locked in the car and she couldn't get out." Then they looked again at the gas can, having assumed that the dead person placed it inside the car, and realized they might be looking at a homicide. But they "had destroyed all of the evidence trying to make sure there wasn't some kid involved in this," said Dr. Bachman. He and Hoeksema extricated the grotesque, charred body and put it in a bag. It was difficult to straighten. Hoeksema had to deliver some paintings and needed to leave, so they took the bag up the cliff wall, secured by ropes raised by Undersheriff Wakefield's Jeep. At one point she stopped to pick up some digits that fell out when the bag snagged and ripped on the rough rock.

On the road she said, "I gotta go. I have to go home now." Because of the art delivery, she missed the debriefing, but in compensation, "I was out of the scene, in a way fortunately, but oh that lady." The grim sensory assaults remained vivid. Bacigalupi felt as if he would barf from the sight and smell of the body, which had fallen apart as they removed it from the car. It took Smith a year before he could eat fried chicken. Hoeksema never ate it again.

Dr. Bachman called the State Patrol and found out that Linda June Greene's estranged husband Raymond had followed her to Delta. Her family reported her missing that morning. The *Montrose Daily Press* reported: "Officials originally thought the car accident was a fiery crash.... However, when law enforcement learned about the missing person report and a purse covered with blood was found ... a homicide investigation began...." The woman's bloody, abandoned purse gave police their clue; the husband was arrested, got out on bail and returned to Arizona where they had recently lived with their two children. He "had murdered her ... towed the car up there on a trailer, poured gasoline into it, shoved it off and thought it would catch on fire," said Dr. Bachman. "It didn't. He had to go down there and throw a match in it for it to burn," The man "went back to Arizona and they found him in the desert in his car with a hose from the exhaust ... dead." OMRT's retrieval of her body never made the papers.

◆ ◆ ◆

On a spring-like Monday afternoon a month later, twenty-eight-year-old Erdme Warswick – whose signature designs, "Erdme Originals," featured fabric she had sourced in Guatemala – took a break from her work in the Ridgway Unicas store that she and husband Nathan owned. Her brother Jens, a "top ranked downhill racer" in training with skiing greats Phil and Steve Maher, had driven from Washington State for a visit. Nathan Warswick drove to Durango that day, March 19, to deal with signage for a new store. On US 550, he saw "huge avalanches everywhere, including freshly cleared ones.... I called Erdme to let her know the danger and urged her and Jens not to go into the backcountry, to stick to the Telluride ski area."

Lured by plentiful new snow beyond the house and gentle terrain, they skied near Last Dollar Road, pausing on a small knoll below a huge cornice. Jens wanted a picture of his sister and her new home, which sat 1.8 miles from CO 62. Erdme skied down the convex, forty-five-degree slope. "When he dropped his backpack after taking out the camera," said Nathan, "the snowpack split in two under his feet and he was carried down the slope on top of the slide."

Nathan returned that evening, skiing in from the highway, aware that three feet of new snow on their roof had slid and there was a fresh avalanche on a small knoll to the south. Jens had left a note on the door – he had come for help and tools. Erdme had been buried in an avalanche. Nathan "couldn't believe it!"

> *Thought they were joking and hiding in the closets. I skied over there to help and found Jens and neighbors Jack Miller and Jay Crowell probing with PVC pipes and digging with garden shovels. Paula Wise had driven to town for help; none of us had phones at that time. The four of us dug a trench at the bottom of the slide, which was twelve feet deep, where we found her body.*

On that inconspicuous knoll south of Last Dollar Road, set against the north end of the Sneffels Range, the fracture line on the cornice was ten feet deep. The slide ran 200 feet and the heavy wet snow, stopped by an oak brush thicket, set up. To the west, a concave slope of twenty-five degrees lay untouched, providing a safe runout to the Last Dollar Road. Paul Hebert, one of many from the Ridgway ski community who came, said that Erdme's three-pin ski bindings "acted as big time anchors. Her skis were bent in an arc from the weight pulling her down."

Dr. Bachman, loaded with sled, blankets and oxygen, drove as far as possible. He "skied in part way, and then snowmobiled in part way ... they had dug her out." With the deep burial and amount of elapsed time, he said, "there was absolutely no chance that she would survive...." Though he had declared people dead in the field many times, this was a much more difficult situation. Morally and ethically, he felt he had to continue CPR "though we all knew it was hopeless." If the husband and brother had not been there, "we would have declared her dead right then and we wouldn't have gone through all this."

San Miguel Sheriff Bill Masters called for a ski helicopter from Sidewinders Helicopters of Telluride, but "for a variety of good reasons, they didn't come and didn't come and it got darker and darker ... pitch black, terrifying to think that helicopter was out there...." When the four-seat chopper landed, he and Eric Berg, head of San Miguel Search and Rescue (SMSAR), boarded with the body. The doctor ended up sitting in the cold woman's lap, doing CPR on her:

"Let's go to Montrose."
The pilot responded, "Where's Montrose?"
"Well, go to Ridgway and you can follow the highway."
"Where's Ridgway?"

Somehow they made it to Montrose, though the nerve-wracking experience remained vivid for the doctor fifteen years later: "I don't like to fly in helicopters much, and I surely don't like to go in them at night. I surely didn't want to stay in that." A young EMT, Bill Dwelley, attended Erdme in the emergency room. "They had given it up, so we were covering her up," he said. He stepped into the hall "and there was Nathan." Dwelley couldn't believe it was Erdme he'd been working on: "They don't look the same when they die."

Even in his grief, Nathan was determined such an accident should not happen again. He created the EKW Fund For Mountain Safety, which supported the Colorado Avalanche Information Center (CAIC) and sold avalanche beacons at cost from his UNICAS store.

◆ ◆ ◆

At the Christmas celebration, Dr. Bachman was elected captain and Scheidegger lieutenant. Kurt Kircher continued as Training Officer, Charlie Ricker as Communications wizard and Koch as Equipment Officer. They intended, Peggy Lyon wrote: "to promote the enjoyment of the wilderness, as well as its safe use, and, when necessary, to help its users back home again." Dr. Bachman, an orthopedic surgeon, ran the Center for Sports Medicine at Northwestern University from 1967-1980, before he and June moved to Ouray. OMRT's training – avalanche rescue, X-C skiing, ice climbing, knot tying, mountaineering first aid, scree and vertical evacuation, orienteering – was used in five searches and seven rescues and he estimated they saved four persons' lives in 1985. Twenty active team members donated 1,150 hours between missions (430 hours) and trainings (720 hours).

◆ ◆ ◆

Five callouts in three weeks began August 15. Seventy-one-year-old Ruth Siemer of Ouray passed out that night while driving her 1977 Jeep up Portland Road. She was thrown out as the CJ7 Jeep flew off the road, banged into a tree and landed twenty feet down a steep embankment. Patty Lyday, her passenger, climbed up to alert Earl Boland, the driver of a second Jeep. He went for help; Undersheriff Wakefield arrived and assisted two other female passengers to the road.

It was after 10 p.m. when Keith Rasmussen got there with the 4WD ambulance. EMTs Mag Keffeler and Pete Smith scrambled down the dark slope with oxygen. Father Bill Doll of St. Daniels Catholic Church, a third EMT, stayed on the road to care for others. Bacigalupi, Koch, Mike Hockersmith and Elwood Gregory rigged a scree evacuation. Dr. Bachman was so impressed with this harrowing night rescue that he publicly urged citizens to stop EMT and OMRT personnel when they saw them and "tell them thanks, we're glad you're here. You might even buy them a beer – if they're off duty."

Six days later, a tourist missed the curve at the bottom of Jim Brown Hill on Camp Bird Road, hit the Uncompahgre Canyon's east wall, and took a bath ninety feet down. On September 10, after looking all night in forty-five degree weather, persistent searchers found seventy-five-year-old Ed Marsh, who had served on OMRT a decade earlier. He was hypothermic and disoriented, but conscious, having wandered from his home in Whispering Pines the previous day. He fell off the road embankment, landed near the river, but showed no signs of trauma.

Days later, a mutual aid call sent five members to a lake south of Silverton and Molas Pass. An eighty-eight-year-old man wandered from his campsite the previous morning. COSAR's call for assistance brought rescuers from three counties for a massive effort that included helicopters, dog teams and searchers on horseback and foot. Peggy Lyon, moving through the woods hollering for the man, found herself struggling to keep up with search leader and legendary runner Rick Trujillo. Just at sunset "Grampa" was spotted from a helicopter "happily walking along … no idea that anything was wrong," said Trujillo. He had hypothermia, but otherwise was in good condition.

The next year, the same Texas man disappeared on the family's annual camping trip. This time the search captain was Terry Morris, a friend of Trujillo's from SJSAR in Silverton. On the third day they found Grampa wandering off road near Purgatory, sixteen miles away from camp. When they brought him back, Trujillo told the family, "You come back next year and he disappears, don't bother to call us. You keep your eye on this guy." No one had ever heard of Alzheimer's. An early sign of the disease is an urge to wander.

Eight days before Christmas, while driving from Farmington to Grand Junction, forty-four-year-old Jim Hester lost control of his car at 3:30 a.m. as he dodged rocks on the road and hit ice a quarter mile north of the emergency phone on US 550. His vehicle rolled three times before it came to rest ninety yards below the road in deep snow. His lights stayed on, a passer-by saw them and used the emergency phone. Sheriff Dougherty took the report at 5:30. Trujillo got to the man first with blankets and checked his physical condition. Though he stayed in the car and never lost consciousness, he was hypothermic and had frost nip on his right foot. By 8:15 a.m. OMRT raised him to the road. EMTs removed his wet clothing and warmed him up with five blankets and four hot packs. He lost a tooth and sustained bruises, strains and soreness. The State Patrol returned his glasses, but the tooth remained lost.

◆ ◆ ◆

At the end of the year, they honored Kurt Kircher. In twelve years, he had been captain, trained most of the team and directed or participated in over 100 rescues. They gave the sixty-eight-year-old a standing ovation and a plaque. At the bottom of 1985's training schedule, he had written: "Our goal is to achieve high competence and become a superior rescue team...." In January 1986 they recognized two more volunteers: Rick and Peggy Lyon. His professional black and white photos of training and rescues captured OMRT in action and her news stories illuminated their activities. Fire Chief Greg Genuit, an early member, joined again at Dr. Bachman's invitation and became Truck Officer. They ordered red "Bubba" baseball caps emblazoned with the original red, white and gray emblem Genuit designed in 1974. The caps became the badge of membership. Bill Dwelley, EMT and midwife, sat in on meetings, encouraged by Capt. Bachman. He became a stalwart, technically proficient rescuer, responding in record time from his Montrose home for the next 31 years.

Training Officer Bacigalupi passed out a personal equipment list and planned indoor sessions, Saturday outdoor work, snow scree evacuation, ice vertical evacuation and Tyrolean traverse. County Attorney Mike Hockersmith realized that OMRT's state incorporation status had lapsed and filed with the state. He obtained 501(c)(3) non-profit status so that those who donated could receive tax deductions. OMRT was paying an unnecessary $316 a year for liability insurance, so Hockersmith got the BOCC to include them in the county's policy. In August a long-awaited Sked arrived. This smooth bottomed, roll up plastic litter could be packed into tight or remote places. When loaded, it was rigid and could be lowered more easily.

◆ ◆ ◆

Hoeksema reviewed ice rescue after the March meeting. At 7:30 the next night plow driver Ted Dorr noticed tire tracks heading over the edge of US 550 and called for help. Fifteen rescuers responded. Four hundred feet below the most precipitous part of the snowpacked road, Ouray resident Mike Svaldi, thirty-five, shivered in his wet truck bed. Hoeksema arrived, descended and watched for the end of the rope, then down climbed another ten to fifteen feet to a snow slope beneath the cliff and waited for teammate Rick Blackford, descending with a second rope. The injured, hypothermic man sat in water running through the bed of his listing 1977 Chevy. Hoeksema and Blackford struggled to get him into dry clothes, a half sleeping bag from her pack, and a full size bag from Blackford's. Lighting for the cold, dark, delicate operation came from dim headlamps until CDOT foreman Jim Warren brought up a portable generator and lamps, which threw some light down the dark cliff. Dorr spread cinders along the highway to keep everyone from slipping. The descent ropes were hauled up so a cable and litter could be sent down, but that didn't happen right away: "This guy was just going out on us," said Hoeksema. Hockersmith and Koch rappelled with the Stokes litter and a warm rescue bag, recently crafted by Lyn Yarroll.

They packaged Svaldi but couldn't lift him over the side of the truck because of encroaching terrain and the river. The Sheriff's 4WD Toyota was hooked to the cable and they decided to weasel Svaldi out through the missing back and front windows. After informing those topside that they were ready to go, they waited and waited, thinking the cable might be caught on a rock. "All of a sudden it uncaught," said Hoeksema, "and that guy just shot like a bullet through that truck." The litter slammed up against the rock wall and they scrambled up behind it, screaming, "Stop, stop, stop, stop, stop, don't crank anymore." Koch said it was a classic case of "how not to do a rescue…. 'Thank God we hadn't attached ourselves to the litter.'" The Toyota was attached to the downhill side of the Z-pull rigging, not the uphill, accounting for the sudden jerk. They hooked onto the litter for "this totally vertical wall," said Hoeksema. Then, on an icy section, the cable halted. She pulled out her radio.

"Why are we stopped? We are on ice!"
"We're letting traffic through."

Hoeksema called Undersheriff Wakefield "every bad name I could think of.... I am never going to do this again … someone was shaking from the cold and so the whole litter was just shaking ... and someone's knees were shaking with the climber's shakes...." They reached the road after 11 p.m. Hockersmith thought it amazing that Svaldi, with a severe head injury, had survived "because there was debris all the way down."

It was her last rescue. Koch said Hoeksema, "one of the first ice climbers" and very good at it, definitely left because of that botched rescue. She had been with OMRT "a long, long time" and was generous with her knowledge. She taught Bacigalupi to climb ice: "I was freaked out,' he said. "She was good at everything ... the only woman involved in technical stuff."

◆ ◆ ◆

A month later, on April 15, an explosion heard four miles away in Ouray led to a massive recovery effort. On August 14, four members recovered a body fifteen feet below the cliff at Inspiration Point on the east end of Log Hill Mesa. Warren Edward Cooper, M.D., fifty-six, of Montrose, lay with a gunshot wound to the head. Charlie Ricker drove the ambulance that night, accompanied by EMTs Janet Peterson and Pete Smith. They needed another rescuer and called Koch. In unintentional irony, they tied off to the cross at the top of the cliff in order to descend safely and retrieve the body. Then, the experience became even more surreal: Koch and Smith were putting the body into the body bag when Dr. Bachman said:

"Put that brain matter into the body bag."
"What brain matter?"
"You're standing in it."

They discovered the dead man fired the revolver twice before killing himself. "They found a cartridge in the cylinder that had the dented primer ... he put this gun to his head, pulled the trigger, and nothing happened, and then he just chambered another one to do the job," said Scheidegger. He had been called for that mission but slept through the call. He had no regrets when he heard about it.

Smith said that these grisly recoveries made them want to just help people, not deal with murder and suicide.

Six days later, they got a live one. Twenty-nine-year-old Gregg Massard was stuck at the top of Silver Gulch 2,000 feet above US 550. The grandson of former Ouray Mayor Frank Massard, visiting from Massachusetts, was one of a party of five hiking from Ironton to Camp Bird. In rainy weather he wandered off an old, rather faint trail and was stranded on a cliff. His sister Wendy hiked to Ouray. The fourteen-person rescue involved rigging a line across "a scree slope that was just like ball bearings," said Hockersmith.

On October 26, Margareta Kircher (Kurt Kircher's first wife) reported hearing a signal gun near Jackass Flats north of town. The shot actually came from cliffs south of Whispering Pines subdivision across the valley. Local grocer Roger Duckett and son Kevin were stranded on a cliff in the dark. Ten searchers found them and brought lights up. Remembering "how shook up I was," Roger Duckett wrote: "I'm sorry it took the whole crew to do the flashlight job but understand it takes a whole crew together to get the job done."

◆ ◆ ◆

Sandy East, director of International Alpine School (IAS), and guide Jerry Roberts of Ridgway taught ice climbing and rescue procedure to Capt. Bachman, Lt. Scheidegger, Bacigalupi and others at the Skylight in December. On that frozen waterfall on Camp Bird Road, East used a pulley rigging to raise Bacigalupi thirty feet. Roberts, who taught for the American Avalanche Institute, shared knowledge: "Basic mechanics of avalanche, basic snow physics ... avoidance of avalanche terrain, recognizing avalanche terrain." He emphasized: "Don't be a victim. Get somebody that knows what the hell they're doing to make some calls, or call in the helicopter to throw some explosives or whatever you need to do. But don't get ten people killed trying to get somebody out...." Roberts said East increased their knowledge by "a big jump."

Undersheriff Wakefield and his wife Jane hosted OMRT and significant others at a barbeque that fall. Her spectacular desserts also highlighted meetings at their house for eight years; people joked they were the motivation to attend. "Jane was just that kind of person," her husband said. "She always had a treat for us." The Christmas party, held at St. John's Episcopal Church, also allowed them to unwind. Peggy Lyon and Hoeksema entertained, playing classical piano music. Otto Scheidegger, Kurt Kircher's brother-in-law, became captain.

Thirty members spent the winter training, gathering equipment and pouring money into the forty-year-old Beast. In May 1987 Secretary Yarroll wrote, "As everyone knows, we are long overdue for a rescue. Now is not the time to get rusty ... and to forget how fellow team members work." Orienteering training on the 16th would build on a map reading session scheduled after the mid-week meeting. Practice would be held in spite of weather, as searches don't always happen on sunny days. Instead of training, however, they spent a harrowing two days looking for a man who disappeared from US 550 early on a Friday morning.

◆ ◆ ◆

At dusk on June 10, a topless Toyota Land Cruiser drove downhill on a private road five miles above Black Lake and CR 17 north of Ouray. It ran off the road, became airborne and rolled several times, stopping 500 feet downhill. Seven victims, five seriously injured, were scattered over 300 feet of steep, dark hillside. OMRT met that night at the Sheriff's house, so when the call came at 9 p.m. they were ready to go.

OMRT and the entire Sheriff's Department, three county ambulances and numerous EMTs responded, with the 4WD Mary E. the only ambulance that could reach the victims. The first two survivors rode down in the back of a pickup to the Ridgway ambulance. The Toyota's driver Ed Gilbert, thrown onto a steep bank, walked 100 feet down with only a scraped left hand.

The Mary E. had "two Stokes litters, blankets, many ropes, backboards.... It was quite dark, even though full moon was out...." Two people were "lying on the road by the dirt bank; they were covered with blankets," wrote Father Doll. "Three were lying high up on the bank in the trees and brush. Ropes were used to climb up ... and to let the Stokes litters down.... Wrecked jeep not visible from the scene." Rescuers evacuated the injured up the hillside and the Mary E. took them down to other ambulances.

Subsequent callouts included three Sneffels rescues and three searches. The first call was the most dramatic: On July 11, Richard Hughes, forty-one, of Corrales, New Mexico, was about to rope up with his climbing companions for a summit push from Sneffels' north face. The helmetless Hughes slipped in a soft patch of snow, fell backward and headfirst and tumbled wildly 500 feet down a rocky, near vertical snow chute. His stunned companions watched him bounce out of sight. He slid another 500 feet. Some of the party climbed to the summit and descended to Yankee Boy Basin for help. Two downclimbed the snow chute, expecting to find a body. Forty-five minutes later, they found Hughes alive but unable to move so they laid him in a sleeping bag. He was in such intense pain, however, that he got up and walked around.

OMRT had just practiced for seven hours on the Golden Crystal cliff. The 3:15 p.m. callout had a muddled accident report – it was either a jeep over a cliff or a man falling 2,000 feet down Sneffels. Once they found it was Sneffels, they assumed it would be technical. A storm was moving in and they didn't want to leave an injured person overnight. From Willow Swamp, Burt Metcalf flew Bacigalupi and Smith into the basin, setting the chopper down with its tail rotor perched only a foot or two above a boulder. A second team was ready to go in, but Lt. Koch received a report: "He's alive and walking." Hughes was evacuated with only "a big raspberry on his chest." In intensive care the next day, he said the climb had been a bit more challenging than others he had done. He had a bruised pericardium, the sac surrounding the heart. Considering that he had gone down like a bobsled, his survival seemed miraculous.

On Labor Day, they mobilized at 8:30 a.m. Two brothers from Albuquerque, New Mexico, climbing Sneffels the day before hadn't returned. Doug Gregory and Thad Spaulding searched from Yankee Boy Basin. On the chance that they might have crossed to the north, eleven members hiked into Blaine Basin. A CAP plane searched along the north side. At 2:45 p.m., Spaulding spotted them fifty feet from the summit. They weren't moving. Charlie Ricker, managing communications, radioed the Blaine searchers, who drove two hours to Yankee Boy. They met the climbers walking out.

Four weeks later, Lt. Koch, his wife Beth and fifteen-year-old step-daughter Alicia climbed Sneffels' southeast side. His wife was leading and yelled "Rock!" when she accidentally dislodged a basketball sized one. At first it looked like a miss, "but it took a bad bounce and curved" toward the girl. Koch covered her, but her hand was out. The rock hit it on the third bounce, nearly severing her thumb. "I saw it hanging off, only held on by a piece of skin and felt it against my arm. I started screaming," Alicia Koch said. From the only patch of snow, Koch packed her thumb and hand in ice, hurried down to his car and found a vehicle blocking the road. He "almost throttled the tourists who had stalled a Jeep in the narrow road below Wright's Lake. They wanted me to stop and assist them!?!" He ran until a passer-by picked him up and took him to town. Three friends who were ahead of the Kochs turned back and they descended. A tourist picked them up and Capt. Scheidegger and Rick Lyon met them at Camp Bird. The captain took Alicia Koch and her mother to the clinic. Dr. Bachman bandaged her thumb, an Air Life helicopter ferried her to Denver and she was rushed to surgery. With the help of a hyperbaric chamber, her thumb regrew its connections, though it took a long time to heal. Today, the small, rocky passageway where the rock took a bad bounce is called Finger Couloir.

On the last call of the year, they spent 225-man hours recovering sixty-seven-year-old hunter L.A. (Johnny) Johnson. When he didn't meet his companions at noon on November 5, they figured he was tracking something. At 4 p.m. they mobilized family and friends. By 8 p.m. Undersheriff Wakefield had Charlie Ricker on radio and Capt. Scheidegger and Dr. Bachman at Thistle Cabin searching. At midnight in heavy rain, they postponed the rescue until morning. At 5:30 a.m. a dozen members, several lawmen, family and friends searched. At 8 a.m Johnson's brother-in-law, Mark Nash, saw a signal flag and spotted his dead body in a ravine. He had apparently slipped on the muddy incline, cutting his head badly during a sixty-foot fall. "He had a half-eaten apple in his hand," said Rick Lyon, "his hunting rifle was in the mud." Lyon stayed with the body while others got the wheeled litter. He unloaded the hunting rifle. OMRT brought the body of the *Plaindealer* editor's ex-husband to the trailhead. An initially quiet year had consumed 1,000 hours over eight missions whose hallmark was beautiful teamwork.

CHAPTER SEVEN

Kissing the Gorge

PETE SMITH PERCHED UNCOMFORTABLY on top of the smashed car, his feet in icy, churning water, hands aflame with nettle stings. Under dripping canyon walls, he cradled a tourist from Santiago, Chile, who lay shivering under a wool blanket. Smith, thirty-seven, a normally unflappable county EMS director, was unexpectedly irritated with this man.

◆ ◆ ◆

Carlos Barros, also thirty-seven, had gone sightseeing along Camp Bird Road and was returning to Ouray when he lost control of his rental car near the old Box Canyon turnoff at the bottom of Jim Brown Hill. The car missed the Uncompahgre Bridge, flew off the road and slammed into the opposite wall of the gorge. It fell ninety feet to the bottom of the canyon and landed upright in the river. Barros unbuckled his seat belt and crawled out of the 1985 Chevette. When Smith first saw him, he was perched on its roof, just inches above turbulent brown water.

Barros saw Smith and ambulance driver John Richardson peering down at him from the canyon rim and shouted, "We need help!" Thinking another person was trapped in the car and about to die, Smith scrambled down an eastside gully, holding onto whatever he could – mostly nettles growing in the loose gray rock. He waded through a deep pool of icy water downstream from the car, plunged underwater and searched, but found nobody else. He pulled himself to the top and asked Barros if he was alone. Then he realized the man did not speak English and resorted to hand signals – one finger? two fingers? Barros was alone.

Smith resigned himself to being responsible for keeping this hapless tourist alive and warm until he could be evacuated. The cold water had partially relieved the stinging in his hands, but he, too, was dripping wet. Then Richardson and three other EMTs – Sharon Berry, Al Glines and Mag Keffeler – made the first of several trips down the gully, hoisting blankets and medical supplies as they made

Pete Smith shelters Carlos Barros under a blanket, waiting for rescue. The wet tourist had to be carried through foaming water to the right and up a west side gully.

Photo by Rick Lyon

their way through the river. Charlie and Elaine Ricker and Lyn Yarroll kept communications going from the canyon's rim, despite the river noise. On top of the gorge, Kurt Kircher, sixty-seven, assisted by men from the city and county crews and some bystanders, rigged a rope and pulley system for a scree evacuation. Ouray Police Chief Richard Zortman, Sheriff Art Dougherty and Deputy Pete Peterson kept the swelling crowd away from the edge. Everyone wanted a view of this extraordinary event.

Eight OMRT members, EMTs and other citizens descended with the litter to the water. David Koch said it was "kinda spooky" as they waded upstream, chin deep in pools of water that smelled of gasoline. When they reached Barros, he suddenly became animated, talking and pointing, wanting to get something out of the submerged glove compartment, which of course they couldn't let him do. The men strapped him in the litter and started back, struggling to stay upright against the force of the river. They "nearly half-drowned coming out," said John Fedel.

Once Barros was safe, Smith realized that he was so cold from his two-hour ordeal that he couldn't help anyone anymore, including himself. His teammates returned, put him in a harness and guided him to the top. Site commander Jerry Wakefield later praised the smoothly run rescue, performed in dangerous circumstances. Koch said that it looked more dramatic than it actually was, and Fedel joked that some people wade through water like that for fun.

Two hours after kissing the gorge, Barros was in the county ambulance enroute to Montrose. He had only minor injuries – a few bruises, contusions and scratches – and was cited for careless driving at unsafe speeds. The totaled Chevette was retrieved from the canyon the next day.

CHAPTER EIGHT

Dynamite, Curves and Cliffs

US 550 OVER RED MOUNTAIN PASS is legendary for sharp turns, steep grades, overhanging cliffs and deep gorges, though its hazards have been miti-gated to some extent by modern road building. An essential travel corridor in a daunting environment, it exacts a toll on the unwary or the unlucky. Since 1974, OMRT has responded to the pass, at any time, in any weather, in most years, doing things nobody else could or would do.

◆ ◆ ◆

Nancy Smith was feeding her baby at 4 a.m. when she heard an explosion from Red Mountain Pass and wondered why they were blasting. When the pager went off fifteen minutes later, she woke her husband Pete. Weslie Ehart of Hesperus, Colorado, was driving a mile north of the explosion when he saw and felt the blast. He continued to MM 90, registered the carnage, turned around and headed for Ouray. Undersheriff Wakefield took the report: an air-plane had crashed on Red Mountain Pass, with debris all over the road. He "got chills up and down my spine."

◆ ◆ ◆

It was still dark that morning, April 15, 1986, when Keith Rasmussen parked the ambulance just north of MM 90 at Ruby Walls, a large pur-plish rock outcropping over a notoriously precipitous stretch of the Uncompahgre Gorge. Rasmussen, Smith, and three other EMTs got out. In the eerie, moonless darkness Rasmussen and Smith went first, but could see scarcely ten feet ahead. Clutching two teeny flashlights, they left the ambulance lights on and moved cautiously. They saw wreckage on the road and found an electrical wire, which Rasmussen, a pilot, said was not from an airplane. Smith said they spotted a shoe-less foot, a license plate and a man's head, arm and shoulder. For this grisly scene, the ambulance wasn't needed and returned to Ouray. Smith stayed, covered body parts with ambulance sheets and took charge of the scene until Capt. Dave Bachman arrived. Undersheriff Wakefield ordered the gates outside Silverton and Ouray lowered, closing the highway for the next five and a half hours.

The blast left a pothole one to three feet deep and wreckage scattered over 300 feet of highway. Small pieces of a car lay on the road with larger ones scattered over a steep talus slope to the west, hundreds of feet below. More parts were discovered fifty feet up the east side. The license plate number was processed; it belonged to Melvin Bower, 63, of Montrose. Colorado Bureau of Investigation (CBI) agent Roy Taylor said "a friend who had talked with Bower prior to his death had warned the Colorado State Patrol (CSP) about his mental attitude.... Bower had talked about going to the Red Mountain Pass area." Undersheriff Wakefield found out that a case of dynamite was missing from the family's storage shed on Log Hill.

OMRT members search US 550 at MM 90, the Ruby Walls, after a blast heard four miles away in Ouray.

Photo by Rick Lyon

◆ ◆ ◆

CBI asked OMRT to assist pathologist Dr. Michael Benziger with an evidence search. Capt. Bachman, his wife June, Lt. Otto Scheidegger, Elwood Gregory, Greg Genuit, Bob Harvey and Rick Lyon combed the road and cliffs. Even tiny bits of paper that might have been on the dynamite were salvaged. Outside of a violent war zone, the scene they worked would be exceedingly rare. Many parts were unrecognizable, though Lyon found a right shoulder and head with red hair and beard. Capt. Bachman said, "We've got to put his head in the bag." Lyon was told remove viscera from a tree above the road so that people driving by wouldn't see it, but the cliff was so rock-strewn and steep that he couldn't get there. Rick Trujillo spotted a shapeless blob of skin and hair – part of a face and scalp – lying directly on the asphalt. Tod Bacigalupi, David Koch and Trujillo descended into the gorge to search for paper, body parts, anything, managing the task with black humor. They found parts of the Mazda GLC clear across the river. A twisted piece of the front chassis was the largest remnant of the car and the largest human remain appeared to be part of a man's upper torso, which by the time most rescuers arrived, was covered by a sheet. Lyon said someone brought up "a tennis shoe that still had the foot in it."

Everyone was affected: Some lifted the sheet, Lt. Scheidegger had no desire to look. At one point he reminded everyone that this was a human body and should be treated with respect, but the scene was so gruesome that Rick Blackford insisted it was no work for volunteers. The county loader scraped the highway before it was open to traffic. Members were driven back to Ouray and given posttraumatic stress counseling by Dr. Bachman. Lyon, a hunter who butchers his own meat, went to counseling. He said what bothered him most was that "I came away feeling like … human beings are just … a bunch of meat."

◆ ◆ ◆

Scott Williams hadn't buckled his seatbelt, perhaps because he was in a hurry to get home. At 1 a.m. May 15, 1987, the twenty-eight-year-old miner missed a curve several miles south of Ouray at Windy Point, just north of the East Riverside snowshed.

Later that morning, Undersheriff Wakefield noticed skid marks off the road, investigated and called for help. It took a while to spot Williams' 1984 Ford one hundred feet below. It sat upright in foaming water, its windshield missing and no sign of Williams. OMRT

Searching for Scott Williams: Elwood Gregory just wanted to make sure he wasn't still in the car.

Photo by Rick Lyon
Courtesy *Ouray County Plaindealer*

used the Undersheriff's Jeep to anchor ropes and rappelled to the riverbank. They arranged a plank extending from a boulder jutting out of the river to the car's broken windshield. Stepping off the debris-strewn east bank, Elwood Gregory, forty-seven, stepped out onto the board, crossed inches above the raging water and checked the car. He realized that nobody had looked inside the vehicle and wanted to make sure Williams wasn't there. The car was empty.

OMRT searched both sides of the gorge from the snowshed down to the hydroelectric dam nearly three miles below the accident site. They assumed the body would float if it reached the reservoir, but it wasn't there. In many places it was impossible to hike, and fearing for their own safety near the roiling water, rescuers turned back, climbed out, and searched with binoculars from the road. Then they focused on an icy snow bridge – fifteen feet deep and 150 feet long with the river rushing underneath – some fifty feet below the car.

Thinking he might be trapped under the snow, Scheidegger started probe teams downriver. He said they "figured that maybe if we blew the snow bridge that we'd find his body." Thad Spaulding and Tod Bacigalupi probed under the ice bridge, but found nothing. Five members of San Juan County Search and Rescue (SJCSAR) helped, including Sheriff Greg Leithauser.

Just before noon on Saturday, two dynamite experts, Ron Williams and Eric Schoenebaum, blew the snow bridge with 250 pounds of explosives. The first charge did nothing but after the second one, Spaulding saw that "the ice squeezed off a portion of the river." As the water level dropped, Bacigalupi spotted a body slumped over a rock at the top of a waterfall. It was "pure luck," he said. "I happened to be looking in the right direction at the right moment." For sixteen-year-old Spaulding, it was the first time he had ever seen a dead body.

Michael Foxx, Bacigalupi, Lt. Koch and Mike McPeek rappelled 150 feet to the river, carrying an aluminum extension ladder that Bacigalupi brought along from his fix-it business. They extended it and it fell across the river to a rock island mid-channel, fifteen feet from the body. They put a man with a rope around his waist into the river from the island, but quickly realized he might be pulled under and drown in the turbulent water. Compounding the challenge, the river roared so loudly that it hampered radio communication.

Scheidegger said they had "no river rats on the team – we weren't equipped to do river rescue," so they called SMSAR. Whitewater expert Sgt. Eric Berg and Tom Meehan, a Norwood EMT-I with whitewater experience, responded. They discussed using a helicopter, but decided against it. Sgt. Berg assessed the very hazardous scene and prepared to decline the rescue. When he heard of their plan to get Williams' body to shore, he said, "You guys are crazy!" Undersheriff Wakefield took Sgt. Berg aside, said that Williams had just cashed his paycheck – a lot of money that his family needed. The money lay in a wallet on the body. The Undersheriff feared that someone else, desperate for money, would die trying to get to it.

Sgt. Berg agreed to try, read the water flow and estimated which way the current would take the body. He thought there was a very good chance that they could lose it since it lay under foaming water at the top of several small waterfalls. OMRT members watched closely in case the body washed downriver. Clad in wetsuits, the SMSAR men crossed the ladder, which was a little bouncier than Sgt. Berg thought it would be, and joined Foxx and Bacigalupi on the island.

As they moved into the river, secured by static anchors, Sgt. Berg said they knew that if they made a mistake they could pay with their lives. Fortunately, they found the vigorously foaming water less dense and powerful than expected. With a fully extended fireman's pike pole, Sgt. Berg hooked the corpse's leather belt, pulled it off the rock at the top of the falls and swung it with pulses of the water to an eddy near the side of the island. A Tyrolean traverse (a fixed rope line used for crossing open space) was strung from the island to the bank in order to move it to the cliff. A litter team on belay raised the load.

By 8 p.m. the deed was done. It had taken five to seven hours to get the ropes right, to get "people in the water and to get this guy back up the scree slope," said Scheidegger. "Anyway, we got him up and outta there." SJCSAR and Sgt. Berg praised OMRT. The *Silverton Standard* wrote that it was "an extremely hazardous rescue operation that required high technical proficiency, resourcefulness and courage."

Williams' paycheck was "in his pocket, all in cash," said the Undersheriff. "It was all soaking in a glob ... [we] dried it all out ... put it all right back in with his stuff.

CHAPTER NINE

1988-92
Out of the gorge "on an icicle"

IN THE LATE 1980s, ice climbing, mountaineering, backcountry skiing, hiking, backpacking, mountain biking and high altitude running brought more adventurers to the San Juans. Mt. Sneffels and Red Mountain Pass claimed victims and caused increasingly difficult retrievals.

1988's callouts began with a miserable predawn search on a cold March Sunday. At 4:30 a.m., fourteen rescuers scoured snowpacked US 550 for a truck reported off road. After five and a half hours of searching canyon and roadway, they abandoned the effort. It was the first of four false alarms. Eleven days later, they headed for US 550 again after a Denver couple rode a Mother Cline avalanche 400 feet into the canyon and lived to tell the tale. Eighty-year-old Ray Cushman saw it coming and accelerated through falling snow, but the slide smacked the right front of his 1982 Oldsmobile, twisting it ninety degrees, "quicker than you can blink." The car slid over the edge; Cushman and his wife Florence calmly navigated the sixty-degree downhill. He steered the car through heavy snow washing over the windshield and when it stopped, he got out and began to climb to the highway, but made it only 100 feet before falling in the slippery tire track and sliding back into the car "like a regular sled ride without the sled."

Dr. Bachman arrived, rappelled and asked if they were all right. "I just kept steerin' her so it'd stay straight," Ray Cushman said. Another slide rolled down, fifty feet to the north. Just fifteen minutes before, spectators were moved from under Mother Cline, a cliff notorious for repeating slides. OMRT carved steps in the snow and

Mike McPeek descended with harnesses: "We just walked them right up the hill...." The Cushmans spent the night in Ouray; it was their first trip over Red Mountain Pass and first snow slide. "Thanks aren't enough," they told the *Plaindealer*. Dr. Bachman called them "real troopers," for staying calm through the experience.

◆ ◆ ◆

All went quiet on the mountain front until the second Saturday of June. While OMRT practiced vertical evacuation on the 200-foot Golden Crystal cliff south of town, a jeep veered off road, reportedly at Box Canyon. A six-man team checked in but found that the rescue scene was actually near Yankee Boy Basin. A twenty-two-year-old Texas driver with five teenagers on board missed a curve on a steep downgrade, skidded across the dirt road and plunged 100 feet.

When OMRT arrived, two teens lay trapped in seatbelts in a rental Jeep stuck in the middle of a short waterfall, its roll bars barely visible. One teen lay in the stream. Three more perched on the rocky, tree-strewn bank. With help from some of the people in a five-Jeep party, OMRT got the teens to the road. All survived. Michael Foxx, who dragged the last one from the water, said, "Any time you take a Jeep into that canyon, if you survive it, you're lucky."

A call at 5:30 a.m. on the Fourth of July sent eighteen rescuers scrambling to find a twenty-four-year-old Denver woman dressed only in shorts, shirt and light raincoat. The day before, thinking it was a one-day hike, she started up the strenuous 17.1 mile Horsethief / Bridge of Heaven / Bear Creek loop without food or overnight gear. Foxx and Ken Miller hiked the Horsethief, Thad Spaulding and Rick Lyon drove to Engineer and hiked American Flats, and Rich Huss and Jim Hollis searched Bear Creek. A base radio station at Mineral Farms allowed for radio contact in upper Bear Creek, where Huss and Hollis spotted the woman at 9:45 a.m.

Two backpackers saw her wandering at 12,000 feet in a rainstorm. Thinking she might be disoriented, they followed her, invited her to spend the night at their camp and steered her to the right trail the next day. She had been walking northeast toward Difficulty Creek, into one of the most remote, confusing areas of the Uncompahgre Wilderness. Undersheriff Wakefield marveled at her good fortune: if "those backpackers hadn't found her, we would still be looking...."

At the end of July, a hiker spotted a flannel shirt on a bush, triggering a fruitless search. Two overdue hikers on Mt. Sneffels sent

Undersheriff Wakefield to Yankee Boy, where he found them coming out after camping overnight in bad weather. A third alert on August 17, however, was the real thing as OMRT performed a 300 man-hour technical retrieval of an injured climber near the top of Sneffels.

Twelve days later, Dawn MacConkey of Grand Junction fell off Bear Creek Trail below the Yellow Jacket Mine and broke her ankle. After a 2:30 p.m. alert, a first response team of Foxx, Bill Dwelley, Bill MacTiernan, Greg Genuit and James Lupp headed up the trail. Six more volunteers hauled the wheeled litter and medical gear up the first thousand feet of the narrow, shale-covered trail and along the precipitous gorge track. Undersheriff Wakefield set up communications at the trailhead. Medical packs and oxygen arrived at 4:45 as MacConkey's swollen ankle soaked in the icy creek. As Dwelley and Foxx splinted it, she wondered how they would get out since she lay in a ravine. They moved her thirty to forty yards downstream for better access to the trail, now only fifty feet above them. They set up a rope system and MacTiernan tied in. Using a fireman's carry, assisted by Genuit, he hauled her to the trail.

Inching along the narrow ledges of Bear Creek Gorge, OMRT members haul a wheeled litter bearing Dawn MacConkey.

Photo by Mike Hockersmith

Dr. Bachman came from the clinic, hiking in penny loafers. He checked MacConkey, strapped into the wheeled litter, and they headed down. At a sharp, washed out switchback, "the litter and handlers did slide down the wash for a few feet, but without incident, since the litter was belayed both front and back with McPeek and MacTiernan running two separate braking systems." MacTiernan, who initially thought a belay (a rope safety system for the litter, patient and handlers) wasn't needed, was very glad they had it. "In setting up that belay system on those washes in Bear Creek.... I thought in my mind, 'Well, let's just roll over this.' And people went 'No, no, no.' And we did slip ... and it was good that we spent the extra ten or twenty minutes it took to set up a rope. My bad." The steep downhill track also felt safer after Miller, Peggy Pass and Mike Hockersmith cleared the trail and filled in washes to widen narrow spots. It was dark when they reached the highway. Genuit said it was the longest day of his life.

◆ ◆ ◆

Early in 1989 disaster struck. On March 11, they discovered that $581.43 worth of equipment was missing from the Beast, parked in the Emergency Services Center. Among the pilfered items were the vertical evacuation stretcher, a double rescue pulley and thirty-six carabiners, a serious technical, logistical and financial blow to the team. A month later, most of the missing stuff mysteriously appeared, parked on the hood of a Ouray Police vehicle. "'Wet and muddy, having apparently been kept in a damp location,' and encased in a large plastic bag, were carabiners, ascenders, webbing, figure eights, the 'spider,' [a special rescue sling for evacuating litters from difficult locations], and several lengths of climbing rope." New equipment had been ordered, but they examined and tested the old gear to ensure it remained safe to use, too. They had a record $8,000 in the bank, so they spent $900 on avalanche beacons, shovels, ascenders, rescue pulleys, a brake tube and a spine splint. A Region 10 grant and a $1,000 donation from the Colorado 500 motorcycle group bought five new pagers – individual Motorola radios for quick communication. Sandy East suggested they pre-rig their gear. "We had built systems," said MacTiernan. "There's a bag for the spider. It's got everything in it. There's a bag for scree evac, everything's in it. Let's make kits that apply to different things.... We had never had an avalanche kit or a whitewater kit...."

Everyone sold ads for printing another 300 cookbooks and on July 2nd Outlaw Restaurant chef James Lupp premiered a new fundraiser: "This breakfast could save your life," Capt. Nick Leva told the *Plaindealer*. "Please attend." It was so successful that it became an essential part of every Fourth of July, providing good income for twenty-eight years.

◆ ◆ ◆

An idealistic twenty-five-year-old adjunct professor at Long Beach State University with "a gift for climbing," came to the May 1989 meeting only a week after arriving in town. Bill Whitt was unloading his truck when Capt. Leva, who was on the Ouray Police force, pulled up in his patrol car. Leva had heard of this young man's seven years of climbing and five years of guiding from Whitt's in-laws, Gary and Debbie Wild, and OMRT "was short on climbers," said Whitt. In the next few years, he, like MacTiernan, became an essential technical member. Both climbed constantly for recreation and had done so for years. MacTiernan would spend twenty years rescuing people; Whitt, thirty. That year, OMRT also voted in a ninety-day membership trial period. In November, outdoor specialist and wilderness instructor Randy Gerke, a Montrose resident who had spent years wishing he had time to join, finally did.

A December ice climbing seminar became a seminal training event. Instructor East was "a great guide ... a really good climber," said Whitt and helped build "the knowledge base of the team." Lt. Foxx said that East worked with Bacigalupi, MacTiernan, Whitt and himself. They "were climbing rocks with crampons on way back then. Sandy had to teach us how to do it, because in a rescue you can't stop and change your crampons, and change out of your boots all the time ... that was kind of a new thing...." OMRT had minimal equipment for ice rescue, so Lt. Foxx and MacTiernan recommended purchasing $2,000 worth of screws, footfangs and ice climbing aids from East's Alpine School. He "was able to get a bunch of stuff on ProBuy and basically sold it at his cost," said Whitt.

◆ ◆ ◆

Three callouts, beginning in late April, were serious and time-consuming. In the first, John Richards, sixty-seven, and his wife Margery, seventy-one, driving from their winter home in Arizona to a summer home in South Dakota, died on impact when their car skidded on the icy Red Mountain Pass Road and ran over the edge below the Engineer Pass turnoff. The car flipped one and a half times, coming to rest on the riverbank. Because of the steep grade and extensive damage, it had to be hauled out of the canyon before their bodies could be retrieved.

On June 17 while glissading down Coxcomb Peak's snowfield in the Big Blue (now the Uncompahgre) Wilderness, Laura Anderson broke through crusty snow, injuring her knee. Her companion, Glen Lathrop, set up a tent, helped her into a sleeping bag, hiked two and a half miles to the trailhead and drove twenty rough miles to Ridgway. A quick response team — Lt. Foxx, MacTiernan, David Koch and Dwelley — headed into the wilderness. Two hours later and 2,000 feet higher, they splinted the thirty-year-old's leg, packaged her in a lightweight Sked and lowered her down steep snow chutes to the trail, where they snugged her into the wheeled Stokes litter. Dr. Bachman, Capt. Leva, Bacigalupi, Rick Trujillo, June Bachman and Gary Miller had flagged the forest trail as they brought in the litter, knowing everyone would be coming out in the dark. Undersheriff Wakefield, Walt Rule and Thad Spaulding built a fire and had hot coffee waiting for them, thanks to Janie Wakefield, who drove forty miles to deliver it. They loaded Anderson into a vehicle and took her to Montrose. They reached the barn at midnight.

Three weeks later, fifteen teens and two adults from Oconomowoc, Wisconsin, left the Bachelor-Syracuse Mine for a seven day hike on the Horsethief. Six hours and several miles later, they camped at Cascade Creek at 12,000 feet. One girl had a sprained ankle and another severe back pain and breathing problems. At dawn, leader Jon Minze and two boys hiked back for help. Given the "extremely remote" location, OMRT estimated that fifteen men and twenty-four hours would be needed to retrieve the girls by foot, so Minze authorized a helicopter. None were available so they requested help from San Juan Guest Ranch. MacTiernan, Whitt and trail guide Dwain Beamer, loaded with first aid, communication and rescue equipment, set off on horseback at 11:30. Their mission was to find the camp, treat the injured and locate a LZ. Early that afternoon a chopper arrived and mountain guide Bill Crawford boarded and located the camp. The girls were extricated and the men on horseback, contacted by radio, turned around.

◆ ◆ ◆

On March 7, 1990, a former member was buried in an avalanche a quarter mile east of Red Mountain Pass. Before the search for the experienced backcountry skier concluded, five neighboring counties sent help and seventy-five people worked for 1,500 hours. On Labor Day La Plata County called for help. Dwelley and Gerke volunteered to search for a thirty-eight-year-old climber from Albuquerque, missing since Friday in Chicago Basin in the Weminuche Wilderness. They drove to Purgatory Ski Resort and flew into Chicago Basin in a Thunderbird helicopter on Tuesday. Ralph Lopez, Jr.'s "tent, backpack, and personal items" were found that afternoon near Hazel Lake. Severe weather moved in and thirty-three rescuers endured heavy rain overnight. Clouds prevailed the next morning, so teams searched upward from Hazel Lake. At 2:20 searchers aboard a Chinook helicopter spotted Lopez's body at the base of 13,600-foot Grizzly Peak. He had died before the search began.

The Chinooks began evacuating everyone from the high basin to Purgatory. Eventually, only three were left: Dwelley and Gerke and a man from Durango wearing a very loud coat, "a bright ass thing, hot yellow, hot green coat," Dwelley said. Their Chinook, however, had to return to Durango for fuel. The weather was "shutting in ... the pilot is saying we don't think we can make a trip back," said Dwelley. In rain and snow, they began building a place on the rocky lakeshore to live that night, figuring they'd have to hack out the next day on their own. Suddenly a helicopter was overhead. The pilot was breaking all the rules, said Gerke, "coming in fast" and the guy in the bright coat ran over to the other side of the lake to a cliff 400 feet above the water where he stood on the edge waving his arms. Gerke and Dwelley watched:

> Gerke: *"These guys aren't even landing, they are coming down and the back door is open and they just barely touch the back door to the ground."*
>
> Dwelley: *"The back wheels are over the water. Water is being sprayed and we are loading."*
>
> Gerke: *"The crew member in the back is going, 'get in here, get in here.'"*

They saw a yellow / green flash as the third man ran down the cliff, around the lake and dove in the back door. "As soon as he hits the deck," said Gerke, "they are off, I mean, out of here." The pilot maneuvered between two peaks in the mist, "with just ten feet on each side of the rotors," said Dwelley. They heard a crewmember sigh. The "bright ass thing" had been useful after all.

Three weeks later, a man slipped climbing near Cascade Falls and injured his back. This late afternoon call morphed into a four-hour technical night rescue. Capt. Leva, Lt. Foxx, Whitt and Rich Huss scaled the cliffs and belayed the twenty-four-year-old from a difficult spot. Leva said: "It's all rotten rock up there, and in the dark it's an extremely hard place to do this."

◆ ◆ ◆

In the 1970s and early 80s, OMRT was part of the MRA. In 1989 they applied again. Vail Mountain Rescue Group sponsored and trained with them. The December evaluation emphasized vertical and scree evacuation, snow and search, all part of OMRT's training and rescues. Chief evaluator Dan Aguilar praised the team as a "very small, tight-knit, highly skilled group" and said the technical evacuation from a snowy cliff was "one of the best he had ever seen." He was also impressed with Sheriff Wakefield: "If you've got that type of willingness to cooperate, which is rare in many counties, you've got a good thing going down there."

◆ ◆ ◆

Capt. Foxx and Lt. Whitt led OMRT in 1991, which began and ended with fatalities on US 550. On January 25, a sixty-one-year-old Albuquerque man driving to Ouray on a dry, sunny road somehow went off the Ruby Walls. He plunged 600 feet to the canyon floor and was thrown from the car despite wearing a seatbelt. Eight rescuers retrieved his body. Eleven months later, they responded to another serious accident. On a November morning, a semi roared northbound through the curves above town. A semi ahead of him pulled over on the narrow shoulder to allow a pass, but to no avail. That driver could only watch as the first semi flipped sideways, leaving 143 feet of skid marks and "a cloud of white smoke." The 101-foot sideways slide in the opposite (southbound) lane ended against a guardrail at the edge of the canyon. The sixty-year-old driver, whose chest was crushed, died a half hour later as rescuers and medical personnel worked feverishly to free him. It took them and the Montrose Fire Department another two hours to cut open the roof and window and free his body from the wreck.

◆ ◆ ◆

By January 1992 OMRT had a new Bulldog rock drill, two 165-foot static ropes, medical packs, throw bags for river rescue, MRA patches and decals. Huss went to Whitewater training in Durango. Capt. Foxx, MacTiernan, Whitt, Gerke and Huss crafted membership requirements, hoping to encourage young people to join. Truck officer Walt Rule created an inventory system. Martha Bille redid the reliable cookbook, they sold ads and cashed a precious CD to pay for 1150 books. The publisher threw in a new cover since the old design was lost. By summer's end, good T-shirts sales and receipts from the breakfast replaced that CD.

Unfortunately, they also had a $7,500 medical wish list but only $9,258 in the bank. A request to the Emergency Medical Board yielded $3,256; they spent $3,500 on necessities: a new Sked, Oregon spine splint, rescue sled and Thomas advanced life support pack, which was so heavy, a member groused, that it needed a "gorilla to carry it around." They bought a second vehicle, a used ambulance from the San Juan Guest Ranch, for $5,000 with $2,500 down and the balance due after the summer's fundraising. Refurbished and painted, the ambulance took over rescue duties and the Orange Beast went to Grand Junction for new springs.

◆ ◆ ◆

Aficionados had been climbing ice in the Uncompahgre Gorge since the 1970s, but the newly burgeoning sport would mean rescues. They needed to be able to respond to accidents, so Whitt suggested hosting a Rocky Mountain Regional Ice Seminar in 1992, followed by a first Ice Festival. On the first weekend of February, they hosted an Ice Climbing and Rescue Seminar for the Rocky Mountain Region. Thirty rescuers from Salt Lake City, Vail, Aspen, Colorado Springs, New Mexico and Wyoming met in sleepy winter Ouray. East brought two of his Alpine School instructors, who earned $50 a day. Whitt, MacTiernan, Huss, Gerke, Foxx, Scheidegger and climber George Gardner also taught. Gary and Debbie Wild, who had purchased the Victorian Inn with Whitt the year before, thinking that ice climbers would need a place to stay, provided rooms. Tom and Tammy Kenning, proprietors of the Western Hotel, fed the crowd. Twenty-two years later, Whitt remembered the very big gamble they made in buying the Victorian and dreaming about multiple climbs lining the gorge.

Back in '91, that first winter in January, if we didn't have a zero for that night, if we had one room that was a big deal ... back then there was nobody in town in the winter. It was dead. All we wanted to do

*was turn the four or five climbs into ... six ... so we troughed one and
made it go two different directions, now we have two. The next year
we thought ... maybe we can put some hoses on this big pipeline and
make four into eight.*

He and Wild created the 'Schoolroom' climb and moved north
toward the bridge over the Uncompahgre at Camp Bird Road where
'Tangled Up In Blue' was already a known route. Wild got permission from Eric Jacobsen, who owned the three-foot penstock, to tap
into the plentiful water it carried to the hydroelectric plant. That
allowed them to create more climbs, but the water was so heavily
mineralized that it froze orange.

For the next few years, instead of one or two climbers in town
on weekends, the Ice Park "might have a dozen." Climbing gyms
became popular "and the climbing boom in general spilled over
into ice climbing," said Whitt. The Ice Park became the "right place,
right time." February's Ice Climbing and Rescue Seminar featured
ice safety, belaying, anchor placement and climbing techniques.
The beautiful ice inspired great reviews. Rocky Mountain Regional
Chairman Tim Cochrane pronounced the seminar "the best I've
ever been to." MRA president Dick Bethers called the experience
"absolutely fantastic." Financially, the team broke even.

◆ ◆ ◆

A test of their ice rescue skills came February 15, two days after a
Denver TV station featured Ouray ice. On the 'Schoolroom' climb,
John Meier, fifty, fell sixty feet from a short rope to the bottom of the
gorge. A climbing partner, Jan Studebaker, was sorting gear at the
bottom and "not paying a whole lot of attention." Meier's gurgling
sounds alerted a nearby climber, paramedic Craig O'Connell, who
manipulated his airway with a jaw thrust, allowing him to breathe
easier. Chris Brislawn ran for help. Twenty rescuers reached the
bridge within an hour. Lt. Whitt and MacTiernan heard the page as
they groomed the Ironton Nordic track and hurried back to Ouray,
knowing this might be "one of the first ice rescues in forty-eight
states," said MacTiernan. He remembered Lyle Dean saying, "It's less
about building big anchors, it's more about eliminating the weight
... you could almost do a counterweight."

Four members rappelled 100 feet to Meier, stabilized him and
secured him in a litter. As they debated the best way to get him out,

MacTiernan wanted a simple raise using a counterweight with tag lines. They could pull back on those and raise the litter. After some discussion, however, they decided to raise Meier with Gerke attending to save weight and gain speed. He was lowered down the cliff on a pulley system.

MacTiernan was counterweight, descending from above, as they slowly hoisted the litter and Gerke. It was a difficult raise. At that time of year, a lot of ice had formed and four to five pound chunks cascaded down. "By the time we were done, we had a lot of people on there," said MacTiernan. Whitt "built one heck of an ice anchor ... or we would all have been laying in the bottom of that gorge." Once they got to the top and headed out, it became "very, very difficult to stabilize the litter on top of the pipe." Whitt built more strong anchors for the snow and ice-packed trestle they had to cross. It was a 200-foot vertical drop to the canyon if anyone slipped.

They were only a few hundred feet from the road, but it wasn't easy to get Meier out. Wielding shovels and ice axes, the rest of the team cleared a trail to the ambulance. The patient lost and regained consciousness several times, but as he was transferred to St. Mary's Air Life helicopter at the Hot Springs Park, "his eyes were open and he was speaking." Flight Nurse Marcia Millar, who had never seen an ice rescue, was in awe of the professionalism and calm of the rescuers. Meier survived hypothermia, six broken ribs and a punctured lung. "I'm very, profoundly grateful to them for what they did," he told *Rescue 911*. Incident Commander (IC) Whitt later acknowledged the difficulties: "It wasn't a slam-dunk rescue." It had been a one of a kind, five-hour team effort. For MacTiernan it was, "One of my highlights ... to get somebody out of that gorge on an icicle." OMRT had aced the first Ice Park rescue.

◆ ◆ ◆

In late July, Whitt and Gerke drove two hours south to Durango to assist La Plata and San Juan Counties. A German mountaineer and scientist, Walter Eidelloth, thirty, had not returned to his camp in Chicago Basin. They checked in with La Plata County Sheriff Bill Gardner and were given black and white chunks of map before they boarded a chopper at Animas Air Field for the Weminuche Wilderness. The weather was bad so they couldn't see much as the pilot zoomed in and dropped them on a ridge. Whitt asked where they were: "I couldn't even tell you!" the pilot answered. Since they were supposed to return to the same spot for pickup, they decided to climb the ridge for a better view and found themselves on the summit of 14,084-foot Mt. Eolus. Other searchers were dropped off around the basin and base camp was set up with giant cook and sleep tents flown in from Durango.

Eidelloth's companion, Bill Cosper, of Alexandria, Virginia, stayed at their Twin Lakes camp with altitude sickness. When Eidelloth wasn't back by Sunday morning, he and other climbers in the basin searched without success. Cosper hiked out ten miles to the remote narrow gauge train stop at Needleton in the Animas River Canyon. He reached officials late on Monday. Burt Metcalf of Thunderbird Helicopters, whom La Plata Sheriff Bill Gardner called one of the best search pilots in the state, began flying at dawn Tuesday morning over three 14,000-foot peaks, Windom, Sunlight and Eolus. A Chinook helicopter from Fort Carson joined the effort. Several ground teams searched Tuesday. Wednesday at 4:30 p.m., the Chinook flew over Eolus's ridgeline and someone spotted a body

A portion of northside of Eolus in foreground extreme left

The north side of Mt. Eolus, left. Walter Eidelloth's body was found in the notched gully on the opposite side of the snowfield.

Photo by Dan Bender

1,000 feet below, wedged in a "real narrow waterfall," said Whitt. It lay in a sixty to ninety degree gorge of rock and ice.

Early Thursday morning a helicopter flew Whitt and "renowned alpinist Charlie Fowler" of SMSAR to the scene. They were dropped off with a Sked on the shoulder of the mountain and climbed the snowfield, finding Eidelloth's body at 9:30 a.m. They "weren't sure they could get the body back.... With the amount of loose shale, it was quite dangerous.... I was beamed by a rock on the leg. It was probably one of the hardest rescues I've been on," Whitt said. In an "extremely hazardous operation," they did manage to get Eidelloth's body out of the crevice. Unfortunately, they didn't have much rope and it had been almost a week since he died. The body "was not exactly real pliable" and they had to work to get it into the Sked. At 11:30 they started down the snowfield, sitting astride the load and digging their feet into the snow to manage the descent. They "rode him like a sled down this huge snowfield to the base where they could get us with a helicopter," said Whitt. Assisting in the recovery was former OMRT Capt. Leva from the La Plata Sheriff's Department.

Sheriff Gardner said the technical descent was "the most dangerous extrication in the history of La Plata County's search and rescue teams." Eidelloth was the fifth fatality on Eolus' ridges in ten years. He "had fallen off the ridgeline," said Whitt. "He was one of these super athletes and he was going to nail all three [mountains] in the same day and he just never came back ... the weather was bad and I think he was just crossing those ridgelines and ... slipped off of wet rocks and pitched." Eidelloth had ascended two of the three fourteeners in Chicago Basin within an hour: Windom Peak at 11:30 a.m. and Sunlight Peak, at 12:30 p.m., as evidenced by his signature in the summit registers on Saturday. His name didn't appear in the register for Mt. Eolus. "For Eidelloth to reach the summit of Windom and Sunlight peaks within an hour of each other is unusual," Sheriff Gardner said, "and it bears out friends' description of him as a world-class climber." On his way to a job in California, he had detoured to climb in the San Juans.

◆ ◆ ◆

In August Ouray County needed help. An Arizona hiking book author, who intended to walk Bear Creek Trail back to Ouray, hired a jeep tour operator to drop her off at Engineer Pass. When she failed to show in town, a three-day search, with assistance from the

San Juan and La Plata teams, was organized. In September, a twenty-four-year-old California tourist, checking out Bear Creek Falls from a dangerous perch with friends, slipped on the grassy slope, "fell into the canyon, hit the wall and landed in about three feet of water." It took twelve rescuers, four EMTs, the Sheriff's Department, the Posse, CDOT and County Road Department employees to get him out. Among other injuries, he suffered a hip fracture and a punctured lung. It was a treacherous rescue site, said Capt. Foxx. The scree evacuation up and over two ledges had the litter in a vertical position instead of the normal horizontal alignment.

Randy Gerke, left, and Bill MacTiernan haul a patient up vertically over a rock ledge at Bear Creek Falls. Some anchors show at lower left.
Photo by LW (Warren) Chilton III
Courtesy Nancy Kendrick and Jennifer Burnett

◆ ◆ ◆

East organized the first U.S. ice climbing festival outside of Alaska, with assistance from OMRT and guides Mike O'Donnell and Lyle Dean, said Whitt. It drew climbers from across the country – and rave reviews. "Turning the natural environment into a festival

... was a stroke of genius," Cameron Burns wrote in the *Aspen Times*. From December 11-13, eager climbers attended clinics and negotiated ice in the Uncompahgre Gorge.

1992 was a year of chilly firsts: an ice climbing seminar, the first Ice Park rescue and first Ice Festival. It also had a sobering first: A new member was driving a tour Jeep in the Sneffels area when a page went out for a fallen teenager. Acting on his own, without authorization, the driver took his clients up the mountain. MacTiernan recalled that:

> *They basically grabbed this thirteen-year-old kid by the hair, drug him down the mountain ... he put this young man's body in the back of a Jeep with clients and drove them to town.... No sense that he had forced his paying clients ... to endure a dead body in the back of the Jeep.... It was wrong in so many ways.... That's not how you respect a body. That's not how you respect a father. That's not how you do these things.*

In executive session, OMRT's officers asked the man if he would do that again. He said he would, that he had no regrets. They dismissed him for grossly inappropriate behavior. The incident, said MacTiernan, became a good reason "to vet people over a period of time...."

CHAPTER TEN

"The Good Lord Has Blessed Me"

SAN JUAN GUEST RANCH, nestled in the Uncompahgre Valley between Ouray and Ridgway, offered a variety of outdoor experiences, including climbing 14,150-foot Mt. Sneffels. So on a fine August day in 1988, two guests left their families to climb with guide Bob Freiburger, a college student from Iowa. Rocky Koga, a forty-six-year-old aerospace engineer from Palo Alto and forty-year-old Earl Ellis, a lawyer from Pacific Palisades, summited just before 10 a.m.

After a brief rest, Koga and Freiburger descended the mountain's south face, heading toward a steep rock notch, the entrance to the southeast couloir that they had ascended earlier. Ellis lingered on the summit, taking photos of a very rugged vista, the north face. When he realized the others had disappeared, he didn't know exactly where they went. He didn't call out because "grown men don't ask for directions." He felt a bit light-headed and crawled down to a two-foot square ledge just above where they had climbed up. He saw a bigger ledge three feet away and moved toward that, gently placing both hands on a six-inch point of rock for stability, barely weighting it. A boulder almost as big as he was broke loose, fell on him and carried him down a steep slope. The pain was unbearable and he blacked out for a few seconds.

When consciousness returned, he was still tumbling and heard Freiburger's voice. The young man had jumped out of the way as the 300-400 pound rock and Ellis swept by. He shouted to Ellis to spread-eagle himself to slow his descent. Ellis dragged himself to a stop with his arms and hands. Lying on his stomach fifty feet down the slope, in great pain, with a badly crushed left leg, he realized that another big slope fell away just below him. He would have been killed had he not stopped himself. Freiburger scrambled to where Ellis lay moaning on a rocky incline and assessed his injuries, dressing a cut on his forehead. He said he would go to a mine several miles below where there was a phone. He left Ellis with Koga.

◆ ◆ ◆

The weather changed, they were fully exposed to wind at 14,000 feet. Koga covered Ellis with a poncho, the only outerwear he had, and weighed it down with rocks. Rummaging in Freiburger's pack, he found a plastic trash bag and fashioned a makeshift poncho just as an icy fog moved in. Still conscious, but chilling rapidly, Ellis lay in great pain on the rocks and thought about not making it. Several climbers appeared above them and Koga called out. When they realized what had happened, they gave the men a coat, sweatshirt, stockings, mittens, poncho, food and water. David Jenkins, a rescue instructor from Salt Lake, climbing on his honeymoon, bent over Ellis and said he would survive. "Men have crawled off of mountains like this with legs like yours. You can get through this." Somewhat reassured, Ellis "manned up."

Jenkins left for thirty minutes in order to assist his new bride, who had vision problems, safely down the mountain. When he returned, he splinted Ellis's broken leg with a couple of aluminum bars. He and Koga slid rocks under Ellis to prevent his rolling down the slope.

◆ ◆ ◆

Freiburger raced down the mountain, drove to Camp Bird Mine and alerted the Sheriff at 10:45, who called Flight for Life from St. Mary's Hospital in Grand Junction. By 11:30 the first rescuers and jeeps left Ouray. Walt Rule and Thad Spaulding, in the Orange Beast, made it to lower Yankee Boy Basin by 12:35, along with the 4WD county ambulance. Ten rescuers set up critical base camp operations a quarter mile beyond the Yankee Boy Mine. At 1 p.m., a first response team – Lt. David Koch, Michael Foxx, Nick Leva, Mike McPeek and Bill MacTiernan – heavily loaded with rescue and medical equipment, jeeped to the upper Sneffels trailhead. By 3:15 they reached Ellis and the technical phase of the rescue began.

The five-hour wait blurred time for Ellis. He saw a helicopter fly over the valley and thought about it waiting for hours. Then the rescuers came. Foxx assessed his medical condition and radioed Dr. Dave Bachman, waiting at base camp. He hooked Ellis to the oxygen tank but the heavy canister was empty; they didn't know it was used the night before for a cardiac patient at the pool. The men immobilized Ellis, wrapped him warmly in blankets and packaged him in the Stokes litter. The slope falling away below them was much too dangerous to lower the litter directly down. Instead, they had to maneuver it horizontally to the main climbing route.

MacTiernan, twenty-seven-years-old, had been with OMRT only a year but had lots of rock and ice experience and knew the mountain. He saw that the best descent would be to pendulum the litter to a small finger couloir connected to the notch route, now lying above them. Assisted by McPeek and with the advice of Foxx and others, MacTiernan used his own rack of climbing aids to anchor the litter, since the team didn't own enough of the right gear.

Once they managed to move the litter to the Finger, the problem became one of lowering it manually to the notch and the main couloir with only one 165-foot rope. One anchor at a time, the belay team lowered that litter. At each pause, MacTiernan scouted out good cracks in the gully's rotten walls and floors, scratching down through layers of snow and scree to sounder rock beneath. Into cracks he judged would hold, he forced his stoppers and secured the rope. Working with two to four handlers, depending on the steepness of the pitch, MacTiernan and McPeek lowered the litter with a Figure 8 braking system. Total weight on the system, including litter, patient and attendants, was about 1250 pounds, though no one knew how well the rope would absorb such stress. The attendants assessed the patient's medical status at the end of every pitch while McPeek and MacTiernan descended to set up the next anchor.

Ellis's condition necessitated careful handling to prevent pain, shock and further injury to his head and leg. Inadvertently, while reaching for the litter handles, someone grabbed his injured leg. Ellis remembered it hurt badly. The attendants had to move carefully to avoid showering rocks on the relief team below. At one point, some men held a very unstable, refrigerator-sized rock in place while others maneuvered the litter around it. More than eight hours after Ellis fell, at 6:25 p.m., they reached the end of the couloir and the very welcome relief teams waiting on Lavender Col. From there, they could descend the 800-foot steep scree more rapidly. Deputy Sheriff Dominic Mattivi, Elwood Gregory, Bill Dwelley, Firemen Steve Duce and John Fedel waited in the cold with food and water which county administrator Pat O'Donnell brought up from local restaurants. The famished rescuers were deeply appreciative.

Eighteen volunteers drove to Yankee Boy Basin after Ouray's city siren sounded. Assembled in their work clothes were OMRT and

EMT volunteers, the Sheriff's Posse, the Road and Bridge crew and some of the Fire Department. "They were desperate to get people to help. We had the whole county up there," MacTiernan said. "Some were wearing cowboy boots."

◆ ◆ ◆

For the descent from the 13,500-foot saddle to the base, rescuers used a 735-foot rope, knotted together from several lengths and anchored it around a huge rock which thrusts upward in the middle of Lavender Col. MacTiernan said they improvised a creative and probably unorthodox knot passing system.

Before they could lower the litter MacTiernan had to clear volunteers scattered around the scree slope, waiting to help. They were in danger from rockfall once the litter and rescuers above them descended. He attempted a radio call, but the situation was so frantic that people stepped on the radio traffic. Many volunteers had no radios and couldn't hear him. Finally, he yelled for them to get the

Daylight lingers on the mountain walls beyond the southwest ridge of Sneffels as rescuers prepare to lower Earl Ellis from Lavender Col. The dark shape in the lower right corner is the huge rock they will use to anchor the 785 foot belay. From L to R are John Fedel, Mike McPeek, Thad Spaulding, Bill Dwelley, Otto Scheidegger, Nick Leva and Bill MacTiernan.

Photo by Rocky Koga

hell off the mountain. That did it. The lowering proceeded.

By 8:10 p.m. the rescue was a race between waning daylight and dark. At the bottom of the slope, relief litter bearers ran a rough half-mile track through the boulder field to the trailhead and helicopter. The Beast's headlights illuminated the area. MacTiernan, searching for the right spot to load, accidentally shone his flashlight in the pilot's eyes, prompting an instant, profane reaction. For Ellis, "the door to heaven opened, except I was alive." Amid the fierce pinnacles of the range, the helicopter lifted off just before total dark, when it would have been unable to fly.

◆ ◆ ◆

Ellis thought he was going to a "hick town" hospital. In the hospital, his wife didn't recognize him until he called out. Later he realized he'd gotten superb care in Montrose and that Dr. Bachman was a famous sports medicine physician and former doctor for the Chicago Bulls. Koga did not expect to be off Sneffels until the following morning and was surprised by the fast response time, speed and effectiveness of OMRT in deteriorating weather amid dangerous rock. Their rescue was possible because of the presence of Ouray's emergency infrastructure. Ellis said a rescuer told him that they didn't find many people alive. Before he left for home, Foxx gave him a gray OMRT T-shirt featuring several victims. He wore it as he recovered, his wife washed it at night. His broken left leg had a two-inch, fist sized pulverized mass of bone in the main fracture zone several inches below the knee. An external fixator with three rods and connectors and seven bolts drilled into the bone held it together. At Christmas he wrote: "The good Lord has blessed me. With the modest help of two crutches, I am now able to walk a mile on both legs.... morning air strikes my face and tickles my nose, the sunlight colors the horizon, and the joys of life and health are prized. " A year later, he sent a welcome $300.

◆ ◆ ◆

Scheidegger said that for such a small team to engineer this rescue, it had to reflect their training ethos; if there had been "ego play," it wouldn't have happened; Jenkins' help wouldn't have been welcome. MacTiernan said his first major rescue taught him how monumental such an effort is, how much time it takes. He was a wreck for three to four days afterwards, knowing they had been "right on the edge of our knowledge."

CHAPTER ELEVEN

The Blue Room

EIGHTEEN INCHES OF POWDER shimmered on the mountains after the biggest storm of a dry season. A bluebird day beckoned skiers with a special intensity, for the low-density (seven percent) storm came on the heels of one of the worst snow droughts.

In Living (and dying) In Avalanche Country, John Marshall and Jerry Roberts challenge backcountry skiers: "Instead of looking at a situation and trying to figure out how safe it is, one should be assessing the dangers. How unsafe it is." Colorado snow remains unpredictable, so experts analyze it by digging snow pits and performing mechanical strength tests. They follow a protocol – carrying and using avalanche beacons, probes and shovels, skiing one at a time in hazardous terrain. Avalanche schools teach these procedures.

◆ ◆ ◆

Mid-morning that day, March 7, 1990, avalanche forecaster Roberts, Tyler Van Arsdell and two companions parked on the Silverton side of Red Mountain Pass. Van Arsdell was "very excited to go up," knowing "that we weren't going to ski anything that would slide." They put on skis and skinned a quarter mile up the rapidly warming south side of North Carbon Mountain to check out the terrain. They knew the danger of such a hair-trigger day and intended to ski only Carbon's low angle south slope. Van Arsdell followed two Montrose skiers breaking trail. They had watched these "Powder Shock Club" skiers – Jim Hollis, a blue-eyed, dark-haired, six-foot science teacher, and his companion Gary McDonald – for years, so their presence wasn't unexpected. "I was talking with them on the way up and listening to their conversation," said Van Arsdell. He could hardly believe what he heard. McDonald asked Hollis if he had his avalanche cord. He didn't. McDonald replied, "Oh well, 'Ski to die!'"

Since these skiers did not follow protocol, Roberts and Van Arsdell avoided skiing with them: "All of us that skied together realized that in the event of an avalanche, we're relying on someone else to save our lives," said Van Arsdell. There was "a little animosity" between the groups – Hollis and McDonald called them "the elitist skiers from Ridgway."

At 11 a.m., Roberts saw that "the low density powder was rapidly densifying into heavy, wet mashed potatoes." Van Arsdell said it stuck in globs to their skis "five, six, seven inches thick," making the ascent difficult. A Powder Shock man asked about snow conditions on the north side avalanche gully, 'Oh Boy,' which Roberts had named and skied years before. He discovered the slope one day when he and a fellow INSTARR (Institute of Alpine and Arctic Research) San Juan Project worker, Tim Lane, were working. They "found this beautiful little shot of open north facing terrain protected from the SW wind in the trees. I looked down the slope before making my first turn," said Roberts, "looked at Lane and said 'Oh Boy.'" They warned Hollis and McDonald they were taking a big risk: This "high density warm spring snow" covering the thin snowpack was dangerous. Hollis and McDonald headed north anyway.

◆ ◆ ◆

Hollis and his partner of nineteen years, Nancy Winkler, met as teachers at Oberon Junior High in Arvada, Colorado. She was in her thirties, with three daughters, had just finished college and was teaching math. Hollis's outdoor persona drew him to her, and after her divorce they traveled, living in Vermont and Colorado. He taught her to ski and they backpacked, skied and climbed together. "A fantastic skier," she marveled that Hollis "was one of those guys that just floats down the mountain." In 1989, on their way home to Montrose after visiting her parents in Denver, they stopped to ski some of his favorite snow chutes, which ran from the top of Loveland Pass to Arapahoe Basin on the west side. After they skied a chute, they would catch a ride back to their car, parked at the top.

The Front Range was especially beautiful. They had "no thoughts of avalanche in our minds...." They hiked to the ridge and she skied first. The crusty snow made the run hard. She stopped part way down to watch his descent. Hollis "pulled up next to me and just as he did, the whole slope ... went." They had several more avalanche paths to ski. It had become "a horrendous day for me," she said. "I said to him that I am not doing this anymore. I will go skiing with you but I am not going where it is scary ... that is how he came to be alone." She realized that for him, part of the fun was that "he lived on that edge."

On this March morning, Hollis woke early to help a friend move. Winkler had worked at a local restaurant the night before but agreed to substitute when the phone rang. The Montrose School District wanted one of them and she was ready to go when Hollis came home. He offered to take the job, but she said, "No, I am up – I had my breakfast – the hard part is over. I will just go." Hollis acquiesced and mentioned that he and McDonald thought they might go up to Red Mountain and do a little skiing.

They took a first run on 'Oh Boy' at 11:30. They went back for a second. Part way down, they rested on a snow bench. Hollis descended first, stopped to adjust a ski binding. McDonald, watching, saw snow run to the left of him. Hollis took off across the slope. "The last thing he saw was Hollis running," said Winkler, "and then all the snow let go, which forced him to pay attention to what he was going to do for himself." McDonald lunged across the slope and grabbed a tree. Secure, he looked for Hollis, but he had disappeared in a huge snow cloud.

◆ ◆ ◆

Just after 1 p.m. Roberts, Barb Wheeler and Paul Hebert were at the truck parked near US 550, relaxing with a cold one after two runs on Carbon's south side. One of them wrote on the Montrose skiers' dirty windshield, "Ski to die!" Another noticed that the Longfellow slide path to the east had run while they skied. Van Arsdell was still out there since he had circled around the west side of Carbon on the way back. "I just had this sixth sense," he recalled. "I said something like, 'You know, I am just going to go this way. I'll see you at the parking lot.'"

The Longfellow slide path, with a vertical drop of 400 feet, begins at 11,600 feet and runs for a total of 721 feet. It includes "several broad gullies, cliffs, large rock outcrops, light to moderate coniferous and grass." The runout zone is a "bowl-shaped slope, talus, boulders and bare ground." Van Arsdell skied the road toward the 'Oh Boy,' rounded the steep Longfellow terrain, with its rock beds and cliffs and looked up and saw a ski track buried by an avalanche:

*probably one of the biggest, most severe avalanches I had ever seen
... the fracture line started at Longfellow and wrapped all the way
around the north face of Carbon ... adrenaline pumps in and I just
start going as fast as I can and I'm rounding Carbon and I get to
'Oh Boy' and I've never seen anything like it in my life. It looked like
a bomb destroyed the mountain....*

At the bottom he encountered an eerie silence and began yelling. From the relative safety of the tree, McDonald heard him, moments after "two large class-4 avalanches had released and run the
skier over like a freight train." Van Arsdell heard, "I'm right here.
I'm okay," but he couldn't see. Then realized McDonald was in the
dead center of the run. Van Arsdell asked,

> *"Where is Hollis?"*
> *He says, "I know right where he is."*
> *I say, "Get down here and show me where you think he is." I
> start putting my probe poles together ... when you are alone and in
> this huge avalanche debris field, you have no idea where to begin. I
> didn't even know how deep it was ... Gary eventually makes it down
> the debris and kind of points to where he thinks he might be ... and
> starts shoving the ends of his skis in ... the debris is so dense that his
> skis are only going in this far [about twelve inches].*

He told McDonald to go back to the parking lot and get everyone. For thirty-five minutes, he worked the twenty-foot debris field
with his seven-foot probe pole, thinking he might get lucky.

◆ ◆ ◆

When McDonald appeared, the party at the parking area "knew
what had happened without him speaking a word," said Roberts.
They quickly erased the message on the dirty windshield, put on
their skis and headed for 'Oh Boy.' On site, they transformed their
LifeLinks ski poles into probes. Hebert couldn't get the rubber
handgrips off his, so he took out his Swiss army knife and sliced
them off: "They were never the same again." Eventually, Wheeler
skied out and alerted a passing snowplow driver, Ralph Merwin.
At 2:15 San Juan Sheriff Greg Leithauser received a report of
a skier buried on Red Mountain. He drove to the top of the pass

and met Merwin, who said a skier was buried about a quarter mile east. It wasn't clear at that point whether the accident was in Ouray or San Juan County, but rescuers came from both sides. OMRT was alerted at 2:30 and the first responders left the barn twenty-three minutes later, arriving at 3:25. There was still no sign of Hollis. George Pastor from Silverton and his K-9 Spots were working the debris field.

Undersheriff Wakefield approached Walt Rule, OMRT's truck officer, now taking mission notes. Someone needed to talk with McDonald, who stood there mute – in shock, cold and miserable. In the late afternoon warmth of someone's truck, "kind of a private place to sit and be warm," said Rule, they sat silent for a minute or two. The survivor finally relaxed a bit and "opened up and willingly talked." His friend Hollis, an accomplished skier who sought out challenging slopes in the Tetons and other places, wanted to ski 'Oh Boy' that day and he went along. They had safely skied it before. McDonald carried an avalanche cord and thought Hollis had a shovel. He estimated the slide covered 270 degrees around the slope. After the interview, Rule walked him to his older model, black Ford pickup. Before he left, McDonald requested that the Sheriff notify Winkler, as he said he could not.

The avalanche dog had gone "down to the very toe of the slope and sat there," said Bill Whitt, but no one believed Hollis would be found there. More help arrived, people parked wherever they found space. Rule noticed that many vehicles were parked headfirst into a steep 100-foot slope on the side of US 550. Sometime later, he went back to get his stuff and noticed that the "whole slope slid, kind of down into the bumpers of the cars that were there."

The rescuers were evacuated at 6 p.m. because the area was still unsafe and avalanche control was needed. Local ski guide Chris George, who ran the St. Paul Lodge on the south side of the pass, had just arrived from working with the Silverton kids' ski program at Purgatory Ski Area. When the ski bus pulled into town at 4:30, his wife Donna was waiting.

"You need to get up to Red Mountain ... there's been a burial." So I went up there and met with the sheriff. He told me what had happened and that rescue teams had already been in looking, trying to find the victim. He asked me could I go in ... do avalanche control on the area that we call North Carbon ....

George immediately "set off towards the lodge," where people had been up and down to use the landline.

I set off probably about 5:30 … on a snowmobile with Pat Owens on the back, carrying our skis in his arms. We get just round the corner

'Oh Boy' slide on the north face of Mt. Carbon during the search for Jim Hollis' body. Rescuers probe at lower left.

Photo by Tyler Van Arsdell

from the parking lot ... and we triggered a huge avalanche ... ahead and above where I was, and I killed the snowmobile and I jumped off and just literally ran back down the track. Pat was sitting there looking at me as I went by and I said, "What are you waiting for?" He hadn't even noticed, but the avalanche had released and was coming down through the trees to this area called Marmot Town ... so we turn around and we go back to the parking lot to inform the sheriff .... When we got to the parking lot another sympathetic avalanche ran off the little hill that overlooks the parking lot. That's how fragile the snowpack was....

They regrouped and left for the lodge on skis with George's small Golden retriever Ginger. It was 8:30, full dark and cold as they finished assembling the one-kilogram pentolite explosives. They wanted to hit "half a dozen potential avalanche paths" which people had worked under, "one of which we had triggered sympathetically with a snowmobile." They worked:

around the west side of North Carbon .... We had to break trail to some really rocky outcrops and then throw bombs down the face ... at one point we're in a very precipitous place.... I want him to throw a bomb down [behind them] because I'm not going to throw a bomb over his head.... I prepared the fuse, I said, "Pat, just toss this bomb down between those two trees ... down that slope and that'll take care of it." So I give him the bomb ... he hit a tree and the bomb bounced back towards us.

They had a minute and a half before the bomb, just fifteen feet away, would blow. They hit the snow and waited. After it blew they were completely covered with snow, branches and leaves. Ginger, though used to being with George on patrol, decided they were crazy and left. George and Owens "traversed the entire top of the hill, bombing everything that we could."

The searchers went back to the slope and a dog that was with them "went down to the very toe of the slope and sat there." Nineteen searchers were sure that the dog was wrong and probed higher up the hill. The search, under the command of OMRT Capt. Nick Leva and SJCSAR leader Larry Raab, continued under moonlight until 10:40, when it was called off for the night. Everyone headed home to Silverton and Ouray for a few hours' rest.

◆ ◆ ◆

The next morning George surveyed his night's work to make sure he could see the black holes left by the explosives. He noticed a precariously hanging slab of snow on the west side of 'Oh Boy,' where they hadn't been able to bomb before. While everyone watched, he skied up to a lone tree on the edge of a bench. Here he hung a four to five kilogram garland of explosives ten feet above the snow and attached a detonating cord which he ran down the hill. He set off the garland from below and the air blast "went kind of south and southwest.... I felt secure enough to have folks go back into that area and then start digging and searching for the victim."

◆ ◆ ◆

OMRT regrouped at the barn at 7 a.m., went back to Red Mountain Pass and continued searching after George cleared the slab. Four avalanche dogs from San Juan and San Miguel Counties also worked the area. One was turned loose halfway up the slope and it went down to where the first dog had sat the day before. Still, no one believed the dog, and rescuers from five counties probed higher on the slope. Everyone thought there was "no way he was this far down," Whitt said later. "Turned out, the dog was right."

Searchers from two counties work the probe line, hoping to find Jim Hollis.
Photo by Tyler Van Arsdell

Van Arsdell checked in with Undersheriff Wakefield and dug ten-foot holes wherever someone on the probe line hit something under the debris. All they found were rocks and the trunks of trees. Then, at 1:15, San Juan searcher #1 had a strike. He had found the body, six feet downslope from where the dogs so insistently alerted. It was "under nine feet of snow, both skis, with non-releasing bindings, strapped to his feet, 300 feet from where the slab released from its crown and over 100 feet" from where Hollis had stopped in the middle of the run. Van Arsdell dug him out, "a pretty emotional event" until "his torso and his pack and his head" appeared. It was his first dead body. When it was finally freed from the snow tomb, Roberts noticed that his "glasses and hat (were) still on, with ski poles wrapped around his wrists." The body was "loaded onto a sled and taken down the hill to Dr. David Bachman, who pronounced him dead."

Hollis had found the Blue Room, the interior of an avalanche debris pile, "referencing the color of snow with visible light penetrating ... but the color Hollis found was black ... and he could have been DOA because of the vertical fall and distance he traveled with the movement of the snow." It was "an unnecessary accident," wrote Roberts. "The red lights should have been flashing in their heads. It was an extreme-hazard day that resulted in one of the largest avalanche cycles I'd seen in ten years of working in the San Juans."

◆ ◆ ◆

McDonald's wife Sheri finally located Winkler at Sakura, the Japanese restaurant where she worked in the evenings. She drove her to Ouray; she saw McDonald in the street and ran up to him, hoping that:

"maybe he was alive and I remember saying something like, 'How bad is it?'"
He replied, "No, it is bad, Nancy."

She stayed with Vivian Pilkington. Her husband Jim, a good friend of Hollis, worked the probe line. The next day she heard her friend say that they had found his body. It was in the Mountain Rescue wagon and did she want to see it? They walked to City Hall. Someone led her to the truck. He had all his clothes on: "It was like a lamp that you have turned the light out...."

◆ ◆ ◆

Thirty people climbed Mt. Sneffels that June to spread his ashes. They had lived in Ouray three years before the accident, just down the road from Box Canyon Lodge, which they managed in 1987. After Hollis died, Winkler came back to Ouray for six years, finding solace in proximity to the mountains they both loved. She regretted that Hollis "would not spend money on his gear. I talked myself blue in the face trying to get him to get a new pair of those bindings." Van Arsdell, who had been there immediately after the slide propagated, thought that as massive as the avalanche was, even if Hollis had worn a beacon, he would have been "dead in minutes."

George took avalanche expert Art Mears to do a post-mortem three days later. "You would think that things would settle down," he said. "We bombed the hell out of the whole area, there had been hundreds of people skiing everywhere, moving around everywhere." He dropped Mears at the burial site and rode his snowmobile east over the debris field. He turned back and a small slab ran over his trail. He could hear branches breaking. "The snowpack was still very fragile."

CHAPTER TWELVE

"It was my life I was working on"

HIKING NEAR TUSCON and in the Grand Canyon kept Betty Leavengood fit during Arizona's mild winters. Summers, she hiked Ouray's trails. In 1992 she'd hiked Weehawken, Upper Cascade, Twin Peaks and Blue Lakes. The fifty-three-year-old author of the *Tuscon Hiking Guide* visited every summer with her husband John and usually hiked with friends. This time, though, her tired, aching companions bailed on her latest plan – taking a jeep ride to Engineer Pass and hiking back to US 550 via Bear Creek Trail.

She decided to go alone, despite the advice she gave hikers, and carefully examined a map at the Bear Creek outdoor store. On Thursday, August 20, San Juan Jeep driver Alan Stahle dropped her off and pointed to the old jeep road "I needed to take to intersect the trail. It all looked perfectly simple. I walked over the Engineer Pass, walked down the road to Lake City a short distance and then turned left .... I followed the old jeep road, saw a trail going off to the left between two mountains and away I went."

◆ ◆ ◆

Her husband was at Bear Creek trailhead at 3 p.m. By seven, she hadn't arrived, so he reported her missing. When there was no sign of her Friday morning, OMRT mobilized. Fifty people from five counties and a pilot searched Friday and Saturday. "Five ground teams from Ouray Mountain Rescue spread out in different directions," said Randy Gerke. "Ouray Sheriff Posse members on horseback headed toward a sweep of Horsethief...." Silverton SAR teams searched. "Sheriff Frank Wilcox of Lake City searched the Hinsdale County side by jeep...." Those hiking Bear Creek and Horsethief Friday found no sign.

◆ ◆ ◆

Leavengood was dressed lightly, in shirt and shorts, and carried a pack. She had "two liters of water, a water filter, candy bar, rye crackers, potato chips and an apple … a poncho, extra sweatshirt and pullover, first aid supplies, ace bandage, Bic lighter, two packages of matches, sewing kit, large plastic garbage bag…." She passed a beautiful waterfall and took pictures of wildflowers, then realized that she hadn't seen the Yellow Jacket Mine near the high end of Bear Creek, but thought she just missed it gazing at the scenery. "Although this should have been a big clue, it wasn't," she wrote. "I lost the trail in this large meadow that was filled with wildflowers. I checked the map and decided that I should be following the creek."

As the sun waned, she thought she was too far from the creek and headed lower down, thought she saw a trail in "a boulder field and foolishly started across it. I started to slip and my pack got in the way so I tossed it. It tumbled over and over until it reached the bottom. It came open on the way down and I could see my sweater come out. I started to slide and for a moment I thought I was history." She retrieved her billfold, camera and pack, found a group of pines, built a fire ring and gathered wood. Sleeping with the garbage bag over her legs, the poncho as a blanket and the extra shirt for a pillow, she woke to feed the fire and think about her husband.

◆ ◆ ◆

Friday afternoon, Sgt. Dan Bender from La Plata Sheriff's Department in Durango and his SAR K-9 Zahn checked in. He reviewed the maps and talked to "a couple of searchers who had returned to the CP [Command Post], I suggested that I be allowed to search a drainage about three air miles from the main search area. Due to the remoteness of the area, I ... spent Friday night east of Engineer Mt. at about 12,400 feet." He figured that "if they could not find her where she was supposed to be, I wanted to look where she wasn't supposed to be." He drove Engineer Pass jeep road, his Blazer hitting bottom and Zahn bouncing to the floor from the back seat multiple times. From there, he hiked to the Horsethief trailhead and pitched a tent.

◆ ◆ ◆

Leavengood's food was gone Friday morning. Convinced she was on Bear Creek and on track to reach the highway, she continued down the canyon. At one point she thought she heard the motors of trucks. "I thought I could scramble around any falls and make it. Wrong. I spent most of the day working my way down the creek and got hung up in one spot ... and decided to retrace my route and get myself back up to Engineer Pass." A storm approached. Under an overhang created by two massive boulders, she built a fire: "I huddled in this cave with hail, thunder, lightning and rain and fully realized that it was my life I was working on." The storm ended, she climbed some more, but had lost her route. She descended and followed the stream upward until she saw a large patch of snow and the game trails she had taken earlier that day.

> *My intention was to top out in a level pine area and build a huge fire and spend the night. By now it was getting late and I was very tired. I missed the correct place to break through the cliff and by the time I found the correct spot, I was so weak and tired that I was afraid to try ... found a semi-level spot ... a lot of wood plus some huge logs. I started a fire and for quite a while was content.*

The fire flared up, the logs caught and rolled down the mountain. She had to stay awake to keep from rolling downhill, thought about John and wished she had gotten to the top of the cliff.

◆ ◆ ◆

Leavengood had been out for two nights. Sheriff Jerry Wakefield, Capt. Michael Foxx and others narrowed the probable search area. Using standard procedure and thinking outside of where her friends thought she was, Wildhorse Creek became their "number one priority," said Capt. Foxx. On Saturday, a Chinook from Fort Carson flew searchers to the area. A jeep carrying men from the Posse went to search Cow Creek.

◆ ◆ ◆

At 6:25 a.m., the man and dog set out across the tundra, surrounded by high peaks. Sgt. Bender carried wool clothes and rain gear, two days' food for him and Zahn, water and fire starter, First Aid and signal devices. He saw clouds racing "overhead, carried by winds that accelerated as they clawed over and around the mountains and passes that connected them. I was confident that I was prepared." He crossed American Flats to the southwest base of Wildhorse Peak and "found tracks similar in size and style to Leavengood's at about 0830." He checked in with Ouray's CP from a perch between two peaks above Bear Creek Trail, the only place he could get a radio signal. He was the only one searching. Others waited for the Chinook, which was late. "CP told me to continue on the trail and they would get help to me as soon as possible. That was the last time I was able to talk directly to anyone by radio for about nine hours...."

For two and a half hours they followed her tracks into Wildhorse Creek Canyon, below timberline and steep slopes loaded with loose rock. They crossed wildflower meadows, "slogged through bogs, and finally entered a dense forest that hugged the edge of the timber." Around 10:30 he lost her tracks. He figured "that Betty had nowhere to go but down," and so he kept moving. "The farther we went the more the canyon narrowed and the cliffs fell hundreds of feet down to Wild Horse Creek." A half hour after he lost her tracks on the west ridge of the gorge, Zahn alerted to the east and tried to go down the edge of the cliff. Thinking that Zahn had Leavengood's scent, Bender called across the gorge. There was no answer. "I was beat by now so sat down to have lunch. Twice more, Zahn went to the edge. I yelled again. No answer. Finally, far across the gorge, I thought I heard a faint voice. A few minutes later, I could see Betty crawling over some rocks." He "told her to stay put until I could get to her. I couldn't call for help because the radio signal couldn't get out."

◆ ◆ ◆

Leavengood began walking at daybreak and gained the top of the hill, berating herself for not having done it the night before. She built a fire for warmth and a signal. She became optimistic.

I could see in the distance the mountain that I had passed beneath and the one on the other side. I could visualize the meadow and the flowers ... thinking how this was my free "Outward Bound" program! A storm was approaching and I built still another fire and waited it out.... I hit another obstacle – a ravine on one side and a cliff on the other.... I followed the elk tracks up to a break in the cliff. There were two places that looked like they had gotten through and that I might manage.... I was halfway up one of the spots and had determined that I could not go on that route, when I thought I heard something. Someone was calling my name. I blew my whistle and yelled, then climbed over to a spot where I could see better ... and there sat someone in a bright orange vest. I really yelled and he finally heard me.

♦ ♦ ♦

Sgt. Bender descended the gorge, forded Wildhorse Creek and climbed to Leavengood. He told her about the search; she was surprised but "happy to see us." Zahn was all over her in his excitement. It was her third day in the wilderness and she was exhausted, bruised, scratched, cold and hungry. "All the adrenalin and energy" she had disappeared as she realized she was found. He gave her food and drink, his extra wool balaclava, shirt and pants.

He wanted to find an LZ they could move to, but she said she couldn't go any further and built a fire. Sgt. Bender looked for a clearing where he could use his flares and finally "climbed to a rocky opening in the trees and waited for a search plane to fly over." The Chinook flew into sight around 12:30 and he fired a flare. Nothing. He fired three more. Then he fired off a smoke grenade, normally used to allow an approaching helicopter to gauge wind speed and direction. Randy Gerke had stuck his head in one of the rear observation bubbles that faced downward: "About the third pass, I see green smoke coming up through the trees, signal smoke."

Found: Betty Leavengood warms up with Dan Bender's spare wool clothes and balaclava.

Photo by Dan Bender

Sgt. Bender returned and extinguished the fire with the last of his water. He moved their packs to the clearing and tied Zahn, who thought a Chinook was "a demon from Dog Hell," to a tree. Because the helicopter couldn't land there, "the Chinook came into a hover and lowered the jungle penetrator...." Lt. Whitt rode it down: It "was windy and raining and the crew sent me down first. Then I strapped her in and we rode up together. The rotor wash blew my helmet, which I gave her, off her head during the ride up and it was a pretty rowdy ride due to the buffeting."

The chopper was supposed to "pivot to the edge of a talus field" so that Sgt. Bender and Zahn could board through the rear door. It didn't turn out that way. He watched them:

> *disappear into the belly of the Chinook and then veer sharply to the right and fly away.... I looked over my shoulder ... wind created by the 30-foot blades had not only rekindled the campfire but had also spread embers to start four other fires ... [it] left me with no water, no warmth against the approaching storm and five fires to fight alone. The exhilaration in finding Betty and the glamour of Search & Rescue were gone.*

◆ ◆ ◆

OMRT celebrated a rare "live one," said Sheriff Wakefield. Relieved that she wasn't hurt, the rescuers who had " been there for a day and a half or two days ... can't wait to get home and take a shower," said Gerke. MacTiernan, "who was really good at wrapping things up," asked, "What about Dan Bender ... it dawns on us, he's up there by himself and his dog." Gerke and MacTiernan realized they weren't going home. They tried to raise Sgt., Bender on the base radio; there was no answer, the weather was going downhill and Leavengood had his warm clothes. Another officer thought Bender would be fine, but MacTiernan said, "There's a name on the chalkboard.... "This isn't right. I have a gut feeling." He remembered this as a personal turning point; it was the prelude to his bid for captain the next spring.

They tried and failed to get Sheriff Wakefield on the radio for permission to use his jeep. Finally, said MacTiernan, they stole it: "It had the keys in it. And we needed a 4WD, and we kept trying to contact [Sgt. Bender] on the radio. We knew we had to get close...." They found his Blazer and with the Sheriff's Slim Jim, they broke into it just as a couple of jeepers came by. Questioned, they said they were on a mission. Then, with Sgt. Bender's extra clothes in their packs, and Sheriff Wakefield's radio, they walked into the storm.

◆ ◆ ◆

That afternoon Sgt. Bender fought the fires with his hands and an old ski pole with no foot that he used as a walking stick. "I moved from fire to fire.... The biggest one was in a fallen dead tree leaning against a standing dead tree. I knew if it went up that ... it would get into the branches and all I could do would be to get out of its way." An hour later the fires were contained, he shouldered both his pack and Leavengood's and began the climb to the Blazer, parked "six air miles and 3,000 feet above me." By 3 he had hiked up and down the gorge again and as he moved into the open area of Wildhorse basin, the full force of rain and wind hit. Though he wore Gore-tex rain gear, both his hat and feet were soaked from the rain and stream and bog crossings. Repeatedly, he tried and failed to reach someone on the radio. As he climbed higher, "it got colder and windier until I was in a mixture of sleet and rain with gusts along the ridges so strong that it almost blew me off my feet a few times."

◆ ◆ ◆

At the top of American Flats, Gerke made contact with Sgt. Bender. By then he and MacTiernan were slogging through a storm with horizontal rain, forty-five MPH wind and descending cloud ceilings. Sgt. Bender said he was just coming out of Wildhorse Canyon. Gerke asked if he had a compass. He did, but when asked to point it to a specific bearing and describe what he saw, it didn't make sense. Gerke told him to keep coming on the bearing, which was the reverse of the one they were on. They checked with him every five to ten minutes, realized his responses were slowing and not making much sense. They had to find him fast.

Gerke asked, "'Can you see Engineer Mountain?' There was a crane up there and they were doing some mining.... 'Can you see the equipment up there?'" He said he could and Gerke asked again for a bearing. Then he asked him to watch for an aerial flare in that direction but he didn't see it. After Gerke asked him to walk for five minutes more, the rescuers ran to a spot where they could see better. Bender didn't see the next flare, so Gerke asked him to walk another ten minutes, gave him a bearing again and shot his last flare. This time he saw it. They were in the vicinity and asked him to keep coming on the bearing.

Bender was "using both hands to press the key on the radio microphone because my fingers and feet were numb from the wet and cold. I was showing signs of hypothermia.... Just hearing their voice on the radio was a wonderful feeling." That kept him going. Gerke:

> thought we are going to come in sight of each other because we can't be that far.... I'm talking to him and he's not responding appropriately ... we see off in the distance ... this little pile of basalt rocks and thought, "Let's just go over there." What it was, was a little shelter that somebody had built ... we get closer to it and then we go around to the front of it and he's in there with his dog ... and they are both shivering.

In the dim late afternoon light on the bare upland of American Flats, sleet turned to snow. They dragged Bender out and discovered his heavy service revolver strapped to his hip. It was something they hadn't imagined he would carry into the wilderness. Gerke said he was "at the bottom end of mild hypothermia heading into severe ... would not have survived the night ... we gave him some food. We pumped water down him. We made him change his clothes ... we just put our arms around him and we said, 'We are going to walk out of here.'" They had a couple uphill miles to go, but the food, dry clothes and exercise had an effect. He was "burning calories so he was feeling a lot better by the time he got to his vehicle." He insisted on driving, so they followed him down Engineer Pass Road in the daylight that was left. It was pitch dark when they got to Ouray. The Silver Nugget Café fed him and the two OMRT men insisted he check in at the Cascade Falls Lodge, which put him up free of charge.

Sgt. Bender wrote afterwards that lack of radio contact and the fear that a search would be launched for him were part of his decision "to go on a forced climb in poor conditions to reach a high point." He still had food and water and could have sheltered in the forest with a fire. "In retrospect, it would have been more practical for me to seek shelter, rest, and start out the next morning." He named his mission "The Search": "In fourteen hours, I had walked fifteen air miles, climbed up and down numerous steep slopes, found Betty, fought a forest fire, and trudged through rain, sleet and wind for five hours with two back packs. It was something I hope I don't ever have to do again."

◆ ◆ ◆

MacTiernan realized that he "was no longer a bystander but was starting to practice leadership ... watching Randy find this man was incredible." He knew that "not going to look for him [meant] he would die."

It's pitch dark," said Gerke, "and Bill and I get back to the barn ... [and we] realize that was the real rescue."

CHAPTER THIRTEEN

1993-1998
"Let's not forget why we're here"

IT TOOK A FEW RESCUERS five hours to raise John Meier to the Ice Park rim in 1992, carry him across the icy pipeline and out to the road. The 1993 Hollywood version required the whole team, a nine-member film crew and eight workdays. Lt. Randy Gerke contacted the TV show *Rescue 911* a couple months after the incident. They didn't reply right away. When they did, they wanted photos. He took pictures and "pasted them together ... so they could see the whole canyon. They were really excited because most of the stuff they do is off the road." Such a unique rescue was a big deal and OMRT knew it, but during negotiations, Katy Film Productions never talked money. "There wasn't a rescue team in the country dealing with an Ice Park in their backyard," said Bill MacTiernan. *Rescue 911* was famous for making rescue and EMS teams donate time, but we said, "We don't donate our time if you're making money." MacTiernan and Bill Whitt had worked with production companies, so Lt. Gerke knew the pay scale.

Talks continued up to the show's departure from Los Angeles, when a woman from the office called. "So they get everybody scheduled," said Gerke, "they are two hours from getting on their aircraft ... they bring up the money thing." He responded, "Oh, I've talked to my guys.... "This is what we want for the main characters that are going to be on the ice all day.... It was Screen Actors Guild rates ... 400 and some bucks a day." After a long silence, she coughed. "Well, I tell you what, if you change your mind, give me a call...." Ten minutes later, Gerke got a phone call: "I'm sure they went to the production people and [they] realized that these office people had never bothered to make arrangements with us." She offered $350 a day plus $75 for equipment rental. Gerke, ever the negotiator, said, "Well, I'll need to talk to the rest of these guys and see what they think...." He called Whitt.

> *"Here is what they came back with."*
> *Whitt laughed.*
> *"I can't get ahold of anybody else."*
> *"It's fine. Tell them it's a go."*

In a quiet mountain town 300 miles from any big city, with few opportunities for making a living in winter, this was a princely sum for a day's work. On January 16, 1993, Katy Film Productions set up shop. OMRT recreated the rescue "the way it happened, except we improved," said Gerke. "Safety was a priority. We didn't want to have to rescue the rescue team." The "toughest challenge ... was getting the people and equipment down in the canyon and back out," including "a five-man crew, plus a stunt coordinator and three stunt men, field climbers and staff." Box Cañon, as the park was called then, stumped the Angelenos. They needed someone to scout for a stunt platform and asked Gerke if he knew anyone.

> *"Sure."*
> *"And who's that?"*
> *"It's me."*

So it began. OMRT built everything. At one point, the astonished crew asked,

> *"You guys do everything around here?"*
> *"Yeah, that's kind of the way it is."*

Gerke was "in charge of the whole thing. If I feel like it's unsafe that day, we're not doing it and we still get paid." The crew were "scared to death ... had never been in that environment...."

They built a stage for the stunt man to take a twelve to fifteen foot fall backwards to the plywood platform, standing on legs resting in the river, now deeper than during the original rescue. It had eroded the bank, so they used ice screws to fasten the legs to the gorge. "Tons of boxes" were used, said Dwelley. They put "one

box inside of a bigger box and bigger box," stacking "all these things [to] break his fall." Whitt set anchors on top, the cameras were ready to roll, and the "Prima donna" stunt man took a look. Instead of driving cars into boxes, he was falling off a rope toward an ice-choked river. "I need to talk to whatever his name was. Get him up here. I'm not doing that for that amount of money. I got to have more...."

Negotiating in front of everybody worked, the stunt man rappelled to within fifteen feet of the river, let go of the rope and fell backwards into boxes stacked above the icy orange Uncompahgre. The take wasn't good enough and the director wanted a redo; but they would have to replace the boxes, that took time and time was money. He decided it was good enough.

The first ice rescue was an initiation for OMRT; now they knew what not to do. Gerke said there weren't "all that many people on the

The Iceman Falleth *from the end of the rope to boxes below the 'Schoolroom.' A cameraman to the left records the one and only take.*
Photo by Bill MacTiernan

rescue," so some climbers helped. Now, everyone turned out. "The guy only lived because we brought him up vertically," said Dwelley. The litter hung up repeatedly on the ice's irregularities: "It was a plow. There was nothing smooth, it had these runners that [went] crrr, crrr...." They wrapped a plastic Sked around the litter the second time and aced the ice. In the real rescue, they carried the litter holding John Meier across the icy penstock to the safety of the trestle. Now, with a dummy inside, they slid it along the pipe. They wore crampons, of course, and they had it roped; it was still a far cry from the secure catwalk that Ice Park climbers and rescuers use today.

Nothing could be as gripping as the initial event, nor could it show their dedication. The finished show was clearly a Hollywood production, but "It was close," said MacTiernan. "You can rarely tell somebody a story and have it come out the way you thought it went." He was counterweight in the initial rescue and hung upside down again for the simulated one. In freezing January weather as the filming progressed, a page crackled over the radio for a missing woman, Ida Seaberg. Eighteen members packed up. An astonished film crew protested the work stoppage; a $300,000 camera was rolling. MacTiernan said, "We're sorry, we have a mission and we have to go." Shortly after they got to Log Hill, they heard that Seaberg had been found in good shape miles away, so they rejoined the film crew. *Iceman Falleth,* aired May 11, 1993.

◆ ◆ ◆

Capt. Michael Foxx, 1992's Volunteer of the Year, resigned in February. Four likely replacements were young: MacTiernan, Whitt and Gerke were knowledgeable climbers and guides and Dwelley was a top-notch EMT and midwife who loved water sports. OMRT discussed "who has time, who can delegate, technical expertise not necessary, who can do political...." MacTiernan became captain and Lt. Gerke stayed. Barbara Morss became Secretary and Jane Wakefield, Treasurer. Dr. Patty Ammon stepped in as medical officer when Dr. Dave Bachman, a legend since 1980 – medical officer, captain, lieutenant and training officer – announced his retirement. He and June moved to Denver, near their grandchildren. Training Officer Sam Rushing, a glass-blowing artist in everyday life, created a special bowl for them.

Two bays at City Hall stored the truck and equipment and served as bad weather training space. Rushing worked "on safety and systems": Rock, scree, swiftwater, ice self-arrest, search. He persuaded City Council to give volunteers a fifty percent pool pass / gym discount for rescue readiness. The Fourth of July breakfast, T-shirt and cookbook sales raised $6,497. Another $2,600 in donations poured in from grateful victims and families. OMRT monitored weather and provided support to those who were "WADAO (weak and dizzy all over)" at the Imogene Pass Run. They made $2,500 in addition to gaining logistical, communications and medical practice. By December, their assets totaled $19,976. $2,100 bought seven pagers for first responders and Whitt found a deal on red coats at Wild Country, the rescuers' first professional clothing.

◆ ◆ ◆

On February 1, an eighteen-year-old Montrose man drove off US 550, 100 yards north of the tunnel. A small tree arrested his Ford's sixty-foot descent. Jason Hinman hit his head on the steering wheel, was conscious when rescuers reached him in four feet of snow, but blacked out in the litter. After his hospital discharge the next day, he said, "It got my head a little bit." Six weeks later, another Montrose youth was stuck on a rock in the Uncompahgre River 120 feet below the bridge on Camp Bird Road. Cody Charron, sixteen, rappelled using two dog collars for a harness and a rope tied to a truck. His friends tried to pull him up but the rope broke five feet above the river. It took ten rescuers over an hour to retrieve him. At the bottom, Sandy East checked Charron's vitals and put him in a harness. Five rescuers pulled backwards to lift him to the bridge. Mission coordinator Foxx marveled that he had come "within a whisper of dying."

At the end of July, a call came for an injured climber on Sneffels' north face. At 9:30 a.m. Doug Matthews and two companions were descending when three anchors pulled loose and the thirty-eight-year-old SAR from Durango fell forty feet onto scree. He showed his companion how to use the radio and a ham radio operator in Nucla picked up. Deputy Sheriff John Radcliff and Dwelley hiked into Blaine Basin. Rushing, Rik Lane and Whitt hauled in the litter and gear. By 3:15 p.m., Matthews, who had multiple contusions, was carried a quarter mile to a waiting Thunderbird. An hour later nineteen rescuers and gear were out. Capt. MacTiernan said the radio call made a huge difference: "without that early notice, it would probably have been too dark to get a helicopter in on Sunday ...

Monday was too windy." In August a sixty-four-year-old woman on Sneffels' southeast couloir fell in terrible monsoon weather. In late September a Texas tourist stopped at the Idarado Mine on US 550 to take pictures, fell thirty feet, slid twenty feet and broke his leg. OMRT lifted him to the road.

◆ ◆ ◆

Capt. MacTiernan, Lt. Gerke and Rushing defined OMRT's mission as a "backcountry ambulance ... technical and non-technical search and rescue." They were not a mountain club; they dealt with lost or dead people in "wilderness settings with long physical hours." Emergencies required knowledgeable personnel, ski equipment, shovels, beacons and winter camping gear; this had long been unwritten code. Members were classified as Logistical Support, Support, Rescue and Technical. Everyone had pagers, so it was " a whole lot easier than having to contact twelve or fourteen people individually...." said Capt. MacTiernan. The Sheriff's Posse – a resource for twenty years – disbanded, though members were still available for searches. Warren and Nancy Chilton, Foxx and Lane managed cookbook, hat and T-shirt sales. After the Fourth of July breakfast, OMRT had $9,000 in the bank, so they purchased a GPS, heavy-duty carabiners, rescue pulleys, a new sled and another ground to air radio. A sixty-four-hour, $350 Wilderness First Responder (WFR) course was offered free to members who weren't EMTs. Rushing and Karyn Carr reported eight new Ice Park climbs, mapped and named by Whitt.

◆ ◆ ◆

Nine callouts began when a single-engine 1969 Piper PA-28 Cherokee carrying three Canadians to air races in Phoenix, Arizona, left Montrose late on a March afternoon. It flew southwest toward the Uncompahgre Plateau, more than 4,000 feet above the town, failed to gain sufficient altitude and crashed in rough terrain. After it was located fifteen miles away in Spring Creek Canyon, OMRT was called. Early the next morning a helicopter dropped Dwelley "a crummy mile" away. "I had to go up, get on top, work my way over." At 6:45, he found three survivors. "The crash cut off both the wings ... the fuselage stopped on the edge of a cliff. The pilot lost an eye and they had him in a tent...." The young couple with camping gear, who had hitched a ride, set up camp, made a fire and tended the pilot.

The chopper returned and dropped a man with a chainsaw 100 feet away. He cut a LZ out of the trees and two EMTs dropped in to package the pilot and fly him out. Dwelley tried to hustle a ride without success, so he started walking with the hitchhikers. The Montrose Posse picked them up and they were out by 10 a.m., "in time for breakfast," said MacTiernan. The pilot, in serious condition, was airlifted to Grand Junction.

In June, an Iowa boy was stuck "only inches from the raging Bear Creek above the bridge." Even with a broken tibia and in danger of being swept over the 228-foot falls, fourteen-year-old Ronald Lamb "remained calm during the entire ordeal." Rushing descended and the boy's father, who had gone to his son's aid, was raised. Rushing had "my arms wrapped around him so he doesn't go into Bear Creek under the bridge...." He looked back to the road and "his mama standing there and it's like there's no way I'm going to let this kid go." "It was a tricky but very satisfying rescue," MacTiernan said. "We got down there, told him that he was in a pretty unique situation, and that he should just enjoy it while he could. He was a pretty good hero during the whole thing." Rushing took Lamb to his mother: "The feeling that you get when you give a kid back to his mama ... you just can't measure it, you can't explain it...." Some years later, the Lambs returned. Rushing looked up from his work; "a big guy" who was "playing football down in Texas" had returned to thank the man who saved his life.

On July 5, a ten-hour rescue unfolded. Twenty-nine-year-old Maura Matthews and friends were near the top of Sneffels' southwest ridge when a "large rock dislodged by a fellow hiker" smashed her ankle. Her companion Tim Fitzpatrick reached town at 1 p.m. Carr, Rushing and Whitt hiked Yankee Boy to Blue Lakes Pass, looked for people on the ridge and realized someone was signaling. "All of us were like, 'Oh this is going to be a good one,' Carr said. "We knew they were prepared." After two pages and a callout, eight more rescuers showed up, but they needed more help, which other climbers provided. With Matthews snug in the litter, they roped her down the serrated ridge "through the rocks and talus slopes" to the 13,000 foot pass and upper Blue Lakes Trail. They attached the wheel for the 5.7-mile downhill to Willow Swamp, 4,000 feet below. Carr and Matthews talked. Shortly after 7 p.m. Matthews was in the ambulance; OMRT reached the barn at 11. Carr, who worked at Montrose Memorial Hospital, "went out of my way to see her because she was such a neat lady" and gave her an autographed OMRT T-shirt.

◆ ◆ ◆

Perched above Bear Creek's spring runoff just feet from the 228-foot falls, Capt. Bill MacTiernan rigs a rope. Sam Rushing holds onto fourteen-year-old Ronald Lamb.

Photo by Ed Thompson
Courtesy *Ouray County Plaindealer*

Another Sneffels' callout July 15 was for Blaine Basin. A twenty-eight-year-old Texan slipped descending the Snake, caught a crampon on rough snow, fractured his right ankle and twisted a knee. In considerable pain, Michael Doyle, assisted by companion Pete Nolan, managed a 200-foot descent to their tent. Early the next day, Nolan hiked out and drove to the main road. Paged at 7:20, ten rescuers met at Sheriff Wakefield's house in Ridgway. Shortly after 9 a.m. they mobilized at Willow Swamp. Posse leader and lawyer Robert Burns and EMT Kathy Barnes came too. Burns brought two Missouri Foxtrotters and Barnes a one-eyed horse. Lt. Gerke rode in with them. Sheriff Wakefield unlocked the gate so everyone could drive the gentle first mile before packing the litter two more rough miles.

The first three got to Doyle's light blue tent at 11:20 a.m. They put a large "immobilization splint ... on his leg," said Burns, which "brought him significant pain relief." They could go out by horse or wait for the litter. Doyle decided to ride, so they lifted him onto Burns' gentle mare Velvet, just as a monsoon thunderstorm appeared over Sneffels' jagged crest. Doyle rode "the horse down ... sitting in the saddle with the splint on his leg kept the two broken ends ... from touching each other.... I will always remember," said Burns, "how gentle the horse was, and very careful with her footing placement. It seemed the horse knew it was transporting an injured person." Rescuers had hauled the litter for a mile and two awkward stream crossings, now they hauled it back. Doyle rode to East's 4WD, which took him out. Capt. MacTiernan debriefed them. It had been a well-executed mission, the extra people and horses very welcome.

◆ ◆ ◆

A night search a month later closed out the summer. Friends reported Mary "Liz" Coyne lost on August 24. Cam Adibi last saw the twenty-six-year-old below Twin Peaks' summit. Pagers went off shortly after 2:30 a.m., by 3:25 everyone was briefed and four first responders left to scour Oak Creek and Twin Peaks. At 5 a.m. the Sheriff's office called pilot Richard Dick. His helicopters were flying for DOW early that morning but one would be available after six. East and Rushing called from Twin Peaks, three miles and 3,000 feet above town. Coyne had not signed the summit register. Whitt and Carr found nothing at 6:15 when they reached the 10,700-foot high point on Oak Creek, three miles from Ouray. At 7:45 the chopper arrived and flew along the cliffs. Forty-five minutes later, Warren Chilton, waiting at a trailhead, radioed that he had her. She had not followed the trail from Twin Peaks, ended up on the edge of Corbett Creek to the north, turned around and spent the night somewhere below Twin Peaks.

◆ ◆ ◆

That fall, Dwelley suggested using Incident Command (IC) to free the captain, "often a valued technical member, from always staying at the barn or staging area." This made sense with several past captains available. Capt. MacTiernan turned the team over to Capt. Gerke and Lt. Whitt: "Let's not forget why we're here; to save lives and help people who get in trouble."

In March 1995, *Plaindealer* reporter Samantha Tisdel explored the Ice Park's beginning. For this "spectacular and utterly unique winter attraction," the 1992 brainchild of Whitt and Gary Wild, Eric Jacobson had offered "to install spigots with hose attachments along the length of the penstock" he owned, and gave a fifty-foot easement on both sides. The three-foot metal penstock carried water from his dam on the Uncompahgre south of the city to the hydropower plant at Third and Oak Streets. The county, with the consent of all parties, hoped to take jurisdiction eventually. Access to the park now bedeviled everyone, from the rescue team, which needed to practice, to businesses with eager climbers from around the world.

Quiet Ouray had become a winter destination; motels and restaurants opened and guide services multiplied, generating discord among some guides who had birthed, nurtured and enjoyed climbing in the early years. East, who had taught some rescuers to ice climb through his International Alpine School and organized the first Ouray Ice Climbing Festival in 1992, was unhappy. He wrote that too many guides and climbers had commercialized the experience, making it dangerous. Wild responded: "Please consider becoming part of a positive process...."

$9,000 from cookbook sales boosted OMRT finances, so Capt. Gerke, Lt. Whitt, Rushing and Warren Chilton gathered ideas for an "ultimate rig" to replace the aging ambulance. They bought batteries and radios, 9,000 lb. pulleys and a new rock drill. The captain and lieutenant got cell phones. Nancy and Warren Chilton, Karl Thees and Whitt, became Wilderness First Responders (WFRs) thanks to Gerke's "very grueling" certification class. In an unconscious nod to a future whose shape they couldn't know, the January 1995 practice featured rescue on the Dexter Ice Slabs, a popular climbing area north of town. Climbers walked in on an unplowed road from the Bachelor-Syracuse Mine. On February 25, the first callout was for a climber injured on the Slabs.

On June 16 a woman's call about her missing husband triggered an unusual rescue. The man hadn't returned from mountain biking on Spring Creek Trail at the north end of Ouray County. Gerke, Whitt, Dwelley, Jackie Hattan, Rushing and Thees met at 6 a.m. on Dave Wood Road. "To save time in the search effort," said Gerke, "we decided to go in on mountain bikes." They "started backwards and tried to trace where he might have gone in two or three different directions.... The weather was really bad, some snow and a lot of rain and mud."

Riding amid snowdrifts in deteriorating weather added to the sense of emergency, said Thees. Steady rain turned everything to mud, forcing them to portage the bikes. At 9:30 Gerke found the man on a side trail. He had settled down with a fire at dark, had water and a raincoat, but no food. "He was surprised we were out looking for him. But he was appreciative," said Gerke. He gave the man his new cell phone and said, "Why don't you call your wife?"

On August 11 they searched with the Montrose Posse for a man missing in the Big Blue Wilderness. "Some people stayed low and then we just fanned out," said Thees. "Three or four of us on that hillside ... tried to look in little cave areas...." They found nothing, but that fall hunters found the man in a tree well covered with camouflage. It appeared he had killed himself. Seven rescuers responded for a second search the same day for a Telluride boy, twelve-year-old Tyler Love "separated from his mother" on Dexter Trail. They found him before dark. Whitt, Carr, Dwelley, Jackie Hattan, Rushing, Lawrence Sanderson and Thees had had a very long day.

◆ ◆ ◆

In 1996 Dr. Dave Sherwood became the team physician. Karen and Bob Risch joined and the next year began training OMRT's first search dog. Internationally acclaimed ice and rock climber Jeff Lowe sponsored the first Artic Wolf Ouray Ice Festival in January. For Wild and others it succeeded "beyond our wildest expectations:" over 200 climbers came. Steve Lance demonstrated avalanche transceivers Friday night to sixty ice climbers: "It may not save you," he said, "but at least your friends will find your body." Avalanche forecaster Jerry Roberts showed 140 slides documenting local dangers. Saturday evening OMRT served a lasagna dinner that brought in $819 from 150 hungry climbers – so many came that the food ran out. A gear auction raised over $1,000 for the Ice Park. Lowe presented a slide show of worldwide first ascents. People from Argentina to Australia and all over the U.S. climbed the frozen wonders of the Park. Local business boomed as Ouray had visitors, lots of them, and a "major winter attraction."

OMRT acquired more gear, a fire extinguisher for the truck and a dozen lockers for gear storage. Thees proposed a command center for SAR operations and $1,000 was approved. He installed a phone and lockers and hung everything up. "We did everything we could with no money," he said. "We made it so it was a good place to come back and debrief." They ordered T-shirts, koozies and vests and bought navy fleece vests, emblazoned with the team logo and individual names. At the end of a quiet spring, Lt. Whitt told everyone to get packs together for the backcountry and emphasized that no one acted alone: "Teams do not have individual heroes.... Teams work together to insure everyone's safety."

◆ ◆ ◆

Ouray resident Joe Salette and friend Bob Thistlewaite left for Mt. Sneffels shortly after dawn on June 15. They had climbed hundreds of summits together, including all the Fourteeners. Thistlewaite drove from Denver the day before, spent the night at Salette's house and was determined to climb, despite unexpectedly poor weather. They parked at the outhouse in lower Yankee Boy around 5:30, but by the time they hiked to Wright's Lake, they were enveloped in "pea soup fog.... I got lost walking around on the tundra," said Salette. They were "missing half the fun," but it was a rare lonesome day on a popular peak. At Lavender Col, they saw only one other couple. They scrambled up the rock wall just south of the Col to the broad moonscape ridge that overlooks the southeast couloir.

Salette was a bit ahead around 11 a.m. as they neared the summit, 150-200 vertical feet away in heavy fog. "I see this sleeve, fleece jacket-like sleeve. I thought, 'Wow, there is somebody else up here!' So, I'll never forget, it's pretty funny, and I yelled out.... 'Hey, how you doin?' He didn't say anything.... I'm maybe twelve feet from him.... I saw a pant leg....' He inched closer, yelled again, figured maybe the guy wasn't friendly. A few feet away, he realized the man was dead, his arms out, head bowed to one side and skin white from freeze-thaw cycles. "His ear was gone, there was just a little hole in the side of his head.... His eyelids were gone ... his eyes were real bug-eyed out," he said. "It was really gross."

After he descended to Thistlewaite, he asked how Salette knew the man was dead. They climbed up together and stood silently for a moment. "At first we didn't know how he was killed because there was a lot of snow and ice up there and we figured maybe he had fallen in the rocks," said Salette. He looked at his friend:

> *"Maybe he's not dead. Maybe we should check his pulse or something."*
> *Thistlewaite looked at him. "Nah, I know dead when I see dead."*

The only way to the summit from that narrow place was to step over the body. That felt like a desecration, "didn't seem appropriate" said Salette. "So we didn't summit that day."

At 3 p.m., looking "kind of white," he found Rushing, blowing glass in the shed behind his store. "Sam, there's a dead guy up there on Sneffels." Salette thought varmints had been chewing on the body. Rushing called Whitt and asked Salette if he wanted to go back. He said no, he was feeling "freaked out."

When Rushing and Whitt got to the mountain, it was still fogged in. They hiked the standard route, veering a bit left near the top. Rushing, kicking steps in snow, went first. "All of a sudden, boom! I'm out of the fog. I can't see my legs because the fog is so thick from my waist down…. I hollered down. 'Whitt, you're not going to believe … this is crazy.'"

Whitt said they had run "into the victim by accident," away from the normal climbing line:

> *it was an obvious lightning strike as his bootlaces had disintegrated and his boots were blown apart. The victim's wrists that were exposed – hands were in his jacket pockets – had all the flesh blown off and the victim's skull was partly denuded … from the strike. The victim had been sitting in a depression and it appears that ball lightning had splashed into him, causing his demise.*

At 7 p.m. they roped the Sked holding the body and slid it down. Lance and Tim Eihausen met them on the big scree field below Lavender Col. Eihausen's first rescue was bringing down a dead man – he had been voted in three days before.

They got to Ouray at 10:45, the pizza came and they dug in. The coroner arrived and unzipped the body bag. For the first time many rescuers saw the effects of lightning. "So here's all these rescue people with a pizza in one hand," said Dwelley, "bending over the body."

Carr saw that the man's wrists were reduced to bone and tendon and the side of his skull lay open. She and Dwelley looked at the body "very respectfully," she said. "How many times will we have the opportunity to see a brain…. It was such a learning experience for me." Gerke remarked later on this "interesting culture, this rescue mentality."

Rushing had felt safe on the mountain with Lt. Whitt, whose head was going "a million miles an hour and he's observing every possible problem, solution…." Four hikers reported seeing Edward McKinney of Nederland, Colorado, climbing during a severe early monsoon storm on June 12. One of his legs was shorter than the other and seemed to slow him down, though his boot had been built up, said Whitt. The hikers tried in vain to talk McKinney into turning back. "It was almost like he had something to prove," said Dave Conklin of Ouray. After an investigation by the Montrose DA, the story took another, sadder twist. At the July meeting, Whitt reported that the DA's office said the man had been fighting with his buddies and they had a falling out. "In the end they never even reported him missing," said Whitt. "I believe they thought he got off the mountain and found his own way home."

Ten days later, Adam Beale, descending Sneffels' north face by a different route than he climbed, slipped and slid 1,500 feet down the Snake at 7 p.m. His partner climbed down to the rocky runout, checked him over and walked down to a climbing camp. Two climbers from Denver "gave him a flashlight, water, food and blankets" for his friend and walked out for help.

At 1:36 a.m. ten rescuers assembled. Rahn Zaccari tried to call others. Climbing veteran Mike O'Donnell knew a shortcut down the north face and was sure he could get to the victim before a second team could on the trail to Blaine Basin. "I can't go alone," he said. "The lone climber, lone rescuer thing doesn't work." Dwelley volunteered; they were on the way to Yankee Boy by 3 a.m., intending to climb to the ridgeline and descend the north side.

The rest of the team arrived at Willow Swamp forty-five minutes later. EMTs left at 4 a.m. and a litter team at 4:10. By 5 a.m. O'Donnell and Dwelley had jeeped to Wright's Lake and jogged to the ridge. They made excellent time, considering that Dwelley's stomach was upset from spicy camerones he'd eaten that night at the Buen Tiempo. They roped up to descend, which slowed them down, said O'Donnell. Karl and Louise Thees reached Beal just before 7 a.m.

and radioed that he was pretty banged up and his wrist was swollen. He wanted a helicopter to get him out pronto. A short time later, O'Donnell and Dwelley arrived. St. Mary's Air Life landed shortly before 8 a.m., loaded Beal and was airborne by 8:50. The rescuers got back to the truck at 11 a.m. An hour later they debriefed over lunch at Pricco's in Ouray, tried to pay the bill but the meal was taken care of by "an anonymous rich dude," a doctor. OMRT sent a thank you.

A July callout for a car over Ruby Walls at MM 90 on US 550 turned out to be a case of mistaken wreck identity. This had happened before, so Lt. Whitt descended to the river and spray-painted all the abandoned wrecks bright orange. An August rescue of a couple stranded on Cascade to the right of the falls brought a heartfelt response from the victims. Zaccari descended to Donna and Fred Clarke with harnesses and they were lifted to the trail. The pair realized they had "tied up six to eight people" and thanked them "for being there for everyone...."

A harrowing night rescue on September 17 sent OMRT to Black Canyon National Park. At 4 p.m. a Nebraska fisherman fell forty feet off the precipitous Duncan Trail in the Gunnison Gorge Wilderness Area, landing on a four-foot ledge 500 feet above the river. His companion managed to get to him, leave clothing, water and food, climb out and alert the Delta Sheriff. Montrose and Delta County teams got close enough on that rainy, dark evening "to make voice contact but couldn't see him," said Gerke. At 2 a.m. he and Matt Elitis got there first since they lived in Montrose, followed the trail almost to the bottom, cut off and went down to the river where a strobe light was set up. They traversed a half-mile to a scree slope under a 100-foot rock face. Local rescuers waited near a fixed line they had installed. They had climbed within 200 yards of the man, but "weren't going to put anybody at risk beyond their skill level, so they called us," said the captain. He and Elitis climbed fifty feet above the rope on "crummy, muddy conglomerate rock." They could hear the man 200 feet above them.

After trying several dead ends, they found a crack system. Gerke ascended to a hollow and belayed Elitis up. They got to the man at 5:15. He had been there for fourteen hours, had a punctured lung and was in severe pain. Gerke marveled that for his companion to have gotten out of the canyon from there was "almost a superhuman feat."

After he radioed GPS coordinates, a small turboprop Soloy from High Country Helicopters flew in at dawn and dropped a litter. By

7:30 a.m. they had the man strapped in and the chopper returned. Gerke attached himself to the litter since he was "not comfortable with ... having a helicopter just haul this guy up, because I've got a tagline on the litter and I'm concerned about it getting caught" in the trees. He hauled the line up after him. At a LZ on the river bottom, St. Mary's helicopter waited. Through that cold, muddy night members stood by at the top in case a lift operation was needed.

Two unfortunate travelers went off US 550 near the Idarado Mine that fall. Robert Barton's Buick Riviera passed a box truck at MM 82, returned to its lane and "probably hit icy slush and lost control," said Undersheriff Radcliff. "You couldn't have controlled a 4-wheel drive under those conditions." Coroner Gary Miller pronounced both Barton, 68, and his wife Mary, 73, dead at the scene. They suffered such traumatic injuries in the 300-foot plunge that Lance said, "They wouldn't have survived even if they'd landed on the operating table."

◆ ◆ ◆

The Ice Park nearly doubled in size that fall of 1996 and the catwalk on the icy penstock was lengthened to 250 feet. Workers added bent steel anchors, spigots and an information kiosk. In December, Whitt became captain and MacTiernan lieutenant. Capt. Whitt's meetings were short, to the point and thorough. He and Training Officer Zaccari expected everyone to be on time, prepared and present unless they were notified otherwise. They practiced ice and scree rescue with the capstan, avalanche drills with new beacons, swiftwater exercises and searches. 1997 was also financially remarkable: The Ice Festival dinner fed 300 climbers and netted $1,000; the Fourth of July breakfast fed 1,200 people for a gross of $7,526. T-shirt sales were good. OMRT began the year with $25,104, a sizeable balance built up over several years, and by December they had $9,098 as well as a $20,000 truck, mostly paid for. In October Whitt, MacTiernan, East and Rushing had finished specs for the new vehicle. Two months later, OMRT bought "a three-quarter ton, 454 cubic inch, 5-speed, 4-wheel drive truck ... completely redesigned just for our rescue purposes," said Rushing. "We modified the back by taking the regular pickup truck bed off ... putting in a utility box system that helps us store all our gear in a logical fashion." The custom alteration included "an innovative bumper system.... "All our systems work off the front, whether it's lowering or raising, and it's evolved to use fewer people and work more safely." They kept useful items from the Beast, "designed by people long since gone and our hats are off to them.... Now we can pass it on ... there's no better compliment than students getting better than the teachers." The white ambulance sold for $3,500; the Orange Beast became a distant backup.

Years of Fourth of July breakfasts, two Ice Festival dinners, T-shirt sales and frugality resulted in a truck "that every rescue team would dream about," said Rushing. "It's been bailing wires and pliers up until now." The 1998 Ice Fest dinner was intended to help pay it off. Early the morning after, however, the cleanup crew discovered $1,000 was gone. A two-hour SAR mission found it — in a box in the trash. "We always find our man," deadpanned Rushing. "This time we found a bunch of dead presidents ... one of our best search and rescue men [Dwelley] found the money."

◆ ◆ ◆

1997's nine rescues included people with broken ankles on Cascade Falls and Box Canyon trails in June and a multi-day search on the Uncompahgre Plateau for a Montrose man. Tim Moore and fiancée Kay Hyle camped under a full moon Saturday, September 16. They hiked the next day until Moore left to track animals. A bear chased him and he became disoriented. Hyle searched the woods, found a cabin and dumped her gear. A sow bear surprised her and she didn't return. She found a ranch on the Divide Road and called for help.

Moore stumbled across the cabin, spent two nights and survived on soup and beans while hiking in different directions to find Hyle. Montrose and Ouray Posses searched Monday but found nothing. Tuesday, OMRT was called and Lt. MacTiernan organized a grid search near Moore's last seen spot. Sgt. Dominic Mattivi spotted a mirror signal from the air twenty minutes later. Jim Kendrick loaded two "Mountain Rescue guys on my four-wheeler and drove 1/2 - 3/4 mile." After he was found, Moore wolfed down a sandwich, but was otherwise in good shape.

A second "slam dunk" search on a misty October morning found Bill Ormsbee, forty-two, of Little Rock, Arkansas, in an hour. The hunter "did what he was supposed to," said Rushing – built a fire and stayed put. OMRT mobilized at 7 a.m. and was back at noon. Getting to Deer Creek at the county's north end and back took a while. MacTiernan led this one; Rushing said he "grew up in these mountains" and knew where "a lost person would probably not go."

A call for a motorcycle accident took Karyn (Carr) Whitt to Engineer Pass on September 8. John Lyon, thirty-seven, of Oklahoma was riding from Animas Forks to Ouray with friends. At one point he rode ahead and when his friends caught up, they found him unconscious on the ground. It was not clear whether he had an accident or fainted and fell over since the motorcycle wasn't damaged. Lyon was transported at 10 p.m. by St. Mary's helicopter. Unfortunately, he "went downhill fast and was in extreme intensive care," said Sheriff Wakefield. After he died, Karyn Whitt learned that he had "a Factor 5 deficiency ... which causes the patient to bleed easily." She wondered, "Why would someone with this condition be on a dirt bike on Engineer Pass?"

On December 21, OMRT responded for an Ice Park climber, Mark Turner, thirty-five, of Dallas, Texas, who was soloing when the ice broke. He grabbed bushes, they gave way and he fell eighty feet. Twelve rescuers hiked in, set up rigging and a mechanical capstan on a tree. He was raised and taken to the snowbound road, where Dick

A rare team photo, May 1997: Back row, standing L to R: Bill Dwelley, Bill MacTiernan, Bill Whitt, Steve Lance, Nancy Chilton, Rahn Zaccari, Mike Gibbs, Rick Zortman, Bob Risch, Dr. Dave Sherwood and Mike O'Donnell.
Kneeling in front: Karyn Whitt, Barb Kurlan, Randy Gerke, Louise Thees, Karl Thees, Joanie Gibbs, a very young SAR-K9 Lyra, Karen Risch and Warren Chilton.
Photo by LW (Warren) Chilton III
Courtesy Nancy Kendrick and Jennifer Burnett

Fowler ferried him in his small Caterpillar to the ambulance. He was airlifted to St. Mary's from the Hot Springs Park. "The fact that he bounced on the way down is what saved him," said Dr. Sherwood, who treated Turner in the gorge. "If he had fallen straight to the ground he wouldn't have made it." Turner suffered no paralysis, though he had compression fractures to three lumbar vertebrae and a fractured pelvis and tailbone. It was "just incredible," he said. "I have nothing but praise for all the guys." Ten months before, the guys and gals had practiced for such a rescue.

◆ ◆ ◆

March 1998 brought a very serious Ice Park call and July "A massive search and rescue operation ... over what was feared to be an airplane crash turned out to be just that – except it wasn't a real plane." Two residents heard sputtering sounds before a plane went down at sunset near Sims Mesa, but local airports reported no departures. A helicopter searched before dark but found nothing. Twelve OMRT members began a three-hour grid search at 6:30 a.m. Jeeps, trucks, four-wheelers and a helicopter scoured a larger area. A deputy thought he heard a woman crying in the forest. The mysteries resolved a day later. Neighbors owned peacocks and a man admitted flying a "remote control model plane" with a six-foot wingspan from the top of the mesa Friday evening. "It probably ran out of gas," said Sheriff Wakefield, adding that it "was more remote than controlled." Also uncontrolled was the impact on his $2,000 search and rescue budget; it cost $1,100 for two helicopters for a "'model' of folly."

Another strange rescue unfolded August 18. Shortly after sunrise tourists heard cries for help and saw something blue waving from a rock wall on Hayden Mountain's northwest flank, high above Canyon Creek. Stranded in a narrow cleft of rock, unable to move up or down, Chris Sanchez, twenty, of Grand Junction, "spent the night standing up on a ledge." He camped with friends Trisha Dettrick and Bill Longworth Saturday before leaving to hike and climb, intending to be back Monday morning. When he hadn't returned by Tuesday, Dettrick reported him missing. Sanchez encountered hail and running water on Sunday as he climbed down a notorious couloir, Bird Brain Boulevard. His belongings were soaked. He "came to a huge waterfall and couldn't climb down," he said. "The only thing to do was to climb back up the mountain ... but I started climbing up the wall and eventually got to a place where I couldn't go up or down." Many people looked at the waterfall, but no one saw him Monday, though he tried to get their attention. He pulled on his wet sleeping bag that night, sleeping "for a few hours with his feet braced against a log and his back against the rock wall, in an almost vertical position."

Eight members responded to a 9 a.m. page, arrived at Weehawken at 9:50 and realized they needed a helicopter and more technical support. East was the only technical member responding. Joanie Gibbs called others with technical experience from the truck radio. Gerke responded from Montrose. Whitt, O'Donnell and Mike Gibbs checked in but couldn't stay. They were climbing and guiding a corporate client, the Cimarron Group, and were put on standby.

By 11 Ed Tracey arrived, East boarded his helicopter to look around and realized it was the most technical rescue of his twelve years with OMRT. He had a concrete job scheduled that day and was going to play tennis afterward, but when the page came he cancelled the concrete truck and swung by his house to get his kit. The call was for a missing hiker, so he didn't get his boots and climbed in bright white tennis shoes. East and Eihausen were dropped into Fall Creek Basin, followed by Rushing and Joanie Gibbs. As Sheriff Wakefield tracked the operation with binoculars, East radioed, asking if he could see him, if he was in the right spot to descend. Bob Risch brought his telescope and he and Gerke moved up the road to help with spotting.

A net loaded with rescue gear was dropped in on a 100-foot line. With Rushing belaying him, East descended 100 feet from the top of the gully to a game trail, then moved out of the fall line and asked Eihausen to descend. East couldn't see where Sanchez was, so he called Gerke, who told him to go east 200-300 yards on the ridge, that Sanchez was 75-100 feet below. At 2:22 p.m. East asked for slings, ropes and water. Zaccari descended part way with two 200-foot ropes, which he lowered on a fixed line. East rapped off to the couloir where Sanchez was stuck. Eihausen joined him and East decided to rappel down. At that point, Zaccari headed up, retrieving the fixed lines. He, Rushing and Joanie Gibbs packed up the gear.

East, Eihausen and Sanchez rappelled the rest of Bird Brain. At 6 p.m. they reached the bottom, crossed Canyon Creek and climbed to the road. The chopper brought out the other rescuers. OMRT reviewed the ten-hour rescue in the barn. Because Sanchez had a fishing license, eight expensive hours of helicopter time were covered by

COSAR. A month later OMRT replaced two short ropes used on the Bird Brain with two 16-millimeter, 600-foot static ropes.

It was the second major rescue in a week. Four days earlier, forty-two-year-old Betty Connerly "suffered head and ankle injuries when she slipped and fell fifty feet … climbing over loose scree and rock" on Mt. Sneffels' southwest ridge. Tracey's helicopter was essential. He asked Rushing and Dr. Sherwood to move her to a ledge to facilitate the rescue, which "had to be quick" since "a storm was approaching," said Rushing. Tracey delivered the litter and equipment in gusting winds to the 13,600-foot site. Dr. Sherwood said they were surprised when it banged into the rocks below them. They secured Connerly and attached the litter to a fifty-foot cable dangling from the chopper. By 5:30, she was at 12,200-foot Wright's Lake. Ten members waited as backup in case the helicopter couldn't fly.

◆ ◆ ◆

December brought a memorable changing of the guard: the three Bills – MacTiernan, Dwelley and Whitt – related events, often humorous, from early rescues. Sheriff Wakefield "expressed his confidence in the team and the incoming officers and congratulated them." Whitt transferred the captain's hat to Rushing. MacTiernan gave him sundry necessities, among them a bottle of aspirin and a crystal ball. Lt. Thees "assured members that he and Rushing had inherited a Ferrari and were not going to crash it."

CHAPTER FOURTEEN

Calling a Rescue

PEAK BAGGING, climbing all of Colorado's 54 Fourteeners, is a popular leisure activity for many residents and visitors. Ouray County hosts two: Wetterhorn Peak in the Uncompahgre Wilderness and Mt. Sneffels in the Mt. Sneffels Wilderness. John Houston, sixty-seven, had three Fourteeners left on his list. His wife Peggy, sixty-four, came along for Sneffels. The Colorado Springs residents had done six Fourteeners together. They lodged at Columbus House on August 26, 1993, intending to climb the next day.

For thirty-two-year-old Capt. Bill MacTiernan that particular Thursday was the kind of day where he woke up and "you KNOW you don't want to be in the backcountry – it's a rainy day ... and, of course, about two o'clock in the afternoon the pager goes off and the anxiety lifts and off you go to Mt. Sneffels once again."

As the couple rested on the drenched summit, monsoon clouds enveloped them. Disappointed, Peggy Houston wrote in the register that she couldn't see anything. Nevertheless, they used the automatic timer on their camera to snap a picture of themselves bundled up in parkas, rain pants and hats for their next Christmas letter. On the way down in the fog they deviated from the standard route, descending just south of and above the main couloir. Near the bottom, at the crux of the route where it jogs to meet the main passage, she slipped on a loose rock and fell 100 feet into the gully, rolling end over end past her husband, who was leading. He climbed down to help, but she lay motionless. He covered her with a solar blanket, went for help and encountered a USFS ranger patrolling the area. He reported the accident and kept walking.

Later, John Houston sat in Sheriff Jerry Wakefield's jeep: "I would appreciate it if you guys could rush up there, but maybe there's no need to rush." The first response team – Bill Whitt and Sam Rushing – headed for the mountain at 2:20 p.m. After more than three hours of slogging uphill in rain and fog, they confirmed Peggy Houston's death. She lay where she had fallen. Rushing felt "the serenity of the moment," his first experience with a deceased person. He spoke some nice words to her and they roped off the place to protect her body.

◆ ◆ ◆

Coroner Dr. Dave Bachman described her injuries for the *Telluride Times-Journal*: "fractured skull, ribs, elbow, tibia and a hanging fracture in the vertebrae, which, coupled by internal bleeding, ultimately lead to her death. The hanging fracture of the vertebrae impinges on the brain stem, which controls cardiac and respiratory activity. Houston died soon after her fall."

◆ ◆ ◆

The steady rain became snow. MacTiernan and the Sheriff discussed the situation. The captain was ready to retrieve the body, but Jerry Roberts, who was called in by Whitt, said, "Look, the mountain just killed, and it would be happy to kill again. Are you sure you want to go up there?" He continued, "I know this sounds rude, but it's not…. The woman's dead. We can get her tomorrow." He had seen people injured on big mountains in bad weather and "worried about the rescuers becoming victims." People aren't loose when they move on mountains in rain or snow. Even with gear on, he said, "it's like you're stiff." Roberts checked the weather forecast before coming up and told them it would be clear tomorrow. It was now almost dark; it would be better for a helicopter to evacuate the body the next day, rather than call one so late. The captain asked Dr. Bachman if they could leave the body. They could.

So they called the rescue. Two men stayed overnight in a cabin near Wright's Lake to safeguard it. Realizing how hard it would be for John Houston to spend the night in a hotel, Roberts took the grieving husband home to his warm adobe, made him dinner, listened to him, and put him up in a spare room upstairs.

The next day, MacTiernan and Whitt flew into the basin with pilot Richard "Stick" Dick, a Vietnam veteran, "and got a few clouds and things." Dick surprised them by landing at Wright's Lake, at

12,200 feet, well below the 13,500-foot saddle near the body. "I don't think I can do it with the two of you in here," he said. What they didn't know was that this was "the Volkswagen of helicopters," not designed to fly at 13,000 feet. They bailed out of the chopper and noticed Dick digging around in the bird for vice grips. He started torqueing his blades, not exactly reassuring behavior. He flew Whitt to the saddle, then the captain. Toed in at the rocks, the nimble pilot kept the small chopper running at maximum speed and loudness as each man jumped out. When MacTiernan hit the ground, he suffered vertigo and his head spun for an hour.

They performed "the nasty work" of bagging Peggy Houston's body and hooked it to the helicopter's highline. When the chopper and its noise disappeared and the wilderness took over, it was a sudden relief as "an incredible silence in a beautiful space" enveloped them.

CHAPTER FIFTEEN

"A Short Haul"

CARROLL ROBINSON AND DAN MAYES were friends, nuclear engineers who worked for Duke Energy in North Carolina. In 1992 they joined guide Steve House for six weeks of rock and ice climbing in Ouray, the Cascades and the White Mountains. In February 1995, they celebrated a week's climbing at the Ice Park and Skylight over Friday night dinner and a couple of cognacs at the Bon Ton. Their last day, Saturday February 25, dawned cloudy and relatively warm – thirty-two degrees and snowing lightly. They left for the Dexter Ice Slabs later than usual. Robinson didn't feel much like climbing. The Slabs, visible from the Uncompahgre Valley, hang 750 feet above the Bachelor-Syracuse Mine and Lake Lenore a couple of miles northeast of town. Climbers hike in on an unplowed road to the fat, moderately steep ice.

They completed the climb and rapped off the Slabs before 1 o'clock. Standing on a ledge with his clients, House heard "the growl of the falling stone" before he saw it.

"Rock!" he screamed. "Lean in. Lean in!"

Mayes, tied in on one side of him at their belay stance, leaned in and glanced upward. They watched as thirty-seven-year-old Robinson lifted his head. House wrote:

I see the rock, but there is no time to feel anything. It is roughly the size and shape of a small microwave oven ... dark, dark brown, nearly black. One end of it is crusted with shiny dark mud that had been holding it to the mountain ... laced with crystals from the morning's frost. The rock is more trapezoid than square. Bits of snow spin off of it as it flies…. The corner of the trapezoid goes into the turquoise blue helmet.

Robinson's broken carabiner lay on a ledge, webbing flapping loosely, the ice screw V-shaped from the force of the hit. Unanchored, he sprawled thirty feet below, at the lower edge of the wide upper ice slab. Below him was another drop of 120 feet. Fortunately, the "rappelling device locked up" as he fell," Steve Lance said, and "brought him to a slow stop."

House's training took over: "Take care of the survivors, allow no more victims." He rebuilt the anchor, placed a new ice screw, secured Mayes and rappelled to Robinson. He was breathing but unresponsive. His split helmet oozed with blood and tissue. The twenty-four-year-old guide gently removed the helmet, staunched the skull depression with a roll of gauze and wrapped more around Robinson's head, repositioning the helmet to secure everything. He rigged a system to allow him to rappel with Robinson, hauled the inert weight of the larger man to his feet and placed his right arm over his shoulder to descend. Robinson suddenly swung, pummeling House with "closed fists … wide and round to hit the back of my head." For a startling moment, House saw Robinson's eyes looking at him, but realized the aggression might be linked to brain damage. Swiftly, he altered the rigging so that he held the man from the rear. As they dropped off the edge of the ice the descent grew easier.

He called for Mayes to descend. Only after a second command did he clip into the rope. Together, they dragged Robinson "to the far side of the waterfall, clear of the possibility of more falling rocks. Dan sits with his legs outstretched and holds Robinson's head in his lap…. Search and Rescue will get here soon and we'll get Robinson out of here and to the hospital." House made the accident call from Timber Ridge gas station at 2:15. When Sheriff Jerry Wakefield arrived, he begged for medical supplies, but the Sheriff had only a couple of blankets. Racing back to the Slabs, he found Mayes hugging his friend, who lay on his back on the ledge. He wrapped blankets around them.

◆ ◆ ◆

Eight rescuers responded to the Bachelor-Syracuse Mine and divided into two groups. Rescue 1 set up base camp: Bill MacTiernan, Sam Rushing, Lawrence Sanderson and Karl Thees arranged for necessary supplies, equipment and transport. Rescue 2, headed by Lt. Bill Whitt, took off for the Slabs. He called Capt. Randy Gerke, teaching survival on Grand Mesa 100 miles north and heartsick he couldn't be there.

"Don't worry," Whitt told him. "I've got it."

A hike to the Slabs takes forty-five minutes to an hour, depending on how deep and firm the snow is. Rescue 2 followed the climbers' track, but postholing is a miserable way to hike and they kept breaking through crusty footprints. "It was painfully slow getting to the scene," said Karyn Carr. "The more I tried to hurry, the more out of breath I got and it felt like slow motion." They reached the Slabs in thirty minutes, even Bill Dwelley, who set off without crampons, and ran back for them.

Bloody ice hung in the air before them. Two men huddled together, anchored to a narrow ledge near the bottom of the first slab. Climbing through jumbled junk rock and ice at the bottom, Whitt radioed base that Robinson had not regained consciousness and his vital signs were very poor. It was forty-five to fifty degrees that afternoon and rocks fell from the melting tree line at the top of the Slabs. Whitt set up creative anchors to secure the rescuers, using multiple ice screws, ice axes and pickets. He made sure everyone had crampons on and scrambled to ensure no one came off the slope. The ice was crappy from the warmth and tumbled rocks. "Down at the bottom ... ice isn't as consistent as it is on the vertical," he said. "I just punched a huge hole in the ice and then put an ice axe in like a dead knife, threaded the ice axe into the hole sideways and then tied off mid-shaft."

Dwelley, who noticed Robinson was slumped forward in agonal respiration [gasping, labored breathing], immediately tilted his head back to give him an airway. The man showed fleeting signs of life, but the side of his head was trashed, said Lance. Dwelley examined him and with Lance's help got him out of the ropes and over to the cliff so they could "run him down." Dwelley radioed team physician Dr. Patty Ammon. She and her husband caught the initial callout as they moved their belongings to a new home. They dumped stuff, turned around and headed for the mine. She listened to Dwelley's description and made suggestions. Dwelley and Lance intubated Robinson and gave him oxygen. Lance said they "knew that we had to act pretty fast and the normal extrication ... would have been to lower him to the next little ledge and then walk him out.... " Carr said their goal was to get him "in the helicopter still alive."

At 4:41 Ed Tracey's Bell 47 flew into sight. Dwelley, Lance and Carr packaged Robinson. Whitt drove more ice axes into the snow and they lowered Robinson down a fixed line. Tracey flew over the Slabs, then to the staging site, where the litter was hooked to the fifty-foot cable. Within minutes, it hovered over the rescuers. Suddenly, the backboard they hauled in to the site, but didn't need, was airborne. It was "one of the weird things," said Whitt. "The rotor wash picked it up and slung it past us and just flung it sideways ... [it] levitated ... into the rocks.... Nobody got smeared by the board." He warned the pickoff "was going to be sketchy because the helicopter blades would be close to the ice and the litter would likely swing once we released it." He guided the chopper in and detached the litter. Lance made sure they had "all the harnesses hooked up to it so we could fly him out ... it was pretty dicey ... we got the basket hooked up and then just held on to it and made the helicopter pull it away from us." Just after 5:20 p.m., in dwindling daylight, the litter swung in the air, headed toward the staging site and ambulance. It was the first time they used "a short haul to get somebody off," said Whitt.

◆ ◆ ◆

EMT Jim Kendrick responded to the callout in his pickup, the back end full of sheetrock pieces. When Robinson, packaged in the litter and dangling from the helicopter, came into view, Kendrick started toward it. A deputy sheriff stopped him, saying he would get the shock of his life if he touched it before it was grounded. They loaded Robinson in the ambulance for transport to Hot Springs Park and the Air Life from Grand Junction. Kendrick followed in his truck. At 5:30, just east of Deja Vu Lane, the ambulance stalled. Kendrick offered his truck, which had a shell on back. He dumped the sheetrock mess onto the road and helped Dr. Ammon and Flight Nurse Teresa Bagshaw transfer Robinson into the truck bed. Red lights flashing, a sheriff's car escorted the makeshift ambulance to the park. In 6 o'clock twilight, the chopper lifted off.

Back in his truck, Kendrick glanced at his gas gauge. It read empty. He filled up and went back to pick up the sheetrock. A good neighbor, Gary Miller, had hauled it off. The next day, at his home on CR 17 across the valley, Kendrick looked toward the Slabs. The ice was still pink.

◆ ◆ ◆

Despite being rushed into neurosurgery that night, Robinson's condition remained critical. Monday afternoon the doctors declared him brain dead and his family donated his organs. The next weekend, his young guide, in tears, aching with his perceived failing, spoke at Robinson's funeral in Charlotte, North Carolina. "I know he loved climbing, that he was at peace when he was in the mountains.... I think that his last days were joyous ones." Robinson's family and friends donated $2,500 to the team. Rushing sent Robinson's wife a handmade glass angel. Dr. Ammon praised OMRT for a "phenomenal job" in dangerous territory.

◆ ◆ ◆

There had been no other casualties by late afternoon when five people downclimbed the ice gully to the base. They packed up the broken backboard and retrieved their gear. The four rescuers brought Mayes with them as they postholed back along the road in the fading light.

CHAPTER SIXTEEN

"Rule No. 1: Take Care of Yourself"

MORE THAN 200 CLIMBS overhang an icy mile of the Uncompahgre Gorge. Novices often get a first ice experience in the easily accessed 'Schoolroom.' Many climbs require rappelling to the canyon floor, often blindly, but by 1998 climbers could walk down a snow path to climb the 'Schoolroom.' Its appealing routes are visible to climbers. Belayers may encounter falling ice but can stand away from the wall. One method of climbing an ice route is that a doubled rope is secured at its midpoint to an anchor at the top of the wall. The rope ends are dropped to the bottom. The climber ties into the rope and ascends the route; the belayer takes in the slack rope through a belay device so that a slip or fall can be arrested quickly.

The trouble began with the ropes. It was the last week of the Ice Park's fourth climbing season, a bluebird March morning. Two friends drove from Telluride to practice in the 'Schoolroom.' Thirty-nine-year-old Greg Kowalski was proficient and had free climbed the difficult 600-foot Ames Ice Hose the week before. His thirty-year-old friend Andy Mowery, wearing lightweight ski boots, a helmet and crampons he found in Telluride's Free Box, was climbing ice for only the second time.

They hauled gear through deep snow on the shaded west side road. At 9 a.m. they tied off at big trees overlooking the "Schoolroom." Kowalski asked Mowery to go first and he tied in. But when he dropped over the wall to rappel to the gorge, he realized he couldn't see the bottom because of the overhang beneath him. Even worse, his inner voice, a premonitory presence since childhood, was active, warning him not to continue. He "felt like death was right around the corner" and knew with certainty that if he took "one more step, I'm going to die."

As he hung over the edge, Mowery told Kowalski he was uncomfortable starting from the top. He climbed up, they broke everything down and walked down the path to the gorge. Then Kowalski hiked back up to set up the rope. That's when they discovered it was too short. Had Mowery followed the plan, he would have rappelled off the end before reaching the bottom. Kowalski was upset with the delay since he wanted a certain amount of climbing that day. He decided to tie two ropes together, but even then, when Mowery set off for the first climb, the combined rope was short enough that both climber and belayer stood against the wall.

They traded off climbing and belaying, until finally Kowalski had time for only one more climb. He ascended the wall so fast that Mowery had trouble keeping the rope taut through his belay device, which he noticed he was using backwards. Kowalski reached the top before Mowery got all the slack in and spent some time making sure his friend was belaying him correctly. Guide Dave Bangert listened as he tested equipment nearby.

Kowalski leaned back on rappel and Mowery saw him falling, his body twisting. His back hit a rock ledge two-thirds of the way down, he ricocheted off, rotating in the air, and hit the ground in front of Mowery – his spine curled like a shrimp, his throat making unpleasant sounds. Mowery "went into Boy Scout / First Responder mode," checking Kowalski's breathing amid the gurgling coming from his mouth. Four climbers, one a doctor, took turns giving CPR to Kowalski, who moaned but did not respond. Someone called 911. Bangert climbed out and sprinted three-quarters of a mile down Box Canyon Road to the Victorian Inn to alert Capt. Bill Whitt. Mowery heard the woman doctor say Kowalski's spine was broken and the EMTs would need help. He took off his harness, walked out of the gorge to his car, removed his ski boots and crampons and put on hiking boots.

Thirteen rescuers mobilized at the Ice Park. EMTs and technical climbers rappelled into the gorge. Some hauled gear to set up rigging. Within an hour of the accident, Dr. Dave Sherwood arrived, donned climbing gear and rappelled to the patient. Mowery walked back to the Ice Park, where rescuers kept him busy, sending him to the truck to retrieve helmets. At first he thought Kowalski would live, but he looked down and saw his friend turning blue, his shirt open.

EMTs were performing CPR. Mowery made another trip out and an EMT walked toward him and said, "Your friend is gone." He hugged Mowery, "already distant: 'OMG, what was to happen now. I dropped my friend, and now he was dead. And, he died alone, without me there. Crushed from a long fall.'" He knew he was responsible, he had belayed Kowalski incorrectly.

◆ ◆ ◆

Whitt wasn't so sure. Studying the piled up ropes next to Kowalski, he asked Mowery:

> *"Did you untie him?"*
> *"No."*
> *"Okay."*

Later, going over the scenario with Bangert, Whitt realized that the Figure 8 knot, which climbers use to attach themselves to an anchor while on belay, was pinched tight, as if it hadn't been finished off properly. Normally, he said, a climber threads the rope attached to the anchor through his harness, then back through the Figure 8 knot holding the anchor, creating a "Figure 8 Follow-Through." Because of the unfinished knot, when Kowalski leaned back on rappel and placed his weight on the rope, it popped up through the upper anchor and fell free to the gorge. Meanwhile, Mowery built a whole scenario in his mind, saw the rope flying loose at the top and Kowalski falling. He was certain that he had dropped his end of the rope. After coroner Gary Miller came and drove him to his office, he went over every detail, drawing diagrams and sorting through memories of what had happened. "I had dropped him, and it was all my fault. I was starting to take ownership of this, realizing my life may be over as I knew it."

The captain "came to the office," said Mowery, "and told me I had to go back to the scene. We drove up there, and he pulled out the rope. He showed me the end of the rope, and asked me if it told me anything. I was clueless." Whitt pointed out the Figure 8 knot one foot from the end. "It was super tight," Mowery remembered. "I still had no clue." Whitt told him:

> *what I thought I saw did not happen. The rope was still through the belay (although backwards) on my end. It was impossible for me to*

have dropped him since I was still physically attached to the rope. What actually happened was that Greg did not double back on his knot, and was not tied in. When he leaned back to rappel, he simply outpulled the rope, which cinched the original knot, but the end came loose. The flying rope was from his end, not mine.

Whitt wrote an account of the incident for the *American Alpine Journal*, pinpointing the inadequate knot Kowalski tied as the cause of the accident. The "newbie ice climber" was not at fault. The more experienced one forgot "'Rule No. 1: Take Care of Yourself,'" and his partner being new to this, didn't know what to look for."

◆ ◆ ◆

Mowery returned a year later, March 16, 1999. He "placed a stone lapis knot of life in the crevice above where we tied our ropes off ... it was a means of letting go...." It took him "seven years to let go enough to not have the replay of the events appear in my head when I did not want them to and the guilt has never really left. The depth of this experience still overwhelms me ... to this very moment."

CHAPTER SEVENTEEN

1999-2002
"It's pretty dark down here"

NEW YEAR'S DAY 1999: An ice climber with a history of shoulder problems was accidentally lowered into the river and popped his shoulder trying to reach the bank. OMRT set up as bystanders took videos and traffic crossed the Camp Bird Bridge. Three men descended, trussed his arm and helped him out of the water. Unfortunately, they had to work beneath the 'Verminator,' where climbers threatened them with falling ice. They decided to walk the man 200 feet upriver to a trail out of the gorge rather than try to lift him out. Capt. Sam Rushing and Lt. Karl Thees hurried up the Ice Park Road to the trestle and fixed safety ropes. During the debriefing, OMRT decided that in the future the Sheriff needed to clear the scene, including the bridge. Climbers would be directed to finish and move away, extrication had lights they would request for night rescues, and they wanted the Ice Park cleared at the end of each day.

Seventeen days later, Jeff Wiltfang fell 75-100 feet from Box Canyon Bridge, landed on his feet and fell backwards. OMRT got there just as it was getting dark. Wiltfang lay on a rocky island with "a pretty significant pelvic fracture." Dr. Sherwood said, "Probably the only reason he's still alive is that the rope was going through the belay device ... the friction slowed him down." Mike O'Donnell spoke with the belayer, who said he turned to put friction on the rope anchored to the bridge, but Wiltfang jumped off before he was ready. He fell straight down and didn't bounce off the wall. Otherwise, said Dr. Sherwood, "he would have spun ... would have landed on his side or back or chest, and that would have killed him."

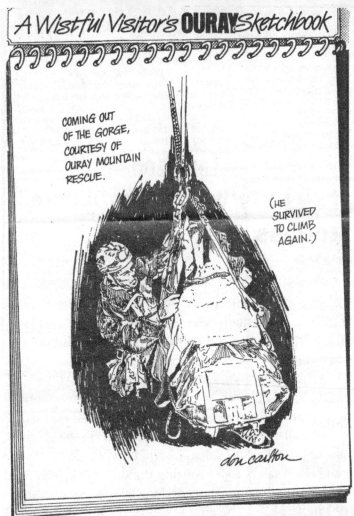

COMING OUT OF THE GORGE, COURTESY OF OURAY MOUNTAIN RESCUE.

(HE SURVIVED TO CLIMB AGAIN.)

don carlton

You needn't have a very vivid imagination to realize the dangers that continually exist in Ouray's mountains. So, when a visitor like me chances on The Ouray Mountain Rescue Team, there's a temptation to "romanticize" the work of these hardy volunteers dedicated to life-saving situations hereabout. But when you review just a few of the many rescue snapshots in their files, you realize that only those willing to undergo regular skill-training in alpining techniques can safely perform when the call comes. And, that call comes several times each year, on average, out in Ouray County – lost hunters, injured climbers, et al.

Mike O'Donnell brings Jeff Wiltfang out of the "hole." Don Carlton sketch, October 7, 1999.

Courtesy *Ouray County Plaindealer*

San Miguel Power's truck, with an extension arm, arrived and parked in the middle of the bridge, but its rope only extended fifty feet. IC Bill MacTiernan said they "had a real problem." Then, someone had a brilliant idea: "Put a pulley on it." They strung rope from the truck's capstan west of the bridge to the power truck's metal boom, attached the litter and lowered it. Extrication installed a "2,000 watt light system" on the east wall and lit up the dark canyon a bit.

"We need to get him out," O'Donnell radioed. "He's bleeding." Rahn Zaccari monitored Wiltfang's vitals, relaying them to Dr. Sherwood. Zaccari stabilized Wiltfang and Thees brought his knees up and strapped them together. Rushing told O'Donnell to ride the litter, but when he clipped in, he experienced weightlessness. "One of the power truck guys started to move the hook before I even was ready. It was really dangerous. We swung and smashed into a wall ... and I screamed, "Who the fuck is moving that hook?" and it came across the loudspeaker.

> *Everybody stopped and Bill Whitt said, "It's okay, big daddy."*
> *I remember saying, "When are you gonna start?" and I looked down and we were like twenty to thirty feet in the air already, it was so smooth.... Jeff looked at me....*
> *"Are we going up?"*
> *I said, "Jeff, this is amazing. Yeah, we're like halfway up, dude. You all right?"*
> *"Yeah, yeah, yeah. No."*
> *I talked to him all the way ... and that was one of the cowboy rescues.*

Ninety minutes after callout, the extension arm put the litter on the road. OMRT moved Wiltfang to the ambulance, but it took another hour to get the rescuers out since the river flowed directly against the cliff and they couldn't move upstream. Mike Gibbs placed a directional line to the capstan on the rescue truck and threw a rope to them as they climbed ice in the dark. In forty-five minutes, they were out. Thees, an experienced EMT, was pleased when he heard that the hospital staff asked who packaged Wiltfang's knees; that had saved his hip.

A monsoon flood on Dallas Creek on July 31, fueled by intense rain north of Mt. Sneffels, stranded five members of the Colby family

OMRT's 25th Anniversary, July 4, 1999: Members new and old cover the Orange Beast.

Photo by David Mullings
Courtesy *Ouray County Plaindealer*

and two friends. "After it started coming over the bank," said Grady Colby, "me and my youngest son tried to divert it ... but it was rising really fast.... I told him, 'We're not going to hold it.'" They hurried to the barn "to get equipment off the ground and take care of the animals." Colby noticed the water was up a foot in just a few minutes. "We kicked the doors open and ran the steers out the back corrals, but the water was already raging through," he said. "They swam across to the pasture, but the big sow wouldn't go." When they got back, the barn was waist deep in water and their pet ostrich was gone. It "hit the fence and was drawn down under the water. I managed to get his head up, but with all that water pressure he suffocated against the fence."

Seven people in the barn scrambled to the second story. Neighbor Marcus Wilson and friend Kyle Easley had hurried to help and were trapped. Wilson's wife Pat called 911 from the road. OMRT was paged, but most of the bridges in the area were gone, so "it took a little while to get there," said Steve Lance. Erin Eddy noticed the "bridge over the county road had become clogged with flood debris which caused the water to back up and flood their property." Lance watched: "Little Dallas Creek – you can cross it without getting your feet wet most of the time – was like forty MPH mud ... threatening the barn. They were so focused on what they were doing, they did not realize that they were being turned into an island...."

From the shallow inside curve of the water, Rushing could see many people watching from the opposite bank, where the flood moved faster. "It was a tense situation ... there was this feeling of helplessness when you don't really know what to do." Lance also saw the river cutting away the bank: "We were trying to get someone over there to get them away from the edges because it was just a matter of time before someone fell in.... If they did, there would have been nothing we could have done for them. They would be gone."

Eddy said they "considered wading through the creek or using a kayak," but "those two approaches were deemed too risky." So OMRT flung one end of a lightweight line on a throw bag to the barn with instructions in a plastic bag. They should pull in the rest of the line, which was attached to a rope, and anchor that properly to the structure. Swiftwater specialist Eddy was chosen for the traverse because "if he ended up in the water, he would have a shot and he was light," said Lance. Wearing helmet, dry suit and life vest, he "was sent over on a Tyrolean. He took an extra helmet, harness and life jacket; secured a rigging anchor; harnessed the people and lowered them "one at a time across the water." Lance stood "eighty yards away, knee deep ... in water by a regular fence.... As they hit the fence, I grab them and walk them still on the line to the rescue trucks till their feet can touch, disconnect the harness and then it is pulled back up."

"The underlying danger was that the building might be undermined," said Lance. "There were big trees coming down the creek battering the backside." Darkness threatened as the rescue played out; extrication set up lights so they could see to get everyone out. Then Rushing noticed chickens heading home for the night, moving down the bank toward the barn where the creek licked furious at the door. One by one, they marched into the brown river. People tried to stop them, but the determined fowl went around, only to be swept away. It was a "smooth as silk" rescue, said Rushing; besides the suffocated ostrich, the only fatalities were the chickens.

"It could have been a lot worse," Colby told the *Plaindealer*. The barn's north wall gave way and hung over its foundation by a foot. He watched as a large trampoline, a snowmobile and an 800-pound cattle chute were swept away, giving him pause about his family's safety. "I have no idea where that chute is," he said. "It could have been my house and my family is OK." Denean Colby said that riding the line in harnesses was "kind of fun, especially for the kids." The barn survived and they built a cement barrier a few feet away to prevent water from reaching it again. The Army Corps of Engineers said they had been caught in a 1-in-500 year flood.

A month later, seventy-two-year-old Penny Loerke and friends hiked down Oak Creek after a Twin Peaks excursion. The veteran hiker sidestepped some manure on the trail, stumbled, twisted her ankle, felt and heard it break. Jill Von Delden hiked a mile to the road and an hour later OMRT assembled at the trailhead. Eddy headed up with medical supplies and others followed with rescue gear, including the wheeled litter. Loerke "wondered how they'd get me down the seven switchbacks below.... One carried a heavy, rolled up stretcher, another a huge wheel, and others ... heavy packs of equipment." She was "hoisted up and on, an ice pack on the ankle, heat packs on the leg muscle in spasm...." O'Donnell radioed that the patient was "dry, slender and stable" as he set up a two-person belay. A tiny woman with a determined air, Loerke refused to lie down, said Jenny Hart, sitting instead. Hiker Cynthia Boxenhorn wrote about "12 unbelievably fit men and women ... working together like a well-oiled machine. This one smooth operation illustrated hours and hours of drills and rehearsals and training...."

On October 25, CDOT workers saw skid marks near the Ruby Walls. Roy Largo, heading north at 5:30 a.m., swerved to avoid rocks on US 550 and his 1990 1-ton Chevrolet skidded 127 feet, ran off the left side and rolled several times during the 450-foot drop. It landed on its wheels at the bottom. CSP Trooper Chris Sandoval estimated the truck was going forty-eight MPH in the twenty-five MPH zone. The rocks "weren't that big, but when they hit the road and shattered ... it was kind of like a patch of ball bearings," said Rushing. Before Mike Gibbs and Eddy descended, Lance asked Gibbs if he'd done a body recovery.

"I said 'No."

"I will give you a tip…. Don't look at the face because you will never forget it."

At the bottom, the men realized they could just pull the large dead man out of a window and put him in a body bag, but it took an hour to raise him to the road. The skid marks from the dual tires were visible for six months, said Gibbs.

◆ ◆ ◆

OMRT met in the aptly named Echo Chamber at City Hall, which allowed for training in the barn afterward. Randy Gerke created a website and Jenny Hart took over as treasurer when Warren Chilton, who had managed the books since 1995, resigned. "Under his tenure, the team raised enough money to purchase the new truck and … and remained solvent as well." The old white truck was last seen heading to Argentina. When last heard of, it was in Venezuela.

The turn of the century brought unanticipated changes. Fred McKnight became sheriff after Jerry Wakefield resigned in October 1999. The previous March Undersheriff John Radcliff and longtime Deputy Leroy Todd had been "arrested on suspicion of providing protection to a methamphetamine ring." The BOCC asked Log Hill resident McKnight, a twenty-five-year veteran of the Los Angeles Police Department with "14 years as a television police-show writer and investigative reporter for *60 Minutes*, to fill the remainder of the term. Severing a twenty-year relationship was a shock; OMRT had worked creatively and productively with Sheriff Wakefield; used his jeep for towing, training and backup, held meetings and BBQs at his house. That August, Deputy Dominic (Junior) Mattivi was elected sheriff.

A boom pole was fabricated for the truck and a new lift kit and trailer hitch were attached. That spring, its engine blew, so the officers took out a $3,000 loan from First National Bank, bought a new engine and clutch and paid the loan after the Fourth of July breakfast. Bob Risch learned that $15,000 in Tier III Rescue Fund grant money was available and applied; the money bought pagers, helicopter training and a litter with a head shield.

A March inspection of the emergency services barn by Sgt. Tony Chelf and officer Ted Wolfe, requested by Ouray Mayor Art Fox, found both full and empty beer cans in the OMRT and Fire Department bays. Capt. Rushing vociferously protested the intrusion, which was illegal since the bays were leased by Ouray County. The issue became moot, but not completely finished, as the community reacted in letters to the *Plaindealer*. Charlie Ricker wrote:

> *I thought having our Big Brother in Washington breathing down our collars was all the overseeing and watchdogging we needed.... For more than fifteen years I was active as EMT, ambulance crew and member of the Mountain Rescue Team.... One of the most valuable training sessions and morale building, camaraderie bonding sessions was the debriefing that always followed a completed mission. A beer or two ... served to slow the heartbeat and dilute the adrenaline level.... I guess those more sedate citizens sitting at home in their easy chairs listening to their scanners wouldn't know about that....*
>
> *In all that time there was never a single instance of alcohol abuse.... Saving lives is not an activity one takes lightly ... rest easy in the knowledge that if you have need of an emergency team, be it fireman, EMT or rescuer, you will be well taken care of....*

OMRT changed its bylaws to require that members be twenty-one years old.

◆ ◆ ◆

On January 13, 2000, Ridgway engineer Brad McMillon, climbing twenty-five feet above the river, asked his belayer to give him slack. Then, one of his ice axes ripped out, McMillon saw "a little hole in the ice," and fell "right into it almost like one had aimed." He knew the current could pull him under the waist-deep water and his axes were still attached so he hooked the slab and hauled himself out. "I thought the worst of it was, I was just soaking wet, but then I just had this very distinct pronounced throb in my right foot." Blood oozed from his boot and he couldn't stand. Eddy rappelled in, said the litter was coming. McMillon wanted to stay under the radar and wondered aloud if Philippe Wheelock could back his truck up to the bridge and "maybe I can get out somehow." Eddy said no. "Hell," McMillon thought, "they need some more training."

Lance and Wheelock arrived, found McMillon alert and responsive, checked his vitals, began an IV and packaged him into a vacuum splint and litter. Sean Hart, David Mullings and Mark Miller placed tag lines east and west of the bridge. O'Donnell descended with seven ice screws to anchor a guideline from the truck to the ice. Anchoring to rock would have been his first choice, but "there was nothing down there," he said. "There was no rock. It was all covered in ice." Extrication's lights went on, they raised the litter to the bridge and Whitt, Tim Eihausen and Rushing maneuvered it over the railing. By 5:40 p.m. McMillon was in the ambulance. It took another hour to get the rescuers out of the dark canyon.

A June incident involved tourists who unleashed their Chesapeake Bay retrievers while walking a greenbelt area east of the Uncompahgre Gorge. The dogs smelled water and leapt off the cliff. The owners couldn't see them in the gorge so the man climbed over the edge to look and got stuck ten to fifteen feet down. His wife called for help at 6:20 p.m. Ten members responded, set up a rappel and sent observers to the west side. One dog stood at water's edge below the man, the other was missing. Karen Risch went home for K-9 Lyra and a spare harness. When she returned the man was out; Eddy rappelled with the harness to Eihausen. Twenty minutes later, both were out along with dog Rosco. His companion Conro was still AWOL. Lyra searched and alerted along the east side while Thees walked the west and spotted Conro 100 feet upstream lying at the base of the eastern cliff. It took the rescue truck, Eddy, Eihausen and a vertical evacuation to get him out. His owners took him to the vet.

A harrowing Blue Lakes rescue and a Chief Ouray assist for a hiker with heat exhaustion happened in July. In early August another hiker broke a leg on Blue Lakes Trail and was carried out. Three days later, on Mt. Sneffels, OMRT responded for a fourteen-year-old boy with knee and head injuries. When Lance got there, he found him walking slowly down the scree with his father and a friend. A 200-pound rock had rolled on him, damaging his head and knee. Lance checked him out, made him stop walking and rest in a litter on the way out.

Another death-defying rescue unfolded August 24. A motorist stopped Ouray policeman Mike Hendrix at Bear Creek Overlook and said there was a car in the canyon. The 7:30 a.m. callout reported no observable activity around a crushed Explorer, perched 350 feet down a sixty-degree slope. Lt. Thees had responders meet at the scene; they arrived in fifteen minutes. Dr. Sherwood was already there. He was up early, heard the page and jumped in his truck. "I remember getting there, looking down, seeing the vehicle," he said. "It was just a steep slope, so it was something I could walk down."

The car was empty. He looked around and spotted a body lying in rocks thirty to forty feet above him. He walked over, the woman had no color and he felt for a pulse. Miraculously, it was there, but weak. "Her head looked like it had bounced on the rocks all the way down. Both her lungs were collapsed and several ribs were broken. The badly broken bones of her left arm were exposed." She "was not only alive, she was conscious enough to tell him her age ... able to nod when he asked if she was Nancy Shippy, a name he found on a piece of paper near the wreckage, and shake her head when he asked if anyone was with her."

Lance told everyone to stay left while descending since everything above Shippy was unstable. He needed a C-collar, backboard, ice bag and as many bottles of oxygen as they could get. St. Mary's Flight for Life went on standby. Shippy, on her way home to Durango, had driven off US 550 south of Engineer Pass sometime the night before. Eddy had seen "a fair amount of trauma" and knew she "was in really bad shape ... when people have significant head injuries ... you have this leakage of brain ... it balloons out, and she was like that. I remember saying to myself, 'Man, if this gal lives, if we can actually keep her alive, it's going to be a miracle.'" She slipped in and out of consciousness and was somewhat combative as they packaged her. Seven rescuers talked to her, told her what they were doing. "Even though their wits are not all about them," Eddy said, "it's important to let them know what you're doing. 'Okay, we're going to do this. We're going to get you out of here. Look, you got to keep breathing for me. You got to.'"

The southbound lane closed immediately. She lay so far down that a large unused spool of rope was unwound to get the rescuers and gear down and then back up. When the magnitude of the rescue became apparent, the entire road closed. Air Life arrived at 8:55 a.m., maneuvering "into a tight spot between telephone wires at the turnoff to Engineer Pass." From the rocks below, Gibbs, Hart and Eddy raised the fragile load. Gibbs realized the angle of the slope was steepening and they "needed to get rid of the third person ... the capstan had to work too hard ... Erin peeled off ... so it was just Sean and I ... and then the capstan failed."

The capstan, an electric winch mounted on the front of the rescue truck, normally provides lift for litter, patient and attendants. Thees ordered a direct lift and OMRT, Extrication, ambulance and CDOT personnel lined up on the highway and literally dragged the

After a long night lying on rocks 350 feet below US 550 near Engineer Pass, Nancy Shippy is rescued. Mike Gibbs, left, and Sean Hart, right, lift the litter. Rob Holmes and others give a hand up as they approach the edge.

Photo by David Mullings
Courtesy *Ouray County Plaindealer*

ropes through the winch. The litter and attendants came into view. Rob Holmes, who ran the lifting operation, and others helped drag it up and over the edge to the pavement. At 9:20 the ambulance delivered her to the helicopter waiting at Engineer Pass. The helicopter for "this tiny landing spot was so small there was no room for EMTs to work on stabilizing Shippy during the ride. They had to do their work on the ground." OMRT packed up and returned to town; the rescue, so intense while they lived it, consumed but two hours. The recovering exercise physiologist mailed a painstakingly scrawled message on a thank you card in pencil:

OURAY MOUNTAIN RESCUE,
Please know how much I and my family thank you and appreciate your wonderful help. Your time and knowledge spent assisting people

does good for those of us in need. Thank you for the grateful days that remain for me to grow, journey, and hand forward your kindness to others.

Nancy Shippy

Bob Risch's Ford Ranger was the backup anchor for the failed capstan. "When we looked at the site where she had gone off," he said later, "we thought it was unsurvivable."

◆ ◆ ◆

Long after dark on September 23, Jeff Schlundt of Durango told Ouray Police that fellow students Benedict and Luke were stuck on cliffs west of Cascade Falls. He had turned around in heavy rain at 4 p.m. while his companions kept climbing. OMRT responded in ten minutes. When Bob Risch plugged a bright hand light into his truck and aimed it west of the falls, shouts rose from the snowy cliff. Two lightly dressed young men were stuck in the left hand gully. Shortly after 9 p.m. Capt. Rushing sent a hasty team – Gibbs, Dwelley, Wheelock, Eihausen and Eddy – up an old mine trail to the falls. Extrication arrived at 9:18 and aimed intense lights at the cliff, but the generator was so loud that no one could hear on the radios, so it was turned off. Risch kept his beam on the subjects. By 9:30 Gibbs reported they were at Cascade Creek but couldn't hear because of roaring water. The subjects were lit up 200 feet above him. The party flagged the crossing and continued upward.

Clouds and fog moved in again; visual contact was lost in heavy snowfall. At 10 Risch asked if they were in the steep couloir. Dwelley said yes and he told them to descend the gully and follow a game trail. They later reported shitty conditions but could see town lights. By 10:40 Gibbs radioed that he had a route. They were all together, heading toward the subjects a quarter mile away. Risch, Holmes, Jonathan Rice and Rushing took the truck to the Amphitheater Road curve at Lower Cascade Trail. From Cascade Falls, Whitt could see Gibb's headlamp and told him to go southeast. The men should take cover in case of rockfall. Rescuers fixed ropes to the cliff and by 11 p.m. they were thirty feet above the men. They rappelled down, belayed them fifty feet up the cliff and led them over fixed rope to where they could hike out. Risch, who knew the cliff well since he had grown up in its shadow, hiked in to meet them. By 12:15 Gibbs reported they all were hiking out. At 12:35 a.m., OMRT cleared the scene.

Two nights later an even stranger rescue evolved at lower Box Canyon Bridge. Box Canyon Lodge proprietor Barbara Uhles reported a man walked into the motel at 9:45, said his companion had fallen into the east side of the gorge just upstream from the Third Avenue bridge, and then left. When OMRT assembled there at 10, Police Chief Richard Zortman and Sheriff Dominic Mattivi, Jr. were already in the gorge. The man who reported the incident was there, too. He had returned to the bridge and fell in, hitting his head.

IC Whitt ordered members to scout both sides of the gorge for the best position for the truck, which turned out to be the west edge. They set up the boom and lowered the line seventy-five feet to the river. O'Donnell, Eddy, Wheelock and Lance climbed twenty-five feet down the east bank to the injured men. Extrication set up lights at the gazebo just up the road, but it was still hard to see, so they moved them further down. EMS Steve Svaldi asked for an update on the second patient. Lance replied that he was stable, with a laceration on his head. He thought the man was bleeding, but "It's pretty dark down here." Shortly afterward, O'Donnell, trying to get the man into a litter, was sucker punched.

> *I stepped back and I thought, "God, I'm gonna punch this guy,"*
> *he was a drunk cowboy.... I said, "Is that how you wanna play it?"*
> *and I grabbed ... both his hands and I hogtied them in two seconds*
> *and he couldn't move. He's lucky I didn't punch him in the head. I*
> *wanted to. But he punched me right in the mouth. Whack!*
> *Junior goes, "You gotta show me that."*

The combative one was raised to the bridge just before midnight and placed in the Ouray ambulance. O'Donnell and the more seriously injured man came out twenty-five minutes later. The Ridgway ambulance took him to the Air Life helicopter. Just before 1 a.m. OMRT left for the barn. Today, the place where the men fell into the gorge is known as Two Drunk Overlook.

Saturday evening, September 30, *Plaindealer* editor David Mullings was "reading in a chair next to the front door" of his house on Fourth Avenue. "Suddenly I heard an awful screech and cacaphony of noise. I looked up and saw a huge dust cloud up by the overlook. The page went out shortly thereafter." A semi rig northbound on US 550 lost its brakes, "rolled near the start of the corner, leaving a trail and gouges in the asphalt" at the Switzerland of America curve.

It skidded on its side through the guardrail, dumping its "flatbed of huge pipes," Jenny Hart said. They "spilled all over the hillside under the road." Forty feet down, driver Michael Harbin, fifty, lay in the wreck. Passenger Lori Ann Horton, thirty-six, crawled out and sat on the cab with a broken shoulder. Several rescuers and two doctors descended through twisted pipes to the victims. At one point during the lift, the tension on the rope was extreme and Capt. Rushing sent Hart down to raise the ropes. By 9 both patients were safely out. OMRT packed up, left and spent an hour debriefing. For a while the curve had been "the most popular place in town ... as all the gawkers and looky-loos came out to gander at the twisted steel on the hillside."

◆ ◆ ◆

Rushing was reelected captain and Eihausen became lieutenant in December. The next year, 2001, saw eight rescues, two searches and a stand-down. Four-year-old SAR (Search and Rescue) K-9 Lyra searched twice that summer for missing persons. Doonesbury INK artist Don Carlton became an honorary member; his *Plaindealer* sketches illuminated rescues, trainings and personnel.

◆ ◆ ◆

On January 13 and New Year's Eve they raised injured climbers from the 'Schoolroom.' In the first incident, a twenty-year-old belayer from Colorado Springs was hit by ice raked off a pitch without warning. He was packaged with heat packs on his broken leg, raised to the top, and carried out. In December, a climber's ice axes popped out, he fell fifty feet and dangled upside down while his wife, the belayer, carefully lowered him to the ground. Fifty-four-year-old Steve Jones of Murfreesboro, Tennessee, had a deformed clavicle and back pain. Darkness fell as five rescuers, working with headlamps, put him on a backboard for extrication.

Four days after the January rescue, a thirty-five-year-old experienced climber fell 135 feet on 'La Ventana,' just east of Box Canyon parking lot. Pete Ro, of Concord, California, a "public affairs manager for the American Chamber of Commerce in Tokyo," was part of Jeff Lowe's Masters Ice Series, the last of the group to make his climb. "As twilight filled the shadowy gorge and most of the twenty-two-person class packed up, Ro elected to take on a challenging 140-foot pillar of chandelier ice." Belayer Lucy Creamer, George McEwan, Ro and Lowe "all discussed and agreed that Pete would climb to the anchors on the road at the top to finish his climb," said Lowe. "The rest of us would scramble out an easy gully on the side." Lowe stood at "a point where he could see both the top and bottom of the route."

Five feet from the top, perched on fifty-degree ice, Ro twice yelled what sounded like "Off belay" or "Okay" to those listening. Lowe and English climber Tim Glasby saw that he had not clipped into the top-out anchors five feet above him and yelled to him to continue climbing. He did not hear them. Lowe yelled down to Creamer, telling her not to take Ro off belay. She did not hear his voice, which was hoarse with bronchitis. "Hearing the command, his belayer went off belay, so when Mr. Ro leaned backward or lost his balance, he fell off, hitting a ledge on the way down."

Climber Dana Berry was walking out of the Ice Park, "looked up and saw a man falling off of the ice. He fell approx. 70 ft. when I lost sight of him. I ran over & yelled to neighboring climbers":

> They said, "He needs an ambulance."
> I then jumped in my friends van & drove into town. We stopped at the pharmacy & called 911 – this was approx. 5-7 min. after the accident. The time was 5:00 pm.

Glasby ran down the canyon road to the Victorian Inn to report the accident to Whitt, who called 911. OMRT, the ambulance and police were dispatched at 5:03. Eddy reached Ro first and took over CPR from other climbers. "It was very, very cold," he remembered. "We were performing CPR ... because he still had a pulse." Gibbs and O'Donnell descended with the litter. Coroner Gary Miller pronounced Ro dead at 6:05 and his body was raised and transferred to the ambulance. A doctor at the scene explained to Eddy that Ro suffered a dissected aorta and was clinically dead even though he had had a pulse and was being given CPR.

Ro's widow Hiroko traveled from Japan to Ouray, arriving on Sunday, January 21. After a memorial service above the accident site, she was "lowered to the position on La Ventana from which her husband fell," but was talked out of climbing the route. They had been married just two months before. Chief Zortman noted in his report that "All of the witnesses described the same events from their different vantage points." A $5,000,000 wrongful death lawsuit (RO v. San Juan Mtn. Guides, et al) filed on November 29, 2001, on Hiroko's behalf was dismissed with prejudice on April 7, 2003. For Jeff Lowe, Ro's death was a turning point. One of the world's leading climbers, he said it was the first time "I've even come close to losing a client.... I've decided not to charge for teaching.... Money is not worth it. I want to transmit my love for the mountains, I am keeping climbing pure."

◆ ◆ ◆

In the middle of a blizzard, Sunday, April 22, a car plunged 100 feet from US 550 onto the Ruby Walls. The driver, Jeremy Mattingly, twenty-four, had minor head injuries but managed to crawl out of the crushed vehicle and up to the road. OMRT, two ambulances, and Support 11 responded. The scene "was pretty miraculous," said Sean Hart, who grabbed his snow goggles as he ran out the door – a good move, since snow blew horizontally in the canyon.

Dr. Sherwood reached Michelle Hoffman, twenty, who was thrown from the car, first. Doug Gregory and Chris Miller from Support 11 helped stabilize her. Hart and Jeff Skoloda took the litter up, secured by ropes from the rescue truck. At one point, Lt. Eihausen looked in the car to make sure no one was left behind, but realized it was so crushed there was no room for passengers. In heavy snow and strong winds, CDOT crews plowed and sanded to give ambulances safe travel. Another motorist took care of the couple's dog.

Three days of monsoon rains closed Camp Bird Road August 7 and rocks cascaded off steep overhangs, damaging three vehicles. Rocks and a mudslide hit three people, including the driver of a topless tour Jeep. Two bruised passengers were hospitalized, one with a concussion, a hole in her back and a broken hand. The county ambulance and OMRT stood by while Road and Bridge crews scraped rock debris off the road. Over fifty motorists were stranded. A two-vehicle accident on Dallas Divide and an ambulance call came in at the same time, straining the emergency system. A Montrose ambulance came to help, and then, as if there weren't chaos enough, a helicopter crashed in upper Canyon Creek. Pilot Mark Young of Montrose had volunteered to fly despite heavy rain and wind, made a hard landing, and walked away.

◆ ◆ ◆

A nine-hour rescue of a badly injured climber "in a steep scree-littered couloir" below Mt. Sneffels' southwest ridge occupied seventeen members, several USFS personnel and a protest group. Sean

Spinney, a twenty-one-year-old Ft. Lewis College student climbing alone, fell fifty feet onto a sixty-degree slope. Falling rocks alerted USFS Ranger Ron Trujillo, on patrol in Yankee Boy Basin. He made an emergency call, providing information vital to Spinney's rescue. OMRT was alerted at 1:50 p.m.

By 2:15 eight rescuers, two on motorbikes and the rest in trucks, roared up Camp Bird Road. In thirty minutes, Gibbs, Sean Hart, Eddy and Skoloda ascended the crux of the climb, a steep notch at 13,500 feet where Spinney had fallen. Zaccari, already with the patient, radioed that he had a head injury and needed oxygen. Gibbs plotted the rescue and called for both litters, 1,100 feet of guiding line, several 200-foot ropes, all thirty-meter cords, webbing, carabiners and pulleys. More rescuers arrived and packed oxygen and gear a mile up the ridge. Spinney was fading, his carotid pulse faint. Multiple IV attempts were unsuccessful and rescuers called for a paramedic or nurse and an LZ for the helicopter.

More oxygen and a vacuum mattress, a kind of beanbag, arrived. Gibbs saw Spinney "recover a little bit when he got in that vacuum mattress. [It] does a good job of providing some insulation because he stopped shivering." Air Life landed twenty-five minutes later with a nurse and a paramedic, who started up the trail but then turned back. The patient would be on his way down before they could get to him. Hart fired the line gun twice – on the first attempt the wind caught the thin line, but the second shot put it where his wife Jenny, stationed with Bob Risch in the middle of the gully, could catch it and climb down to attach big ropes for pulling up. At 5:30 they connected the ropes and dodged falling rocks as big as basketballs in the unstable couloir. A half hour later, the litter travelled up the massive gully.

At the bottom, Jenny Hart rested a bit:

> *The sun started to set, and the colors were just incredible.... I stopped and I looked around and I was like, "Look where I am. Look where I find myself." And it's this little present. It's this tiny little gift. Here I am setting my whole life aside to run off into the wilderness to go save somebody. And I have this moment of "Wow. I'm so lucky. I'm so blessed that I got to be here, right now, in this very special place."*

At 6:50, the roll call of rescuers complete, Mark Miller managed the tension line and pulley system from below, Jenny Hart and Risch monitored it part way up, vectoring the line and dodging rocks. Eddy started down the unstable gully attached to the side of the litter, his feet sometimes flying above the ground, sometimes barely touching. Rocks whizzed by, one of them softball size: It made "this awful noise like the weed eater," he said. "It's just crazy noise. And you know, anything this big will kill you." He prayed, "Please, get me out of this one."

The litter began scraping two-thirds of the way down so Gibbs, controlling the descent with the main line, had Jenny Hart scramble upslope to provide a high directional by lifting the tension line. The helicopter pilot radioed Gibbs that they had to take off in fifteen minutes or be out of daylight. Eddy cleared the gully with the litter, fresh volunteers grabbed it and ran across the talus field to the trail. High on the ridge, Gibbs and Skoloda watched it race through the switchbacks. The chopper lifted off at 8:32: "It was right out of the movies," said Gibbs. As it was "turning the corner by Stony Peak over the Camp Bird you could just see the last bit of light disappear." Under a full moon, everyone packed stuff off the ridge and dragged rope bags across the talus to the trail. By 9:20 a line of motorcycles and trucks snaked down the canyon. At 10:45 everyone dug into pizza at the barn.

A very lucky Spinney left the hospital on September 3. He owed his life to a fortunate series of events and people. "Everybody drops the political stuff because we've got a guy whose life was in danger," said Capt. Rushing. "That gets down to the real important stuff": Protesters and federal rangers worked together ferrying ropes and rescuers. Spinney's family placed an ad in the *Plaindealer*, thanking everyone. Three years later, Rushing was notified that Spinney was lost in the desert outside of Durango. An expert tracker, he offered to search, but was told they had too many people. He was certain Spinney would be found close to his tent, but searchers on ATVs didn't find him. His body lay in a ravine 100 feet below the tent. When Eddy heard of his death, he "was so discouraged," he said. "We went to all this work ... we're so happy and you're alive, and that's what's rewarding for us. And then you go and do it again."

◆ ◆ ◆

Whitt took over for 2002, the last year of Capt. Rushing's second term. He "had done everything I wanted to do." The team didn't vote and there was some unhappiness, so in January Whitt offered the position to anyone who wanted it. Skoloda offered to do it, "but stated that if Bill was happy, then it could wait until next election." The Imogene Pass Run, September 7, was memorably wet, with ten runners needing assistance. Buckskin Booksellers sold the last cookbook, twenty-five years after its creation. Don Carlton offered *A Wistful Visitor's Sketches* to support the team. Jenny Hart oversaw the project.

At the end of 2001, Ice Park Board president Eddy told the BOCC that they no longer had the resources to handle guiding in the park. Ice had become gold for the historic mining town and people came from around the world. "The growing popularity of the unique facility," wrote *Plaindealer* editor David Mullings, led to "concerns that competition for routes might lead to 'ice rage' and crowd out individual climbers." Eddy suggested designating "a single entity to regulate commercial guiding." Three companies applied: San Juan Mountain Guides' (SJMA) owners Gibbs and O'Donnell had a "demonstrated track record," and got the concession.

In summer 2001, South Park opened with thirteen climbs. The Ice Park Board and SJMA raised $38,000. With that money, Superintendent Mark Miller built "a new, more efficient system " to create ice. The City allowed the park to tap into the bottom of the water tank for a new pressurized system to replace gravity water flow. Miller, who moved to Ouray with his wife Colette in 2000, after wintering here over four years, said he "had the two best jobs in town"; he was also a guide for SJMA.

Over 2,000 spectators and climbers thronged the park for the five-day January Ice Festival. As everything was being set up a sixty-one-year-old man fell forty feet while leading 'Pic o' the Vic.' John Ohlson, in his first season of ice climbing, had climbed mountains for thirty-five years. The swift hour and a half rescue utilized a winch to raise him, encased in a body splint, on a litter. It "caught everyone's attention" said Gary Wild. "Spectators and sponsors told me that they were extremely impressed by how that job was done." The Ice Park "was hailed as perhaps the best ice climbing venue in the world."

More ice climbers were rescued at 'Gravity's Rainbow' above Engineer Pass Road on February 2 and at the lower bridge February 23. The backcountry rescue involved thirty-five-year-old Bob Kentenhafen of Boulder. After leading a first pitch on poor ice, he lowered off a cam, a spring-loaded climbing device, to find a rock anchor. The cam popped, he fell thirty feet and pendulumed twenty. His partner, Michelle Kranz, lowered him to the base and left for help.

The rescuers came in by snowmobile, Jeff Skoloda climbed to Kentenhafen and found he had broken ribs; Kranz said he lost consciousness. Nicole Skoloda climbed up with oxygen and put him in a C-collar. Kentenhafen complained of hypothermia and severe back pain. They removed his helmet and saw a bump on the right side of his head. Lance arrived, they pumped up a vacuum body splint, packaged him and his vital signs improved. Eight more rescuers hiked in with litter and gear. Jenny Hart, Rushing and Eihausen rigged ropes, lowered the litter part way and established a second anchor. They delivered Kentenhafen to the snowmobile at 2:40, three strenuous hours after callout. An ambulance waited on US 550.

An icy two and a half hour rescue on Camp Bird Road unfolded at 4:40 p.m. Sunday, February 10. Mike Sanders, a member of Western State College's Rescue Team, driving the last of three vehicles near the Drinking Cup, noticed that the snow berm on the east side of the curve was gone. He and Stephen Johnson got out to look. Two tracks led over the edge; finally they spotted a truck 200 feet down near the creek. They stopped a car and had the driver call 911 for the rescue team and ambulance. The Gunnison men clambered down the embankment, gathering bags and gear along the way. Three men were conscious, though one had been knocked out earlier. Sanders and the driver, Renan Ozturk, twenty-one, of Colorado Springs, hiked to the ambulance.

Rescuers walked down the slope, cared for patients and set up rigging. Sanders helped Eddy carry medical supplies. Support 11 brought lights so they could see. Jeff Skoloda helped Zack Paquette, twenty, of Foxborough, Massachusetts, who sprained his ankle while climbing earlier that day, walk out of the gorge. A helicopter was ordered for a third man, Evan Horn, twenty, of Colorado Springs, who had been riding in the back of the truck with the gear when it hit ice and skidded. By 6:05 Horn, with broken ribs and collarbone and pulmonary contusions, was in the ambulance heading for the Hot Springs Park. At 6:45 Care Flight lifted off for St. Mary's. Eihausen said it was the best rescue he had been involved in. "Repetition is paying off," agreed Capt. Whitt.

◆ ◆ ◆

April through October's seven incidents included two missing women; four injured / lost hikers, climbers and a hunter; and two off-road accidents. The K-9 team deployed four times. Sunday, April 7, saw an 8 a.m. ground search. Sheriff Mattivi briefed IC Whitt and fifteen members, including the K-9 team. Karen Brennan, forty-four, of Bear Dance River Ranch, a bed and breakfast north of Ridgway State Park, was reported missing the night before. Thom Wells, her husband, gave permission to search, so at 9:15, Karen Risch retrieved a scent article from the woman's bedroom, harnessed Lyra and let her sniff it before sealing it up. Lyra searched the woman's room, her stepson's bedroom and Thom's office / storage area. When she came outside, Sheriff's Officer K. Morehouse quietly told Risch that something had been found at Ridgway State Park, but to carry on searching the premises. After checking out a building, corral and trees, Lyra took a trail to the river, alerting at the top of the bank.

She turned south, went through barbed wire and deadfall to a fence separating a lawn and dry irrigation ditch from US 550. Mark Miller, K-9 support, and Risch followed Lyra east to the ranch house road and then the highway. She headed south to the park, went around a closed gate, alerted on air scent and headed toward the river. At 10:25 the K-9 team stopped at the top of a trail leading to the riverbank, waiting for the coroner and law enforcement to finish their work. A state park ranger had found the body just after Lyra searched the house.

At 11 the K-9 team descended to the body, which lay partly submerged at the river's edge. Lyra turned her head toward the bloody corpse to indicate the find, then moved away. Dwelley and MacTiernan lifted the body out of the water and put it on a litter. Lance and Dwelley retrieved water-soaked evidence. Eihausen, Russ Harvey, Holmes, O'Donnell and Nicole Skoloda took the litter up the trail. Risch praised Lyra and unharnessed her a short distance away to signal the end of the search. It was the four-year-old dog's first real world human "find." Her reward was play and treats.

On June 22, an open Jeep plunged off Camp Bird Road at the Waterhole Slide. The passenger leaped to safety before it went over the edge. The Jeep landed in Canyon Creek on its roof. OMRT was called at 5:15 p.m. The eighteen-year-old driver, Greg Young, was crammed under the dashboard and steering wheel. Eddy, the first medic on scene, was amazed he was alive. "That kid was a mess. He was really combative, too." Sean Hart, Nicole and Jeff Skoloda,

Harvey and Eddy raised the litter over seventy-five feet "really fast, trying to get the guy out of there." Young was loaded in the ambulance at 7:10. Air Care flew him to the San Juan Regional Medical Center in Farmington, New Mexico. As they packed up, Eddy looked down the cliff and said, "Oh my gosh. That's my rental." Young's parents had rented the blue Jeep from Eddy and his wife Tracy who owned the Riverside Motel. Young wasn't authorized to drive it. "I was pretty patient focused," said Eddy.

CHAPTER EIGHTEEN

"That black, black sky"

TED AND MARIANNE ZEGERS passed several hikers, July 17, 2000, on the way to Blue Lakes, a favorite trail. Ted Zegers noticed a couple hauling a tripod and photographic equipment as he passed them on his way to the lower lake, where he waited an unusually long time for his wife.

As she crossed the last wooded stretch of the Blue Lakes Wilderness a mile below the lake, Marianne Zegers found a man lying on the trail, his entire body seizing every twenty minutes. She had never seen anything like it and pulled a space blanket from her pack to cover him. Sherri Cameron had never seen her companion, fifty-three-year-old Bob Ogle, like this either, but she held his head firmly in her lap as he convulsed. He took medication daily and hadn't had any epileptic seizures for twenty years. Other hikers tried to call for help but couldn't get cell service. A woman hurried down most of the trail before she finally found a place to call.

Ted Zegers joined them just as a monsoon thunderstorm moved in over Mt. Sneffels. It was an awful storm, Marianne Zegers remembered, with "that black, black sky" and torrents of water. "We sat there with our hands over our heads in the hail." Water collected on the trail and she dug a little ditch in the dirt path above the sick man to keep water from running over him.

◆ ◆ ◆

The 1:30 p.m. callout brought but five people to the barn. Twenty-five minutes later, on the fifty-minute drive to the 9,400-foot trailhead, Capt. Sam Rushing asked the Sheriff's office to send another page. By 2:23, seven rescuers assembled at the trailhead;

six more were enroute, two riding the ambulance. Rushing put St. Mary's Air Life on standby.

At 2:30 he sent first responder Philippe Wheelock 1,400 vertical feet up the trail with oxygen to "help prevent neurological damage from the seizures." Sheriff Dominic Mattivi saw him take off running and tried to get him to slow down, fearing he wouldn't make it to the patient. Afterwards, he was amazed he did. Wheelock ran those two uphill miles in thirty minutes and later reported the patient was on oxygen and conscious. When Marianne Zegers saw him running toward them, she felt "glad there was somebody who knew what to do."

After Steve Lance left with medical supplies, Tim Eihausen and Lt. Karl Thees, who were hauling the litter, called for a tire pump. Members assembled equipment at the base. Mike and Joanie Gibbs arrived at 3 after finding a babysitter for their nine-month-old child. Forty minutes later, they hiked in with loaded packs. Ogle was having seizures every forty minutes now and Lance called for Valium. Paramedic Steve Svaldi arrived and headed up the trail since he was the only person authorized to administer the drug. Air Life was fifty to fifty-five minutes away. Finding a good LZ became a priority, but when they searched the truck, the GPS was missing. Wheelock radioed that he had both smoke and a possible LZ a quarter mile above the creek in a flat meadow. Bill Dwelley found another LZ, a swampy one, 100 yards east of the creek crossing. Mike Gibbs radioed coordinates for one nearby at 10,600 feet. Bob Risch drove north down CR7 to spot a base LZ at Willow Swamp and radioed that he had it and smoke ready.

Just before 4 p.m., dispatcher Penni Berry called to say that the National Weather Service reported a strong thunderstorm coming toward them from Norwood, twenty miles west. At 4:05 Air Life asked for the patient's location. As thunder rumbled, the rescuers picked up Ogle, his level of consciousness deteriorating, and hurried toward Thees in a meadow a quarter mile above them. For thirty minutes the helicopter tried to land in gusting wind, cloud and rain. It finally headed downhill and landed over a ridge to the west. Clouds descended as the crew scrambled out of the chopper with needed IV fluid looking for the patient. Somewhat later, they realized they were on a game trail.

The patient's medical condition deteriorated even though he was tied into the litter, a head shield and blankets protecting him. Eihausen said they started down as "serious inclement weather" set in, with thunder, lightning and hail drumming against their helmets, drowning out radio traffic. Mike Gibbs set up rigging for the steep switchbacks. The patient was "medically unstable, with continuing seizures," he said. "We needed to have a sense of urgency, but there's only so much you can do. It's not a fast process to get him out of there." He anchored ropes ahead of the litter in the hazardous stretches, waited for five attendants to pass with the load and stop, broke down the belay, ran downhill around them and repeated the process.

The descent was "a nightmare," said Thees. "It was so muddy and slippery and twisty." At one point they had to step around a log that rolled onto the trail. Keeping the litter level during the patient's five seizures was extremely difficult, said Eihausen, as the man's severe convulsions torqued it repeatedly to the side. Luckily, this happened on the more level stretches. Joanie Gibbs, hoisting the IV bag, was forced to walk off the trail. Sometimes, at the very narrow places, she switched positions from one side to another. "It was difficult to be a little bit off the trail," she remembered, "and then some sections we couldn't really do that."

By 5:30 the Air Life crew realized they were somewhere above the litter and gave up. They radioed that they were heading back to the chopper and would land at Willow Swamp. The patient's level of consciousness was acute and the medics, anticipating a new set of seizures, called for more oxygen. Bob Risch, one of three rescuers left at the trailhead, took off with a tank. Mike Gibbs asked for a description of a nearby meadow. They tried to contact Air Life and get them to land, but the chopper crew didn't respond. For another ten minutes they trudged on, finally hooking up with the oxygen. They needed IV fluid too, so Karen Risch took that up the trail. Ten minutes later, she met Wheelock, who took the fluid in exchange for his pack and empty O2 bottles. The helicopter crew radioed that they were in the chopper. Bill MacTiernan waited for them with smoke at the lower LZ.

At 6:10, an hour after they crossed the wilderness boundary, the captain met a weary litter team; twelve minutes later, Air Life lifted off. Thirteen rescuers packed up and left for home. Three weeks later, Ogle wrote: "Words cannot express the gratitude I feel for what you guys did for me that day," he said. "I'm a very lucky man ... and the OMRT is deserving of all the help it can get, too. So please accept this donation along with my deepest thanks...." Enclosed was $500.

OMRT upgraded the litter with a sixteen-inch bike tire that had a hand brake fixed to one handle to allow for slowing down or stopping immediately in steep or dangerous places. Looking back, Eihausen said this incident provided "a real learning curve" for them all. For Mike and Joanie Gibbs it brought change too: It "was the last time she responded to a rescue for years, because she thought this doesn't make any sense for me to hire a babysitter to go volunteer."

◆ ◆ ◆

The Zegers hauled Ogle's heavy photographic equipment out of the wilderness, passing the litter on the main switchbacks. He drove Cameron's car to Grand Junction that night so she could be with Ogle; Marianne Zegers followed in their car. A couple days later, they hiked Blue Lakes again and marveled at the hand marks on the steep dirt walls of the switchbacks where the litter crew had steadied themselves. Three days later Cameron and Ogle returned to Ouray and took them to dinner at the Silver Nugget. Marianne Zegers didn't recognize Ogle at first – "he looked so different" from the intensely ill person she had seen during seven grand mal seizures. "He would not have made it out without the rescue team," she said. "The response was unbelievably fast…. He was lucky he was on a busy trail."

◆ ◆ ◆

Several years later, the Zegers were sitting in the National Gallery of Art in Washington, when Wheelock walked up to them and asked, "Are you those guys from the Blue Lakes rescue?" Marianne Zegers was delighted to see the incredible young athlete who had responded by running full bore up the trail with heavy oxygen bottles.

CHAPTER NINETEEN

K-9 Lyra – Following scent, finding people

BOB AND KAREN RISCH BEGAN training an inquisitive Labrador / German shepherd puppy in May 1997. Lyra was eleven weeks old, just fifteen pounds, shiny button black with deep brown eyes. Her K-9 training included mountain, rural and urban search; snow, water and cadaver training; ATV, helicopter, ski lift and snowmobile work for three to five times a week until her retirement nine years later. Lyra and handler Karen Risch trained in seven western states, driving thousands of miles on backcountry roads. Lyra's search career included eleven missions undertaken at the request of six different law enforcement agencies.

Hundreds of people from all walks of life, OMRT members and other SAR people set trails and hid for her. She found volunteers of all ages, becoming a keen, focused search machine. A plucky seven-year-old neighbor, Zina Lahr, became one of her youngest and most frequent finds on land, in water and under snow. Zina's grandfather, Keith Lahr, was one of her oldest.

Karen Risch and Lyra trained with Search and Rescue Dogs of Colorado (SARDOC) and many fine dog handlers. Sue Purvis of Crested Butte, Carla Wheeler of Aspen and KC Harmon of Mancos, all extraordinary K-9 people, were instrumental in the final stages of Lyra's training as they planned and set up her trailing certification.

Lyra located a missing hunter in the Cutler Creek drainage, three lost hikers in the mountains around Ouray, two suicides in Ouray County, and two drowning victims in San Juan County. She searched Mountain Village for a knife in a crime scene and a location in the west desert of San Miguel County for a missing teen. His

185

remains were found several years later, having been dumped many miles away from his last seen point. Other missions included a hunter lost in a snowstorm on the Uncompahgre Plateau in Montrose County, who found his camp during the search. In two water searches in San Juan and Ouray County, Lyra worked alongside other SAR K-9s. She was deployed for five weeks of searches in Ouray and San Juan Counties for a wandering Alzheimer's victim whose body was finally located by hikers. In a bit of irony, the K-9 team was never summoned for the original disaster scenario which prompted Lyra's training: avalanche / snow search. The time and financial commitment required to train and field a search dog is considerable and deters many individuals and smaller teams from completing the process. The value of a trained dog, however, is demonstrated by two of Lyra's successes.

◆ ◆ ◆

June 2001: A twenty-two-year-old Montrose woman had been missing for nearly twenty-four hours when a sheriff's deputy noticed her small white truck at the turnout for Eldredge Pond, at the north end of Ouray County between US 550 and the Uncompahgre River. Her husband saw it the next morning as he drove to work in Telluride. Sheriff Dominic Mattivi called at 1:20 p.m. At 2, the K-9 team, the Montrose Police, DOW and Sheriff's personnel stood in the sun waiting for CBI to arrive. The tightly locked truck cooked in eighty-five-degree heat. No one knew whether the woman walked away or left in some other manner. Four-year-old Lyra sat patiently in the shade. Her subdued behavior suggested she knew this was for real, not just another training session.

When CBI finally arrived, a local deputy picked the lock. Karen Risch harnessed Lyra at 2:55 and led her to the stuffed truck. Carefully inserting her hand into the outside of a clean, unscented Ziplock bag, she retrieved a scent article – one of the woman's sandals. Lyra sniffed the sandal and the driver's seat, then walked around the front of the truck to the passenger side. She sniffed the dirt near the truck, alerted and ran full bore to the south end of the parking lot and down a dirt path leading to an overgrown, tree-strewn riverbank. Twenty to thirty feet later, she veered left into some willows and undergrowth, heading northeast to the river. Running behind her with a long leather leash, Karen Risch tripped over downed trees and fell flat, but managed to restrain the excited dog long enough to regain her footing. Bob Risch brought up the rear of this wild chase with radio, map and sealed scent article.

At the river, Lyra waded in a few feet, turned around and ran northwest through swampy willows. Bounding up the riverbank, she headed through small narrow-leafed cottonwoods to a beaten-down dirt track encircling the pond. Suddenly, she slowed, sniffing at two shallow gullies east of the pond. Just beyond its north end, she alerted again and headed down a packed dirt gully, jerking the leash downward.

Karen Risch raised her head and simultaneously tightened the leash. A swollen body in gray sweatpants and a short-sleeved green T-shirt hung high in a tree twenty-five to fifty feet away, the noose an awkwardly tied, bright yellow plastic rope. The woman's waist-length, wavy blonde hair shone in the slanting light. Holding the leash taut, Karen radioed her support, Bob Risch. "Tell the Sheriff we have found her." It was 3:03: The search had taken eight minutes. The law officers were impressed. It was not an always hoped for live find, but the quick resolution was a relief.

◆ ◆ ◆

Two years later, Karen Risch was working in her yard on an Indian summer day when Capt. Steve Lance strolled across the grass. San Juan Sheriff Sue Kurtz wanted the K-9 team. The night before she received a report of two men overdue on a fishing trip to Clear Lake. Concerned about the possibility of foul play, Sheriff Kurtz wanted the K-9 team to clear the remote high altitude lake's perimeter. It was possible that someone had walked out and she hoped a search dog would pick up that scent.

◆ ◆ ◆

Clear Lake is an intense blue oval, 2,000 feet long and 1,000 feet wide, filling an alpine rock bowl at 12,000 feet, accessible by a tortuous, narrow jeep road. The major axis extends E-W with the outlet descending east over coal black rocks. A fisherman's footpath defines the north shore. Forbidding dark cliffs edge the south and west. A cold body of water, it is more than 100 feet deep at its dark western end.

Sheriff Kurtz knew the importance of preserving a scene for K-9 search and prevented people from entering the area. The only exception was Deputy Brian Jacobs, who investigated that morning. He found an unlocked Jeep Wrangler with two personal flotation devices inside, parked on the northeastern shore. A paddle and a foam cooler floated in shallow water just west of the jeep. Another 400 feet west a capsized canoe lay a bit offshore. The deputy pulled it in and checked underneath. It was empty. He left it upright against the shore. In the next 500-600 feet of shoreline, he found other debris – a second paddle; loose, floating cans of beer and the carton; ripped potato chip and pretzel sacks; apples, cheese and meat slices. A couple of apples and a snack bar wrapper lay on the trail a few feet above the water, probably scavenged by animals during the night. Beyond that, the west end cliffs offered no other clues. Jacobs saw no tracks or other sign that the missing men had left the water.

◆ ◆ ◆

The K-9 team left Ouray at 12:20; Clear Lake was twenty-nine miles away over Red Mountain Pass, above the Mineral Creek valley in San Juan County. Their mission was to rule out the possibility that either or both of the men had left the area by foot. They arrived at 1:30 and found a well-preserved scene. Deputy Jacobs assured them that the Jeep remained untouched and the trail along the lakeshore was uncontaminated except for his footprints. Bruce Conrad, from SJCSAR, was grid searching the lake from a kayak, but had found no sign of the missing men. At 12,000 feet it was a clear, sunny day, the temperature forty-five degrees with a light breeze from the south. The previous day had also been Indian summer with typical south-southwest winds – perfect fishing weather.

Lyra was harnessed, taken to the driver's seat of the Jeep, and told to "Find Fred," her cadaver command. She sniffed the seat, put her nose down, moved deliberately to the lake, entered the water, drank and returned to the trail. She headed west along the north shore, stopped at the canoe, jumped into the water, circled the boat and sniffed its interior. Back on land, she continued west, entering the water occasionally until she reached the debris field Deputy Jacobs saw earlier. She, too, checked out every bit of litter. They searched the west end of the lake, moving upward over rock cliffs until the terrain became too steep. At the sheer cliff's edge, Lyra stood a few moments, sniffing over the forty-foot drop to the water. She turned back, moving down to the debris field along the lake shore, checking each item again as she passed.

A rising wind pushed insistent waves toward them. Lyra entered the water twice, alerting at two articles not present on her first pass

– a brown and black hiking boot and a black ball cap with a gold logo floating just offshore. A quick radio check with Deputy Jacobs and Conrad confirmed that neither had seen these items. The cap, with its dark bill upwards, lay partially concealed among sharp black rocks at the water's edge. The boot floated near the beer carton first seen that morning and would logically have been noticed by everyone had it been present earlier. Because Lyra meticulously sniffed every other object on the first pass, it seemed likely that both the boot and the cap floated to shore while she searched the west cliffs. Bob Risch flagged nearby rocks and stayed to work with Conrad (still in his kayak), setting up a grid to examine the water to the west of the floating boot.

Lyra still needed to clear the south edge of the lake, so the team worked east to the outlet, hopping rocks to the southern shore. Near the middle of that side, snow-covered cliffs dropped steeply to the lake. The dog showed no interest anywhere, a marked contrast to her behavior on the north edge. They turned back and as they passed the Jeep, Karen Risch opened the passenger side to let Lyra sniff that seat, just as she had previously done with the driver's side. A dive team was enroute from Durango, fifty plus miles of two lane roads and two mountain passes away. Another contingent from SJCSAR now searched the east end of the lake in a second canoe.

Divers Perry Tucker and Bart Mangen arrived at 3:30 and donned their wetsuits. The K-9 team headed for Bob Risch, waiting near a large rock protruding from the water. Small waves generated by the increasing wind splashed the rock. As they approached, Lyra alerted, barking sharply, her tail a windmill. She jumped into the shallow water, barked and whined. Furiously, she dug the sand underneath that rock as if it were a snowfield and a victim lay buried out of sight. Sheriff Kurtz was told that she had a strong scent alert. The K-9 team suggested the divers search the deep water upwind (southwest) rather than spend time in the shallow eastern end.

Responding to Lyra's insistent barking and pleading eyes, Bob Risch finally took off his shirt, reached into the water under and around the rock to see if anything lay there. There was nothing but sand and water, despite her intensifying certainty. Lyra dug, paced and whined excitedly. She could not be persuaded to leave the water for the next hour. Conrad and another observer from SJCSAR confirmed her extraordinary behavior. Everyone thought that upwind of this spot was the logical place for divers to search. There, two hundred feet offshore, the lake deepened to over 100 feet and a body could not be seen from the surface.

The divers – 600 feet to the east – swam slowly westward, searching as they went. Conrad waited 300 feet offshore, marking the likeliest area. At 4:30, within 100 feet of the kayak, they located a first body 400 feet offshore on a rocky shelf twenty to forty feet deep. The divers surfaced, recharged their air tanks and warmed themselves in the waning sun. They found a second body twenty minutes later in the same area. Though it was difficult to do in these circumstances, Karen Risch called Lyra off the search, walked up the hill from the lake and played with her. Her reward, as always, was "Good Girl, Lyra," treats and ball throwing.

The low October sun set behind the mountain ridge southwest of the lake just after the first body was found and the air temperature dropped dramatically. Sheriff Kurtz radioed that the parents watched from a knoll near the eastern edge of the lake, so Lyra and Karen Risch walked east along the lakeshore. She introduced the dog and herself and said how sorry she was for their loss:

"Which one was yours?"
"They both were," Trish Davis answered. "They were all we had."

For many years, brothers Jeffrey, thirty-one, and Richard Davis, thirty-three, had fished together in this favorite spot. Their father, Gary Davis, said they had given their sons life jackets for Christmas the year before. Stunned, Karen Risch asked if they had any grandchildren. Trish Davis' face brightened. She said they had four. Belatedly, the handler realized what a gamble she unwittingly had taken in asking such a question.

◆ ◆ ◆

This search provided several lessons. The shifting night winds scattered debris along 2,000 feet of shoreline. Deputy Jacob's initial catalog of the debris location proved invaluable when Lyra found new evidence. Her subsequent alert at the rock and her insistence that someone was in the water dramatically narrowed the search area and focused the final effort. "I thought that was a very amazing rescue," Sheriff Kurtz said. "Your dog finding those two in the water ... it saved us so much time." Her decision to use a K-9 team to rule out the possibility that the missing men had left the lake produced results she hadn't anticipated: "I didn't know dogs could do that," she said. Lyra's insistent behavior at the rock provided a graphic demonstration of canine detection of human scent, even that rising from deep, cold water.

For Sheriff Kurtz this had been an especially gut wrenching mission. Her two grown sons were almost the same age as the lost brothers. Especially hard was the aftermath. She brought the parents to the Carriage House in Silverton where the bodies lay. "A lot of times … they want to see the body. And so the Mom wanted to see them," she said. "Dad wasn't sure he wanted to …. I talked to him: 'I understand how you feel and you need to make your own decision, but this is the one chance you're going to have to do this.'"

Gary Davis decided he wanted to see his sons. He "was very nervous, he was very shaky…. I walked into the Carriage House where the bodies were with one of them on each arm and just held on to them while they viewed the bodies of their sons. And it's that kind of stuff that really, you know, you never get used to."

SAR K-9 Lyra sits on a knoll northeast of Clear Lake, 2004.

Photo by Karen Risch

CHAPTER TWENTY

2003-2006
"We composed ourselves and then looked"

OURAY COUNTY EVICTED the Orange Beast from the Community Center in 2003, needing room for a third EMS vehicle. The BOCC appropriated $1,000 to revamp the remaining bay for Rescue 11. OMRT decided to build a rescue barn and the BOCC provided an eighty-year lease on the Rio Lode near the Ice Park. The City of Ouray offered sewer, water and power connections. Unfortunately, the Rio was solid rock – prohibitively expensive to blast. "We found a place where we could get it done pretty much by moving dirt," said Capt. Steve Lance. Engineer Brad McMillon created building plans. OMRT knew they needed a building with three deep bays – Rescue 11 barely fit in the Community Center. A New Year's Eve fundraiser and $100 bricks raised money. Locals volunteered time and expertise: Contractor Joe Kersen initially oversaw the project and master electrician John Kropuenske, OMRT's first youth member in 1975, wired the entire building gratis. The team decided to pay as they built, so they could afford future maintenance and insurance.

◆ ◆ ◆

Seventeen missions began with a quick ice rescue in January and ended with a K-9 search in San Miguel County in November. A two-day ground and water search on June 11 sent the team to South Mineral Creek in San Juan County. Two days later, six-year-old Evan Johnson still hadn't been found in spite of the efforts of divers, rescuers and dogs. For Silverton Sheriff Sue Kurtz, it was a sad thing to remember: "By the end of the first day, we had like 100 people in that field," she said. On June 13 Johnson's family held a memorial service in Silverton. Four days later, SJCSAR members and James Burwick's K-9 in training, Kai, found a sandal and then his body in a deep pool flooded with logs and foaming spring runoff. Durango diver Bart Mangen retrieved his body three days later when the water level dropped.

A late June rescue of a sixty-two-year-old Georgia woman who tore her leg open while climbing to Lavender Col on Mt. Sneffels, inadvertently created an expensive second retrieval – of Rescue 11. It slid sideways into deep snow on the 4WD Jeep road to the trailhead and stuck. OMRT hauled gear a hundred feet up to the 12,600-foot trailhead and then to Lavender Col, 900 feet higher. Rescuers packaged the patient, set up anchors and lowered her down the scree slope. Five hours later, Cathy Spraetz was loaded into McMillon's truck and driven to the ambulance. That evening, Timber Ridge proprietors Steve Duce and John Fedel freed the truck from dense, wet snow. At 10:30 everyone reached the barn. The second rescue – of the truck – cost $1,000. Bill Whitt's motorcycle at the Sneffels trailhead also needed rescuing. Eight marauding marmots were spotted eating his seat, goggles and helmet, initiating a $500 repair bill.

On August 20 a motorcycle skidded off the Drinking Cup curve on Camp Bird Road. First responder and avid cyclist Jeff Skoloda looked at the skid and knew there was no chance that the rider was alive. Jeff Black, thirty-four, of Suwanee, Georgia, was "going really fast ... that corner comes up on you and if you hit your brakes, especially your front brake, the bike wants to stand up straight. You can't turn. You can't lean into a turn, so if you panic and grab ... your front brake ... his skid mark was right off."

The cycle plunged 105 feet to a steep rock embankment, throwing the rider another eighty-five feet toward the river. He lay face down, "It was so visible from the road, and so bizarre," said Erin Eddy. As seventeen rescuers worked to bring up the body, word came that the cyclist's father was on another road three miles up the gorge. Milton Black asked to stay there until his son's body was retrieved. A grateful family stayed in touch and donated $500. Skoloda made a memorial for the Drinking Cup wall at the widow's request.

A climber's rescue, a water search for two men missing in San Juan County, and a K-9 land search in San Miguel County closed the year. On October 20, Jack Palmer, thirty-one, of Ridgway, took a 100-foot free fall on Ouray's popular Pool Wall climbing area, then cartwheeled sixty to eighty feet on scree. He wore no helmet but remained conscious, suffering only lacerations. On November 4, the K-9 team spent a day searching a steep hilly area in Little Gypsum Valley at the west end of San Miguel County. A nineteen-year-old Michigan man was missing under murky circumstances. "In spite of good conditions (a cloudy day, favorable wind, fifty degrees)," Lyra found nothing. "It does seem likely that the missing person is not in this area," Karen Risch wrote to Sheriff Bill McMasters. Four years later, a hunter found the young man's remains in a canyon six miles to the northwest.

◆ ◆ ◆

By February 2004, OMRT had $12,500 in the building fund. Capt. Lance estimated that four-dozen bricks had been sold. In April the BOCC "approved the special use permit and declared its desire to work with the City of Ouray to review the annexation proposal." The

Eight principals in the effort to build the barn turned out for Groundbreaking Day, August 1, 2005. L to R are Rob Holmes, Capt. Tim Eihausen, Lt. Jeff Skoloda, Steve Lance, Bill Whitt, Garry Schalla, Nicole Skoloda and Sam Rushing.

Photo courtesy *Ouray County Plaindealer*

Building and Expansion Fund contained $18,000. Four bids came in for the building; the lowest was $135,000. By June McMillon had drawings for architect John Nixon. After the Fourth of July breakfast, they had $25,000. In January 2005, OMRT had $67,500 of the $250,000 needed. Another $10,000 in bricks came in by the end of July. It was time to build and a jubilant team broke ground August 1.

Two local guides, Clint and Ryan Cook, joined that February, bringing team strength to twenty-four members with eight in reserve. Former captains Randy Gerke, Whitt, Bill MacTiernan and Rushing provided a wealth of information and experience. From May to November, OMRT responded for six injured hikers, a lost hunter and two stand-downs. One August rescue was the most traumatic in team history.

One of the most frustrating searches in Sheriff Mattivi's experience began May 17 when Cynthia Gottschalk, a fifty-seven-year-old Missouri resident visiting Ouray for the first time, took her dog Shadow to the Uncompahgre River Walk. She and her husband were staying at the Riverside Inn. A veteran walker, she "had early stage suspected Alzheimer's disease," said George Gottschalk. He "had confiscated her car keys and driver's license a year before when she became lost while driving to work and was unable to find her way home."

He reported her missing at 6:30 p.m.; two hours later a missing person page went out. OMRT responded immediately. Members searched upstream through town, at Box Canyon and the Ice Park. Karen Risch interviewed the husband, scented Lyra on his wife's slipper and searched the room, the motel and part of the River Walk, but found nothing. A couple reported seeing a woman walking a dog near Rotary Park north of town at 4:30. At the park Lyra alerted immediately, crossed the road and headed south toward Skyrocket Basin. Darkness had fallen when Sheriff's deputy Ed Torres pulled up alongside the K-9 team and said that a woman and dog were seen south of town at 6:30. He gave them a ride to the first switchback on US 550. Lyra entered the driveway of a stately cream and blue Victorian house tucked into the hillside; checked the doors, decks and landscaping; and moved to Lee's Ski Hill two blocks away. She lost the scent on the highway above the hill. At 12:30 a.m. OMRT stood down.

At 6 a.m. searchers learned that the woman's family said she "was unlikely to wander away from roads, so rescue parties concentrated on areas around the highway." Even though Lyra found scent at opposite ends of town, Capt. Lance explained that dementia sufferers could head "in opposite directions ... appear confused to anyone who was dealing with them, but would, in themselves, have an idea of where they were going." So they searched the river, US 550 to Engineer Pass turnoff and west side trails. Lyra was taken again to the Victorian house and Ski Hill where she alerted once more, but showed no interest in US 550 to the south.

Barbara Staehle, who lived on CR 14A north of town, reported that a wordless woman walked up her driveway near noon and dropped a glove. Staehle walked toward her, but "she waved her off and continued up the road." Lyra was uninterested in the glove and George Gottschalk did not recognize it. Sheriff Mattivi, Colette Miller and the K-9 team searched Thistle Park, Cutler trailhead to the creek, the lower gorges of Cutler and Dexter Creeks and the 4WD road to Baldy trailhead. Lyra showed interest only in a grassy swale at the Thistle Park entrance.

The third day a frantic Border collie was reported on CR14: Bob Risch searched Gold Hill while Karen Risch and Lyra walked an historic wagon road into Jackass Flats. Bill Dwelley and George Kenney kayaked from Whispering Pines to the Ridgway Reservoir. Rushing, Rob Holmes and Jeff Wiltfang searched Canyon Creek from the Victorian Inn to Box Cañon Park. At noon, policeman Tony Chelf asked the K-9 team to search Box Cañon Park, after George Gottschalk remembered they visited there the day she disappeared. Lyra alerted on the loop and upper bridge trails, inside the Visitor's Center and in the women's bathroom. Officer Chelf confirmed Cynthia Gottschalk had been there. Lance, Rushing, Holmes, Karen Risch and Lyra went to the river near the Inn. The men probed the rapids. Lyra sniffed the probes without interest.

The fourth day, May 20, Lance and the K-9 team drove toward Red Mountain Pass. George Gottschalk had snapped a picture of his wife and Shadow the day she disappeared. They found the curve where the picture was taken, but Lyra detected nothing along the barren, hot roadside. She later searched CR 361 from Mineral Farms to the Hayden Trailhead. Sheriff Mattivi deployed a helicopter along the river from Ridgway Reservoir to Red Mountain and Dexter / Cutler Creeks. Finally, he suspended the search.

Three days later, May 23, Log Hill resident John Cappis returned from a five-day trip, picked up the week's *Plaindealer* and recognized Cynthia Gottschalk. He had "passed her and her dog a mile up the Cutler Creek trail Monday evening. She was hiking in and he asked how she was doing. She did not respond, so he thought she might not speak English." When he got back to his car, he realized it was the only one there. OMRT fanned out early the next day in the Cutler/Baldy trail system. Lt. Mark Miller and his father hiked Okeson Trail to 10,400-foot Baldy Ridge and its hunt camps, finding intermittent footprints and small dog tracks along the ridge. Cappis and the K-9 team searched Cutler Creek to the 11,200-foot junction with Dexter Trail, hiked along Baldy Ridge and finally turned back in thigh-deep snow, finding nothing.

Rushing, Holmes and Tim Eihausen searched Left Fork and found footprints near the ridge. They descended via Storm's Gulch, seeing human and dog prints above the snow line. It was unclear if the tracks were from Cynthia Gottschalk and Shadow since other hikers had used the area and runoff was heavy. Kenny walked Cutler doing radio relay for the far-flung searchers. At 3:40 they called it a day. Lance estimated OMRT had spent 500 man-hours searching for the missing woman. "We've been all over the county and haven't found a single piece of evidence." Her husband checked animal shelters from Montrose to Durango as well.

On May 30, a black and white Border collie limped into a camp in the ghost town of Eureka, fifteen to twenty miles away in San Juan County across the still snowbound San Juans. The campers recognized Shadow from missing person/dog posters in the area. She wore a collar and tags, though her leash was gone. Two days later, they found a Bureau of Land Management person who informed Sheriff Kurtz. Shadow was ten pounds lighter, hungry, tired and sore, but not malnourished. The family retrieved her, said she had been over-weight. The mystery deepened. No one thought a small dog could negotiate the high mountain trails between the Cutler/Baldy area and Eureka in the current snow conditions and Shadow had not been seen on US 550, Engineer Pass or any Silverton area roads. Sheriff Kurtz requested the K-9 team. On June 2, they searched from 9 a.m. to 1:30 p.m., covering territory from Eureka north toward Engineer Pass. Lyra, scented again on Cynthia Gottschalk's slipper, which had been sealed up since the night of her disappearance, checked empty buildings, roads, creeks and woods as far as the snow allowed. Even in the rocky area where Shadow was found, Lyra showed no response except to cats in the old boardinghouse. Whitt rode his motorbike to Engineer Pass and Lance took the rescue truck to Corkscrew and Brown Mountain Roads but found nothing.

Shortly after noon on June 11, twenty-six days after Cynthia Gottschalk disappeared, Ridgway runner Kelly Day spotted a body twenty feet down to the right of Shortcut Trail in the Cutler / Baldy system. Ridgway residents Nancy Hartzog and Peggy Spindler also hiked down the trail that day. Halfway down, Hartzog told Spindler she saw a dead body.

"We composed ourselves and then looked," said Spindler.... They stayed five minutes to observe ... Nancy tied a red shirt to a pine tree to identify the spot. They described the body as mangled, decomposed and shirtless, lying head down in the creek in front of an aspen tree. One boot was near and over the shoulder of the corpse, which was face down. One hand was splayed at an odd angle. The body had short dark hair and the overalls it wore were wet. The backside was bare; they did not know if it was a man or woman. Some dark clothing was lying nearby.

Cynthia Gottchalk's body lay west of the trail at 9,660 feet. When he got there, Lance realized there was only a short window from which it was visible – and only to downhill hikers. Rescuers waited two hours at the trailhead for CBI to arrive, hike in and catalogue the scene before they could retrieve the body. Sheriff Mattivi said that of his twenty-five years of rescues and searches, "that one still bothers me a little bit because of the unknown ... we always deal in the known and you know the fact that the dog kept going south ... would lead us to believe that she was going south." The body lay several miles northeast of Ouray; she died of hypothermia and exposure.

◆ ◆ ◆

At 9:30, the first morning of the Ice Festival, January 15, 2005, Paula Wilson leaned back on rappel at the 'Scottish Gullies' below Box Canyon Bridge. Eihausen said that both the woman and her belayers missed the fact that her anchor rope was not attached. Her college buddies watched as she fell eighty feet, landing on ice and snow. Ice Park president Eddy registered shock. "All these bystanders observing this.... I needed to be out there. I had to act on behalf of the event, and the patient ... trying to coordinate resources and probably the entire rescue." EMS and OMRT were on scene, reached Wilson in minutes, packaged her and hauled the litter up a nearby gully to the ambulance. A helicopter waited at the Hot

Springs Park. She spent almost two weeks in critical condition at St. Mary's in Grand Junction, with what was thought to be major head trauma, a broken pelvis and internal injuries. She finally went home in mid-February.

An unusual pair of rescues called the team to Red Mountain Pass and Whitehouse Mountain and Corbett Peak that winter. Three July callouts included a thirteen-year-old boy with an open femur fracture and head injuries at 13,100 feet, just below Lavender Col. Paged out at 4 p.m. on July 1, "a six-person OMRT crew climbed through a snowfield, stabilized the patient and set him in a litter, then lowered him down the couloir." He reached the helicopter "as daylight waned."

The last July callout was for a local man, Tom Sullivan, who disappeared from his home above Canyon Creek Tuesday, July 27. His wife Bobbie Sullivan last saw him at 3 p.m. trying to fix an antenna on the roof. She eventually called the Sheriff, who searched for him that night. OMRT was paged before dawn. Lyra was scented on the man's clothing, alerted on the outside deck and followed the scent to the edge of the steep, overgrown ravine above the river. The nine year-old K-9 was now stiff and arthritic, so Karen Risch kept her from descending the bank in the dim light. Later, ten rescuers searched around the household and the immediate Canyon Creek area and Rushing found traces of blood down the bank. More search dogs arrived from Dolores, approached from the other side and indicated the man was in the river.

"We searched for him all day," Garry Schalla remembered, "and we finally found him under the first trap created by logs in the river." He waded across and put a rope around Tom Sullivan's arm and leg. His body was caught under a large log pile, but by pushing him down and working him under the obstructions, he finally popped out. Schalla belayed the body into the river current, which carried it to the bank, where OMRT pulled it out.

A last rescue, for a lucky driver who slid down Sullivan's Gully on December 27 and lived to tell about it, closed out the year. "Amazing. That's the first word that came to mind as a second set of vehicle tracks headed down Sullivan's Gully ... and another live person walked out," wrote *Plaindealer* editor David Mullings. "An orange tag was attached to a tree so the wrecker crew could find the van. That tag confirmed that for the second time in ten months, a vehicle had taken the plunge.... And for the second time, with a happy ending."

One resulting conversation went like this.

Question: "Well, do you think CDOT will get around to putting up a guardrail now?"
Answer: "No. Nobody's getting killed.

◆ ◆ ◆

The barn's footprint was poured on February 9, 2006. It was time to fundraise – Schalla realized quickly that they weren't going to build the Barn with T-shirt and brick sales. "We got the initial private kind of matching grant, we got some smaller grants and then we used that private grant to go to the big three in Denver: El Pomar, Boettcher and Gates." Schalla, Rich Wojciechowski and Lance, the marketing committee, mailed information to potential donors. Lt. Skoloda announced in May that when the bills were paid, they would have "virtually no money left in the building account." Mark Miller suggested they borrow money for the Tyvek wrap from the operational account. Everyone agreed; the barn's "drying in" was finished that month.

◆ ◆ ◆

2006 brought fourteen callouts, starting with two ice park rescues in six days at the 'Schoolroom' and 'New Funtier.' Under the bright light of a full June moon, OMRT spent a weekend night on cliffs south of the Neosho Mine across US 550 from Bear Creek Falls. That evening, travelers reported cries for help to the west, across the Uncompahgre Gorge. Bob Risch knew the combination to the locked gate on an old mine road in the Mineral Farms subdivision and notified residents that OMRT needed to use the road, drastically shortening everyone's hike to the mine. After they got to the cliffs where the injured man was, they set up a belay to lower him to the river and take him across to the highway. Rushing and Karen Risch guided his young daughter back to the Neosho's well-preserved blacksmith shop, the pair's original destination. She signed the historic logbook and they walked out to the road. Her father had taken an unorthodox route through cliffs that he thought led to the mine.

A week later, ten people on a Sunday hike to Mt. Sneffels heard rocks fall and someone scream high above Yankee Boy Basin. Jesse Kirvan, Amy Foss and Allison Laramee were among those descending the mountain. Kirvan thought he saw a man fall from Gilpin Peak's ridge. A woman screamed bloody murder – "Someone help me!" Laramee headed for a saddle in the range, hoping for a cell phone connection. She and several other hikers managed to alert authorities, but they initially said the fall occurred on Mt. Sneffels.

Kirvan and Foss took off across the basin. Forty-five minutes later, they found sixty-four-year-old David Lauer's body in a snowbank on the side of Gilpin Peak. They had nothing to cover his gruesome head injuries, so they arranged their backpacks to shield his body. They saw Anna Milburn-Lauer, his daughter, climbing down the snowy couloir 1,600 feet above them, realized that she was in danger and would cliff out. They stayed and talked to her for four-and-a-half hours "about everything they could think of, including teachers" that she and Kirvan shared at Fort Lewis College in Durango. Milburn-Lauer repeatedly asked about her father, but they did not answer. Later, Kirvan praised her courage and composure. "She was amazing. I don't know how she was in such control. She was a rock star."

Twenty rescuers responded to the 12:37 p.m. callout. Philippe Wheelock and Jacob Nacht ran Wrights' Lake Trail to the basin, ascended the steep snow couloir and reached Milburn-Lauer at 2:20. They "set an anchor and harnessed her in so she could rappel down the cliff," said Capt. Eihausen. A thousand feet below, the recovery team placed the body in a bag and packaged it into a Sked. They erased a visible trail of blood, which extended 200 feet up the couloir, with snow. "We had to bring the girl, the daughter out the same way," said Eihausen. At 4:42 Lauer's body was placed in an ambulance waiting below Wright's Lake.

David "Running Cloud" Lauer's obituary read: "He lived for climbing high and dancing long and walking with purpose." A "long-time political and environmental activist," he died on a Father's Day outing with his daughter. "On the trail that morning, looking around at the high green grandeur, he had said with a deep sigh of gratitude, 'I live for this.'"

Five July backcountry calls included two injured ATV riders and two Jeep accidents. James Parker, sixty-two, from Rowlett, Texas, was in a line of Jeeps descending Camp Bird Road when a seventy-five-pound rock from the cliff above the road pierced the Jeep's soft top, "killing him instantly." His quick-witted passenger, Nancy Ingle, fifty-six, grabbed the steering wheel and turned the vehicle to the mountain. She suffered a broken arm but saved the Jeep from tumbling 400 feet down a cliff. Rescuers got her out of the overturned vehicle as smaller rocks fell around them. "This truly was a freak accident," said Sheriff Mattivi.

On July 17, Shannon Higgins called San Juan County Sheriff Kurtz from Molas Pass trailhead. Her twenty-nine-year-old husband Brent, "an experienced free climber," was twenty-four hours overdue from a solo climb in the Weminuche Wilderness. His passion for climbing was evident to those who knew him: "A good climber, a great guy," said MacTiernan. Brent Higgins had participated in OMRT operations in 1994-1995, when he was still a teenager. On Saturday morning, July 15, he left his wife, her parents and his infant son "to walk down Molas Trail, across the Animas River to Elk Park Trail and up to Vestal Valley to free climb one or more peaks. He would stay overnight and then return the next morning to his family at the Molas trailhead. Higgins had hiked and free climbed in the area previously."

Sheriff Kurtz called out SJCSAR. Over the next four days, OMRT, La Plata and Mesa SAR units, CAP, and K-9 teams from Dolores joined the five-day search, aided by helicopters and the Durango & Silverton Narrow Gauge Railroad, which shuttled rescuers to and from the area. Level 3, the Utah firm where Brent Higgins worked, "even brought in an airplane with infrared search equipment." Matt Hepp said he and Jeff Skoloda were helicoptered into Kite Lake to search the north side of the wilderness and Balsam Lake on the south. Eihausen and Nicole Skoloda drove to Kite Lake and searched the upper Elk Basin. Nothing was found. By the fifth day Sheriff Kurtz had to tell the family that that day, July 21, would be the last day of the search. OMRT trackers Rushing and Holmes worked with SJCSAR trackers Patrick and Amy Swonger and Scot Jackson. Searchers flew over Balsam Lake and reported "campers waving crazily at them from below." They had found a camera, "thought it belonged to the missing man ... hadn't realized its importance when they saw it busted up at the bottom of Vestal Peak's Wham Ridge...." Then searchers flew over and dropped leaflets: "When they looked through the pictures, they realized what they had. The camera showed the climber and his whereabouts."

The search team landed, retrieved the smashed camera and memory chip, the ripped bag and attachment loop, a plastic water bottle. The chip was downloaded at Molas Lake rescue base. "The search ended at 1307 when climbers [Jerrod] Campbell and [Chris] Leriso found the body ... in the fall line at the base of the cliffs below

Vestal Peak." Clad in a neon yellow-green jacket, Brent Higgins lay in a crack green with lichen. He died of injuries "sustained in a long fall, probably 1,000 vertical feet or more." The body was long-lined out. SJCSAR Capt. Mike McQueen was on the chopper and on a private ham radio connection told Sheriff Kurtz that Higgins' wife shouldn't see the body after a bad fall and a week's exposure to the elements. Sheriff Kurtz "told Shannon this was not how she would want to remember Brent, "but she still wanted to do something and so we decided we could put the body ... over in the trees next to the landing area in the body bag." That way, "she could see his feet, but she couldn't see his face." Shannon handed the baby to her mom and asked the Sheriff:

"Would you go with me?"
"That was just heart wrenching ... one of the rescues that sometimes makes you cry," said the Sheriff. "I just stayed there with her."

CHAPTER TWENTY-ONE

Imogene

ON THE OURAY SIDE OF 13,114-foot Imogene Pass, Dan Glucklich pulled his 1998 Jeep Grand Cherokee "onto a steep embankment, on the high side" of the road, giving way to an oncoming vehicle. A military contractor from Colorado Springs, Glucklich was doing what he loved that summer afternoon – exploring a mountain road with his wife Jeanine, their eleven-year-old son Cole and a friend, seven-year-old Ian Nordstrom. As the fifty-year-old driver turned his SUV back to the road, it "put the vehicle off-balance and it rolled onto its top." As the driver's side slowly hit the road, the window glass fell out perfectly shaped. John Bright, from Mobile, Alabama, was "lining up a photograph of Telluride Peak just behind Imogene Pass when the Jeep started its plunge." It "appeared to be overloaded and top-heavy … rolled for about 70 feet, then started to tumble end-over-end. Then, it just exploded." Later, Sheriff Dominic Mattivi said that the Jeep "may have hit a large rock or dropped into a hole" and tipped over.

◆ ◆ ◆

The responders have not forgotten *Imogene*. "It was wildly catastrophic," said Sean Hart. "I thought about that one for years, a long time.... I don't know where you can throw a car off and have a bigger fall...." Thirteen hundred feet of rock lay between the upper road and the crumpled Jeep at the bottom of Imogene Basin. The devastation was surreal; gasoline drenched the hillside. The truck "divotted a trail on the way down," said Hart. "You could see one place where it went off a cliff and then went 'bang' … a big scratch on the rocks … pretty scary."

First responder Bill Whitt rode his motorbike up to where the Jeep went off. Fifty feet below, he found Cole Glucklich, ejected shortly after the Jeep rolled. The boy's skull was fractured, his brain exposed. Whitt held his head together, waiting for medical personnel.

Jeff Skoloda stopped his motorbike at the stream crossing in the lower basin and found a "chaotic and definitely high adrenaline" situation. The radio traffic "showed massive trauma … multiple victims." Surveying the scene, he saw that the hillside sloped down "between big rock outcroppings." He rode in "on one of those lower roads that dead ends at an old [mine] adit." On the rocky hillside, he found Nordstrom in a cleft in the rock in the arms of a nurse "who had scrambled down the entire cliff." The boy was "conscious and breathing …. incredibly broken and he had bones sticking out. He had an open femur fracture … gravel in his mouth. I cleared his airway and he was conscious enough that I asked him his name and he could tell me."

The nurse asked Skoloda if he was okay with the boy because she wanted to check for other people. He said yes, stopped some bleeding with the minimal medical supplies he had and sat for "what seemed like forever." He knew there were other victims but since he had touched Nordstrom "he was my responsibility. So I was going to care for him until I was able to hand him off to a higher level of care." He saw his wife Nicole and Capt. Steve Lance climbing to him. Lance started an IV on the boy and sent Nicole Skoloda to search for more victims.

EMT Colette Miller, on her first day back from knee surgery, scrambled up rock ledges, her hands full with jump kit, splint bag and other equipment. Others helped her carry some of the stuff; she climbed past the crushed Jeep and a covered body. Someone asked if she wanted to check it out. She replied, "If you say he's dead, he's dead." She got to the rock crevice where the boy lay, broken "like a rag doll." Advanced Life Support provider Kim Mitchell also scrambled to check him. There was enough help. She heard about a second boy and knew she "needed to get to Cole." Sheriff's Deputy Shane Kavanaugh gave her a lift to the upper road.

Nicole Skoloda radioed that she had another victim. The radio traffic asked if the person was alive; she said no. Her husband asked if she was sure and she said, "positive, because she found half of one of the people," the legs of a woman. "It was awful," she said. "It was such a … surreal experience to come across part of somebody…." She searched uphill until she "came across Bill Whitt and he is holding the poor little boy's head together." She stayed with him.

Hart rigged a system to get Nordstrom down to the mine road. It was time to package him. Jeff Skoloda "was a pretty fresh Wilderness First Responder" and when Lance said to put the kid in the litter, he was "trying to deal with how, and I was going about it very gingerly." "Pick him up and put him in the litter," the captain repeated. "And I grabbed him by his chest, picked him up and everything just fell into place. I laid him down. I thought, 'Oh My God, this is what has to happen.'"

Miller and Lance sat on the tailgate of the deputy's truck as he backed down to Camp Bird Level 3, the stream crossing. She asked Nordstrom to look at her "and his eyes would drift that direction, and they would start to focus, and then you could see them unfocus again."

Sam Rushing sent Mike O'Donnell to search the cliffs. He "found the torso of the woman and no arm.... I walked right past her and I didn't see it. And then I turned down and looked, and it looked like an Annie doll. It just didn't look real. And I walked back to her.... 'Oh, for God's sakes. Holy shit.'" He told Rushing: "You do not need to send people up here to see this."

Dr. Dave Sherwood heard the page while helping his wife at the Ridgway Pharmacy. "I grabbed my stuff and just hopped in the truck and just hauled ass ... when there's kids involved ... everyone's adrenaline goes up.... I beat the crap out of my poor truck hauling up Imogene." He stopped to check Nordstrom, who "was relatively stable," then drove up to Cole Glucklich: "It was just bad ... a depressed skull fracture." He asked about the parents and was told they were dead. "All I remember was just looking across, down the slope and just seeing blood."

Jeff Skoloda rode up, they put the boy on a backboard and hauled him to the ambulance. Dr. Sherwood and Mitchell rode down with him to the stream crossing where the helicopter would land. His teeth were clenched and he could not be intubated. His breathing was very fast – fifty-eight breaths per minute, a result of his brain injury. Mitchell ventilated him.

◆ ◆ ◆

The first Flight for Life helicopter landed as the "sun was well on its way down," said Dr. Sherwood. It carried only one gurney, so one boy would have to wait. Triage was the senior medical person's responsibility: Dr. Sherwood "sent the younger kid because he just had extremity fractures.... He had the chance of actually surviving. I didn't think the older boy was going to." The pilot, concerned about the aircraft's ability to lift off from the very warm 11,300-foot elevation, asked Miller to ride the helicopter since she was lighter than the paramedic from Farmington, who was also needed to drug Glucklich and intubate him before he could be flown out. When they unloaded at St. Mary's, Nordstrom's eyes focused, he spoke in complete sentences and he knew he was in the hospital.

Dark shadows and shifting light from the setting sun made Mitchell wonder if another flight was possible, but then a second helicopter came. Bob Risch climbed to the Jeep lying on its side like a piece of crumpled tin foil, but couldn't see anything inside it and moved on. He helped bring Dan Glucklich's body down – he appeared to have been thrown out last. They loaded it into the covered bed of Risch's Ford Ranger and he drove down to US 550 and a mortuary vehicle.

Jeff Skoloda returned to the lower hillside and "searched the vehicle and there was a child seat in there.... Everything was so compact that you couldn't even stick your hand" in. He resumed searching with Hart and Rushing, horrified that they might have missed a baby, and "spread out over the entire slope and we worked our way down." Rushing found a child's crayon colored pages as he searched a marshy area near the crumpled vehicle. Later they learned that Jeanine Glucklich, forty-seven, had been a day care provider.

Dr. Sherwood "drove up to St. Mary's the next day to visit with the extended family. I just let them know what happened." Several years later he got a card from Cole Glucklich. "He had made an impressive recovery." At their next meeting, OMRT found a catered meal, courtesy of chefs Lisa and Jason Nelson, Meagan Rule and Chris Fairchild. Rene Leonardi brought flowers. Sheriff Mattivi thanked them for a great effort and gave Capt. Lance a key to the gate at the lower Camp Bird Road for future rescues.

Imogene was O'Donnell's last rescue: "It was probably the most dramatic one the team has ever been on ... kids, dead parents, guts, blood.... I got down to Junior, and he's like, "You all right?" and I said "Yeah.... I've got enough tissue retrieval in my life ... in Yosemite, I picked up a lot of tissue, not really bodies, but pieces."

The searches for survivors, the body recoveries and the horribly injured children remained with the rescuers and medics. Jenny Hart couldn't leave her eleven-month-old son but monitored *Imogene*.

"I'm hearing Bill Whitt on the radio ... master rescue guy, superhero of all rescues. Always cool, always organized, always collected, total professionalism," she said. "He's holding this little boy's brain together and his voice was cracking.... He's having a hard time even talking on the radio."

For Jeff Skoloda *Imogene* became a seminal moment: "What cemented it for me," he said, was that "this was important volunteer work.... I could keep doing this and that it served a good purpose. It was hard but at the same time it was totally worthwhile." Later, "the vindication was the first Christmas card that we ever got from Ian."

◆ ◆ ◆

Karen Gluklich Braun and her husband Bob brought her brother's daughters, Chloe, fifteen, and Corinne, eighteen, to their home in West Bloomfield, Michigan. They transported Cole Glucklich to Children's Hospital in Detroit for $9,000. "Their family suddenly expanded from three to six children, from no canines to two golden retrievers, and from three cats to six cats." She looked forward to "three more weddings and a bunch more grandkids."

CHAPTER TWENTY-TWO

Sullivan's Gully

IT WAS AN UNUSUALLY WARM February day as a 2000 Pontiac minivan headed north from Durango on US 550. Two Montrose High School freshmen – Tessa Sullivan, fourteen, and Stacia Holman, fifteen – crashed in the third row after a strenuous varsity girls' basketball game. Tessa Sullivan's mother Linda sat in the middle right seat with son Tyrel, seventeen, to her left, just behind his father Joe Sullivan, who was driving. Stacia's father Terry Holman had the front passenger seat. Both men were pumped. "The girls won an amazing game," Joe Sullivan said. "They were down sixteen points and they won in overtime."

The weather had deteriorated and the road was wet when they crested 11,018-foot Red Mountain Pass. Joe Sullivan glanced at the temperature gauge – thirty-two degrees. A thousand feet below in Ironton Park, the rain became slushy snow on the two-lane road. Familiar mountain ridges were invisible. North of the valley, the van slowly negotiated tight fifteen-mile an hour curves leading to the Uncompahgre Gorge. It was now twenty-eight degrees.

Curiously, a Chevy Suburban, which had followed them from Durango, disappeared when they emerged from East Riverside's snowshed. Joe turned the wheel right, into a dark curve where the sun never shines in winter, but the road felt different and he touched the brakes. They locked up and the van slid sideways, "just drifting. Nothing was happening."

Suddenly he spoke, "I'm sorry, we're going to go off."
Tyrel, behind him, was "looking right over that edge. He screamed."

◆ ◆ ◆

Skip and Terry Garcia looked for the white minivan as they drove out of the snowshed, momentarily puzzled when it wasn't there. Skip Garcia "glanced down and noticed tire tracks in the fresh, slushy snow headed over the embankment." He pulled the Suburban over and got out. Father Nat Fosage of St. Daniel's Church in Ouray, in his Roman collar headed south to say evening Mass in Silverton, also saw tracks. He parked his Ford Focus, got out and walked to the edge. A man ran down the road, yelling:

"Did you see a white van?"
"I said no. Skip hollered that the van was there and I ran down and it looked like it just got there."

The men stood in awed silence, staring over a berm into the white depths of the ravine. Hundreds of feet below, a van lay tilted on its side near the river. The priest noticed a dark blue jacket and a newspaper lying on a ledge just below the road. The van lay "on the driver's side and the passenger side was sticking up." There was no sign of activity and the windows were gone. "Oh my God, they're all dead," he said.

Tiny figures emerged from the van. Skip Garcia "yelled down the gully" that help was on the way and the figures waved at him. Father Fosage watched, amazed. "I thought it was all kids popping out the way they were excited and fine…. I was just unbelieving that anybody could be that lively and coming out and not wounded."

The men shouted, asking if anyone was hurt. "One girl yelled that her mom was caught." Terri Garcia pushed the On Star Emergency button in the Suburban. "On Star Emergency, this is Terri. We are going over Red Mountain Pass and a car just went off the highway right in front of us and we need emergency vehicles up here." The operator asked if anyone was injured. She said, "They're moving around. There's a big drop off so we can't tell." On Star's GPS data pinpointed the location and notified Montrose Dispatch. Ouray Deputy Keith Sanders answered their call and paged out OMRT and EMS.

◆ ◆ ◆

We "rolled and rolled and rolled and rolled and rolled," said Joe Sullivan. "You know, if you were going end over end that would have been the end…. It hugged the mountain. We hit it at the exact right speed." Eyes shut tight, he heard the van thud every time it rolled a full circle and the tires hit. About 300 feet down, it rested momentarily, long enough for everyone to hope it might have stopped.

"We are still alive. I better cover my face," Linda Sullivan thought as they began rolling again. "I think that is why my hand got cut." The van flipped again and again, finally at rest across the river, 340 feet below the road. A high school wrestling match played on the radio as six dazed humans realized they were still alive. None of the airbags, side or front, had deployed.

Stuck on the windowless van's downside, Joe Sullivan was buried in snow as high as his chest and thought they must have been in an avalanche. He smelled exhaust from the still running engine and searched for "the ignition key to shut it off," but it was "down below my knees somewhere." Terry Holman helped him find it, then pulled him out and got him across the river. The teenagers jumped out in a hurry and dug in their suitcases for warmer clothes. Joe Sullivan realized that his wife lay unconscious in the van. Tessa Sullivan saw that her mother's right hand was caught in the sliding door. Her dad watched as she spread apart the metal, pushed hard to free her mother's hand and helped her out of the van. Linda Sullivan remembered, "They all had me sit down and covered me up."

◆ ◆ ◆

When Mike Gibbs heard the page, he thought, "no way anyone is surviving MM 88, because I knew that was … a precipitous part of the gorge." He wondered how they knew there were six, but had no time to think about it. "I remember thinking we didn't have enough body bags…. Turns out, we didn't need any of them."

Thirty minutes later, OMRT, EMS, Extrication and law enforcement arrived. US 550 was shut down. Medic Steve Lance, who expected a "way ugly" scene, found only "one significant injury, enough to litter out, so that changed the whole nature of the call." Under Gibb's direction, members set up the rigging. Below them was a "soft chute and a snow bank at river's edge…." It was incredible to "find all survivors," he said. "If you're going to take a ride off 550, you probably couldn't have done much better than that. A lot of places along there, you might cream into some trees or go off a series of cliffs."

Sam Rushing was also "expecting the worst, and in my wildest imagination I would never have expected this scenario." In thirteen years with OMRT, he had never encountered anything like it.

The van went off in a relatively clean area, said Gibbs, "just kind of slid down through the snow until they hit the gully ... loaded with snow...." and landed in a huge white pile on the river's edge.

Joe Sullivan saw that Lt. Jeff Skoloda's 300-foot rope hung just part way down the gully. When he got to the end, the tall young rescuer simply walked down the slope. "The first thing he did was triage and he put an auxiliary on Linda ... on her finger," said Joe. "It was at ninety some percent." Four rescuers rappelled with a litter and supplies. The two women noticed the young girls had no gloves and gave them theirs. After Linda was packaged with a C-collar and spineboard, Clint Cook littered her to the road. Wearing harnesses and armed with jumars, the other survivors jugged upward on a rope with the rescuers' help. The snow lay so deep, Joe Sullivan said, that they "stepped in and sunk." His daughter's jumar kept slipping, but eventually she made it up, too.

Rushing watched "the other five ... jugging up the slope in a line. I just couldn't believe what my eyes are telling me ... five people are walking out of this canyon. They've got a heck of an angel watching over them."

Rescuers package Linda Sullivan for the long lift to the road.

Photo by Mike Gibbs

◆ ◆ ◆

Sullivan rode the ambulance with his wife, who worried about the treacherous road. "Don't go too fast," she said. "We just went off and we were going slow." EMT Kathy Elmont told the driver to slow down and stay behind the snowplow: "We did not want to become an accident ourselves." When three ambulances pulled up to the emergency ramp at MMR, the survivors were startled to see the basketball coach, team members, the Sullivans' parents and their friends. The team bus had been caught in the halted traffic on the road. Coach Laurie Brooks didn't know who had gone over. "I knew it was one of us, but I had a gut feeling they were okay."

The medics "thought Stacia had broken her nose, but decided it was from [an injury] earlier in the season during a basketball game," said Linda Sullivan, whose blackening eyes and scrapes on her nose were also checked. She was told she was "good to go," but the back of her head still felt wet. "You have not checked my head yet," she told them. She sat up and the pillow was bloody. When they got home at 11 p.m., she had five staples in her scalp. At midnight, an EMT came to their door with Joe Sullivan's CPAP breathing device. He was amazed: "It had blown out of the van and it was somewhere on the mountainside and they went back and looked for it."

◆ ◆ ◆

Three days after the "miracle on the mountain," the *Today* show set up in Montrose and interviewed the survivors, all wearing OMRT T-shirts and looking a bit weary. TV stations and newspapers across the country picked up the tale. General Motors set up an interview: Capt. Tim Eihausen emphasized the huge part that weather plays in a winter rescue in the San Juans. Even for victims who survive their injuries, the threat of hypothermia is largely dependent on "a quick response time."

Joe Sullivan decided to contest his ticket for improper mountain driving, so he and his wife drove to Ouray in April, gave Capt. Eihausen a $600 check and went to Ouray County Courthouse to argue the case before Judge David Westfall. State Patrol Officer Keith Oletski and Father Fosage showed up as well. Joe Sullivan pled not guilty. The patrolman insisted the road hadn't been that bad when he arrived around 5 p.m., that the driver must have had bald tires and that he was going too fast. He wanted an accounting.

Father Fosage disputed the patrolman's account of the road, noting that he had been there at three, just after the accident, and the road was black ice. It had been graveled by the time he returned that evening from Silverton. Joe Sullivan conceded nothing, said his tires, while not new, were good. He was familiar with the road, having driven it for eighteen years.

Judge Westfall instructed them to sort it out and went to his chambers. The four of them argued for forty-five minutes. Officer Oletski finally said,

> *"There is no points off and only a $15 fine."*
> *Joe Sullivan responded, "No."*

Linda Sullivan laughed.

> *Father Fosage said, "For God's sake, Joe, we have been here for forty-five minutes. I'll pay the damn $15 fine.*
> *Joe Sullivan smiled, "Okay, I'll pay it."*

The judge returned and the Irishman spoke.

> *"My chaplain advises me to accept this."*

Everyone laughed – except the patrolman.

CHAPTER TWENTY-THREE

"No Place To Run"

FLYING TO HIS SECOND HOME in Elbert, Colorado, was routine for Robert R. Ford, fifty-nine, of Chino, California. He took off from Cable Airport on Wednesday, May 11, 2005, with three family members, landed his single-engine Cessna 210 in Page, Arizona, fueled and headed for Colorado. He did this a couple of times a month in a plane with "every instrument in the world…. It was in perfect condition," said his brother-in-law Terry LaCuran.

◆ ◆ ◆

At Ouray's 8,000-foot elevation, wind gusts exceeded forty MPH. Moist lenticular clouds continuously formed and dissipated over the surrounding high summits, their deceptive saucer shapes concealing fierce rotor winds aloft in the San Juans. It was not a day for mountain flying.

◆ ◆ ◆

On May 12, relatives reported the plane overdue to the Federal Aviation Administration (FAA). Telluride Airport's (KTEX) radar return for 12:48 p.m. Wednesday showed the Cessna at 9,078 feet, nine miles southwest of Whitehouse Mountain. The FAA Incident Report a year later referenced several radar returns: The Cessna experienced extreme turbulence at 12:56, its altitude abruptly veering from 17,500 to 19,200 feet, its ground speed zooming from 124 to 314 knots. An AIRMET (Airman's Meteorological Information) for occasional moderate turbulence below 18,000 feet was in effect. Ford neither obtained a weather briefing nor filed a flight plan.

The FAA report said the right wing was .8 miles west of Corbett Peak at 11,175 feet, the left wing .5 miles west at 11,500 feet. The debris path led to the propeller at 12,800 feet, above the fuselage, engine, horizontal stabilizer and elevator. There was no evidence of fatigue or preexisting fracture in the wings. The pilot lost control in adverse conditions, which exceeded the design stress limits of the Cessna and led to structural failure. Inadequate preflight and in-flight planning and decision-making, severe turbulence, and the mountain wave factored into the crash.

◆ ◆ ◆

Wednesday afternoon two people walked into Sheriff Dominic Mattivi's office: "We don't know what happened, whether to report this or not, but we're working up in Panoramic Heights, we heard this boom." On Friday CAP pilot Mark Young called the Sheriff: "I think you might have had a plane crash in your jurisdiction." The Cessna's Emergency Locator Transmitter (ELT) signal alerted CAP. Around 1 p.m. Young flew over the northwestern San Juans, finding "a debris trail about a half-mile wide and a mile-and-a-half long indicating the airplane broke up in flight." The Sheriff met him that night. "There's debris scattered between 10,000 and 12,800 feet." A tracking device on Patricia Ford's cell phone located the plane on the Corbett Peak spur of Whitehouse Mountain, but getting to the remote site posed serious logistical problems. Recent spring storms had piled snow twenty feet deep. Though it was but four miles west of Ouray, the site was accessible only by aircraft. Young reported: "Jagged, steep cliffs and deep snow make traversing the mountain nearly impossible." A National Guard Chinook flew in, saw the debris and confirmed there were no survivors.

Bodies were spotted from the air. A Sheriff's deputy looked at Corbett Peak from Panoramic Heights north of town and saw "a waterfall that just kept flowing." Lt. Jeff Skoloda told him that what he had seen were huge snow avalanches that flowed down the mountain on warm days. Monday afternoon, after both CAP and the National Guard said they couldn't help because there were no survivors, Sheriff Mattivi, Capt. Tim Eihausen and Lt. Sloloda met "to weigh the dangers of lowering men from a helicopter onto avalanche-prone slopes...." The next day, conditions prevented safe access, though the Sheriff hoped to deploy searchers that week.

On Wednesday, the captain and lieutenant flew with pilot Devin Felix of Olathe Spray Service, to "the crash site in the predawn hours, before the steep slopes have time to become warmer and less stable," said Sheriff's spokeswoman Penni Berry. On the mountain, however, the snow was still too unstable for the helicopter to land. "Every time (the copter) set down," the Sheriff reported, "it would start sliding down the mountain." The chopper's landing skids had no traction in the bulletproof snow, said Skoloda. Hiking to the wreckage was impossible in such rugged terrain – technical climbing was required. "It would have been a nightmare to have to go in there on foot," said Bill Whitt. OMRT hoped to get a larger helicopter to lower rescuers to the site.

When the weather improved, Felix picked up Skoloda at the Jossi ranch north of Ouray, in a Bell B2 helicopter equipped with a jet turbine. At first light, 5:30 a.m., May 19, Felix dropped Skoloda on a big flat spot at 12,600 feet on the north ridge of Whitehouse Mountain. With crampons and ice axes, he climbed the 13,072-foot summit of Corbett Peak and descended 2,000 feet along the snow-filled eastern couloir, the icy source of Corbett Creek. Above a prominent cliff band, he dug a trench so that Felix could make a toe-in landing.

"By the time he was set down," Skoloda said, "there was about a foot between his rotor" and the slope. There was a boulder in front of the trench for stability and for landings. "We would let him set down and then he would ... wiggle the helicopter around and make sure it was stable ... give us the sign and we would run over and get in." There was no place to go if something went wrong. Massive rock walls framed the bottom of that tight couloir and the sketchy LZ. Eight days after the crash, however, they could land and search for bodies: Whitt said they found the pilot and his wife still in the fuselage, strapped in their seats, at the base of a frozen waterfall near the top of Corbett. The Cessna's wings sprawled west of the peak, the propeller stuck out near the top. The helicopter long-lined the bodies out.

The bereaved relatives didn't really understand how Ouray's mountainous terrain and extended winter season prevented the recovery of their loved ones. Eihausen said:

> "We'd have to have regular meetings with the family, and [they] didn't understand avalanche terrain."
> 'It's right there. Why can't you find them?'
> "We'd have to sit them down and tell them what we're doing and how we're dealing with the avalanche hazard. Because they didn't even know what an avalanche was."

Corbett Peak was visible from Whispering Pines Bridge and Panoramic Heights north of town. Terry LaCuran, Patricia Ford's brother, spent thirty-eight days in Ouray and brother John LaCuran, visited twice. It took multiple meetings for them to realize that it wasn't like searching a parking lot. Rescuers were dropped off at a precarious LZ to search the tight couloir with avalanche probes. Erin Eddy said he and Mel Rajkowski went up with Whitt to the huge debris field, which stretched across and down a hidden south-facing couloir. They put what debris they found in body bags, sliding them down the slope to the helicopter. Time on the mountain was limited by the rapidly ascending May sun and every day new avalanches flowed. The rescuers "started at first light," said Skoloda, "and by noon stuff was moving again."

◆ ◆ ◆

Sheriff Mattivi got a call from a Senator who represented the Ford family's district, wondering why there wasn't more being done to find the family.

In the couloir: Brad McMillon and Capt. Tim Eihausen search the rough, avalanched slope for more bodies. A piece of the plane lies in the foreground.
Photo by Jeff Skoloda

"Can I send you some pictures of the area?"
"Please do."

The Sheriff emailed the pictures and the Senator called back.

"I am so sorry. I didn't realize that the area's so rugged."

Skoloda also got a call – from a Colorado Senator.

"This family wants me to check to see what you guys are doing."
"Well sir, you send us a helicopter, we'll get it done."

Shortly thereafter, a Lama with an absolute altitude record of 40,814 feet flew in from Fort Collins. One day's search used both helicopters, though rescuers were surprised when the Lama showed up. The family's attitudes also underwent a shift when Eihausen found Patricia Ford's purse. They were super appreciative when "I brought a purse down and gave it to the kids."

For a week they searched for bodies, but finally realized they were spending "all of our time ferrying people in and out and we weren't getting anything done," said Skoloda. "We decided we needed to just wait." The family hired the Olathe helicopter and on one flight spotted five-year-old Matthew Ford's body, which had melted out near the toe of the avalanche. On May 29, Skoloda retrieved the body. He waited as it was long-lined out, studying the walls surrounding the LZ. "There was no place to run if something went wrong."

◆ ◆ ◆

The first two weeks of June were mostly wet and cold, but by mid-month the weather stabilized enough to search for the fourth victim, Richard Ford, 36, son of Robert and Patricia and father of Matthew. Whitt contacted Sue Purvis, who had an avalanche / cadaver dog, Tasha. The K-9 team arrived from Crested Butte Saturday night, June 18, and Whitt put them up at the Victorian Inn. The Uncompahgre River roared outside her room, so Purvis kept the black lab in, safely away from high water. Ten-year-old Tasha had already located a drowning victim in a water search that day and they were both tired. Purvis had delayed a trip to the Dominican Republic for her work as a geologist: "I had to decide, 'Do I go to my job or do I try to help somebody out?'" she said. "In my heart I knew it was the right thing to do.... I'm so glad I did."

At dawn on Father's Day, June 19, Whitt and the K-9 team met Lt. and Nicole Skoloda at Jossi's ranch. The OMRT people flew in first. Nicole Skoloda had never ridden in a chopper and felt extremely stressed. Lt. Skoloda jumped out, chopped out the LZ and the helicopter toed-in on the slope. The other two jumped out. Felix went back for the K-9 team. In the small yellow chopper, Tasha's bum pressed against his right hip, her barrel chest rested on Purvis's lap, furry elbows dug into her thigh. Purvis saw "her webbed feet, spread wide from years of digging in avalanche debris, dangle off my leg and out the helicopter's open doorway." Wearing climbing gear and helmet, she was still a bit unnerved by the terrain, saw volcanic rocks broken into huge spires and bends, every crevice filled with snow. "If the helicopter shifts, we're dead," she thought. At first she couldn't see Whitt, then realized he was digging out a platform for one skid. It was 7 a.m. and rocks were already moving under the summer sun.

Sheriff Mattivi said that if Richard Ford "was up there, he would've moved with the movement of the snow," but continuous avalanches over the last month refreshed the snow in the couloir even as the warm sun created a watery gap between the rock and the snow. Tasha worked her way up the slope, whining as scent came to her from the water. Purvis also caught the smell of decomposition whenever she approached the foot-wide gap. Tasha circled a big rock, and Purvis radioed Whitt, asking if a victim had been found there. He said yes.

The snow had melted dramatically over the past three weeks and plane parts were strewn over the slope. Whitt told Purvis the five to ten foot tall rocks in the couloir had just emerged. As she and Tasha moved upward, a toothbrush, children's books, an oxygen cylinder and tubing appeared: "Doors, parts of the seats … it was all strewn along this half mile path."

Tasha moved north and disappeared. Purvis followed and was relieved to find her sitting in a cave-like area near the top. They had climbed for an hour and she sat to rest. The others came up and rested as well, having a bite to eat. Purvis, who had taught Tasha to sit as her cadaver find signal, suddenly realized that the dog sat there like a good little soldier. "Where is he?" she said. She walked around the quiet, still animal, which neither barked nor dug. Purvis felt overwhelmed with the debris, shoes, socks, pants: "I just couldn't sort anything out." She probed around Tasha in bigger and bigger circles, at one point overwhelmed by the smell of human decomposition emanating from a rock. Tasha moved to her, brought her back, and sat "in the exact same spot." A foot away lay a white sock, almost invisible against the glare of the snow. Purvis walked over and realized it covered a foot; a bit of blue jean and part of a calf were visible.

"I just got on my hands and knees." She started crying: "Tasha, you did it!"

CHAPTER TWENTY-FOUR

2007-2010
"Our Voices of Hope"

ON MARCH 15, 2007, at Ouray's Western Hotel, five captains shared their OMRT years. For Lt. Jeff Skoloda, thirty-four, it had been a "life-changing experience." He had seen sixteen body recoveries in his first six years and "they stick with you." "The only good thing about a recovery is the pressure is off," said Otto Scheidegger, captain from 1987-88. Bill MacTiernan spoke of danger and sadness: "It's really hard to put someone in a bag and watch them fly away." For Randy Gerke, "just being part of this organization has been an important part of my life." Bill Whitt said that in his first year on the team with MacTiernan, he asked, "'Are we ever going to do anything other than body recoveries?'"... that's what we dealt with ninety-nine percent of the time. It's grim, but it gives the families closure, so we do it." Karen Risch's power point featured thirty-three years of rescues. Two non-profits, OMRT and the Ouray County Historical Society (OCHS), split the proceeds – $7,140.

◆ ◆ ◆

That year, none of the eleven deployments involved fatalities. In April OMRT assisted a twenty-four-year-old Ohio woman suffering from hypoglycemia as she descended Old Twin Peaks Trail. In June they extricated an injured man from a Garfield County wilderness. From July to September they responded to ATV rollovers on Imogene Pass. August 24 brought the first of three calls in five days: A fifty-eight-year-old woman hiking Weehawken Trail slipped two miles up and "tumbled about ten feet down a steep embankment." A fallen log above another drop off halted her descent. Hobbled by an ankle injury, she got to the trail and crawled to where she had

A January 13, 2007, rescue involved a twenty-four-year-old belayer, hit with an ice chunk packing "enough force to break her helmet, briefly knock her unconscious, chip three teeth and create a cut that required 15 stitches to close," paramedic Norm Rooker told the Plaindealer. *Rescuers lever the litter up the Ice Park stairs. The climbers' catwalk is at top right.*

©2007 Randy Cassingham / ThisIsTrue.com, used with permission.

cell service. The team immobilized her ankle and wheeled her out. Two days later, a call came for a dehydrated hiker on Coxcomb Peak. Another hiker descended and walked out four miles for help. Four rescuers on motorcycles responded, hiked in and brought him out. A helicopter flew him to Ridgway Fairgrounds. Two liters of IV fluid revived him.

Another wilderness call August 28 was for a sixty-year-old Houston man hiking the seventeen-mile Horsethief / Bridge of Heaven / Bear Creek Loop. He had food and water and planned to come out Monday evening. His wife waited all night at Bear Creek trailhead before alerting the Sheriff. The 7 a.m. call and an hour's planning brought a multi-pronged search. Two members rode motorcycles to Engineer Pass and hiked across American Flats toward Bear Creek, two others hurried up Horsethief. As weather deteriorated, a helicopter was called and a spotter saw the man at 10:15; he was airlifted out ten minutes later. OMRT got out much later.

◆ ◆ ◆

In January 2008 the Barn fund totaled $139,000 ($55,000 from grants); but to finish the 2,700 square foot structure, they needed another $107,000. Garry Schalla applied for over forty grants. "Community support for the project has been overwhelming," he said, with "476 donations ... 293 (62 percent) coming from within Ouray County." In kind donations of labor, services and materials from members, contractors and businesses were valued at $96,000. By November OMRT had $105,000, enough to fulfill requirements for a challenge grant of $20,000 from the Gates Family Foundation in Denver. Schalla obtained grants from the Ergen Family Foundation ($35,000), El Pomar ($15,000) and Boettcher ($10,000). He looked back on the fundraising "with great pride ... what a great legacy for the team and for the community ... it's always been very special...." He had the right "skill set ... whenever I go by it, I always smile."

It took five years, longer than anticipated, and cost more than expected, but on November 15, 2008, a jubilant team hosted an open house in the new Barn. Situated between the CR 361 Bridge and Box Canyon Bridge, on the east bank of the Uncompahgre Gorge, the two-story building echoed Ouray's mining heritage. Clad in metal siding, it had board and batten upper walls and a tin roof. Metal stairs on the south led upward from a brick wall etched with hundreds of donors' names. On the lower floor, three twelve-foot high

OMRT's new barn. Sketch by Don Carlton, September 1, 2006.
Courtesy *Ouray County Plaindealer*

vehicle bays sat on a concrete slab behind large garage doors whose extra height accommodated rescue vehicles. The upper level had meeting space, kitchen and bath. Best of all, it allowed for quicker response times to the Ice Park, Mt. Sneffels and Red Mountain Pass. *Doonesbury Ink's* Don Carlton sent regards: "Eat an hors d'ouevre for me tomorrow. Wish I could be there.... My congratulations to the team and its dedication and hard work.... Things do get done in Ouray by Ourayians...."

The 12th annual Ouray Ice Festival, January 10-14, 2008, was a huge success, with seventy-two clinics, 500 participants and 120 children in a Kids' Climbing College. The Ice Park raised $7,500 for a children's and beginners' climbing area. Stories about the park and festival appeared nationally; executive director Erin Eddy gave press passes to "30 different media outlets throughout the country, including a video production company for Warren Miller." A *New York Times* article called it "A perfect microclimate for making ice." Many newspapers from around the country featured the Park before it closed March 26. "We had an incredible year," said Eddy, "particularly with the media attention." A long season encouraged plans for a new six-climb area with ninety feet of "dead vertical" on the east wall of the gorge near the penstock, easily accessible from US 550. This "Got Stump Wall" was the brainchild of Mike Gibbs and took its name from ice climber Malcolm Daly who lost a foot to frostbite in Alaska but continued to climb hard routes. Daly auctioneered an Ice Festival fundraiser dressed in a T-shirt with the logo *"Got Stump?"* given to him by Chris Folsom, who was short a finger. For five years the shirt was auctioned; winners paid a few hundred dollars to $7,500 and the money went to construct the kids' climbing area and a memorial kiosk.

On May 18, in a memorable multi-agency training, a school bus was levered off the overlook above Ouray, turned over and stabilized on the slope below US 550. Twenty volunteers wearing moulage – makeup to recreate various blunt force traumas – with scripts for their assigned roles, were inserted into the bus along with two mannequins. Earlier that day OMRT's Colette Miller applied the "fake, yet realistic-looking, wounds and injuries" so that first responders who might see such injuries once or twice in their careers, "know how to treat their patient when the time comes." The victims were "triaged by severity of injury, provided with basic first aid, packaged and moved up the roadside via several rope systems."

A temporary morgue was established. Victims were warned ahead of time that they would hear loud noises as the rescue squad cut into the bus. Such a nightmare scenario had long worried first responders since local schools, several tour lines and Greyhound buses routinely traverse Red Mountain Pass. The donated bus, obtained by Maggie Graff, transportation supervisor for Ridgway School District, was drained of all fluids by the Road & Bridge Department "to minimize any environmental impact." Chief Paramedic Norm Rooker organized the exercise, utilizing EMS, OMRT, Squad 11 (Extrication), the Police and Fire Departments, the Sheriff's Department and the Montrose Fire Protection District.

◆ ◆ ◆

Sixteen callouts from March through October included four stand-downs for vehicle rollovers, a missing Hardrock Hundred runner and two Ice Park accidents March 5 and 6. In May, at the Sheriff's request, some members climbed cliffs above Camp Bird Road to remove faulty fencing and overhanging rock. Two exhausted hikers were assisted on Silvershield Trail and a young man was rescued after he fell from the Pool Wall in July. For several days in August, Sam Rushing and Rob Holmes tracked an Alzheimer's patient in San Juan and La Plata Counties. The man turned up in Rico "a little dazed and confused," said Rushing. Hikers found him and realized something wasn't right. A flash flood on Corbett Creek in early August drew ten rescuers to help a mother and two children stranded on Dallas Trail by Corbett Creek's high brown water.

◆ ◆ ◆

March 30 began as a beautiful Spring Break Sunday. Shaddow Huston, eleven, and two slightly older friends began hiking around noon on Old Twin Peaks Trail, heading up the cliffs above it after the first big bend. They saw a few remnants of winter snow, but near the top "It just started dumping and then our tracks got covered up," said Huston. "We lost where we were going ... just kind of tried to go straight down." They halted above the American flag on the cliff. They weren't dressed for the weather; Huston's head was shaved, he wore a sweatshirt and tennis shoes. They yelled for help.

One buddy had a phone and called 911. "When dispatch called us, we were then able to call him," said Sheriff Mattivi, and "locate him through the binoculars." Ten rescuers came. At dusk, six "ascended through steep rock and mildly technical terrain made more difficult by snowfall and wet rock," said Capt. Skoloda. They fixed ropes as they went up a ravine so that later they could short rope the boys down. When they got to them, Lt. Eihausen spoke to Huston, whom he knew.

> *Hey, what's up?*
> *Oh, nothing.*
> *Oh, nothing?*

Huston asked if he had a spare pair of socks. He didn't. Gibbs made webbing harnesses for the boys so they could be tied into the rope and lowered down the cliff. In the mud and snow those slick rocks made for an interesting descent, said Skoloda. "That face is pretty prone to rockfall.... A few rocks came zinging down while we were extricating the kids." Huston got home at 12:20. For Eihausen, that one-of-a-kind rescue "was a cool one."

A memorable one for Lance, an active rescuer since 1970, involved kids partying on a dark May night near Portland Gorge. A cop appeared and a "kid decided to dive into the bushes and didn't realize that there is a cliff there. Open fracture, tib-fib, pretty ugly. It was just dumb luck that he didn't drown because there was water running in the bottom." A black rope tied to a tree provided a way down for Lance, Folsom and Skoloda. They couldn't see a thing descending the narrow canyon, but managed to find the kid. They splinted his legs, started an IV and packaged him to be "lifted out of there before he freezes to death.... The thing that stuck in my mind about it," said Lance, "was the kind of damage in the awkward place, and the fact that it was dark." That rescue was just "smooth around the machine. Everybody was doing their thing."

◆ ◆ ◆

On Labor Day weekend, Dr. Doug and Susan Martel of Littleton, Colorado, left their BMW at Dexter Creek trailhead Sunday morning, August 31, walked a mile up the road to Horsethief Trail and hiked southeast from the Wedge Mine over the Bridge of Heaven. At the junction with Difficulty, they turned north toward Dexter, intending to finish their 14.5-mile wilderness loop that evening. Somewhere they missed the main trail. Three to four hours later, they looked across a rockslide to a large pointed peak. Behind them was a sheer rock wall. It was obvious they were no longer on the trail, so they built a fire and took shelter under a tree.

They were in a high spot with cell service to Montrose Dispatch. OMRT called back. Gibbs asked the doctor if he had a compass and knew how to use it. He did, knew the pointed peak was Wetterhorn, and gave him the data point. When asked for another data point, he wasn't sure what peaks he was seeing. They had survival gear and could camp out. "We set up a system where we would call...." said Jenny Hart. "'Turn off your phone, turn off your battery. We're going to call you ... in one hour turn your phone back on so that we can tell you what we're doing.' The plan was, they're going to sit there because we're not going out at night to search."

"They were the perfect rescue subjects," said Mike MacLeod. "They knew they were in trouble but they had packs, they had rain gear, they had a way to start a fire, they had food, they had water." OMRT planned to search the Baldy system and the wilderness; Hart told the couple that " at first light we would be on the road and we'd be looking for them." For the Martels it was "a helpless and fearful time," but after they spoke with her, they felt a "sense of relief.... She instructed us on what we needed to do and, best of all, she told us that search teams would be on the trails before sunrise."

Many members responded and searched Baldy Ridge, Shortcut, Left Fork, Cutler and Dexter trails. Gibbs and MacLeod took Dexter, with the "highest probability of detection," said Gibbs. "We were both pretty fit hikers, we were practically running up that trail." He triangulated the one point he had and thought the hikers were in the wilderness east of Difficulty. It was still dark when they "headed up the trail," at 5 a.m., said MacLeod. "We got up there pretty quick."

Backcountry communication, a longstanding problem because of the 12-13,000-foot high terrain separating the wilderness from the Uncompahgre Valley, was solved with this rescue. "I think it was just sort of necessity being the mother of all inventions," said Gibbs, "we just realized that we needed a repeater ... so where could we get line of sight ... if you just go to Park Estates you're high enough." Miller volunteered her big medical truck equipped with a handheld VHF (very high frequency) and other radio gear. She parked at the gate to Park Estates subdivision high to the west of the valley, listening to the eastern wilderness where her teammates searched. "Of course, I'm nowhere near the scene," she said. "I don't know what happened, didn't see it." Her work successfully linked the valley and the wilderness.

Gibbs said they "were cruising along. I see this game trail going off to the left towards Cow Creek." He told MacLeod: "I bet you dimes to dollars that they were coming along this way and they just forked off that way." MacLeod continued south on Difficulty. Gibbs followed the game trail. Miller picked him up: "We have a good chance of detecting them ... but you are not going to have me on the radio for fifteen minutes. I need to go out and explore this." Ten minutes later he saw smoke: "I don't bother going to them because they are still a ways down.... I get Mike...."I've got them." When they got there, the Martels were "cliffed out but they were still in tree line and they had a little bivy with a fire ... a nice little view of Wetterhorn Peak and a nice view of Cow Creek.... They were tired. It was a slow walk out."

Difficulty is only a link to other wilderness trailheads so it sees much less traffic than other trails. "It was easy to lose it," said MacLeod, "even if you knew where you were going." On the four-hour trip out, they shared food and water, talked about the scenery and kept up the hikers' spirits. Three days later, the Martels sent "a heartfelt thanks to all of you with special thanks to Jenny Hart and Colette Miller for being our voices of hope, to Mike Gibbs and Mike MacLeod for using their exceptional skills and knowledge of the Uncompahgre Wilderness ... and to Sam Rushing for coordinating this extraordinary effort."

◆ ◆ ◆

Matt Hepp, born the year OMRT was founded, was voted in two years before his election as captain in 2009. He grabbed the bull by the horns: "It wasn't bad but it definitely felt like I had to learn a lot quick.... There was plenty of help and experience ... building the Barn had totally absorbed the team for so long that I remember saying, 'Now we can get back from being a construction team to a rescue team.'"

He got his wish: 2009 had eleven callouts from January to December, with a memorable one January 6. Four vehicles with eight members and friends left Ouray at 6 a.m. for powder cat skiing at Purgatory (Durango Mountain Resort), three high passes away. Before they got over Red Mountain, those in the lead truck saw tracks disappearing into the canyon 400 feet below. "A closer look down into the canyon revealed the dim glow of headlights," wrote photographer Jack Brauer. "Jeff (Skoloda) was out of the truck and into his harness and headlamp in minutes, rappelling off a truck hitch to a 50-foot cliff. He yelled to the driver who responded that he was okay." They reported the accident and rescue trucks, an ambulance and firemen soon appeared and set up floodlights. Deep snow had cushioned the truck's descent and the driver wore his seat belt as he drove his semi up the pass, wrote Brauer:

(A) semi-truck came around an inside corner a little too wide. The outside driver gave him a bit too much room, and once the wheels fell off into the soft snow on the edge, it was too late and the truck slid ... into the chasm below ... the semi flipped around and hit trailer first, which was probably an enormous stroke of good luck which may have saved the driver's life ... the truck was completely crumpled and the engine torn out.

Training Officer Kevin Koprek descended to the patient:

was surprised to see the driver of the truck standing and in good health. This is particularly remarkable considering the path taken by the truck.... The Sullivan mini-van experienced a 'gentle slide' down a snow filled gully. This truck entered from slightly up the road (closer to RMP) sending it over ... a seventy-foot cliff. The truck was a complete mess ... only the driver compartment being relatively intact. I was struck by the driver's desire to "walk" back to the road if we could just help him. Due to the mechanism of the event and deep snow conditions, we opted to give him a ride.

Once the driver, who had chest, neck and shoulder injuries, was out of the canyon, the party set out again for the day's skiing. Brauer was impressed: "It was pretty amazing to me how many people were up there so fast to help out. I'm not sure if they all sleep in their clothes or what."

◆ ◆ ◆

On a brilliant late June day, thirty-five-year-old Mike Reddy and longtime climbing partner Arne Bomblies, on their annual Colorado climbing trip from Connecticut, ascended Mt. Sneffels' north snowfield to the Snake Couloir. They planned this as a warm-up for a more challenging climb of Cross Couloir on Mount of the Holy Cross. "The Snake appeared totally within our grasp," Reddy said, "a relatively easy ascent up compacted snow in crampons and ice axes, conditions for which we had trained and felt fully competent." As they approached the narrowest section at 12,500 feet, Bomblies rested on a snow bench. Reddy noticed:

> an ominous sign – water freely running under the snow just next to where I was planning to step and pivot in order to grab a seat beside my resting partner. I remember thinking.... I should plant my next footstep just to the left of the patch of unconsolidated snow. I also clearly remember Arne pointing out the loose snow and mentioning to avoid it ... my crampon grabbed what appeared to be solid foothold and then immediately slipped out from under me as my weight transferred to my right foot. I desperately attempted to self-arrest ... my crampons caught and I was flipped upright and thrown on my back.

He lost control, slid 150 feet, hit a boulder, lost consciousness and came to yelping from excruciating pain radiating from his back. He had a "burst" fracture of the lumbar spine. Bomblies and two other climbers, one a doctor, called for help at 9:30. A hasty team of Skoloda and Clint Cook hurried to Yankee Boy, climbed Dyke Col between Kismet and Cirque and descended Sneffels' north face.

Hepp drove from Montrose "way too fast ... passing people when I shouldn't have and somebody even called to complain." Then, "Scottie [Ridgway Marshall David Scott] ... pulled me over." Hepp said there was a climber with a broken back on Sneffels. The Marshall replied, "Don't make a bad situation worse," and let him go. Hepp and Mike Bryson rode dirt bikes to the first creek on Dallas Trail, then ran. They reached Reddy just before Skoloda and Cook. We "built an anchor," said Cook. "The litter came up from Blaine." Then they did "a series of lowers off of snow anchors down to where it was less steep and we could drag / carry the litter."

Ice and rock blitzed the responders as they trenched snow to stabilize Reddy. They lowered him "maybe 500 feet, in the vac-mattress," said Hepp, got him "out of that shooting gallery." MacLeod and Mark Miller arrived as the hasty teams prepared the first lower, setting up anchors for the next pitch. Kim Mitchell hiked up with pain medication. When the litter reached the end of the snowfield, they wheeled the patient to a medevac helicopter. It was an "all hands on deck call," said MacLeod. "We needed everybody."

Rescuers haul Mike Reddy to a helicopter, waiting across East Dallas Creek in Blaine Basin.

Photo by David Mullings
Courtesy *Ouray County Plaindealer*

Jenny Hart and Koprek arrived at sunset with three Panny's pizzas, courtesy of Sheriff Mattivi. For three miles they balanced large flat boxes, sometimes on their heads, said Hart, arriving just as Reddy was loaded into the chopper. "It was such a huge team effort to pull it off," said MacLeod. "An immensely physical effort.... It required every skill in our toolbox."

Reddy had a spinal cord injury as well as "a fractured right ankle and a diagnosis that he would never climb again." During the surgeries and recovery from the injury, which initially paralyzed his left leg, he wrote: "Extreme pain, mixed with the relief of having survived a near-fatal mountaineering accident," made him realize "that my life was forever changed." By March 2011, however, he was walking again and had climbed ice in New Hampshire. He completed doctoral studies in epidemiology and public health at Yale and travels as a Program Officer for Malaria (Vector Control) at the Bill and Melinda Gates Foundation.

◆ ◆ ◆

On December 16, opening day at the Ice Park, seventy-two-year-old Charlie Winger fell ten feet and hit a ledge on the 'Shithouse Wall.' An ice screw he placed two moves before arrested the fall: "The sun had softened the ice," he said. "I went to pull up and both tools just sheared out and I just went flying backwards." Belayer Randy Murphy lowered him to the gorge.

A page went out just after 10. EMT Tricia Eischied, who knew Winger as a customer at Ouray Mountain Sports, reached him first. Descending via a walk-down, she "found Charlie lying on the ground." He was "alert, aware and denied any pain ... wanted to walk out on his own. Mike [MacLeod] convinced him that we needed the practice and he agreed." They "did very little from a medical perspective, just got him packaged in the litter ... and took vitals."

Koprek, the litter attendant, said he and Winger "had the greatest conversation on the trip up ... future climbing plans, objectives, and the current state of the Ouray Ice Park. He was thrilled to be sharing the climbing life with others. Charlie is one of the most remarkable human beings I've ever met."

The emergency room doctor recognized him immediately.

> *"Oh, I know you. I worked on you last year."*
> *I said, "Ribs or face?"*
> *"I think it was face."*

During multiple scans to see what he had broken this time, Charlie bantered with the docs. Finally he said:

> *"Guys, I'm hurting.... I need medical marijuana."*
> *"We don't do that here."*

He was released from the hospital with two broken lumbar vertebrae, several broken ribs and a big brace; his climbing buddies got him out of the car, but then there were stairs in his house. One big guy picked up the always featherweight Charlie (120 lbs. in good times). "He's not heavy, he's my brother," he said and carried him upstairs. Two days later, Charlie had his wife Diane tape his ice axes to his walker. He correctly predicted, "I will be ice climbing when I'm eighty. I think I might be the oldest guy in the Ice Park.... Today, I put in more ice screws."

◆ ◆ ◆

A record twenty-two rescues, including four fatalities, two avalanche callouts, eight vehicle wrecks and seven falls, consumed January through November 2010. January 2 had two callouts, the first for a snowmobiler with a broken femur on Owl Creek and a second for a fall victim at Ridgway State Park. Twenty members of the climbing community volunteered as haul monkeys on February 5 when "a climber was accidentally dropped on the 'Pic of the Vic' climb just upriver of the bridge," said Hepp. Fifteen members retrieved the man, "conscious and stable throughout." He fell "approximately forty to fifty feet, landing on ice at the bottom."

They had to wait a while for proper gear, a vacuum mattress and blankets, since Rescue 11 wouldn't start. IC Whitt decided to raise the climber with a vertical rope system, a Georgia Haul, since many volunteers were available. They raised him between two lead only climbs – 'Pic of the Vic' and 'Tangled up in Blue,' with MacLeod tending the litter. Hepp said the accident may have been caused by a gear malfunction since the man was roped in and climbing with a partner. It also took place in full view of the upper bridge on CR 361: "It was a great spot to take photos," said the captain. Rushing made a *You Tube* video from photos taken by Lora Slawitschka, a member of the Ice Park Board.

Major avalanches ran in February on the north side of the Sneffels Range and again in March on the northeast side of Baldy Peak, generating prolonged rescues. June began with a call for a motorcycle over the edge at the Drinking Cup curve on CR 361. The young patient, with suspected shoulder and back injuries, was raised using Rescue 12. Another call for a forty-three-year-old male with a broken leg or hip sent OMRT up Engineer Pass to Poughkeepsie Gulch.

Five July callouts included three in the first five days. On July 1, a call for a lost child possibly in the river, ended with relief when the six-year-old was found unharmed. In a second "All's well that ends well" callout July 4, for a family trapped above a waterfall in Senator Gulch, rescuers set up a tree anchor to lower a father and his kids back to the road. At 2:59 that night, the sheriff received a third call for a fall victim at the Drinking Cup, just up the road from the afternoon rescue. When Lt. Gibbs and Whitt got there, one of the young people told them Pete Morss was dead. "Bill got very upset when he heard that because he knew Pete well and he knew Barb [Pete's mother] particularly well." Gibbs told him, "Look, I'm going to be in charge of this rescue here and you need to take a back seat." Whitt was fine with that: "He was very distracted by knowing that he was probably going to have to be the person to inform Barb."

Friends discovered twenty-year-old James Peter (Pete) Morss's body 100 feet below the road. The *Plaindealer* reported that he "was celebrating the Fourth of July into the night with a group lighting fireworks.... Morss may have stepped back and off the cliff after an accidental detonation of a firework." Gibbs said they were told the kids were shooting big fireworks, "operating right near the edge of the cliff." Then, "one of the fireworks either prematurely discharged or it tipped over ... everyone wanted to get away from it and when Pete moved to get away from it, he moved the wrong direction, basically went off the cliff."

"One of the things that we did right off the bat," Gibbs said, "was say this is a body recovery, we need to be respectful but we are in no rush. It's dark.... It's a local kid. We're all going to be distracted by that dynamic and we should really concentrate on doing our jobs well." Eihausen said they rappelled downstream and then walked up to the accident site. A memorial service the next Sunday, July 11, filled the Hot Springs Park. Morss's mother, Barb Sever, had been secretary and rescuer on the team in 1993-1994.

Other callouts included an ATV accident on Imogene Pass and a hiker with a knee injury on Baby Bathtubs Trail. In August local Bonnie Hellman slid on a tree root while descending a very wet Weehawken Trail with the Hardy Hikers. She tumbled through a grassy patch and trees, breaking her leg. Two sister hikers, one a nurse, hurried to her and got her up, but she collapsed. Finally she made it to the trail, where she sat with her arms around a tree. MacLeod responded first, running up with his medical kit, followed by EMT Glen Boyd. Hellman was on her way to the hospital in an hour, "grateful they were there for me." She suffered a spiral fracture, which took a while to heal. That month, a motorcyclist with a broken leg was retrieved from Poughkeepsie Gulch.

September resembled July — five rescues and a fatality. A fifty-year-old fall victim required stitches and staples for head injuries after being carried out from Box Canyon Falls. A second callout the same day was more serious and complicated. A daughter and her mother traveling in a RZR ATV in Sidney Basin at 11,600 feet tumbled down a "very steep forested slope, close to fifty degrees," said Gibbs. They landed 300 feet "east of the primary road." He thought "they might have missed a switchback." The mother was ejected and died at the scene; the daughter needed extrication. Both wore seatbelts. "The survivor was a gigantic (tall) woman," said Koprek. "I remember her repeatedly telling us she played basketball or volleyball. If my memory serves me correctly, she was 6 feet, 7 inches and around 270 pounds."

Skoloda arrived first on his motorbike and performed "a really good ... medical assessment on her," said Mitchell. She had "a punctured lung and some broken ribs." The RZR was "hung up in a tree; it was partially on the ground, partially in the tree." Because the daughter was so tall and lay partly upside down, it was difficult to get her out of the vehicle. They eventually managed to extricate her, but in the litter her feet hung over. Lt. Gibbs "was running the incident for OMRT," recalled Koprek. He found "a nice LZ for the CareFlight Helicopter" at 12,000 feet. "We relayed the patient height and weight ... for load calculations. [The pilot] stuttered a couple times and informed us we would need to transport ... to a much lower LZ."

The lieutenant found it "a little bit frustrating to deal with the helicopter agency." He knew "they could have very easily taken their flight nurse and a couple of other people out of the helicopter and grabbed the subject." Instead, OMRT loaded the patient in Rescue 11. As they descended the steep 4WD road her feet hung out the back. Mitchell, Koprek and Cory Jackson took turns supporting them running behind the vehicle down to the Revenue Mine at 11,000 feet.

Two more rescues were for injured hikers on Mt. Sneffels and Cascade Trail. Sean Hart responded to a call for a Tennessee man thrown from his horse. He fell down the steep scree below the treeless, rocky Bridge of Heaven at 12,300 feet. OMRT hiked in after a 6 p.m. callout, passing the man's guides – on their way out. At the Bridge of Heaven, four miles and 3,000 vertical feet later, they realized the bigger problem would be getting the man to the trail.

Hart "went down to the patient and packaged him up." The only "anchors were a bunch of miscellaneous shrubs and bushes and stuff like that," not exactly confidence inspiring. At the top, they packaged the cowboy into the litter and wheeled him down to a grassy open spot on the ridge where the medevac helicopter, equipped with night vision capability, landed. "It was crazy late," Hart said. They had only their headlamps for light.

◆ ◆ ◆

Ouray County's Climbing Team, sponsored by Voyager Youth Program and coached by Hepp, taught thirteen middle and high school students to climb rock and ice and compete in the Western Slope Climbing League. The captain, an engineer, lived as he taught: He and OMRT Building Officer and local contractor Clint Estes took a long-planned climbing trip / humanitarian mission to Pakistan in 2009.

After days of remote travel, a local brigadier lieutenant summarily denied their climbing permit in the Kondus Valley, said Hepp. After waiting three days for a decision from Islamabad, they decided on "a more approachable location, the frequented Nangma Valley in the Karakoram." In early September, they showed villagers in Kande and Hushe how to build an emergency shelter for six people in just a few hours. They used locally available sandbags, barbed wire and corrugated metal. Their inspiration for designing and building these "post-earthquake hasty shelters," said Hepp, was the dZi Foundation in Ridgway, which works in Nepal, where he had climbed previously. "Thanks to Zack Martin Breaking Barriers Award from the American Alpine Club and our generous community," Estes wrote, "we not only journeyed to Pakistan to climb rock, but more importantly, to spread some love."

The "climbers, along with their cook, continued on to Nangma. Unfamiliar with the area, they scouted potential lines on three peaks under 16,000 feet." After some preliminary climbing, they settled on the south ridge of Denbor Brakk, a 4,800-meter peak just above basecamp. They climbed through "grass-choked wide cracks," Estes said. From the top of "the formation's south tower ... they rappelled off the east shoulder and named the route 'Good From Zafar, But Zafar From Good.'" The name honored their local contact and lampooned the route: "I can't in good conscience ever recommend the route," said Estes, "as it was one of the nastiest, most heinously unenjoyable climbs ever. It was good adventure though." They graded it G3, for "steep gardening."

CHAPTER TWENTY-FIVE

"Blowin' in the Wind"

SEVEN COLORADO SKIERS JOYFULLY tackled the pristine slopes above the Ridgway Hut, the second of five San Juan Hut System cabins. Six to ten inches of fresh powder had fallen over the past several days, but settled heavy and lay over a layer of mush. After one lap under mostly cloudy skies and light snowfall, the friends weren't quite ready to quit and skinned back up the leisurely curving west ridge of 12,980-foot Reconnoiter Peak. Three climbed toward Peak 12,478 near the top of the ridge; four descended a treed slope they had explored earlier. They "decided that this was safer than all being in the same spot, especially since climbing the peak added more exposure," wrote CAIC forecaster Ann Mellick.

At the bottom of the slope, the party of four climbed eastward for a last run. The three top skiers swooshed to timberline, halting above a:

> *tapering cliff band. Skier 1 jumped off the cliff band and stopped below a small tree just below. Skier 2 went down the slope to where there was no cliff showing and stopped roughly 50 feet from Skier 1…. Skier 3 jumped the small cliff and made it almost to where Skier 1 was standing before the slope fractured, taking Skiers 1 and 2 with it. Skier 1 saw the crown and scrambled towards it, but could not get off the slab in time. Skier 3 was knocked off his feet, but not carried downslope.*

None of the seven knew they were all on the same slope. Suddenly, one of the four moving upward in thick timber said, "We have movement," and they hunkered down until the slide passed. One man saw debris flow on both sides of him. Everyone was dusted with snow. After the slide stopped, Skier 3 asked if everyone was okay, but only the skiers in the timber below him responded. "Where are my guys?" he replied. They all switched beacons to rescue mode.

◆ ◆ ◆

At 3:20 p.m. February 11, 2010, Sheriff Mattivi's office took a call for an avalanche in the northern San Juans. "Initial reports indicated that two backcountry skiers" were "buried by the avalanche but were quickly located and recovered by other members.... One victim was unresponsive and not breathing while the other reported hip pain and possible fractures."

Fourteen minutes later OMRT, EMS, Extrication and Ridgway State Park personnel streamed toward CR 5 and the Elk Meadows subdivision mailboxes. The command post, which included a Ouray school bus ... "rehab-station," went operational shortly after 4. A flat parcel of land to the southeast with a view of the snow-blitzed range and Mt. Sneffels became a LZ.

Radio traffic between dispatch and command said that San Juan Hut personnel advised that "snow machines and skis would be required to reach the site ... eight miles south of Ridgway and above 10,000 feet." Two Elk Meadows residents, guide Bean Bowers and Mike Pennings, had skied hugely unstable snow below Corbett Peak and Whitehouse Mountain that day and "very strongly suggested that we look in one of these two drainages" of Beaver Creek, said Training Officer Kevin Koprek. He was familiar with the route, which began at the Burn Hut just east of command. Clint Estes called a local engineer, Chris Haaland, who owned a Polaris 1995 WideTrak that he used to groom the nearby Top of the Pines Nordic area. On the way to command, Haaland encountered the Sheriff: "I'll never forget it," he said. "The only way to get up there is up the road, the dirt road, CR 5.... I've got it maxed out and I'm going up ... the gravel road, and right next to me is the Sheriff." He's "tracking with me, and he knows what I'm doing.... We wave to each other."

Haaland ferried Chris Folsom to the Burn Hut and headed west. Pennings borrowed Haaland's ski gear and hurried toward the Ridgway Hut. Estes and Bowers snowmobiled to the West Dallas Trailhead below Mt. Sneffels and skied east toward the accident. Two Olathe Spray Bell 47 helicopters and a more powerful Helitrax Bell 407 from Telluride with San Miguel SAR personnel were enroute by 4:30.

At the command post "there was a lot happening and it was getting dark," said Operations Chief Matt Hepp. They "had a quick chance and it was great that Helitrax was able to show up," since "they had to do a lot of work to coordinate ourselves up there ... to make sure we just kept the LZ safe ... that nobody did anything foolish." Sam Rushing watched the MASH-like scene; by 5 three choppers had landed. Helitrax flew Koprek along the rugged range, searching for ski tracks. He saw "some other skier traverse slide activity ... and determined that there were equal tracks in and out ... and then we came back [towards Reconnoiter Peak] and sure enough they were right there."

◆ ◆ ◆

His friends found Skier 2, the cautious one, first. "He "was not buried and was visible on the surface." Unfortunately, the slide had slammed Kellen Robert Sams, twenty-seven, of Manitou Springs, into a large tree. His medically trained friends performed CPR continuously for forty-five minutes, but could not revive him. Skier 3 found Skier 1, Dominic Franz Muth, twenty-four, of Breckenridge, as he "honed in on ... [his] beacon signal and felt a positive probe strike."

He and another party were able to quickly dig to his face to establish an airway. Skier 1 began breathing on his own. His face was 1' – 2' below the snow ... total burial time is estimated at five minutes. He was seated in a fairly upright position facing downhill. Party members continued to dig Skier 1 out of the snow ... he had suffered painful injuries to his upper leg/hip.

They called 911 and hauled both men down to an open area below the trees. One man skied to the hut for sleeping bags and supplies to keep Muth comfortable while they waited for rescue.

◆ ◆ ◆

"You would think it would be easy to see people in snow," said Koprek, "especially a group of them from the air, but it's not. It's super challenging. So we located them and then made another couple of passes," to make sure that "the hazard is not still present ... the majority of that ridge slid already." The Helitrax pilot hovered on a skid, dropped him in and flew to command. Minutes later the pilot unloaded Mountain Trip Guides' co-owner Bill Allen, who also worked for Helitrax, and two SMSAR paramedics, Emil and Heather. They brought "a super basic medical kit." It had "life support stuff, a little bit of airway ... narcotics for pain management ... a backboard."

Muth's pain was 10 over 10, so Emil administered morphine before they packaged him with sleeping bags to cushion the backboard. Emil covered his face, loaded him into the chopper and strapped him to the bench. Koprek noticed the tall young man's feet hung out into space where the door had been removed.

Suddenly he realized something was horribly wrong. Each skier had been given a job:

> *Some were assigned to sit on piles of packs.... Helitrax has this sled ... it was sitting uphill ... the one girl was assigned to sit on it because it blows around really easily. And we're about halfway through loading the patient and all of a sudden the pilot starts freaking out —mind you he's hovering. Bill and I look up ... the girl who is supposed to sit on the sled is approaching the helicopter ... from uphill, and she was probably less than ten feet from the rotor disk and it would have got her right in the waist area.*

They yelled at her to stop and to their immense relief she sat down on the sled until the helicopter pulled away. By 5:35, Muth was in the ambulance.

Darkness encroached, the mountains steepened into shadows. Hepp ordered all searchers and snowmobiles to return. On his way back, Haaland stopped to pick up Garry Schalla, who was skiing towards the accident site. Olathe #1 headed home after flying Mike Bryson in and back since they "had enough people to accomplish what we needed and we were super pressed for time," said Koprek. Olathe #2 ferried Jeff Skoloda and Cory Jackson to the site but they too weren't needed. Later, it picked up the deceased skier, wrapped in a big tarp from SMSAR. Koprek, Allen and Heather carried it 150 meters downhill in chest-deep snow to the chopper's side basket. At 5:45 Olathe #2 dropped the body at command and headed home.

They decided to evacuate the skiers. "They kind of wanted to ... ski back to the hut and spend the night," said Koprek. "But a couple of them ... looked pretty hypothermic, they were shivering, their clothes were wet." The rescuers kept them busy putting "ski gear into one pile, their packs and personal gear into another pile in very specific places."

Intermittent snow squalls swept through command; the sun set at 5:47, nine minutes after Helitrax returned to pick up the skiers. "The loading process is really interesting," Koprek said.

A Helitrax Bell 407 descends into the command post at Elk Meadows with an avalanche victim. In the background is the eastern end of the Sneffels Range. The partially obscured ridge at right is where the avalanche occurred. OMRT members wait in the foreground.

Photo by Patrick Davarn
Courtesy *Ouray County Plaindealer*

That's where Bill does his job. So right where the helicopter toes in, imagine the skid. On one side is the pile of packs and the people and on the other side is the ski gear that goes in the basket and it's super narrow. There is not more than a foot or two.... You've got the stuff there to show him where to land.... Bill is on the front of it. And the helicopter pilot literally lands ... right on top of him. He has this bright jacket on and he holds his hand out and the pilot puts the helicopter right on his hand.

Allen's presence gave the pilot depth perception so he could just focus "on that one point ... trusting him ... he's not looking at what is going on around. He's looking at Bill's hand and his jacket," said Koprek. "He comes in nice and slow. It's super gentle. It's amazing."

The skiers loaded and were at command just after sunset, leaving Koprek, Heather, Allen, their personal packs and ski gear. By 6:01 they, too, were back.

Forty-five minutes later, Helitrax was home in Telluride, most of the field people and snowmobiles had left, Crippin Funeral Home was headed to Montrose. The remaining skiers were taken to Ridgway. Then, "just as people are coming out of the field and wrapping up and gear's getting sorted," said Koprek, he, Hepp and Skoloda reviewed the operation with the Sheriff. They realized "that there were seven in the party and we accounted for six." Then, "somebody asked if any of the field teams had connected with the one ... nobody had made contact with this person at all, we had to go do that."

Shortly after 7 Hepp and Koprek gathered their gear and pushed the snowmobile as far as they could past the Burn Hut before putting skins on their skis and breaking trail toward the Ridgway Hut and the missing skier. An hour and a half later, they found the hut – and the man. They had set off not knowing if he would be there, but they knew they couldn't just leave him. Koprek said they discussed what they would do if "the guy wasn't at the hut, if we were going to go look for him. It was a pretty easy 'no.' We were not going to wander around in the dark." Hepp knew the missing man "had an emotional need" and they did find him "pretty shell-shocked. We didn't have to do much convincing or anything." He "imagined the party's perspective ... dealing with everything and then a helicopter shows up and whisks their friends away and then they are just left there."

Koprek saw that David "was a little bit reluctant. I think he was kind of comfortable there, physically anyway. But he just packed up and we packed up a bunch of the deceased's gear. The Sheriff's office wanted that." They had arranged that local resident John Kuijvenhoven would wait for them with his big snow cat. Shortly after 10 he met them at the road portion of the trail and Hepp and David transferred to his big machine for the trip to command. Twenty minutes later they all reached the mailboxes and everyone, including Deb Folsom who was still chronicling the mission, headed home at 10:30.

Night lay peaceful on the range. "Sometimes as part of these rescues," said Hepp, "you wind up being out in the mountains at a time in a situation you wouldn't normally be out and you get to really enjoy some interesting natural moments." Koprek, however, was at the "point of being tired and kind of on autopilot." *Blowin' in the Wind* was on his mind.

◆ ◆ ◆

Six weeks later, on a sunny Tuesday, March 30, Heidi Kloos, a "revered climber and mountain guide," left her friend Sarah Christianson's house on a ranch north of Baldy Peak, east of US 550 and Ridgway, to ski a snow-covered back road toward the peak. She did not return.

That day, the tender snowpack had been on everyone's mind. Clint Cook, who worked for SJMG, said he knew that Kloos "was looking for a new ice climb, but that day ended up being the big warm up shedding day for a lot of the mountains." Spring-like conditions were evident from the west end of the San Juans east to Mt. Baldy and the Cimarrons. Peak Mountain Guides' owner Matt Wade, who worked with Kloos on youth outdoor education programs at Ridgway High School, recalled "several very large avalanches on the north side of the Sneffels range." Bill MacTiernan, who lived near Ridgway, "looked that day across the entire range." The north side "released from Telluride to here." It was "a bizarre day for sympathetic release."

An experienced, AMGA certified guide, Kloos worked for Mountain Trip Expeditions, based in Ophir, Colorado, since 2005. The sturdy forty-one-year-old led expeditions around the world and was one of the "lead guides up Denali in Alaska." She and Rob Durnell received the National Park Service's Denali Pro Award for their "selfless efforts in helping the Park Service with a difficult rescue in 2007." Her friend, co-owner of Mountain Trip Expeditions Todd Rutledge, said, "she received more positive reviews than any other guide here. She was incredible in all forms of climbing." She led trips in "Nepal, Russia, Argentina, Alaska, Thailand, Patagonia ... her sacred Colorado Rockies." She had "climbed four of the Seven Summits, the highest peaks on each continent" and "was one of the first women in the United States to become a certified mountain guide" with the AMGA.

Born in Aspen, she grew up in Old Snowmass and was a two-time state track champion at Hotchkiss High School before joining the Air Force where she began climbing as a member of an Air Force Search and Recovery Team. "But as a guide she was one of those people that is set apart. She could put herself in someone else's shoes," said her boss and friend Nate Disser of Durango-based Southwest Adventure Guides. "She was an inspiration to a lot of people ... to women, to at-risk kids to adaptive sports." A climbing and skiing partner, Sonja Allen, said she was "a rock star in the mountains but seemed to find true enjoyment in enabling others to enjoy themselves and succeed. She had a huge heart, especially for animals, and she was and still is an inspiration for me."

Heidi Kloos gears up for ice climbing in Crack Canyon above Ophir, Colorado. In the background are friends and dogs, including her cow dog Minky playing with the golden retrievers.

Photo by Sonja Allen; Courtesy Angela Hawse

Chapter Twenty-Five: "Blowin' in the Wind"

◆ ◆ ◆

Sheriff Dominic Mattivi called out OMRT the next morning. "High winds prevented deployment of a helicopter" so they skied into the site after setting up command near the Wachle Ranch on CR 12. Trackers Sam Rushing, Charlie Banta and Tim Eihausen followed her ski tracks, working "that thing for two days...." They hoped she might have "just twisted her knee real bad," said Rushing. "I knew I was on a trail. I radioed in.

> 'Did she have a dog?'
> They said 'Why?'
> 'Well, I'm picking up little pieces of white and black dog hair.'"

Cook, who worked with Kloos at SJMG for a couple of winters, considered her a good friend. "We followed her ski track ... up towards Baldy," he said. Under the cliffs was avalanche debris with her tracks leading out, which "then ran into another 'avi' path." He said "her dog quickly appeared ... would not let anyone close to it. We organized a probe line of that path starting near the top. Night fell with no strikes. We had to leave the dog out." She had found this "really cool little ice climb," said Rushing. "It's real remote, but Heidi ... was one of these incredibly strong outdoor women that you read about all the time that just does unbelievable things."

◆ ◆ ◆

The second day, one of her best friends and fellow guide, Angela Hawse, met the team that morning. "I got a call from Clint ... they have found Heidi's dog and they believe she was buried in the avalanche," she said. "They asked me if I could go in the next morning because I was a close friend of Heidi's and I knew her dog really well." Cook drove Hawse, the treats and toys she had brought for Minky, including a favorite toy, in on a snowmobile. The avalanche:

> was split by terrain, so it kind of had two paths that came back together. It was an extremely large avalanche, very destructive. There were timbers, mature timbers ... with a girth of foot and a half, snapped in half. There's no way she could have triggered it because it released well above her on a discontinuous slope that was broken by a cliff band. She was below the cliff band.

Hawse spent an hour enticing the wary little cow dog until Minky finally came and sat beside her so that two ski patrollers and avalanche dogs could work. They had waited some distance away so Minky wouldn't smell their dogs. They "resumed probing," said Cook, found her skis and worked downhill from there. Hawse didn't need to hold Minky anymore so she joined the probe line: "After an hour, hour and a half of very tedious ... pinpoint probing," Kevin got a strike and they found her "near the toe of the avi path." After they dug her up, Hawse said they told her to go sit because "I was really close to Heidi, so I sat with her dog." It "was very, very agitated the whole time, and just clearly disturbed. As soon as they uncovered her body, Minky went over and just kind of checked it out, and totally changed. It was like all happy, like Heidi wasn't there anymore."

Minky trotted alongside Hawse: "Heidi's spirit was gone, and the dog knew it.... It was really kind of liberating for me: 'Oh, that's right, Heidi isn't here anymore.'"

In the spring sky, a golden eagle soared.

CHAPTER TWENTY-SIX

2011-2014
"God's own army gathered around us"

FRIDAY AFTERNOON, MARCH 4, 2011: Mike Gibbs and Mark Miller shook hands with four Canadian military men after a week's Rigging for Rescue training, carried equipment from the Barn and drove a half-mile to their Main Street office. They were "still in full climbing garb ... unloading the ropes and the buckets of gear," said Gibbs: "The pager goes off ... 'ice climbing accident, lead climb area Ouray's Ice Park.'" He looked at Chris Jackson. "I will bet you that's one of our boys from the class." Gibbs, Miller and Sam Rushing reached the barn in two minutes, even before Capt. Mike MacLeod, who was climbing nearby.

◆ ◆ ◆

The Royal Canadian Air Force SAR-techs (Search and Rescue Technicians) "had a hankering for more climbing." Forty-year-old Mark Salesse ascended the worst of 'Chris's Crash,' a lead-only route north of the upper bridge, and thought about his next piece of protection. He saw his left ice tool leave the ice. "It was such a subtle thing.... I looked over in disbelief, thinking to myself, 'That did not just happen.' And I'm slowly leaning back, realizing I'm going to take a good one." He fell past his last ice screw, it pulled out and he watched the opposite wall race up. He hit the wall, bounced off and slammed into a snow-covered boulder: "I don't think I'm going to make this one."

Gibbs saw the "imprint of his body in the snow like a cartoon." Salesse "landed on his back and then he kind of rolled off the boulder ... it was obvious that a person had fallen right there." He estimated

249

Salesse fell forty to fifty feet, ripped out his ice screw and plunged a similar distance to the canyon floor. Three buddies – all paramedics – worked on him. Salesse told them, "I need O2, a C-collar. I need a spine board. I need a pelvic sling. I need a couple of straps to tie my legs." Fellow SAR Christian Morissette yelled the order to the bridge.

Capt. Mike MacLeod ascends to safety with a badly injured Mark Salesse.

Photo by Mike Bryson
Courtesy *Ouray County Plaindealer*

IC Gibbs sent Miller, Bill Whitt and MacLeod to the hole. It was a precise and effective operation, in spite of being for "somebody that I've been working with the last week." Gibbs "was emotionally invested" in the outcome. MacLeod watched as Gibbs lined up Rescue 12 "to a gnat's ear" on the bridge; ropes were lowered through a pulley off the boom pole. Whitt secured a bottom tag line on the ice below the patient so the litter would swing free of the water and the bridge above. "We just needed to get him out of there," said Gibbs. Miller packaged the soldier.

They dangled in mid-air and slowly ascended toward the bridge. MacLeod held onto the litter with one hand, and with his other ... the hand of the victim. "We worked out a signal – one squeeze was good and two were bad.... My job at that point was to deal with any kind of bad situation – for example, if he had to vomit. I just kept talking, telling him, 'Hey, we're halfway there; you're okay.' I had to be his eyes and ears.

"The most painful part was the transfer from the ground to the litter," said Salesse. "I've worked with patient litter loading and setting up for the past six years ... the boys in Ouray have it dialed." After a "smooth ride to the ambulance," he flew to St. Mary's Hospital in Grand Junction and then a Tier I Trauma Center in Denver. Eventually he went to a veteran's hospital in Ottawa for three months' convalescence to heal his shattered pelvis. The rescue "was a tremendous team effort," said Gibbs. From "page-out to Mark being loaded into the AirLife helicopter at Fellin Park was seventy-five minutes."

◆ ◆ ◆

Another twenty-three callouts brought no fatalities until December. Four were complex, serious and time-consuming; others for overdue climbers, hikers and an injured runner. Four were stand-downs. San Juan County called for help March 25 after a car plunged 300 feet over the Silverton side of Red Mountain Pass at MM 79.5. Thirty-eight-year-old Montrose resident James Emery and his girlfriend reported the accident from one of the few spots with cell service. Far below them, twenty-nine-year-old Eric Petranek of Bayfield lay half out of a burning car. Emery slid down "the steep snowy embankment ... in snow up to his chest," but the site was too hot for

him to get within five feet of the car. "Petranek's jacket was on fire …
he 'threw snow on him' to squelch those flames." Then, "grabbing
onto a nearby tree branch for traction," he bent it toward Petranek
to grab and dragged him ten to fifteen feet away. Afterward, the ex-
Marine struggled uphill through deep snow: "Twenty feet from the
top … they threw me a rope."

OMRT arrived in "full blizzard conditions," said Gibbs. "The vehicle was fully engulfed in flames … tires were exploding and the gas
tank exploded right after." Undersheriff Bruce Conrad asked Gibbs
to take over the technical operation so he set up Rescue 12. They
lowered San Juan medic Kyle Mesich with the litter. He took off his
jacket to cover Petranek and worked in his T-shirt to stabilize him.
MacLeod said they "used every bit of a 90-meter rope to get down
to the victim." The car still burned as they packaged and evacuated
Petranek, said Clint Cook. Ouray's ambulance ferried Petranek
over the pass to St. Mary's helicopter. Later, he transferred to St.
Anthony's in Denver, a Level 1 trauma center. Emery, his breathing
normal three days after inhaling smoke, shrugged: "I didn't think
nothing of it. Anybody would of done it."

San Juan County called again July 20. A CDOT worker broke his
ankle in Brooklyn Gulch searching for unexploded ordnance left
by avalanche control on Red Mountain Pass. Half a dozen members
helped SJCSAR retrieve a "forty-year-old, 220-pound big guy, probably six foot," recalled Sean Hart. Rescuers set up a scree evacuation.
Hart and Cory Jackson from Ouray and Andy Morris from Silverton
maneuvered the litter down the slope. "It was a big, long patient
lower in Brooklyn Gulch down to the highway, through a boulder
gully with lots of loose rocks," said MacLeod. More than 100 meters
of rope arched out over the scree field, said Hart, dragging over
rocks as they lowered the litter. Riggers tied ropes together, attendants waited and teammates negotiated knot passes. "It was really
obvious that we were potentially going to get rockfall," said Hart,
who called up to Charlie Banta:

> *"Charlie … If we have rock fall, see what you can do."*
> *He said, "I will take off my pack and I will block it."*

Moments later, a "toaster sized rock" aimed for them. They
dragged the litter up the side of the gully. They could see the rock
slowing down, Hart called to Banta that they were good, but he

"lifted his pack in front of his own body and threw himself into the rock," said Rushing, "and saved great harm to the three litter attendants as well as the patient.... Ouray Mountain Rescue does a lot of dangerous work, but this was a truly heroic act." After the rescue, Morris sent an email to the team: "If you ever need a goaltender, Charlie is your man."

Sunday August 21, three agencies retrieved two women near MM 90 on US 550. Kimberly Leppke, fifty-two, of Albuquerque, New Mexico, southbound, passed Bear Creek Bridge before her car veered off the highway; her seventy-eight-year-old mother, Jean Hall, lay on the back seat. The car "bumped along the right edge," said the State Patrol, then "traveled over the edge ... collided with a tree which pointed the car nose-down into the abyss of the Uncompahgre Gorge. [It] careened into the gorge for another 55 feet before traveling over some large rocks and crashing into another large tree 74.6 feet down." Sheriff Dominic Mattivi estimated the distance to the bottom was 200 - 300 feet. "If the tree hadn't been there to stop them, this would have been a recovery mission, not a rescue." Extrication removed the driver's side rear door. "On a 30-plus degree slope ... it was tricky business getting them out of the car and into a litter," said MacLeod, praising Extrication as "unsung heroes in this county."

The year ended with a cold, difficult search by San Juan, La Plata and Ouray Counties for victims of a bad weather December plane crash on forested Anvil Mountain. The NTSB reported that, a "Socata TB21 airplane, N25153, collided with terrain near Silverton, Colorado. The non-instrument rated private pilot and three passengers were fatally injured." Debris lay all "over the place, on both sides of the road" near Cement Creek, said Sheriff Sue Kurtz. Thirty people from nine agencies helped with the recovery. Four bodies were finally located at 10,000 feet after four days of searching. Kevin Koprek said OMRT assisted with the rigging to bring the bodies out.

◆ ◆ ◆

January through November 2012 brought eighteen callouts. Five complicated big missions began on a gray January afternoon when a climber fell on Horsetail Falls, across the Uncompahgre Gorge from Bear Creek Overlook. He "had too much distance above the last piece of protection," said Gibbs, so that even though his ice screw held, he still hit the ground, injuring an ankle. After calling 911, his partner dragged him to the east side of the river.

Gibbs took charge, sending EMT Tom Kavanaugh and Chris Jackson down to the patient and Lt. Clint Estes and Hart across the river to rig lines. The options for raising the climber were "something fancy," said Gibbs, "or we do it more blue collar and just a get a rope system up through the woods." They went with a guiding line across the gorge, Plan A, with Plan B, manually lifting the load, as backup. Estes and Hart climbed a mixed (ice and rock) rap line, accessed "a little bench area where there are some big live trees," said Gibbs. He plumb bobbed a sight line for Tim Pasek, who shot the rope gun and line across the canyon, allowing Estes to pull ropes across and fix them to a large diameter live tree. They rapped down Horsetail and crossed the gorge for part two of a "difficult and complex backcountry operation." New to OMRT, Kavanaugh watched. "I wasn't really sure what was going on … we had gotten all the lines across and anchored off and back down to the guy and packaged up, then I started seeing everything." He realized they were "pulling him up the canyon off that line that they just shot."

Estes tended the litter as the main and belay lines, fastened to Rescue 12's boom pole, brought them uphill. The raise began "steep, which is great for the guiding line, you can just hover the obstacles," said Pasek, but the hill rounded out and the litter hung up, so he, Gibbs and Koprek hiked down to help. Pasek and Koprek helped push the load over rock bumps. "Mike clipped in as attendant," said Pasek. "The less steep the terrain the more people you need on the litter." "That was another one that was pretty fast," said Gibbs. "I think it was under two hours … for quite a technical operation."

From May 12 to July 31 they were paged out twelve times, seven in June alone. Four vehicles over the edge on US 550 included a miraculous recovery of a South Dakota woman, Phanessa Baril, forty-five, and her two cats. Driving south the evening of June 1, "the lady decided Red Mountain Pass was not for her," said Koprek, and she attempted a turn at a narrow spot. "Her car went over in reverse and she came to a precarious resting place several hundred feet below the road. The terrain was mostly scree and talus slope." Baril was conscious through the descent, called for help and then stayed on the phone with dispatch until rescuers arrived. Fortunately, her car didn't go all the way down, said Sheriff Mattivi. He said MM 89 was one of the better places she could have gone off since "the ground dropped six to eight feet." Her 1998 Buick Century slid backwards through a scree field and stopped, its "headlights shining upwards toward the highway," said the Sheriff. "She just went off into the one place where this would happen."

Patrick Rondinelli said he and John Fedel, from Extrication, worked their way "down to the vehicle, stabilized, and gained access through the passenger side door." They cut off a back door so paramedic Ruth Stewart and Kavanaugh could get to Baril. She ended up in a heap in the back seat on top of the cat carrier, which popped open, said Stewart. In spite of unstable footing, they got her on a backboard and into the litter. Then, in a vehicle precariously perched on a dark talus slope, Fedel and Rondinelli searched for cats. "The cats miraculously just stayed put," said Stewart: "If those cats had bolted, we'd have never found them.... One was under the passenger seat and the other one was in the rear dashboard. So I had a cat here and cat there," she said. Baril, "like many of us pet owners," was "much more concerned about her animals than about herself." Stewart, Tricia Eischied and Kavanaugh took the litter to the road. Baril had leg pain, abrasions and cuts on her head. Had she been wearing her seat belt, said Stewart, she probably wouldn't have been hurt at all.

The others "were left with the cats," said Koprek. Rondinelli and Fedel fashioned a carrier and stuffed "the little beasts in." The firemen used the rope to get up the loose slope to the road. This left Koprek, "the one with severe allergies to cats, to carry them up the hill." Rondinelli said he also hauled up some of their extrication gear. "I think we teased him a little about being the hero to save the cats."

Three more rescues in a week were "all big operations," said Gibbs, "multi-pitch, lots of ropes." On June 24, nine experienced climbers ascended an "exposed, technical route on the north side of Coxcomb Peak" in the Uncompahgre Wilderness. They were high enough on the 13,565-foot peak's rectangular north face to have cell service when "a good sized boulder came popping off," said MacLeod, "the gentleman belaying ... sustained a head injury. It was not a good situation at all, but it could have been worse; he lived to tell about it." The man's helmet took the brunt of the hit. His partners lowered him to the saddle between Redcliff and Coxcomb, which "saved a lot of time," said MacLeod.

They realized the terrain "was too steep to just carry him even with six people," said Pasek. They used "a single rope system because if the rope failed, the surface was rough ... we would all just kind of land on our butts and the litter would just stop." CareFlight landed at 10,800-foot West Fork trailhead; the crew unloaded the heaviest person and equipment since it was a very warm day and they would be landing and taking off at 12,000 feet. "They were a very light-weight flight crew," said Pasek, "which allowed us to get this relatively big climber ... full size, six-foot plus adult male" into the chopper. MacLeod said it was the first backcountry rescue of the summer and "hopefully our last.... That would be okay with us."

Three days later, however, an even more serious backcountry incident involved Marston Doolittle, seventy-five, a Nebraska farmer and cattle rancher showing his extended family a scene from his youth near the Ribbon Ice Climb on Camp Bird Road. He had done this many times before. In 1957, he "etched his name and the year in an old wooden door" of a mining structure. This time, on "steep, loose ground ... one of the kids knocked a rock and it came tumbling down." Unfortunately, "they were staggered on the slope above and below each other," said Gibbs. "The rock hit him in the head...."

"He was at a terrible spot," said MacLeod, but, amazingly, still walking around. Stewart, a tall, fit former firefighter, hiked 200 feet down the gulch and up the opposite slope hauling an awkward six-foot vacuum mattress strapped to the back of her pack, its bulk threatening to tip her backwards. "An immobilization tool," the device was flat and flexible, filled with little beads to cushion a patient when it was secured. Then, air was sucked out to create "a custom fit taco shell." On this steep ground, however, her problem was finding a flat spot. She placed "it below him" and slid "him down into it" with some help. "It was a really awkward spot to work."

Meanwhile, Gibbs, Miller, Rushing, Sean Hart and others set up a guiding line and several pulleys at critical places. "It was one of the worst slopes" anyone could remember working on. Stewart hooked up an IV. Jenny Hart helped package Marston and chatted with him:

> [He] survived a lightning strike when he was younger ... he was as tough as nails and he did not want medication, he did not want help. He just wanted to get out of there.... Ruth had me in charge of him ... letting him know what would happen next and when we were going to do it. As soon as they put him on the rig ... all hell broke loose and he was dying.

In that "crappy, rocky gully," Stewart watched his condition change. "We had him hooked up to the ropes and started moving down ... he got really nauseous. And so I hopped in there to give him some nausea medication. And then within a couple of minutes he was unconscious. He was beginning to do neurological posturing." The men turned the litter to the side and she used a turkey baster so he wouldn't aspirate. They ran downhill with the litter over four or five rope lengths of rough terrain. Riggers at two stations passed knots and made directional changes. Stewart and Gibbs ran alongside with radios, talking to those controlling the ropes from the top.

"Wow, this guy is going to die," Gibbs thought. "We need to go faster, faster, down, down, down, down." It felt like they were flying down "this relatively benign duff-like forested area through the deadfall." MacLeod waited near the bottom and as "they got down towards the end, we just unclipped ... six or eight of us grabbed ahold of it and just ran through the river as fast as we could" and up the opposite bank. They loaded him in the ambulance and drove a short distance uphill to the CareFlight helicopter at lower Camp Bird. He was "circling the drain," said Jenny Hart; it would "be lucky if we can get him to the road before he dies."

Marston died July 5; the captain recalled "the patriarch of a huge, close-knit family.... It really broke the hearts of our team." As the family came through the Fourth of July breakfast line, said Gibbs, they thanked "all the rescue team members that had gotten their husband, father, patriarch down." His daughter Molly Nightingale wrote that they were grateful for "a chance to be with Dad a little while yet, even though he is unresponsive."

OMRT and MacLeod's "heck of a week" included another call June 28. "It seemed like five or six weekends in a row [May-June 2012] we were doing a rescue," said Gibbs. We got "pretty close to half of our active roster [ten to fifteen] on a given call." In borderline weather, they hurried to Lavender Col and up Sneffels' southeast couloir with a defibrillator for a man having a heart attack. David Heitke, sixty-nine, of Minneapolis, Minnesota, an experienced hiker, had climbed fifty of Colorado's Fourteeners, Kilimanjaro and Aconcagua. He went down high on Sneffels; a doctor at the scene "recognized right away he had an issue going on," said MacLeod. "She coordinated CPR but after thirty minutes of valiant and extraordinary effort, they were not able to get him back. We didn't get there in time." The body "had been covered by a tarp ... approximately 100-200 meters up the tourist col," said MacLeod.

"It was a typical semi-moist day in the San Juans," said Pasek. "We had thunderstorms ... did not want to stay up there." They put the victim in a body bag, rolled it into the plastic Sked and hurried down to Lavender Col. They anchored a rope to the big rock block on the saddle and "lowered the body ... as fast as we could because the weather was coming in." MacLeod wrote: "Kudos to everyone for a job well done this week. Three major callouts in the span of six days ... this week has been tough on our work and family commitments." He concluded: "I have never been more proud to be a member."

They comforted Heitke's wife, Kristina Felbeck, at the Fourth of July breakfast. Donations poured in from their friends; she thanked OMRT "for your humanity, your fitness (!), and for your dedication to helping all those who get stuck in the mountains." MacLeod realized the fatalities had "taken their toll.... To have two people passing away, it's tough." Because they were "a small team in a small community," he said, "It's just harder to totally detach."

2012's last calls included an injured Cascade Flume jumper, two local girls lost at night on Hayden Mountain, two injured hunters and a stand-down for a vehicle over the edge on US 550. The most extraordinary, however, came at 3:45 Sunday afternoon, September 16, for a canyoner who had fallen fifty to sixty feet into Oak Creek Canyon.

◆ ◆ ◆

Canyoning – descending alpine cascades in a wetsuit while anchored to a rope – officially arrived in 2010 with the Ouray Canyon Festival, though local cascades were explored before. John Kropuenske had climbed and rappelled Portland Creek "between the Amphitheater Bridge and Sixth Street where I lived.... I spent most of my childhood playing in that canyon and the amphitheater." Now guide services offered clinics and tours of local waterfalls. Aficionado Greg Foy and his wife Connie organized the festival with the American Canyoneering Association, known for promoting "its kissing cousin, canyoneering, which mostly applies to adventures in dry canyons (think the slot canyons of Utah)." A rescue was inevitable; OMRT began training.

◆ ◆ ◆

The Oak Creek victim was spitting up blood and had a compound arm fracture. Both the length of the fall and the severity of his injuries were a concern and fifty-five minutes later, an EMS helicopter was airborne from Montrose and Ground Team #1 was hiking up

Oak Creek Trail. The pilot verified the patient's location but reported no possible LZ. "It was reasonably open," said IC Pasek. There was "a very small kind of bench ... the canyoners had built a fire. That's actually how the helicopter found them." After trying other companies, Pasek called the Air Force Rescue Coordination Center (AFRCC) "to request helo (helicopter) with hoist capability." The center contacted the Colorado Army National Guard High-Altitude Army Aviation Training Site (HAAATS) in Gypsum. They accepted the mission and TALON 39, an H-60A+ Blackhawk helicopter with night vision was launched.

Ground Team #1 – Koprek, Skoloda, Tricia and Blaine Eischied – hiked the steep three-mile Oak Creek Trail in three hours. At 7:40, "just as dusk was sliding into darkness," Skoloda said he and Koprek left the trail at the 10,700-foot high point to bushwack on an old, faint outfitters' trail across Oak Creek Canyon, radioed that they were at the patient. The others should "wait at the trail. Do not try to follow us." They were "in high alpine terrain, with huge gullies and washed out sections which made it challenging to access," said Koprek. They traversed the hillside, climbing to the "11,200 contour, where we found the subject and his party with a fire going." The route was horrible and "there were no air assets available," said Koprek. He told Pasek to keep calling. "We were not moving this patient overland in a litter." The canyon "was a total junkshow." The victim "was in good enough shape to be hoisted out," but "he was very, very cold; they had a fire built for him. One buddy was an EMT and they were taking really good care of him which was fortunate."

Ten minutes later, they had determined he had no spinal injuries with Mitchell's help. She responded from Ground Team #2, who were hauling the litter and backcountry tech gear up the trail. Trying to work around the man's punctured lung, Skoloda said he and Koprek strapped him into a chest harness, which they linked to his climbing harness for the raise to the Blackhawk, which had no litter onboard. Ten minutes later, using its night vision, the chopper hovered above them. They had a spare 200-foot piece of rope, said Koprek, which they used as a tagline to keep the litter from spinning as it was hoisted. By 8 p.m. the enormous twin-engine bird capable of carrying a squad of troops was enroute to Montrose Airport where the hospital ambulance waited. The seventy-foot, 18,000-pound helicopter was far too big to land atop the hospital. Later, the man was transferred to Grand Junction.

Meanwhile, three waves of rescuers – "a whole mule train of people," said IC Pasek, were strung out along the trail – twelve of them hauling everything from the litter and backcountry tech gear to a sleeping bag, stove, fuel, the litter wheel and food. David Mullings and others in the third wave smiled when they "heard the unmistakable arrival of the helicopter."

"Hey, we get to turn 180," and avoid what would have been a long, dark and challenging wheeled litter evac.
So for the third wave, anti-climatic, but we like anti-climatic.

"The Oak Creek ascent, going across the loose dirt exposure part for the first time with a weighted pack," said Mullings, took "a little extra time, no time for a slip-up."

As the Army helo crew safely carried out the "VERY HIGH RISK" mission – "high altitude, narrow canyon, night-time, hoisting ... an unfamiliar area," they had "pristine weather: calm winds, cool temperatures, and clear skies within an hour of sunset." They reported that the campfire started by the distressed party created "massive amounts of infrared light" that washed out their night vision goggles. In addition, 100 MPH rotor wash "blew hot embers into the forest," a concern in dry fall weather. The four people clinging to that hillside got lucky; nothing ignited. "We executed an accident free rescue from a very difficult position," said Skoloda. "We did what we needed to do without any other injuries.... We ended up spending most of the rest of the night hiking the patient's partners out to the trailhead." They scrambled up to the 11,800-foot contour line to find their way out. The outfitters' faint trail had disappeared into darkness. The Eischieds waited for them, said Skoloda, and called to them reassuringly as they worked through blowdown on the hillside. The canyoners, really fried from the day's events, trudged along. By 12:51 a.m. all ground teams were out.

That "nighttime hoist using night vision goggles at 11,000 feet is probably the riskiest mission" the helicopter crew had ever done, said Pasek. OMRT put hoist training with the TALON crews in Gypsum, a four-hour drive from Ouray, on its yearly training schedule. We have "a very good professional relationship," said Pasek. "When we have called them, it's been, we really need you." Two days later, Mitchell sent teammates a welcome message: "Hemothorax on the pt., recovering at St. Mary's with a chest tube."

◆ ◆ ◆

By 2013, Capt. MacLeod was "ready to turn in his clipboard and 'put my helmet back on and do whatever it takes to get a rescue done.'" Pasek, a Coast Guard reservist who was voted in two years before and excelled in several capacities, became the "public face and voice of the team." Cory Jackson was lieutenant. Three new members in two years: Kevin Timm, Kavanaugh and Stewart, added strength. Nicole Skoloda, who had been on reserve and served on the membership committee since the birth of her first child in 2008, became committee chair. They continued to screen applicants, pairing new recruits with long time members for training.

In 2013 the callouts eased a little; from February through November eleven rescues included the Ice Park, San Juan Hut System, Red Mountain Pass, Black Canyon National Park and Camp Bird Road. It became a year for focusing on air resources, training with Tri-State CareFlight, Olathe Spray Service, Helitrax and HAATS.

Whitt, Gibbs and Jackson resigned from OIPI (Ouray Ice Park, Inc.), which reorganized and brought in new talent, including "passionate ice climbers and users … financial management, fundraising, marketing and outdoor recreation industry," said president MacLeod. Jeff Lowe, founder of the Ouray Ice Festival in 1996, had turned it over to OIPI in 2002. He came for the first Jeff Lowe Award for donating "significant time and talents to the Ice Fest," given to Whitt, co-founder of the park twenty-one years before. Lowe, "the godfather of modern ice climbing," was fighting a progressive neurogenerative disorder. His Festival appearance, made from a wheelchair, was a "big love fest." On March 31, a "busy and successful" Ice Park season ended.

◆ ◆ ◆

On February 17, a 6 p.m. call for a skier with a broken ankle on Blue Lakes Trail became a skiing / snowmobiling odyssey. In poor weather, nine members got to the end of four plowed miles of CR 7 leading to Blue Lakes Trail just before 8 p.m. Ahead lay another five miles of snowbound road and 2.6 miles of backcountry trail under three feet of snow, said Capt. Pasek. Fifty-three-year-old nurse practitioner Jean Lein lay at 10,400 feet. She and a companion, Curt Leitzinger, a ski patroller at Powderhorn, had skied under a bluebird sky from the Ridgway Hut toward the Blue Lakes Hut. Descending from Wilson Overlook, her "backcountry touring ski hit or caught on something and before she knew it, Lein was flipping through the air and landed in several feet of powder to the right of the trail." She heard something crack.

They discussed the options. Leitzinger splinted her leg with a ski pole and arranged a wind shelter. She got into one sleeping bag and he put another one along with a safety blanket around her. She was tucked under a tree, "with a tarp, leaves, his warm jacket," said Pasek, "relatively comfortable, she wasn't shivering or anything." Leitzinger "took a GPS reading, reassured Lein he 'would not leave her there forever,'" and went for help. Ninety minutes later he skied into cell range and called 911.

Four expert snowmobilers zoomed through the storm, arriving at rescue base at 8. Steve Duce, Nick Peck, Richard Weber, Jr. and Tony Schmidt picked up Pasek, Blaine Eischied, Matt Hepp and Estes. Twenty minutes later, they met Leitzinger skiing out at MM 7 and he gave them Lein's coordinates on the Wilson Creek Trail. The machines got rescuers and gear to within a mile and a half of her. Just before 11, Weber pushed his machine to the remote junction of Blaine Basin and Dallas Trails and dropped off the toboggan, .3-mile downhill from the patient.

Hepp climbed 400 vertical feet to Lein with a vacuum splint and hypothermia gear; others hauled the toboggan. "She was very, very calm and collected and kind of wiry waiting there," said Pasek. They splinted her right ankle and packaged her in the toboggan with chemical heat packs and blankets, sleeping bags, warm mittens, hat and harness. Purcell Prusiks – adjustable SAR rope loops – held her harness onto the sled to keep her from sliding forward during the three-mile descent. At midnight they moved down toward the first of three creeks, where snowmobiles waited. They lifted her out, said Pasek, and carried her across because the creek surface was too rough to drag a loaded toboggan. At 1:20 a.m. they reached Weber's machine. An hour later snowmobile and sled reached the road.

Lein self-transported to Montrose with Leitzinger instead of riding the ambulance. Fifty minutes later, four rescuers and snowmobiles reached "Elsie," Rescue 11. OMRT got back to the barn at 4 a.m. A few days later Lein sent thanks for her rescue by "people who are working full time and have families … there they are in the middle of the night to help you."

The first of two June callouts was for a rental car on its roof in Red Mountain Creek. Another involved former miner George

Munzing who had pulled his pickup over on a very narrow stretch of road three-fourths of a mile above Lower Camp Bird to let a Jeep tour pass: "his back wheels went off the road. The Jeep tried to pull his truck onto the road but the tow strap snapped, sending Munzing over the edge." The vehicle rolled, coming to rest on its roof at the top of a cliff. Munzing was trapped, his feet entangled in tree branches, but "It didn't go the distance," said Pasek. "He was pinned for a long time," said Mitchell. They finally "gave him a saw ... rather than trying to move the car it was easier to cut the tree." The Fire Department got him out and OMRT raised him to the road. Mitchell took him to town in her truck after he refused treatment.

On July 10, a twenty-five-year-old woman from Missouri fell on a steep, unforgiving talus slope 400 feet below Sneffels' summit after she and a friend wandered seriously off route. Twelve members responded at 2 p.m. When R11 got to the trailhead, Pasek and Kavanaugh took off with first responder and trauma kits, O2 and a blanket. After a fast ascent, Pasek spotted her with binoculars. They reached her at 3:40. The women "had tried to down climb" a "low fifth class section," said Kavanaugh. The patient had fallen and hit her chest: "She thought she had broken her wrist, her chest hurt." They debated calling a helicopter, "but she declined, just wanted to get out of there." She initially lost consciousness after the forty to fifty-foot fall and her O2 saturation was eighty-two percent, so they put her on oxygen, splinted her right wrist and wrapped it with a cold pack. "We rigged up, put some anchor points in, and ... lowered her," said Kavanaugh. At 5:22 they eased the litter through a rock opening and then down to Lavender Col. At 6:30 they reached the trail and put the wheel under the litter. At 7:20 they reached R11.

After a stand-down for a missing hiker in July, everything went quiet until November 17 when a skier triggered an avalanche on Trico Peak. He was "buried up to his chest" but breathing, said Pasek. "His buddy came over, he dug himself out." Don Moden, skiing the ridge to Commodore Gulch, saw it happen and satellite-texted his wife Brenda, who called 911. "We had CareFlight launch from Montrose," wrote the captain, but "the ski party had self rescued and made it to Red Mountain Pass so we stood down." The same day, deadly carbon monoxide gas buildup killed two miners and injured others at the Revenue Mine near Camp Bird Road. OMRT was called; Pasek said because it was underground, they assisted with helicopters and medical work and cleared out the barn for corpse / coroner work.

On November 21 Ouray native Zina Lahr went missing. She was her grandmother Pat Lahr's caretaker after returning in July from Los Angeles. A film animator with Chiodo Bros Productions, she helped "create a whimsical, life-sized pink and purple dinosaur puppet named Lily for the Santa Barbara Zoo." Known locally for her creativity, she studied media arts, animation and graphic design with the Art Institute of Pittsburgh. As a teenager, she had created a wiggling robotic rat and red-eyed flapping raven for a Dracula show.

She went walking in late afternoon, November 20, as wet weather set in. Neighbor Bob Risch saw her going north toward the Hot Springs Park about 4:30 p.m., just at dusk. At 6 she hadn't returned and her mother, Cindy Lahr, contacted friends and neighbors, who searched for several hours before police were called at 10. Officer Justin Crandall searched with them until 3:30 a.m. but they found nothing. After the Sheriff issued an alert the next morning, a private search party spotted the twenty-three-year-old's body 150 yards above the Cascade section of Perimeter Trail, lying in very wet snow from the night before.

OMRT was searching east of town when they heard that she had been found. Everyone converged on Cascade trailhead. Kavanaugh and Stewart hiked up with an AED (Automated External Defibrillator). Kavanaugh had "a sense of urgency that if she was alive, this is our window because there was a storm coming in." It was spitting snow when they got to the body, which lay face down. They secured her in the litter and carried it down steep talus to the north.

She had fallen "from a considerable height (fifty to seventy-five feet) striking the earth below her," wrote the Coroner, detailing traumatic head injuries, a broken rib, multiple lacerations, contusions and abrasions. In her back pocket was a fragment of lichen; Zina habitually brought back a special object for her grandmother from her walks. Kavanaugh said that rescuers always hope that "there is still a pulse," but when a victim is found "the emotions come into play and it's not a rescue anymore." Mourners young and old filled Cedar Hill Cemetery on November 27. Her family, childhood friends, neighbors and rescuers said goodbye. Kavanaugh came "mainly for some closure. I didn't know her but it was a traumatic experience for everybody." It was his first body recovery. Journalist Samantha Wright captured her spirit: "Brilliant, spiritual, and exceptionally creative, Lahr touched the hearts of many people during her brief lifetime."

◆ ◆ ◆

OMRT celebrated its 40th year with twenty-six men and women on the roster, including three on reserve. Two had served twenty-seven years, starting in 1988 and 1989. Seven began in the 1990s, eight the 2000s. Nine had joined since 2010. Six were past captains, able to run a rescue at a moment's notice. They were familiar with backcountry trails, climbing routes and emergency medicine. They could rig a rescue, load a helicopter, extricate people from swift water, icefalls and canyons. "They're constantly improving and working and training," said Sheriff Mattivi. "Their expertise is beyond ... amazing." He had a special word for them: Supererogation. "I always have the captains on speed dial."

◆ ◆ ◆

Several Durango women set out to hike the Ouray Perimeter Trail on a sunny February day. Under the Pool Wall one on snowshoes tripped, fell and was seriously injured. "She didn't just slip and fall and break her wrist," said Pasek. "She came off the trail just a body length ... she was probably 5 to 5 ½ [feet] tall, she fell and ended up going head first into one of those sharp rocks." Because of "Potential danger to the orbit, the eye socket ... possible vision issues," a helicopter was called. OMRT put the wheel on the litter and rushed her to the park and chopper just across the road. Joanie Gibbs, a very fit team veteran, heard the page and response from the Rigging for Rescue office two blocks away. She realized "they didn't have very many people ... the truck was there and they had something more that needed to go up so I hiked it up." Afterward, she "helped break down and then carry stuff down. At that point I wasn't even on the reserve list!" OMRT received a thank you, a donation and an Ouray Brewery gift certificate from Bonnie's friends. She was expected "to make a full recovery after reconstructive surgery in Denver despite multiple fractures around her left eye / temple area," said Pasek.

Fourteen callouts in two and a half months included two responses to Red Mountain Pass. On July 15, a motorcycle went off the menacing Ruby Walls, MM 89.8 on a wet road. "A family parked at an overlook near Engineer Pass turn-off either saw the accident happen or spotted the accident victim in the gorge" and notified authorities, but did not wait for the response. Shortly after 8:30 p.m., rescuers found a body trapped under a 1999 Suzuki DX 650 sport motorbike 140 feet below the cliff. Two hours later, the bike was winched off and Tricia Eischied, Kavanaugh and Skoloda took the corpse to the road. The motorcycle was retrieved the next morning. Nine days later, authorities had not released his name since no next of kin had been found. What they did know was, "based on the skid marks left on the highway, the fifty-year-old victim 'was going too fast'" for a twenty-five MPH speed limit. It was a first rescue for Dolgio Nergui, assisting Mark Miller with the rigging at the top. But because she "didn't really see the patient, it was not as emotional as it would've been."

A second accident had a happier ending. At 9:30 p.m. Sunday, August 31, twenty-five-year-old Caleb Schiller's 4-door green 1994 Chrysler sedan "plunged about 200 feet down a steep scree embankment between MM 90 and 91 before coming to rest in a thicket of pine trees." He got himself out of the car and "climbed about 150 feet up the slope, but collapsed about 40 feet shy of the highway, where he spent the remainder of the night." OMRT responded shortly after 8 a.m., reached Schiller at 8:45 and an hour later he was in the ambulance.

A July 17 rescue drew ten members to Owl Creek Pass / CR 8 and the Nate Creek / Lou Creek trailheads. Stewart said a woman's horse spooked, fell over backwards, crushed her pelvis. Her companions called 911 and gave emergency personnel a GPS reading of the location. The page went out at 2:15 p.m. After a long drive, Stewart and trainee Bill Hall hiked "3.5 miles to the patient." "Like so many of the backcountry things," she said, "by the time we finally get to her, she's been laying ... for three hours hurt." The litter came, they packaged her and started out. St. Mary's CareFlight launched at 4 but no suitable LZ existed in the rolling, forested terrain. Later, the patient indicated she was doing well, so they canceled the helicopter. Members took turns maneuvering the litter. "It was a long rescue, time-wise," said Pasek. "Everyone was hungry and thirsty; it was a warm day, and a sweaty endeavor." At 8:50, they reached the trailhead. Tricia Eischied, unable to respond initially, had brought pizza and wings for them.

An innovative approach to locating a lost hiker that month involved Durango CareFlight. A forty-four-year-old woman descending Twin Peaks Trail lost the route, bushwacked until she came to a cliff and called 911 at 6:57 p.m. "While the cell ping was relatively close," said Pasek, "it's not very reliable in this area. We've had cases where the ping is more than a mile away from the person across the Ouray 'basin.' This is probably due to the signal bouncing off the canyon walls, confusing the direction finder on the cell tower."

Ouray had only one cell tower so Pasek could not determine her location by triangulation – using three towers to determine the location by forming triangles to it from known points. The hiker had a flashlight and could see "the big house up on the mountain," above Wanakah Mine on the east side of the river. CareFlight offered fifteen minutes of free search time and located her flashlight beam at 8:32 "900m northwest of the cellphone ping." The GPS reading helped Pasek and Koprek find her after dark on a steep wooded slope above cliff bands. By 10 p.m. they were on Silvershield Trail, reached the bottom at 11:30 and drove to her campsite. "Without certainty of her location," provided by the helicopter, said Pasek, "the next step would have been to call out the team and deploy people both up Oak Creek and Silvershield."

Four callouts the first two weeks of August were for overdue, stranded or injured hikers. The most serious was a request from Crested Butte for help finding a missing hiker in the Raggeds Wilderness. Moden volunteered and on August 16 he searched the Buck Creek drainage on the Marble/West side of O-be-Joyful Pass with two other Tech Team 1 trackers from Garfield County. A missing fifty-four-year-old electrical engineer was not found after three days' searching by fourteen ground and air teams. Moden reported that "you'd have to be a very committed lost hiker to bushwack the game trails necessary to make forward progress" in the area. His party airlifted out from above the Middle Anthracite Creek drainage; that October, hunters found Sherri Ahlbrandt's remains near Middle Anthracite Creek.

◆ ◆ ◆

Fifteen rescuers met in Yankee Boy Basin at sunset Friday night, September 12, facing a dark climb of Sneffels' gnarly southwest ridge. Travis Simpkins, thirty-six, of Littleton, Colorado, and climbing partner Steve Troyer had descended a few hundred feet from the summit when Simpkins fell, tumbling 250 feet. Troyer stabilized him, climbed to the summit and called 911. He came down, "dug in and held onto Simpkins to keep him from sliding further down."

For thirty-three-year-old Stewart, just getting to the mountain was memorable. Others drove to Yankee Boy Basin, but she and Skoloda rode a CareFlight helicopter so they could locate the climbers' position. They "flew around the peak a few times until they spotted Steve's flashing headlight." They were to be dropped off at 13,000-foot Blue Lakes Pass where the route begins, but altitude was a problem for the chopper, so they unloaded at Wright's Lake.

It was September and "the days were a little shorter," said Hepp. "And the good thing is when you get a call that late, you automatically know … that it's going to be in the dark. It's not like you're racing the clock." For Stewart, who "had never done the mountain before … doing it in the dark, carrying a backpack" made it interesting. "There's a couple of spots on the hike that definitely pushed my ability, where you have to do a couple of climbing moves to get up."

They were "going to just try to find this guy and get him down," Hepp said "Then it became a realization that we weren't going to be able to go anywhere." Philippe Wheelock cautioned: "We need to rethink all this." They "realized if we kept trying to push this extrication agenda," said Hepp, "somebody … was going to get hurt."

◆ ◆ ◆

On the mountain, Troyer and Simpkins talked about their young children, "trying to keep each other's spirits up and pass the time. We knew they were coming, but we really didn't know how long it was gonna take…. The headlamps of the rescuers were moving around below us in the dark." Troyer heard a "voice from nearby, that beautiful voice, saying they were coming … they were just above us, figuring out how to climb down." Finally, "God's own army gathered around us on that mountain, setting ropes, giving first aid, putting together a litter." The first team to reach them realized how lucky Simpkins was not to have fallen further down the loose rock. Troyer sat perched on a rock in front of the prone Simpkins. His feet had been "braced against a couple rocks for like five hours," said Stewart. He was leaning "back against his hips … to sort of pin him in place." "It was one of those spots where if you were to trip and stumble, just like this guy did, you'd go a while before you stopped," said Hepp. It was "incredibly sketchy footing," said Stewart. "We're so lucky that we didn't hurt one of us." They "were definitely exposed, at a very real risk of falling down the mountain."

OMRT's first concern was everyone's security. "It was probably one of the worst settings I've ever been in for a rescue," said MacLeod. "Just the crappiest spot….You can't take a step without sliding five feet and this guy's right [in] the middle of it." They were "trying to get anchors built above him, and he's like right there and you're trying not to kick rocks, and it's dark." They finally got "everybody in on an edge line," said Hepp. "We got all that tied in. Got the patient on a line in their harness and then into the vac-bag ... and packaged into the litter. 'All right. Let's get lines to everything.'"

By 1:30 Simpkins was secure. "Trish and I were the main ones working on medical stuff," said Stewart. Jenny Hart, recovering from a cold, had been "the badass for that trip," hauling the unwieldy vac mattress up the ridge. Hepp, MacLeod and Skoloda did security rigging and it became much easier to work," said Stewart, "because at least you didn't have to worry ... they eventually got various little things anchored in and tied together and got a litter attached." They moved the patient to that secure litter and "clipped into the litter or the ropes."

◆ ◆ ◆

A second wave of rescuers went to Lavender Col, up the southeast couloir, over the summit and down the southwest ridge. The moon was so bright Rushing turned off his headlamp. He had never climbed the mountain in the dark, everything he touched moved, and he injured an ankle, which hurt five days later. The second team left "all their coats and everything because ... none of us have BV [bivouac] kits or anything," said MacLeod. "I had like four different coats on and emptied my pack and did the BV sack with my pack." The second team returned to the summit, descending by the tourist route. When they got back to town, said Hepp, they "regrouped all through the night to get resources and figure out what the options were."

Stewart, the highest qualified medical person, stayed on the ridge with MacLeod and Hepp to care for Simpkins since pain control was necessary and only a paramedic could to do it. Once they got him off the rocks that had been poking him for hours and into the litter he felt much better. He was wrapped in a big space blanket with chemical packs and sweated while the rescuers chilled. "He was actually too warm in the morning," said Stewart. "The rest of us were like: 'Maybe we'll bring an extra one of those next time.'"

His care was unusual since she had to decide what an athlete with a closed femur fracture who had been exerting all day needed to drink and eat at 13,900 feet. She offered him some food and he went with "goo gels." She gave him "drinks out of my water bladder," and then tucked "it under the heat blanket with him … so it would stay thawed out."

It was one of the best nights they could imagine. "No wind," MacLeod said. "It was super mild, so we just got cozy." For Troyer, it had been a superlative experience as he and Simpkins initially clung to the mountainside. "The stars, oh the stars … the Milky Way. The shooting stars, the one shooting star was unlike any I've ever seen before, a long burn and then a pop at the end. I think it was sent just for us."

The next morning, early hikers watched a UH-60 Blackhawk from HAATS fly toward Sneffels. Hepp had recently trained with them, "learning how to do the land side of such a hoist operation." "The helicopter sitting there in the wind," he said, is:

> getting bounced around and the cable's coming down and jumping around … that cable's like a 10,000 pound breaking strength … but it's as supple as a shoelace … you really have to be vigilant … because that thing will try to wrap itself around your head in a second.… One person's on the hook, one person's just doing cable management, keep him safe, and then the third person's on the tag line.

The tag line, which keeps the patient from enduring a flat spin, has to have a weak link, said Hepp. "It could be lighter 8 mm rope, it can be full 11 mm rope. But one of the important things is, it's got to have a weak link … like a piece of shoelace or something like that." The training paid off: "We had him ready to go," said MacLeod, "and boom, boom clip, he was gone."

Early morning on Sneffels' southwest ridge: Ruth Stewart checks Travis Simpkins' vital signs. Ropes secure them on a precipitous, unstable slope. Wright's Lake, a turquoise triangle near the initial staging place, nestles in the tundra 1,700 feet below.

Photo by Matt Hepp; Courtesy *Ouray County Plaindealer*

CHAPTER TWENTY-SEVEN

The End of a Fantastic Season

MAY 2015 BROUGHT HEAVY SNOW to the San Juans. For Gary Ryan, who began climbing rocks at five when his dad tied a rope around his waist in the hills near Manchester, England, the ski season was spectacular. As incredible conditions continued into early June, it became his best in thirty-five years of guiding. It was essential that he know the conditions firsthand, so from May 25 to June 2, he skied off Mt. Sneffels five times. On one trip, for a friend who was getting married, the "boys' party" featured the south side, the bridegroom's "last big ski." Ryan also skied the Snake on Sneffels' north face on a personal ski day, as well as the north chute of Gilpin Peak on the west side of Yankee Boy Basin, said his boss Matt Wade at Peak Mountain Guides.

Wade monitors Mt. Sneffels, a world-class ski "when the snow conditions are right.... It's a beautiful summit and then you come back down the rock and then you ski the couloir, which is fairly steep." Both men reviewed weather reports and photos of the Snake, as well as reports from those who had recently skied it. At 4 a.m. on June 2, Ryan did a last weather check. Thirty minutes later he and Seth Beers, thirty-seven, a lifelong skier and competitive racer who had skied Sneffels' south side with Wade – "an impeccable job" – drove to the end of the plowed road in Yankee Boy Basin. At 6:30 they skinned up the southeast gully and Lavender Col. There was "a solid freeze from the night before," said Beers, "and we were able to make good time on the ascent." They switched to boot crampons for the summit climb, arriving at 10 a.m. After a short break, they built an anchor on the summit block and rappelled 100 feet to the top of the Snake. Ryan "judged the conditions were soft enough to ski.... I positioned my client right there.... started to ski down into the couloir and conditions were fairly firm, but it was in my mind to look down the Dogleg…. It was super variable, with sun dependent spring skiing."

"It was a beautiful morning to be in the mountains, clear and calm," remembered Beers. "We were hopeful that protected, north-facing terrain would still be holding dry snow…. [but it] had gotten cooked from the warm-up that began the previous day … refrozen overnight and we were dealing with a fairly stout melt-freeze crust at the top of the couloir." Surprised and disappointed, they discussed the conditions. They had hoped to ski the Snake in spring powder. Beers "didn't need to ski the line if the conditions were not ideal…. I was perfectly OK ascending back to the summit and returning to the car … if he felt that was the best option. Gary acknowledged but wanted to descend a bit further into the couloir to see if better conditions existed." He watched Ryan ski away and down; communication became difficult, mainly due to the "chatter-noise of side-slipping on steep, frozen snow!" At the beginning of the Dogleg pitch near 13,700 feet, "I lost visual, Gary was still side-slipping down and under control."

◆ ◆ ◆

Ryan sideslipped toward a safe position to look down the narrow, rock-ribbed Dogleg, but the snow became so firm that he "couldn't even hold a side edge and all of the sudden I was tumbling." Surprised, he tried to stay on his side "and get my edges back in" but he "was cartwheeling before I knew it, didn't have a chance to look down the couloir … bounced into walls and went over edges." It looked like nice soft snow and "kind of lured me in a wee bit." A thousand vertical feet later, he sat, looking north, "one ski tip … showing me the tail … my leg was virtually backwards." His K2 Coomback skis still clung to his boots. As usual, before skiing such severe terrain, he had prepped his skis, so the bindings were tight. No skier could afford to lose a ski in the Snake, "one of "the places where you don't fall."

In forty-five years of climbing and guiding, he had never had an accident or even taken an out of control fall. In examining the Dogleg, said Wade, "he was doing what any guide would do." Ryan had "landed and realized my leg's on backwards and I am in agony." He carried two communication tools, a SPOT mobile satellite positioning device and a cell phone. He texted Wade: "Need help. Broke my leg. At bottom of Snake." Then he called him: "I told Matt that I had been hurt…. I might have punctured something, I don't know. I was really having a hard time breathing and talking. I was in a lot of pain. I needed help and most likely heli-evac help." He called Beers, got no connection and realized he must be in a spot with no cell service.

◆ ◆ ◆

Beers, an "experienced, young, very strong, fit skier" wanted to learn more about ski mountaineering. He watched Ryan ski the upper line of the Snake, observing and testing the conditions. When he disappeared near the upper corner of the Dogleg, Beers thought he "heard a yell ... very faint, so I called back and asked if he had said something. I didn't get a response." He "tried yelling to him several more times with no luck.... I realized there was a high likelihood that he had fallen and that what I had heard was a scream." His cell phone hadn't shown a signal on the summit and wasn't showing one now. Ryan had the Spot device so there was no possible communication. Beers thought about his options: staying put; climbing back to the summit; descending to Yankee Boy Basin and going for help; and finally, descending the route. He "had boot crampons and a lightweight ski mountaineering ax." He was "confident that I could downclimb ... my ability to safely get off the mountain was the leading factor in my choice to descend. I simply wasn't going to be of any help ... if I fell and turned into another injured or lost climber on the mountain. So I began to cautiously descend."

◆ ◆ ◆

Wade took Ryan's call at 10:27, as he read the text message. He asked his exact location and if he was in a safe spot. Ryan said he "was safe at the moment" at 12,650 feet according to his watch altimeter. Wade asked what happened. Ryan said he "made a few turns down the couloir to investigate the conditions and then slipped on a patch of ice and fell down the remainder." He said Seth was still at the top. Wade asked him to leave his phone on while he called 911. He would call back. He contacted former OMRT captain Matt Hepp, described the situation and requested assistance. Hepp said he would mobilize the team and that Wade should meet them at the barn. Wade called 911 and provided the same information (age, gender, what happened, exact location, probable injury) and said OMRT was mobilizing for rescue.

He called Ryan back; he was still having trouble breathing and that set off alarm bells. "I told Gary I was doing everything I could to get to him as soon as possible." Wade also called Averill Doering, Ryan's girlfriend, got her voicemail and left a message. Then he called Nate Disser, owner of San Juan Mountain Guides and an OMRT member, to request support and extra manpower if needed. Disser said he would contact his staff right away. Angela Hawse, one of Wade's guides, agreed to come. Finally, Wade called Beers, got voicemail and asked him to stay where he was until a rescue was organized.

OMRT was paged at 11:01. Fourteen members responded. Lt. Tim Pasek conducted the operation with EMS director Kim Mitchell. When Pasek got the latest, "dire" patient report from Wade, "Leg broken (tib / fib), Rib Pain, Difficulty Breathing, High Level of Pain, Reduced Level of Consciousness," he called immediately for a helicopter from the Army National Guard in Gypsum. They also needed "a ground team in case there is a malfunction of the aircraft or whatever and they can't fly." Pasek had some very experienced people, including "a mountain guide who had been in Yankee Boy Basin and he said, 'I have a semi-decent route!'"

By 12:10 a south approach team – Hepp, Dan Hughes, Philippe Wheelock and ski guide Keith Garvey – were enroute to Yankee Boy. If conditions permitted, said Wade, they would ascend Sneffels' ridgeline east of Lavender Col and descend the snowfield on the east side of the massive north face. A north approach team – Capt. Cory Jackson, Jeff Skoloda, Mike MacLeod, Hawse, Disser and Jim Turner – stood by.

◆ ◆ ◆

Focused on safety, Beers slowly sideslipped the first few hundred feet of the shaded couloir. It was:

solid melt freeze crust ... where the couloir initially doglegs and pitches up to its steepest point ... a wet avalanche, likely from the prior day, had stripped the gut ... and basically left a blue-ice runnel ... stripped most of the choke to rock and water ice....These sections were completely unskiable so I stopped, dug a small bench, built a light anchor to prevent a fall in case of a slip, and transitioned into boot crampons. The downclimbing was ... a bit challenging because I had a mountaineering ax vs. an ice ax, and I actually found the downclimb quite a bit easier on the sides. Although it was steeper here, I was at least able to sink my ax in deep enough to feel better about the holds.

He felt the angle of the snow easing, thought about what he would do once he was out of the Snake. "Having downclimbed what Gary had fallen through … the probability was pretty high that Gary would not be alive when, or if, I found him." Then he started seeing equipment and "finally got eyes on Gary." Amazed at how far he had fallen, Beers also knew they were in the middle of avalanche terrain. The snow heated rapidly in the high June sun.

Beer's cell phone had one bar. He called 911 to report the accident, moved to Ryan and called Matt Wade to say he was safe and update him. Wade consulted Mitchell on the best way to care for Ryan and they agreed he "needed to be insulated from the snow, checked for bleeding, and kept warm." When Wade called back, Beers said there was no significant bleeding. He had backpacks, ropes and clothing to keep Ryan off the snow, dug a small platform and moved him.

"Things were warming up and the sun was getting in that face," Ryan said. "We were getting into more of an avalanche concern." "Conditions were terrible," Pasek reported later. Wet, slushy snow "created ideal conditions for small avalanches." Rocks fell around the two skiers. A small slide threw Ryan downslope and "partially buried him with his head facing downhill. Even though I saw it coming," said Beers, "the slide knocked me off my feet and scattered equipment all over. I was able to get down to Gary and get him out of the snow fairly quickly but it was something that we could have done without."

At 12:19 he reported the small wet loose avalanche, which had pushed them "100 feet downslope but the volume of snow was not sufficient to cause harm." Wade asked if the entire slope above their position slid; Beers said it had. Assuming that there was no more snow to slide, Wade told them to stay in place, that the helicopter was on its way. Ryan did his best not to pass out from the pain. For two and a half hours Beers sat next to him, trying to keep him "warm, hydrated, encouraged, and as comfortable as possible." They talked about the possibility of moving to a "slightly safer position on the slope, but it just didn't seem possible given the terrain and the extent of his injuries." Beers kept his skis on in case another avalanche came.

◆ ◆ ◆

Mitchell realized that Pasek faced some really hard decisions if no military helicopter was available. Both ground teams would need to ski for miles in really bad conditions to reach Ryan. A major factor was the afternoon temperature increase on both the north and south approaches to the mountain. They might have to wait until everything began to cool off. If they had to "wait for that snow to consolidate in the evening and do a ground approach, we would have probably flown people into Blaine Basin at the very, very bottom," he said. Fortunately, at 12:54 a TALON 12 Army National Guard UH-60 Blackhawk called – airborne with an estimated time enroute of sixty minutes. At that point command moved to the Ridgway Fairgrounds. Mitchell called for a St. Mary's CareFlight from Grand Junction to meet them there.

Enroute to the Fairgrounds, Jackson, Pasek and Skoloda discussed using the Talon's Jungle Penetrator "as the magnitude of the avalanche conditions became more and more clear," said Pasek. "The JP seemed like a good tool to minimize exposure to the rescuers while effecting a rescue." Otherwise, they would have to get to the bottom of Blaine Basin and wait for conditions to improve before they could get to Ryan and Beers.

◆ ◆ ◆

In Yankee Boy Basin, the south approach team parked at the restroom and skinned toward Dyke Col between Kismet and Cirque Mountains. The steep south slopes were already soft, said Hepp, with "roller balls coming down and ski poles just sinking through the snow." They were aware of the danger but also knew that getting a helicopter to Ryan was not a done deal and they needed to explore the possibility of crossing the Dyke and descending the northeast side of Blaine Basin. They were "traversing, trying to find a way to avoid the slide paths. They were actually going onto paths that had slid that they knew were clear," said Pasek. "They knew they could get into that and then figure out to go up or down to get across the next one." Finally, snow conditions got so bad that they had to turn around, but since they had no radio communication with Operations at the Fairgrounds, they still didn't know how Ryan would come out. "That was a tough decision to make," said Hepp, "because not only is there somebody that needs to be rescued, but it's a local that everybody knows."

◆ ◆ ◆

At 1:49 Jackson and Skoloda boarded Talon 12 with a litter. Twelve minutes later they assessed the scene as the chopper hovered above the skiers. We "were watching wet slabs flowing as we were going in

... and then you look up and there are big rock bands above," said Skoloda. "We're directly below the Snake Couloir ... you can see all of the wet slab debris." They would have to grab the two men from the mouth of the Snake, right where it empties into Mt. Sneffels' prominent snowfield and they realized they had no time for the litter or anything else. "We're all in danger every single second," said Skoloda. Jackson rode the JP and made the first physical assessment of Ryan's condition, but discovered he had no radio contact with the helicopter. The pilot sent Skoloda down.

> *Beers was the first to be lifted out. It was a "surreal experience,"*
> *he said.*
> *Jeff and Cory descended on the jungle penetrator ... one of them came to me to see if I was OK, told me to sit tight while they determined how they were going to handle Gary ... after a quick evaluation they came over and told me they were going to airlift both of us out and that I would be going first. I quickly got on the jungle penetrator, they locked me in and up I went.*

For Ryan time seemed interminable until the helicopter appeared and flew around them. "Cory came down and then I kind of filled him in," he said. "Jeff Skoloda was lowered down ... on this thing that looked like a giant sea anchor."

> *Jackson said, "Can you hang on to this?"*
> *I said, "You bet I can."*

They strapped him into the JP, he was lifted to the helicopter and strong arms dragged him inside. His floppy leg jammed in the door and he screamed in pain. Overriding the pain, however, was "a huge wave of relief.... I was getting out of there." Jackson came next. Then, as Skoloda mounted the wedge-shaped anchor, which was already in motion, the whole slope went. When he got to the airship, he collapsed "in relief ... after watching the slide run right below," said Beers. It was, "quite unbelievable," a class 2 avalanche, he estimated, defined as "big enough to bury, injure or kill a person."

◆ ◆ ◆

At the Fairgrounds, Pasek and Mitchell monitored radio traffic, knowing that everyone had to get off that slope; it could go at any moment. By 2:24, only nineteen minutes after Jackson was lowered to Ryan and Beers, the TALON 12 headed to the Fairgrounds. "They did not have any choice," said Mitchell of the two rescuers: "That was really frightening." She thought of Skoloda's young children: "He's got ... a lot to live for."

At the Fairgrounds an ambulance waited. Once Ryan was stabilized, the attendants transferred him to CareFlight. The medics told him they would take the pain away. When he woke up he was in the hospital. The South team checked in from Camp Bird Mine where they finally had radio contact. By 2:45 they reached the barn, but waited another fifty minutes for the Fairgrounds and North team to arrive.

Pasek debriefed with the pilot on the phone a couple days later. The pilot said the helicopter was facing into the mountain and he had seen the slide coming.

He asks the crew chief: "Is he hooked up?"
"Yeah."
"Bring him up."

The pilot "started raising the helicopter as the hoist operator was taking in cable to get him off the snow." "I almost died up there," Skoloda said, but "from my vantage point, it was the only way that thing was going to happen and he was going to live." Skoloda said that afterwards he just "wanted to go home and see my family."

Ryan "ended up with some very expensive tattoos ... half million dollar tattoos," in addition to metal rods and screws holding his right leg together, the distal fibula feathered like a toothbrush. Skiing is "what I love to do and taking it to the edges has been a very rewarding life ... to be able to do that for work is a whole other ball game.... I have stood on that same edge, you know, a thousand times in my life and that is the one time I slipped ... it's somewhat the nature of the game, for sure." Sometime after the accident, he told Skoloda that:

"He would be satisfied to ski low angle fluffy runs the rest of his life."
I said, 'Yeah, I think anybody would be happy to do that."

On the road to recovery: Gary Ryan, in wheelchair, visits with Jeff Skoloda, left, and the Talon 12 pilot and hoist operator who rescued them.

Photo courtesy Jeff Skoloda

"Uncommon by definition"

FRIDAY, JULY 29, 2015, was a perfectly hot eighty-two degrees in the shade in Ouray. It felt much hotter on the intensely sunny pink cliffs of the southwest-facing Amphitheater where the Chief Ouray Trail snaked up to a high crossing of Cascade Creek. An urgent call came in: a Montrose eleven-year-old had fallen from a sixty-foot cliff into a high Cascade basin. Her father managed to scramble down to her. A couple of hikers called 911. The 11 a.m. callout for the unconscious Abby brought a "skeleton crew" scrambling to her rescue, said Medical Officer Tricia Eischied, who initially directed the rescue from the barn's command post. EMS director Kim Mitchell assisted from the Amphitheater Campground. Among the first rescuers ascending the 2.5-mile trail in ninety-five degree heat were Jenny and Sean Hart, Sam Rushing and Ruth Stewart. Anticipating the worst, Rushing took a body bag. Their radios went dead, but they found a witness who said, "She's alive." A man helped Sean Hart carry gear. A second crew, Matt Hepp, Dr. Patrick Brighton, Jared Vilhauer and Dave Ahrens, hauled supplies.

No one anticipated how high up she lay: 10,000 feet. They "were totally in disbelief it could be all the way up there," said Jenny Hart. Trail runner Sean Hart reached her in sixty-six minutes. "For the Harts, long-time team members, the call carried added urgency because of the severity of her injuries." She was the age of their children, eleven-year-old Mica and twelve-year-old Hayden.

Dr. Brighton scrambled down a forty-five-degree slope to Abby, lying in the spray of the falls, "soaked to the skin." Her father had covered her with a shirt. "She was unconscious, breathing erratically, gurgling occasionally with no purposeful movements," the doctor said, with "fractures to her skull, spine and left ankle, a sprained neck and nerve damage to her left shoulder." On the Glasgow scale of 3-15, used "to help gauge the severity of an acute brain injury," she was a 5. She lay "in extremis" [at the point of death], had a closed head injury, spinal fluid leaking from her ears and a clenched jaw, which prevented giving her an airway. He put an oxygen mask on her face and asked Stewart to have the ambulance ready a tracheal tube.

Hepp dropped his load at the stream crossing above the waterfall and ran half a mile up to a prominent rock outcrop to radio wind speed and GPS position to Eischied, who was going through necessary channels to get a Blackhawk helicopter. It wasn't dispatched yet and more than an hour away. Hepp suggested they wheel Abby down. They needed more oxygen; there was no one fit enough to do it, so Eischied hiked the cannister up the trail.

Sean Hart, Stewart and Dr. Brighton raised the litter sixty to seventy feet to the trail. From there, it was "ninety hot, difficult, downhill minutes" to the trailhead, but it was "one of the smoothest operations" the doctor had ever seen. Dan Hughes packed water uphill to thirsty rescuers; Dolgio Nergui said she, Sean and Jenny Hart dealt with "ropes, backpacks and personal gear all over the place." They packed everything up and hauled it down.

"The ambulance drove from the park with the flight crew up to the amphitheater," Eischied said. "When we got her in the parking area, she was loaded ... and the flight crew was hands on from that point." St. Mary's initially flew her to Grand Junction and later that night transferred her to a children's medical facility in Salt Lake, where a trauma team worked on her until 3 a.m. After a long, and at times uncertain recovery, Abby returned to Montrose that fall. Dr. Brighton, a general surgeon for twenty-eight years and author of the *Hikers' and Backpackers' Guide to Treating Medical Emergencies*, told Jenny Hart that he had never in his career seen a person who was injured that badly recover so quickly. He said one of the primary reasons she's alive is that she was so young. Lying in the waterfall, said Jenny Hart, Abby became "hypothermic rather quickly." That immediate chilling helped, too.

"On November 9 Abby and her family attended an open house at OMRT's barn, with the happy survivor walking and talking and being a normal twelve-year-old." It was very emotional for the team. Thinking back on her rescue, Dr. Brighton said, "It was like we had trained this a hundred times." Everyone acted without hesitation and "that's why Abby is still alive." Jenny Hart, Ouray's fourth grade teacher, still sees her; she "is a part of my life."

◆ ◆ ◆

Keeping backcountry victims alive and safe on the way to the hospital is the second necessity of rescue work; keeping rescuers safe is the first. In the wild and lonesome San Juans, where 357 summits rise above 13,000 feet, these imperatives may clash. The Incident Commander must ensure they are met – and they are. Remarkably, in forty-four years, no OMRT member has died or been seriously injured performing a rescue. Three hundred and fifty-three men and women have incorporated OMRT into their lives since the first members resolved a quandary about who should be captain. Ouray Police Chief Keith Kelley volunteered, said Mike Hamrick. "He basically gave the rescue team any resource." They had "little Mickey Mouse radios ... [that] wouldn't go very long, so he'd ... be the radio dispatch guy." David Mullings, who joined OMRT twenty-five years later, said Kelley, his neighbor, was "down-to-earth, a friend to all, and a jack-of-all-trades ... dedicated and good at any vocation he chose."

One memorable night, Capt. Kelley called Hamrick at 11. "Somebody's gone off Red Mountain Pass, will you help me? I'll come down and get you." They "went tearing back up there ... a motorist had seen this car go off the side of the road.... I don't know where the deputies were, but I think it was a weeknight ... [Kelley] couldn't drive and look down in the ravine," so Hamrick sat in the passenger door window with a big spotlight, looked over the edge, and finally saw a taillight reflection. The captain radioed for help, they grabbed a "little first aid box" and climbed down a scree slope. At the bottom a car "was all crunched together ... collapsed into some alder bushes." Thinking the boy inside must be dead, the captain reached into the car:

> *"Jesus, I sure am cold," said a voice. "You got a blanket?"*
> *Keith kind of pulls this guy out and asks if he's okay.*
> *"Yeah, I'm okay. I'm just cold."*
> *"Damn you. I will take you down and put you in jail. You're drunk like a skunk."*

◆ ◆ ◆

The *Plaindealer's* philosophical editor Mullings once wrote, "Mountain Rescue's assignments are almost uncommon by definition, and thus often end up on page 1." In 1974 a false alarm, two rescues on Mt. Sneffels' north face and another eighteen callouts bonded the rescuers, Ouray and the *Plaindealer's* far-flung readers. It continues today. Kurt Kircher, OMRT's father figure and founding genius was then fifty-six and everyone else considerably younger, but some thirty years his junior couldn't keep up with him. A favorite 6 a.m. hike with Bill Hopkins was the steep six-mile Twin Peaks Trail, with a full pack. Born May 2, 1918, in Malmoe, Sweden, he graduated in 1942 from the Royal Institute of Technology in Stockholm as an Automotive Engineer. From 1939-1945, he was infantry soldier, ski trooper, part of Sweden's first mountain regiment, and a skiing and arctic survival instructor with a rank of captain.

He and his first wife Margareta lived in Argentina from 1946-1949. He climbed in the Andes, including Aconcagua, where he turned around at 19,000 feet because of bad weather. In Colorado by 1951, he became a Ski Touring Instructor. From 1972-1976, he operated Box Canyon Ski School and ski touring program, taught first aid and avalanche hazard recognition. He was Vice-Chair of Region Ten Emergency Medical Systems Council from 1974-1977 and served on NASAR's Emergency Medicine Committee. A Stage II Certified Ski Touring Instructor and EMT, he also completed Silverton Avalanche School four times.

Kircher participated in over 100 rescues, taught survival training, rope handling, mountaineering, evacuation techniques, avalanche recognition and rescue, skiing, winter camping and first aid. In 1974, he was the man for the moment, with a gold mine of knowledge, technique and experience; a vision for the future; and charisma that inspired others to serve. Many members were mountaineers who knew each other's capabilities. "They weren't part of the rescue team as a way of being in the mountains," said Lynn Kircher. "That is what they did normally ... it was a service they thought was needed." "You knew exactly what the other guy was capable of doing," said Kurt Kircher. "You didn't mind hanging at the end of a rope because you knew the guy on the other end."

◆ ◆ ◆

Coincidence warps a thread in this story: in the spring of 1974, thirteen-year-old Bill MacTiernan's sixth grade teacher, trying to interest him in school, gave him Royal Robbins' *Basic Rockcraft* and

Montrose climber Tom Mourey's phone number. Early that summer Mourey fell on Sneffels' north face and was paralyzed, so that climbing session never happened. Thirteen years later, MacTiernan, a self-taught climber and author of *Ouray Ice: The Beta Edition,* joined OMRT. Within six years, he was training officer, lieutenant, and captain at thirty-two, one of several young captains. In January 1978, twenty-nine-year-old Rick Trujillo became the third and last original member to be captain, succeeding Kurt Kircher.

◆ ◆ ◆

Dave Frank was twenty-seven when a high school friend, Training Officer MacTiernan, recruited him in 1989. They climbed on the dump wall together when they could. OMRT meetings were mostly training, said Frank, "so when a call came out, you ... would all show up and you knew each other's habits and patterns.... You knew each other's strength and weaknesses." Like many members, he hoped to "help humanity." His most memorable rescue, though, involved a gentleman who had a stroke at Ruby Walls. The autopsy later said he had probably died before the car left the road. OMRT retrieved the body, but the USFS wanted the wreck out of the canyon, which wasn't their responsibility. MacTiernan and Frank volunteered.

A tow truck with a very long cable showed up the next day and the highway closed. MacTiernan "went down first and he guided the ropes down," said Frank. "I went second, rappelling down and guiding the tow cable. The slope about the first 100 yards is fairly steep." He guided the cable around rocks, trees and stumps; the sun came out and melted enough snow that water ran down his rope, to which he was attached with a Figure 8 device. "I get to the edge, I lean back. I'm in a good rappelling position.... I step back and I zip down about thirty feet." The sun had set behind the mountain and the rope iced, leaving his feet hanging in air. He finally made contact with solid rock and stopped. MacTiernan looked at him: "Bet that was exciting."

The friends hiked to the torn up, blue-gray car, dug around in three feet of snow, and found the only place to attach the cable was to the axle. They radioed the crew to let them get halfway out before pulling up the cable, fearing the car might pop loose and bounce. They hiked out on a little trail, shucked climbing gear, drove back to town and sat in the Elks Lodge with a well-deserved beer. Someone spotted the lights of the tow truck coming down.

"We look as it drives by and there is nothing but the axle on the back of the truck."

Later the Forest Service said, "Well, you guys, you know, you have to retrieve the car."

And everybody said, "No."

Frank had risked his life "to save an axle."

◆ ◆ ◆

In 1976, John Kropuenske became the first high school student to join the team. Unusually experienced in the outdoors, Kropuenske was "just thrilled to be part of the group," happily trained and showed up for rescues. "No one ever suggested I stand back and watch. That was very empowering." He remained grateful to his mentors, Lt. Mike Hamrick and Training Officer Jim Fife, with whom he trained in Bear Creek Canyon. Another student, Thad Spaulding, punned that he joined OMRT at seventeen "to learn the ropes and help people." The young journalist chronicled an amazing live 1988 rescue of eighty-year-old Ray Cushman and his wife Florence from a Mother Cline avalanche. He participated in several memorable rescues, graduated in 1989, "and thus ended what I thought at the time was a long career with the OMR."

◆ ◆ ◆

Early on, women held supporting roles, but Linda Hash, who had been IC at rescues, became the fifth captain in 1981. Mary Hoeksema, a very experienced ice and rock climber from Boulder, taught fellow members to ice climb in the 1980s. She once slept in a snow cave she dug on an eighteen below zero night at Silverton Avalanche School since her male teammates thought it would be improper if she slept in their tent. By the time Nicole Skoloda joined in 2001, much had changed. She aimed for equipment and training officer, which hadn't been done by a woman. "I wanted to maybe encourage [other women]. I think it's healthy to have them hold their weight in a group with primarily men." Mark Miller, who taught Rigging for Rescue (RfR), was particularly helpful. She had taken his class and sometimes previewed a month's training exercise with him. "I always felt respected and appreciated," she said. "I loved being a part of all of it."

Capt. Tricia Eischied (2017-2018) joined after fellow EMT Mike MacLeod recruited her during a 2008 school bus over the edge training. "It looked like a lot more fun to be on Mountain Rescue," she said. During the 2014 rescue of Travis Simpkins on Sneffels' southwest ridge, she lugged gear up the ridge in the dark, despite having just taken Nyquil for a cold. "That's how I define responding on rescues," she said. "It's not about the patient, it's about your team members, it's about not putting them at risk because they don't have enough resources or not being able to carry the equipment that they need.... I couldn't stay at the truck. They were all just piling stuff in their bags." 2017, her first year as captain, set a record. They "responded to 26 callouts, up from recent annual averages of twenty, with much of the spike ... all-terrain vehicles."

◆ ◆ ◆

OMRT still draws mountaineers and outdoor enthusiasts; their rescue time is not duplicated anywhere else in their lives. In 1974, Lt. Hamrick wanted to help people and was saddened when events prevented that. In 2017, thirty-three-year-old Hot Springs Pool Manager Tom Kavanaugh said, "When you're outside ... it doesn't matter what color you are, doesn't matter what gender you are ... it's one human helping another human being in their time of need ... why wouldn't you want to be part of that?"

There are many roles to fill, as in any great endeavor. Someone must log the time, what happens and who is involved. Some mission recorders, like retired USFS District Ranger Walt Rule, become indispensible to their colleagues and to posterity. For eight years he served as truck and equipment officer, secretary and mission reporter. Chris George called him "the perfect scribe," keeping track of who was out, where and when they came in. Rule used his life experience to find the victims' companions and reporting parties, often getting marvelous interviews from a person who was reeling emotionally. Other scribes have worked late hours in miserable conditions. Mission reporters like Deb Folsom have literally turned the lights out after a precarious, cold rescue.

Captains often write mission reports, which may carry an inescapable whiff of amazement, anger or sadness. After a particularly brutal search for hikers high in wilderness tundra in a blizzard, a growling Capt. George Pasek wrote, "the party was terribly ill-equipped to travel in these mountains." That they survived was solely due to rescuers' risking their lives. Once, after the white death of East Riverside claimed yet another highway worker and threatened sixty-seven searchers for thirty-three hours, Capt. Rick Trujillo went to Denver and lobbied Colorado's governor, Richard Lamm, for a snowshed to protect travelers on Red Mountain Pass.

◆ ◆ ◆

Imaginative, innovative, sensitive people are drawn to rescue work. They see practical problems and figure solutions, like putting bike tires and brakes on litters for better control on muddy, steep or icy trails. They utilize a power company's boom pole for an icy night rescue and then craft specialized poles for their rescue vehicles. They use whatever technology is available to communicate, one of the latest being devices "that allow us to send text messages" through satellites when the mountains and canyons of the San Juans prevent other forms of communication, said Capt. Cory Jackson. "We live in a really unique area and because of this steep topography ... we have to employ whatever means we can to stay in touch."

"We have the respect from the community," wrote Capt. Sam Rushing in 1999, "because we do rescues that other people cannot comprehend." In April 1986, OMRT was called out to retrieve what was left of a man who blew himself up in his car at the Ruby Walls. Twenty-nine years later, Trujillo vividly remembered finding the man's face and hair on the road. "We could see it was just the skin like somebody had slit the back of his head and skinned his face and scalp off." Luckily, such horrific scenes are rare.

Rescuers sometimes encounter terrified people in miserable circumstances. "One of my roles," said Jenny Hart, "is patient interaction. I'm often the one who's dealing with the patient and keeping them safe and talking to them." A 4:21 p.m. callout for a twenty-five-year-old hiker with a broken neck two and a half miles up Blue Lakes Trail on May 23, 2015, was particularly challenging. The north side of the Sneffels Range lay under heavy spring snow, forcing rescuers to alternately pack and then wear snowshoes. "Half the way up the trail," Jackson said, "we were on mud and another half we were on punchy snow."

The man had "three fractured cervical vertebrae with changing ability to feel and move," said Eischied. He was hiking with friends who thought they might climb Sneffels — wearing jeans, shorts and tennis shoes. Above the creek crossing, they left the trail and played, jumping off a huge boulder into snow. It was fun until one of them hit his head and "landed face down in the snow," said Hart. "He's screaming and his friends thought he was laughing," she said. "They thought he was clowning around ... realized quite quickly that something was terribly wrong ... got him turned over ... moved him to shelter under a tree." There was no cell service, said Hart, "so it was many, many hours before we got to him." He was terrified, "the most scared patient I've ever dealt with in eighteen years." They couldn't get a helicopter since "snow showers and fog prevailed during most of the evening, " said Lt. Tim Pasek.

Rescuers got back to the barn at 12:30 a.m., slightly more than eight hours after callout. The rescue had taken six of those, including three hours and fifteen minutes to move him down the dark trail. They slid the fiberglass litter over snowy areas and then used the fat wheel litter for the rest of the slippery trail. He was loaded into a warm ambulance at 11:30. Night rescues are often nasty, though one early member, Laszlo Kubinyi, "really enjoyed ... going at night, trying to find these people," who are not "necessarily hurt [but] are some place really miserable."

◆ ◆ ◆

After an emotionally difficult rescue of Canadian SAR Tech Mark Salesse from the Ice Park and his long but full recovery, rescuers were hit hard when he died in an avalanche four years later, on February 5, 2015. He was "on a training exercise with the 435 Transport and Rescue Squadron. A small avalanche swept him sixty meters over a cliff in the Polar Circus ice climbing area of Banff National Park. After a week of poor weather, his body was found under 2.7 meters [8.9 feet] of snow." Mike Gibbs had climbed Polar Circus in 1999 with the Mt. Everest team of Mike O'Donnell and Erik Weihenmeyer.

Gibbs was then in a "tough time" grieving his friend, climbing partner, fellow guide and longtime teammate Mark Miller, fifty, who had fallen 450 feet to his death while guiding First Gully in Eureka Canyon near Silverton on January 30, 2015. Near the top, he was "free-soloing alongside one of the clients to give him pointers," wrote Dougald MacDonald, when "a large piece of ice fractured unexpectedly under Miller and carried him down the route." A climber who was "in his element on ice," said Gibbs, Miller had been on his staff every day since 1998. He "constantly monitored risks and made sure climbs were done smartly and safely." The friends had climbed together the previous Sunday, January 25, "an all day adventure, filled with good conversation." Gibbs hoped "he died on first bounce."

Miller's first rescue experience was on Denali in the early 1990s. He and his climbing partner were somewhere above 16,000-foot Windy Corner when they "saw this guy stumbling around camp and his partner was trying to help and couldn't," said his wife Colette. They radioed the rangers that they would bring him down to the huts, but would need some help getting the climbers' equipment down and couldn't bring their own packs. With the help of a hand line they short roped the sick man, who was so ill that he "would take a couple of steps and fall over." His companion also made it down using the hand rope. Miller and his partner "ended up staying the night there because it was dark ... they were given food and sleeping bags and everything for the night. Then they went back up and continued on their climb. They did summit, but for Mark the highlight was the rescue ... the summit was secondary."

When they got home to Utah, Mark and Colette joined Weber County Search and Rescue. A few years later, they moved to Ouray, he guided for Mike O'Donnell and became Ice Park Superintendent. In 1999 he joined OMRT, learned Rigging for Rescue (RfR) and became an instructor. He was lieutenant in 2003-2004. Mike MacLeod said his contributions to the Ice Park "cannot be overstated." He "established a number of routes ... organized competition routes ... served on the advisory board. He was instrumental in the development of the ice farming system." Hundreds of people attended his memorial services at the Ice Park and Ouray Community Center.

◆ ◆ ◆

"I don't know any rescue team that does what we do, the variety of it," said Rushing, who was responsible for sending members to a first RfR class in Silverton. Chris Harper, a member for a couple of years in the 1990s, praised Rushing's and others' efforts "in organizing the skills required for OMR participation. Rookies like myself suddenly realized the vast array of skills that the veterans possessed."

Dr. Dave and June Bachman, a registered nurse, moved to Ouray in 1980. They ran the Ouray Medical Practice and joined OMRT. As captain in the mid-eighties, Dr. Bachman got rescuers covered by the county's liability policy and workman's compensation. It was a big deal and relieved a lot of worry even though "we never had any significant injuries," he said. There was amazing support for rescuers from the community. Paul and Lois Klein, who ran the Outlaw

Restaurant, sent "cuisine" to rescuers on long missions through Sheriff Jerry Wakefield, who always looked out for the team. "Jerry would go and we'd get steak sandwiches," said June, "just wonderful food."

Ouray County Sheriff Jerry Wakefield and his trademark blue Toyota.
Photo courtesy Sam Rushing

◆ ◆ ◆

In any rescue, no one sees everything. "You end up compartmentalizing what it is that you do," said Gibbs. "The entire rescue involves a lot of moving parts but I don't think anyone has their finger on the pulse of it all." The IC or someone else may keep a timeline and write up the mission, but the individuals involved in the moving parts often tell stories that enhance the portrait. During the difficult rescue of Abby, "It was really cool to see brand new people [Dr. Patrick Brighton, Jared Vilhauer and Dave Ahrens] … who have been on the team less than a year show up," said Sean Hart. "Those guys did a great job."

◆ ◆ ◆

In a 2007 historical presentation, Jeff Skoloda summed up his first six years on OMRT: "There is nothing like the feeling of being a part of something like that." He participated in many body recoveries, even as he hoped for live ones. Tim Eihausen, whose first rescue in 1996 was a grim Sneffels body recovery, has memories more of "haunting than pride." The Bon Ton Restaurant chef joined because "it's so gorgeous here…. I feel … special for being able to live here and this is a way to give something back." "It has been an honor to serve," Kurt and Lynn Kircher wrote upon retiring from rescue work. "Most of all, we have enjoyed the fellowship of the other members of the Team…. We thank you … for all these years." For Sean Hart, as for many others, saving lives is "a really big deal." For Bill Whitt, with thirty years on OMRT, it was imperative that he use his "skill set," that "considering how hairy a lot of the stuff we've done is, it's amazing nobody has ever gotten hurt. It's because we are all very mountain smart, we all look out for each other and we are all technically skilled for the most part."

The characters that call the team home are "part of the reason I stay," said Sean Hart. "You never know what somebody is going to say next…. You've got a lot of real life people that are like Jenny or me or whatever…. Gibbs who runs his rescue thing. You got normal people … and you got all of these characters." While hiking the busy Blue Lakes Trail to rescue a woman with a broken ankle in 2014, some members carried the litter, but "big, tall and strong" Skoloda carried the bicycle wheel that would be used to roll it out. At one point Jenny Hart said he was overheard assuring inquisitive tourists that it was:

> *"his unicycle and he's going to ride back down."*
> *They weren't sure what to make of him.*
> *"Wow! What is wrong with you?"*

The camaraderie, the bond cemented in extreme circumstances, persists long after active service on OMRT. "They are the greatest people," said Randy Gerke, "on the face of the earth."

A lighthearted moment with the venerable Orange Beast, Summer 2014: Topside L-R: Sean Hart, Clint Estes, Jenny Hart, Mike MacLeod. Ladder: Tom Kavanaugh. Foreground: Ruth Stewart
Photo courtesy Duane Raleigh, *Rock and Ice*

Ouray Mountain Rescue Team Volunteers 1974-2018

353 Members 1974-2018

*	**36 have served 10 years**
**	**9 have served 20 years**
** 1/2	**2 have served 25 years**
***	**2 have served 30 years**

Name	Years	Positions
Dr. Patty Ammon	1993-1995	Medical
Dick Arnold	1990-1993	Aircraft
Steve Arnold	1980-1982	
Dave Ahrens	2016-2018	
Rick Axe	1989-1992	
*Dr. Dave Bachman	1980-1993	Capt. 1985-1986, Lt. 1983-1984, Training, Medical
*June Bachman	1980-1989	RN, Cookbook
Tod Bacigalupi	1983-1987	Training, Resources
Bill Bailey	1980-1982	EMT
Dr. John Baker	1983	Medical
Jill Baker	1983	
Charlie Banta	2010-2012	Building, Tracker
Dick Barker	1978	
Earl Bashaw	1982-1986	EMT
Sue Bashaw	1982-1983	
Milt Bennet	1985-1986	
Lloyd Berry	1974-1976	
Martha Bille	1992-1993	Cookbook
Dan Blackburn	1975	
Patti Blackford	1976-1978	EMT
*Rick Blackford	1975-1988, 1998-1999	Secretary, Treasurer, Equipment

Brent Blake	1975	Communications
Tracy Blashill	1987-1989	
Nick Bohurjak	1974	
Georgie Boots	1975	
Jim Boots	1979	
Bob Borchardt	1980-1982	
Frank Brackvogel	1980-1982	
Debra Braden	1992	
Gerald Bremseth	1987-1989	Secretary
Dr. Patrick Brighton	2016-2018	Secretary, Medical
Mike Briscoe	1991-1995	Truck
Jean Brown	1975-1976	Horses
Mike Bryson	2008-2012	
Joel Burk	2006-2018	Ouray County Undersheriff
John Burkdoll	1985	
Mike Burve	1997-1998	San Juan Regional Director
James Burwick	1980-1986	
Don Camerron	1976-1977	
Jim Campbell	1975	
Chris Candee	1974-1975	
*Don Carlton	2001-2018	Chronicler, Cartoonist
Karyn Carr (Whitt)	1993-1998	Secretary, WEMT-I, Cookbooks
Jeannine Casolari	1992	
Mike Casper	1974	
Jackie Chambers	1979	EMT
Nancy Chilton	1992-1998	Secretary
Warren Chilton	1992-2000	Treasurer, Truck, Equipment, Cookbooks
Jason Chulotta	1992	
Kay Colby	1974	
Dr. Nick Cole	1983-1991	
Joe Condotti, Jr.	1979	
Bruce Conrad	2000-2003	San Juan SAR
*Clint Cook	2004-2013	
Kathy Cook	1983	
Ryan Cook	2004-2010	WFR
Warren Cook	1983	
Bob Corey	1975	CAP Montrose
Bill Crawford	1987-1989	

John Dalton	1980	
Kathy Dalton	1980	
Jim Dean	1995-1996	San Juan SAR
Dee Dee Decker	1985	
Shawn Del Piero	1989	
Goss Dembitsky	1999	
Steve Dembitsky	1985	
Larry DeVinny	1983	
Fred Dilly	1978	
Bev Dilworth	1981	
Nate Disser	2016-2018	
*Art Dougherty	1974-1984	Ouray County Sheriff
Steve Duce	1982	
Gary Dunn	1981-1982	
***Bill Dwelley	1988-2018	Medical, WEMT-I, Equipment, SWR, T-shirts
Pam East	1995	
*Sandy East	1987-1999	Technical Officer, EMT, WFR, WWR
*Erin Eddy	1999-2010	Medical, EMT
**Tim Eihausen	1996-2018	Capt. 2005-2006, Lt. 2001, 2007-2008, Training
Blaine Eischied	2010-2018	Building
Tricia Sullivan Eischied	2009-2018	Capt. 2017-2018, Medical, EMT, Membership, T-shirts
Matt Elitis	1994-1997	EMT
*Clint Estes	2008-2018	Lt. 2011-2012, Secretary, Vehicles, Building
Angela Eyre	2000	
Bill Fay	1980-1981	RN, EMT
Harlan Feder	1985	
John Fedel	1982	
Dave Fidler	2001, 2003	Montrose, San Juan SAR
Jeannie Fife	1976-1977	
Jim Fife	1975-1983	Training, Medical, EMT
Tom Fink	1979	
Dave Fleming	1993-1994	Equipment, EMT
Chris Folsom	2003-2010	Equipment, SWR, EMT
Deb Folsom	2009-2011	Secretary, Tracker, EMT
Jack Fors	1974	

Glen Fortner	1975	
Michael Foxx	1987-1995	Capt. 1991-1993, Lt. 1989-1990, Training. Truck, EMT
Dave Frank	1989-1991	
George Gardner	1987-1994	
Gary Garrett	1978	
*Greg Genuit	1974-1976,	OMRT Logo, Truck
	1987-1993	
**Randy Gerke	1989-2010	Capt. 1995-1996, Lt. 1993-1994, Equipment, WEMT-I
*Joanie Gibbs	1997-2010	RfR, WFR
**Mike Gibbs	1997-2018	Lt. 2009-2010, RfR, Equipment, Membership, WFR
Mary Gilles	1980-1982	
Danika Gilbert	2007	
Andy Gleason	1999	
Al Glines	1985-1986	
Chris Goplerud	1988-1990	
Kim Grant	2000-2002	
*Doug Gregory	1976-1988	
*Elwood Gregory	1976-1988	Financial
Rosanna Gregory	1976-1977	
Dick Guadagno	1974-1976	
Dave Hahn	1995	
Dennis Hale	1981	Ouray Police
Mike Hamrick	1974-1979	Lt. 1974-1977, Training, Equipment
Patsie Hamrick	1974-1975	Secretary
Don Hargis	1985-1988	
Noel Harlan	1992-1993	
Chris Harper	1993-1994	
**Jenny Hart	1999-2018	Fundraising, T-shirts
**Sean Hart	1999-2018	Training, Equipment
Bob Harvey	1986	
Russ Harvey	2001-2005	
Linda Hash	1980-1984	Capt. 1981-1982, EMT
Tom Hash	1980-1987	Capt. 1983-1984, Lt. 1981-1982, Truck, EMT

Jackie Hattan	1992-1997	Secretary, Equipment
Jim Hattan	1993	Communications
Alan Henn	1977	
*Matt Hepp	2007-2018	Capt. 2009-2010, Communications
Brent Higgins	1994-1995	
Mike Hockersmith	1985-1993	Attorney
Mary Hoeksema	1981-1987	
Ron Hoeksema	1982	
Jim Hollis	1988	
*Rob Holmes	1998-2010	Equipment, Tracker
Bill Hopkins	1974-1976	Communications, Pilot
Cathy Hopkins	1992-1994	
Mike Hopkins	1992-1994	
Bill Hotchkiss	1974-1976, 1981	Posse
Dave Houtz	1979-1982	Truck, EMT
Alan Hudson	1975-1977	Police, Communications, Horses
Dan Hughes	2016-2018	Media, Website
Rich Huss	1988-1993	EMT
Paul Hutchison	1985	
Pete Inglis	1993	Telluride
Paul Innes	1993	
Jim Irvine	1985	
Chris Jackson	2010-2014	Search
Cory Jackson	2010-2018	Capt. 2015-2016, Lt. 2013-2014, Secretary, Treasurer
Bud Jahn	1975	
Tony Jakino	1992-1993	
Larry Johnson	1974-1976	EMT
Bobbi Jones	1988-1989	
Paul Jones	1974-1975	Communications
Susan Jones	1975	
David Justice	1989-1993	RN
Vicki Kaufman	1993	
Tom Kavanaugh	2012-2018	Medical
Keith Kelley	1974-1976	Capt. 1974-1975, Ouray Police Chief, Communications

George Kenney	2002-2008	WFR
Bob Kingery	1975-1976	EMT
Carl Kircher	1976-1978	
*Kurt Kircher	1974-1988	Founder, Capt. 1976-1977, Training, Communications, EMT
*Lynn Leachman Kircher	1976-1987	Treasurer
Margareta Kircher	1975	
Terry Kishbaugh	1974-1975	
Jim Kitchen	1976-1977	Ouray Police Chief
Grant Kleeves	2017-2018	Secretary
Sherab Kloppenberg	2000	
David Koch	1984-1989	Lt. 1987-1988, Equipment, Truck
*Kevin Koprek	2005-2018	Mission Coordinator, Training, EMT
Harriet Kramer	1975	Nurse
John Krocesky	1985	
John Kropuenske	1975-1977	
Laszlo Kubinyi	1976-1979	
Barb Kurlan	1994-1998	Nurse Practioner
Mark LaGree	1989	
Stan Laidlaw	1982	
*Stephen Lance	1994-2011	Capt. 2003-2004, Medical, Equipment, WEMT-I, WWR
Rik Lane	1992-1995	Truck, Equipment
Quinton Larkin	1999	
Bob Larson	1974-1982	
Ray Ledford	1974	
Jake Leonardi	1992-1993	
Nick Leva	1987-1991	Capt. 1989-1990, Treasurer, Ouray Police
Dr. Larry Lindsay	1980-1982	
Jim Link	2017	4X4
Tracy Lockhard	2007-2010	WFR
Liz Lunt		1983
Paul Lugen	1983	
James Lupp	1988-1993	Chef, OMRT Breakfast
Peggy Lyon	1983-1991	Public Relations
Rick Lyon	1983-1991	Photographer

Mike MacLeod	2008-2016	Capt. 2011-2012, Treasurer, Training, Donations, EMT
Sandi MacLeod	2013-2016	Treasurer, Donations
**Bill MacTiernan	1987-2007	Capt. 1993-1994, Lt. 1997-1998, Training, Membership, SWR
Dr. Bob Maisel	1978-1982	Medical
Susan Maisel	1979	EMT
Paul Malcolm	1989	
Andres Marin	2016-2018	
Ed Marsh	1977-1979	
Alice Martin	1975	
Ken Martin	1974	
Gilbert Martinez	1976-1977	Ouray Police, Mexican Dinner
Viola Martinez	1976-1978	Chef, Mexican Dinner
**1/2 Dominic Mattivi, Jr.	1992-2018	Ouray County Sheriff, Undersheriff, EMT
Shelly Mattivi-Glines	1986-1987	EMT
John May	1975	
*Brad McCardle	1996-2006	
Joni McCullough	1990-1991	EMT
Mike McCullough	1986	
Jim McGuire	1974	
Jason McKeown	1992-1993	
Fred McKnight	2000	Ouray County Sheriff
Karen McLaughlin	1986	
Brad McMillon	2001-2007	WFR
Regina McMullan	1994-1995	
Allan McNeer	1982-1983	
Mike McPeek	1986-1990	Training, Truck
Ron Meecham	1992-1993	
Frank Merling	1974-1976	Ouray County Undersheriff
Rich Miers	1980-1981	
Bob Minnick	1974	
*Colette Miller	2000-2018	Treasurer, Medical, Paramedic
Gary Miller	1987-1993	EMT
Ken Miller	1987-1994	Secretary

*Mark Miller	1999-2015	Lt. 2003-2004, Training, EMT
Kim Mitchell	2010-2018	Medical, Paramedic, County Liaison
Don Moden	2010-2016	Equipment, IT Infrastructure, WFR, SWR
Barb Morss	1992-1993	Secretary
**David Mullings	1999-2018	Secretary, Newsletter
Jack Munson	1980-1983	Equipment, EMT
Jacob Nacht	2006-2008	EMT, SWR
Dave Nerden	1988	
Dolgio Nergui	2015-2018	Treasurer, Website, Facebook, T-shirts
Mark Nichols	1974-1975	Posse
Max Noland	1998-1999	
Chris Nute	1997-2000	San Juan SAR
*Mike O'Donnell	1995-2005	WFR
Bob Olivier	1985	
Helen Olivier	1985	
Dennis O'Rourke	1986	
Steve Osborne	1989-1991	
Tod Pace	1986	
George Pasek	1978-1982	Capt. 1978-1980, EMT
Timothy Pasek	2010-2018	Capt. 2013-2014, Lt. 2015-2018, Secretary, Training, Equipment
Peggy McClarren Pass	1988-1990	Treasurer
Michael Peck	1994	
John Petty	1975	Idadrado
Felix Pfaeffle	1978-1983	Public Relations, Cookbook
Bill Phillips	1979-1982	
Jan Powers	1980-1982	
Annie Quathamer	2015-2018	Facilities
John Radcliff	1979	Ouray County Deputy Sheriff
Chris Rahm	1985-1988	
Mek Rajkowski	2005-2010	Secretary, EMT
Brad Rhees	1975-1976	Helicopter Pilot, Communications
Jen Rice	2001-2002	

Jonathan Rice	2000	
Anastasia Richmond	1992	
*Charlie Ricker	1980-1994	Communications, Radio, Callout
*Elaine Ricker	1981-1994	Secretary, Treasurer, Communications, Callout, EMT
*Bob Risch	1997-2010	WFR
*Karen Risch	1996-2010	Secretary, K-9, Historian, WFR
Norm Rooker	2009-2010	Paramedic
*Jerry Roberts	1985-1993, 1999	Avalanche Expert
Tommy Routt	2001	
Jack Rowe	1992-1993	
Walt Rule	1987-1994	Secretary, Truck, Equipment
**1/2 Sam Rushing	1992-2018	Capt. 1999-2001, Treasurer, Training, Communications, Radio, Tracker, Membership, T-shirts
Joe Salette	1992	
Joanne Salette	1992	
Lawrence Sanderson	1992-1998	Equipment, EMT
Ed Saunders	1983	
Garry Schalla	2005-2010	Fundraiser
Gay Scheidegger	1985-1986	
*Otto Scheidegger	1982-1994	Capt. 1987-1988, Lt. 1985-1986
Lynn Schiever	1985	Documentation
*Babs Schmerler	1989-1999	EMT
Eric Schoenbaum	1985	
Ken Scroggins	1981	
Barb Sever	1993-1994	Secretary, Equipment
Arnold Shane	1981	
Joseph Shane	1981	
Steve Shane	1981	
Roger Sherman	1978	
*Dr. Dave Sherwood	1997-2010	Medical Officer
Kay Shofner	1978-1979	Equipment, EMT

*Jeff Skoloda	2001-2018	Capt. 2007-2008, Lt. 2005-2006, Membership, WFR
*Nicole Oines Skoloda	2001-2013	Training, Equipment, Membership, WFR
Bill Slemmer	1999-2000	
P. David Smith	1980-1983	EMT
Gil Smith	1981-1983	
Rick Smith	2000	
Pete Smith	1983-1988	Medical, EMT
Thad Spaulding	1987-1989	
Ruth Stewart	2012-2018	Medical, Paramedic
Robert Stoufer	1980-1982	EMT
Allen Strickland	1980-1982	Ouray Police
Steve Svaldi	2001-2003	EMS, Paramedic
Jeff Swanson	1980-1983	
Sheila Sylvester	1980	
Tom Sylvester	1979-1982	
Karl Thees	1994-2000	Lt. 1999-2000, Equipment, WFR, SWR
Louise Thees	1996-1998	EMT
Bob Thomas	1985-1987	Legislation
Kevin Timm	2011-2014	
Rich Tisdel	1974	Attorney
John Tjossem	1976-1977	
Mary Tjossem	1975	Nurse
Mark Trujillo	1979	
**Rick Trujillo	1974-1978, 1980-1994	Capt. 1978, EMT
R. Van Trump	1979	
Jim Turner	2016-2017	
Tim Tyler	1980-1982, 1991-1992	EMT
Tyler Van Arsdell	1989-1990	
Jared Vilhauer	2016-2018	Training
Gary Wade	1993	Computers
Jane Wakefield	1991-1995	Treasurer
**Jerry Wakefield	1980-1999	Ouray County Sheriff, Undersheriff, Public Relations
Neysa Wakefield	1989	

Nonie Wakefield	1988-1989	
Benda Walker	1975-1977	
Doug Walker	1974-1977	Medical, EMT
Maldon Wallace	1978-1979	
Jane Wanderer	1975	Nurse
Dave Werden	1989-1990	
*Philippe Wheelock	1999-2002, 2013-2018	
Warren Wheeler	1987-1988	
Marilyn Whelan	1977-1978, 1987	Archivist
*Tom Whelan	1977-1990	Lt. 1979-1980, Training, Equipment, EMT, Fundraising
Adam White	1993	
David White	1993	
Don Whitehead	1983	
***Bill Whitt	1989-2018	Capt. 1997-1998, 2002, Lt. 1991-1992, 1995-1996, Treasurer, Membership, WFR
Bumper Williams	1990-1993	EMT
Mary Williams	1975	Nurse
Oran Williams	1974	
Ross Williams	2007	
Jeff Wiltfang	2002-2005	Equipment
Jeff Wingate	1988-1992	EMT
Richard Wojciechowski	2005-2010	EMT
Tom Workman	1975-1978	Communications
Lyn Yarroll	1983-1987	Secretary, Communications
Pamela Yaskin	1979	
Steve Yaskin	1979	
Ted Yoder	1979	
*Rahn Zaccari	1995-2008	Training
Bob Zanett	1974-1975	
Bob Zimmer	1976-1977	
Rick Zortman	1996-1998	EMT

*

Notes

All interviews were conducted by the author.

Chapter One: 1974-1977 – "Some of us could've gotten killed"
Page
1 "Some of us could've gotten killed": Doug Walker, September 10, 2014.
1 His body accelerated: "Man Injured In Fall On Mount Sneffels," *Ouray County Plaindealer and Ouray Herald,* June 20, 1974.
1 Rocks jutting out of the snow: Doug Walker, September 10, 2014.
1 Sheriff Art Dougherty immediately called: "Man Injured In Fall On Mount Sneffels," *Ouray County Plaindealer and Ouray Herald,* June 20, 1974.
2 "Altitude ceiling": Doug Walker, September 10, 2014.
3 Wearing a big glove on his hand: Kurt Kircher, December 2, 1998.
3 Just minutes of fuel: Doug Walker, September 10, 2014.
3 The first successful helicopter rescue: "Man Injured In Fall On Mount Sneffels," *Ouray County Plaindealer and Ouray Herald,* June 20, 1974.
3 "Horsing around" unroped: Kurt Kircher, December 2, 1998.
4 The teens lay down in the snow: "Louisiana Youth Killed in Fall From Mt. Sneffels," *Ouray County Plaindealer and Ouray Herald,* June 27, 1974.
5 He was indignant: Ibid.
5 *Guide to the Colorado Mountains*: Robert Ormes with the Colorado Mountain Club, Sixth Edition, (The Swallow Press INC., 1970).
5 "A skier and mountaineer": Mike Hamrick, September 10, 2009.
5 I share your serious concern: Bill Gardner, July 4, 1974.
6 Death of Frances "Frankie" Licht: "Fall kills Frankie Licht," *The Silverton (CO) Standard and the Miner,* July 26, 1974.
6 "Making a transition from rock to snow": Mike Hamrick, September 10, 2009.
6 For a few: "Hiker Rescued From Cliff," *Ouray County Plaindealer and Ouray Herald,* August 8, 1974.
7 A five-watt CB radio: Patsie Hamrick, "OMRT Minutes," August 14, 1974.
7 Tired and unable to finish: Mike Hamrick, "Our Readers Write, 'Critical of Cliffhanging Account,'" *Ouray County Plaindealer and Ouray Herald,* August 22, 1974.
7 "A cat hanging on a screen door": "Hiker Rescued From Cliff," *Ouray County Plaindealer and Ouray Herald,* August 8, 1974.
7 "We resent the statement": Joyce Jorgensen, "EDITOR'S NOTE," *Ouray County Plaindealer and Ouray Herald,* August 22, 1974.
7 They were thrown out: "Jeep Accident Victims Suffer Night in Canyon," *Ouray County Plaindealer and Ouray Herald,* September 19, 1974.

8 The first twenty-one rescues: "Additional Members Welcome – Ouray Mountain Team Organized and Keeping Busy," *Ouray County Plaindealer and Ouray Herald*, November 8, 1974.

8 Several people had their feelings hurt: Patsie Hamrick, "OMRT Minutes," November 13, 1974.

8 "Quickly found the 'victim'": "Our Readers Write: Impressed By Team Avalanche Rescue Practice," *Ouray County Plaindealer and Ouray Herald*, January 31, 1975.

9 A hiker was stuck: "RESCUE SQUAD IN ACTION," *Ouray County Plaindealer and Ouray Herald* June 19, 1975.

9 Two Silverton men drove: "Two Silverton Men Injured In Car Wreck South Of Ouray," *Ouray County Plaindealer and Ouray Herald*, August 14, 1975.

10 Attended trainings and meetings: "OMRT Minutes" November 11, 1975.

10 "Not OMRT Members": Mike Hamrick, "Membership List," "NEWSLETTER 1," May 19, 1975,

10 Somewhat skeptical: Rick Trujillo, March 3, 2007. Mike Hamrick, September 15, 2009.

10 Diplomatic: Lynn Kircher, February 8, 2012.

10 Down to $20: "OMRT Minutes," February 19, 1976.

11 New ropes and radios: "OMRT Minutes," April 14, 1976.

11 "This is the backbone of the Rescue Team": "*OMRT NEWSLETTER* 3," February 19, 1976.

11 Three June callouts: Lynn Kircher, "1976 Rescue Missions."

11 Bomb threat: "FOURTH OF JULY, 1976," *Ouray County Plaindealer and Ouray Herald*, July 8, 1976.

11 "Blew their celebration": "EDITORIALS," *Ouray County Plaindealer and Ouray Herald*, July 8, 1976.

11 A young girl: "Two Fatalities Over Holiday Weekend," *Ouray County Plaindealer and Ouray Herald*, July 8, 1976.

12 A 1955 Willys Jeep overturned: Ibid.

12 Were put on life support: Lynn Kircher, "1976 Rescue Missions."

12 A young man drove 200 feet: "Two Fatalities Over Holiday Weekend," *Ouray County Plaindealer and Ouray Herald*, July 8, 1976.

12 A cut-off tongue, respiratory problems and abrasions: Lynn Kircher, "1976 Rescue Missions."

12 Trujillo climbed to the top: "Extensive Search For Lost Hikers," *Ouray County Plaindealer and Ouray Herald*, August 19, 1976.

13 Two boys and a dog reported stranded: Lynn Kircher, "1976 Rescue Missions."

13 "But their description": "Stricken Hunter Rescued," *Ouray County Plaindealer and Ouray Herald*, October 21, 1976.

14 "You guys sure know how to ruin": Rick Trujillo, February 25, 2013.

14 "May have recently had brain surgery": "Hunter Discovers Human Skeleton Near Twin Peaks Trail," *Ouray County Plaindealer and Ouray Herald*, October 28, 1976.

15 "Thought the driver was not telling the truth": "1976 Rescue Missions."

15 "In urgent need": Kurt Kircher, Letter to The Board of County Commissioners, January 10, 1977.

15 Nothing happened: "OMRT Minutes," April 13, 1977.

15 "10 watt Motorola VHF radio": "OMRT Minutes," October 12, 1977.

15 An injured pilot walked: Lynn Kircher, "1977 RESCUE MISSIONS."

16 An argument in a bar: Doug Walker, September 10, 2014.

16 The twenty-four-year-old: Gary Acton and Joyce Jorgensen, "MAN FALLS TO

DEATH ATTEMPTING RESCUE OF WOMAN KILLED IN BEAR CREEK ACCI-DENT," *Ouray County Plaindealer and Ouray Herald,* June 23, 1977.

16 "A four-foot-high chain link fence": Ibid.

16 "Well below the falls": Doug Walker, March 13, 2015.

17 "Extremely dangerous": Gary Acton and Joyce Jorgensen, "MAN FALLS TO DEATH ATTEMPTING RESCUE OF WOMAN KILLED IN BEAR CREEK ACCI-DENT," *Ouray County Plaindealer and Ouray Herald,* June 23, 1977.

17 A large crowd formed: "11-Year-Old Boy Injured in Fall Sunday," *Ouray County Plaindealer and Ouray Herald,* June 30, 1977.

18 A seventeen-year-old boy: "Stranded Youth Rescued From Cliffs," *Ouray County Plaindealer and Ouray Herald,* June 30, 1977.

18 "Well-meaning": "An Urgent Plea," *Ouray County Plaindealer and Ouray Herald,* June 30, 1977.

19 "When they took a wrong turn": "Grand Junction Woman Rescued From Hiking Fall After Grueling All Night Search," *Ouray County Plaindealer and Ouray Herald,* July 7, 1977.

19 Rescue finally ended at 2 p.m.: Ibid.

21 "Difficult area east of Mt. Baldy": Lynn Kircher, "1977 Rescue Missions."

21 "Mr. Magician": Mike Hamrick, August 2, 2014.

21 Fife ands Trujillo met: "OMRT Minutes," July 27, 1977.

Chapter Two: A Vanished Hunter
Page

22 "Low hanging clouds and fog": Gertrude Perotti, "No Trace of Missing Woman In Spite Of Expanded Search Efforts," *Ouray County Plaindealer and Herald,* November 17, 1977.

23 Laid out their maps: Rick Rowan, May 4, 2013.

23 "Where they didn't want to go": Gertrude Perotti, "No Trace of Missing Woman In Spite Of Expanded Search Efforts," *Ouray County Plaindealer and Herald,* November 17, 1977.

24 Estimated the wind chill: David Tuohey, "Bloodhounds join search for missing woman," *Montrose (CO) Daily Press,* November 10, 1977.

24 Local residents assisted: Gertrude Perotti, "No Trace of Missing Woman In Spite Of Expanded Search Efforts," *Ouray County Plaindealer and Herald,* November 17, 1977.

25 7,000 rough acres: Joyce Jorgensen, "PART OF A SEARCH," *Ouray County Plaindealer and Herald,* November 17, 1977.

25 "You're lucky to have him": Gertrude Perotti, "No Trace of Missing Woman In Spite Of Expanded Search Efforts," *Ouray County Plaindealer and Herald,* November 17, 1977.

26 It would have been for several hundred thousand dollars: Joyce Jorgensen, "PART OF A SEARCH," *Ouray County Plaindealer and Herald,* November 17, 1977.

26 "I think I know where she is": Joellean Neilson, March 11, 2012.

Chapter Three: 1978-1982 – "These hills in their darker moments do not forgive"
Page

28 "These hills in their darker moments do not forgive": George Pasek, "Operation #3, 1979."

28 Confirmed with its MRA certification: Rick Trujillo, March 19, 2010.

28 A beeper now streamlined callouts: Lynn Kircher, February 8, 2012.

28 Diners vicariously climbed Mt. McKinley: "Ouray Mtn. Rescue Dinner Benefit," *Ouray County Plaindealer and Ouray Herald*, March 30, 1978.

28 Suggested publishing a cookbook: Mike Hamrick, September 16, 2009.

28 Subscribers: "Send Recipes Now," *Ouray County Plaindealer and Ouray Herald*, March 9, 1978.

28 Cost $636 for 500 copies: "OMRT *Minutes*," April 12, 1978.

28 "Responsible for getting it going": Lynn Kircher, December 2, 1998.

28 Found a green WWII ambulance for $75: Lynn Kircher, December 2, 1998; February 8, 2012.

30 At Dr. Bob Maisel's invitation: "OMRT *Minutes*," April 12, 1978.

30 "Failed to negotiate a sharp left turn": "OMRT Mission Report," June 27, 1978.

31 Boy disappeared: "Child Drowns In Irrigation Ditch," *Ouray County Plaindealer and Ouray Herald*, July 6, 1978.

31 A seventeen-year old: "Michigan Youth Rescued After Fall Above Cascade," *Ouray County Plaindealer and Ouray Herald*, August 24, 1978.

32 At 'Oh! Point': "Several Injured In Jeep Accident On Top Of Engineer Mountain," *Ouray County Plaindealer and Ouray Herald*, August 24, 1978.

32 "Boots off and a survival blanket": "BODY WAS OF MAN MISSING SINCE LAST FALL," *Ouray County Plaindealer and Ouray Herald*, October 5, 1978.

32 "Frozen body of Lea McClain": "Search Dog Finds Missing Woman's Body," *Ouray County Plaindealer and Ouray Herald*, December 14, 1978.

32 "Finally convinced them": Tom Sylvester, "LETTERS," *Ouray County Plaindealer and Ouray Herald*, August 23, 1979.

33 "Led on by one of the victims by searchlight": George Pasek, "Operation #3, 1979."

33 It is extremely comforting: Letter from Jim and Sally Smyth, 1979.

34 "Startled to see you": Letter, Ray Loffholm, August 29, 1979.

34 "Oh shit" descending radius corner: George Pasek, December 27, 2014.

34 Plunged 400 feet: "Survives Plunge 400 Ft. Into Canyon," *Ouray County Plaindealer and Ouray Herald*, September 6, 1979.

34 The twenty-two-year-old: Ibid.

35 Elks Citizen of the Year: "Ouray Elks Choose George Pasek As Citizen Of The Year," *Ouray County Plaindealer and Ouray Herald*, April 10, 1980.

35 Ouray filled with drunken revelers: Joyce Jorgenson, "Citizens Ask For More Control Or An End To July 4th Celebration," *Ouray County Plaindealer*, July 10, 1980.

35 A fourteen-year-old: "Charles Youth Killed In Accident July 4," *Ouray County Plaindealer*, July 10, 1980.

35 In the annual flare parade: "Two Seriously injured In Accident During Flare Parade," *Ouray County Plaindealer*, July 10, 1980.

35 Ouray hunter Steve Martinez: "Mountain Rescue Team Retrieves Hunter," *Ouray County Plaindealer*, October 30, 1980.

35 "A spectacular rescue": Linda Hash, "Letter to Mountain Rescue Association," January 19, 1981.

36 She gave demonstrations: Marti Ottinger, "Emergency Medical Services Board To Be Expanded," *Ouray County Plaindealer*, March 5, 1981.

36 Laughing while they carried out this unusual mission: George Pasek, December 27, 2014.

36 "A place that was inaccessible": "Mountain Rescue Assists Police," *Ouray County Plaindealer*, November 5, 1981.

36 150 feet above Cow Creek: Roger Anderson, "FATHER, SON RESCUED FROM COW CREEK CLIFF," *Ouray County Plaindealer*, October 15, 1981.

37 Loaned gear: "Mountain Rescue Team Out All Night For Missing Hiker," *Ouray County Plaindealer*, June 25, 1981.

37 "Will you look at that kid's shoes": Ibid.

37 There are times: Joyce Jorgenson, "EDITORIAL," *Ouray County Plaindealer*, June 25, 1981.

38 Had to back down: Tom Hash, October 4, 2017.

38 The Jeep slipped: "Woman Killed In Jeep Accident," *Ouray County Plaindealer*, July 22, 1982.

38 The 300-pound woman: Tom Hash, October 4, 2017.

39 OMRT bought a wheel: Dr. David Bachman, December 30, 1998.

39 Two experienced hikers: Roger Anderson, "Busy Weekend For Mountain Rescue," *Ouray County Plaindealer*, July 29, 1982.

39 His crampons snagged on a rock: Earl Bashaw, November 13, 2014.

39 The wary pilot: Roger Anderson, "Busy Weekend For Mountain Rescue," *Ouray County Plaindealer*, July 29, 1982.

39 A heart attack call: Roger Anderson, "Helicopters Lift Heart Attack Victim From Hunting Camp," *The Ridgway (CO) Sun*, October 28, 1982.

40 "Realized that although he could land": Ibid.

40 "Just totally got lost": Tom Hash, October 4, 2017.

41 Rivaled the worst: "OURAY UNDER SIEGE," *Ouray County Plaindealer*, August 26, 1982.

41 "The war began Friday afternoon": Roger Anderson, "OURAY FIGHTS BACK COME HELL AND HIGH WATER," *Ouray County Plaindealer*, August 26, 1982.

41 In a town of 684 people: *U.S. Census*, 1980.

41 "Manned shovels and heavy equipment": Roger Anderson, "OURAY FIGHTS BACK COME HELL AND HIGH WATER," *Ouray County Plaindealer*, August 26, 1982.

42 A scree evacuation: Roger Anderson, "Mtn. Rescue Team Gets Recertified," *Ouray County Plaindealer*, August 16, 1982.

42 A new section on preparing and serving wild game: "MTN RESCUE RECIPE BOOK UNDERGOING REVISION," *Ouray County Plaindealer*, November 25, 1982.

42 Hoeksema leads the climb: Mary Hoeksema, October 13, 2014.

Chapter Four: A Father of Three
Page

43 "The box-cañon": Franklin Rhoda, *SUMMITS TO REACH: Report on the Typography of the San Juan Country*, 1876, ed. Mike Foster (Boulder, CO: Pruett Publishing Company, 1984).

43 "It wasn't until 1919": Jerry Roberts, "RED MOUNTAIN PASS – CHIEF OURAY HIGHWAY: A History of Forecasting and Mitigation, Part I," *The Avalanche Review*, February 2009.

43 "Most avalanche prone": *Colorado Department of Transportation Region Five Avalanche Atlas*, 1995.

43 "Miner Elias Fritz was swept away": Jerry Roberts, "RED MOUNTAIN PASS – CHIEF OURAY HIGHWAY: A History of Forecasting and Mitigation, Part I," *The Avalanche Review*, February 2009.

43 "The highway takes the full brunt": *THE SNOWY TORRENTS: AVALANCHE ACCIDENTS IN THE UNITED STATES 1910-1966*, ed. Dale Gallagher ((Alta Avalanche Study Center, 1984).

45 "Despite phone calls asking him not to come": John Marshall and Jerry Roberts, *Living and Dying in Avalanche Country*, (Silverton, CO: A Simpler Way Book Co., 1993).

45 "The main chute of the East Riverside": THE SNOWY TORRENTS: AVALANCHE ACCIDENTS IN THE UNITED STATES 1910-1966, ed. Dale Gallagher (Alta Avalanche Study Center, 1984).

45 Avalanche mitigation began in 1956: Jerry Roberts, "RED MOUNTAIN PASS – CHIEF OURAY HIGHWAY: A History of Forecasting and Mitigation, Part I," *The Avalanche Review*, February 2009.

45 "A minor slide": Rick Trujillo, "Operation of the Mission," February 10, 1978.

46 I was in a state truck on the Silverton side: John Marshall and Jerry Roberts, *Living and Dying in Avalanche Country*, (Silverton, CO: A Simpler Way Book Co., 1993).

46 The snow lay thirty feet deep: Jerry Roberts, May 13, 2016.

46 A hasty search of several large cracks: Rick Trujillo, "Operation of the Mission," February 10, 1978.

47 "They won't let me come up there": Warren Waterman, May 4, 2013.

48 "Bob Miller from Idarado Mine offered": "Minutes," OMRT Meeting, March 15, 1978.

48 "Due to unfamiliarity": Rick Trujillo, "Operation of the Mission," February 10, 1978.

48 "In a fine cloud": Ibid.

49 Avalanche practice: "Minutes," OMRT Meeting, March 15, 1978.

49 Sixty-seven people searched: Rick Trujillo, "Operation of the Mission," February 10, 1978.

49 "Pleas started for some sort of tunnel or shed": Laura Slavik, "United Western Slope Responsible For Snowshed," *Ouray County Plaindealer*, March 19, 1992.

49 "Plan for a tunnel at the Riverside": Scott Allen, "Searchers attempt to locate East Riverside Slide victim Friday, Saturday," "Same slide killed Robert Miller, Rev. Marvin Hudson, daughters," *Montrose Daily Press*: February 13, 1978.

49 "The killer slide": Rick Trujillo, Letter to "The Honorable Richard Lamm," April 26, 1978.

50 "It tears a guy up": John Marshall and Jerry Roberts, *Living and Dying in Avalanche Country*, (Silverton, CO: A Simpler Way Book Co., 1993).

50 "In the first of two fences": "SNOWSLIDE VICTIM'S BODY FOUND," *Ouray County Plaindealer and Herald*, May 25, 1978.

50 A petition drive: Laura Slavik, "Council Exploring Avalanche Control," *Ouray County Plaindealer and Herald*: March 19, 1992.

50 "Prohibitively expensive": David Mullings, "Longer snowshed cost prohibitive, CDOT tells county," *Ouray County Plaindealer*, January 14, 1999.

50 "The latest chapter in the violent history": Marvin Gregory, "It Didn't Have To Happen," *Ouray County Plaindealer*, March 12, 1992.

51 "And almost swept us from the road": Laura Slavik, "Three Motorists Escape Avalanche; Walk Into Ouray," *Ouray County Plaindealer*, March 5, 1992.

51 Which "landed": Chris Smith, "Riverside Slide Kills Ouray Man," *The Silverton Standard and the Miner*, March 12, 1992.

51 "Eardrums pounded": Craig Leland Childs, "Miracle And Tragedy On Red Mountain Pass–One Dead, Nine Alive After Avalanche Strikes," *Ouray County Plaindealer*, March 12, 1992.

52 "Reach the accident": Chris Smith, "Riverside Slide Kills Ouray Man," *The Silverton Standard and the Miner*, March 12, 1992.

52 "A flashlight bouncing along": Craig Leland Childs, "Miracle And Tragedy On Red Mountain Pass–One Dead, Nine Alive After Avalanche Strikes," *Ouray County Plaindealer*, March 12, 1992.

53 "No further because of avalanche danger": Chris Smith, "Riverside Slide Kills Ouray Man," *The Silverton Standard and the Miner*, March 12, 1992.

53 "Horrendous, with slides": Craig Leland Childs, "Miracle And Tragedy On Red Mountain Pass–One Dead, Nine Alive After Avalanche Strikes," *Ouray County Plaindealer*, March 12, 1992.

53 "200 feet long and as much as 10 feet high": Chris Smith, "Riverside Slide Kills Ouray Man," *The Silverton Standard and the Miner*, March 12, 1992.

54 "An air pocket": Craig Leland Childs, "Miracle And Tragedy On Red Mountain Pass–One Dead, Nine Alive After Avalanche Strikes," *Ouray County Plaindealer*, March 12, 1992.

54 "Talked during the entire ordeal": Ibid.

54 Creating an eight-foot wormhole: Don Castle, September 6, 2016.

54 His first request: Craig Leland Childs, "Miracle And Tragedy On Red Mountain Pass–One Dead, Nine Alive After Avalanche Strikes," *Ouray County Plaindealer*, March 12, 1992.

55 "Clothes were wringing wet:" Chris Smith, "Riverside Slide Kills Ouray Man," *The Silverton Standard and the Miner*, March 12, 1992.

55 When CDOT workers were able to clear the road: Harvey Martinez, "Avalanche Clean-Up Red Mountain," CD, March 7, 1992, courtesy Don Castle.

55 "Simply buried two days worth:" Craig Leland Childs, "Miracle And Tragedy On Red Mountain Pass–One Dead, Nine Alive After Avalanche Strikes," *Ouray County Plaindealer*, March 12, 1992.

55 "IT DIDN'T HAVE TO HAPPEN:" Marvin Gregory, "WINDOW TO YESTERDAY: It Didn't Have To Happen," *Ouray County Plaindealer*, March 12, 1992.

Chapter Five: The Mountain Shook
Page
57 A beautiful sunset: Art Porter, "FALL ON ROCK, FALLING ROCK, OFF ROUTE; Colorado, Mt. Sneffels, North Face," *ACCIDENTS IN NORTH AMERICAN MOUNTAINEERING*, 1981.

57 "Sybaritic delights of a soft bed, a hot shower, and a great meal": Art Porter, April 26, 2013.

57 Thoroughly chilled: Art Porter, "FALL ON ROCK, FALLING ROCK, OFF ROUTE; Colorado, Mt. Sneffels, North Face," *ACCIDENTS IN NORTH AMERICAN MOUNTAINEERING*, 1981.

57 The North Buttress was a nasty climb: Art Porter, April 24, 2013.

59 In a pendulum fall: "FALL ON ROCK, FALLING ROCK, OFF ROUTE; Colorado, Mt. Sneffels, North Face," *ACCIDENTS IN NORTH AMERICAN MOUNTAINEERING*, 1981.

60 Gale force winds: George Pasek, "Rescue Report," 1980.

60 2:30 a.m., he heard men's voices: Art Porter, "FALL ON ROCK, FALLING ROCK, OFF ROUTE; Colorado, Mt. Sneffels, North Face," *ACCIDENTS IN NORTH AMERICAN MOUNTAINEERING*, 1981.

62 The line swung out: "Dramatic Rescue Atop Sneffels," *Ouray County Plaindealer*, September 4, 1980.

62 Stuck out his thumb: George Pasek, December 27, 2014.

62 "The rescue was a textbook example": Art Porter, "FALL ON ROCK, FALLING ROCK, OFF ROUTE; Colorado, Mt. Sneffels, North Face," *ACCIDENTS IN NORTH AMERICAN MOUNTAINEERING*, 1981.

75 "As everyone knows, we are long overdue for a rescue": Lyn Yarroll, Team Letter, April 27, 1987.

75 A topless Toyota: "Seven Injured In Accident," *Ouray County Plaindealer*, June 18, 1987.

75 "Two Stokes litters": William P. Doll, "OURAY AMBULANCE REPORT," June 10, 1987.

76 Fell backward and headfirst: "Climber Survives 1,000-Foot Fall On Sneffels," *Ouray County Plaindealer*, July 16, 1987.

76 He was in such intense pain: Nancy Lofholm and Mary Anne Perez, "Man survives slide down Sneffels," *Daily Sentinel (Grand Junction, CO)*, July 12, 1987.

76 Its tail rotor perched only a foot or two above: Tod Bacigalupi, June 10, 2013.

76 "A big raspberry on his chest": Otto Scheidegger, April 17, 2013.

76 A bit more challenging: "Corrales Man Survives Plunge of 1,000 Feet," *Albuqerque Journal (NM)*, July 12, 1987.

76 Down like a bobsled: Nancy Lofholm and Mary Anne Perez, "Man survives slide down Sneffels," *Daily Sentinel*, July 12, 1987.

76 "But it took a bad bounce and curved": Thad Spaulding, "The Alicia Koch Story," *Voice of Troy*, insert in *Ouray County Plaindealer*, November 19, 1987.

77 Figured he was tracking: "Local Hunter Found Dead," *Ouray County Plaindealer*, November 12, 1987.

77 OMRT brought the body: "OURAY AMBULANCE REPORT," November 6, 1987.

Chapter Seven: Kissing the Gorge
Page
80 On top of the gorge, Kurt Kircher: Harlan Feder, "Man Survives 200-Foot Plunge Into Uncompahgre River," *Ouray County Plaindealer*, August 29, 1985.

80 Was cited for careless driving at unsafe speeds : Ibid.

Chapter Eight: Dynamite, Curves and Cliffs
Page
81 She heard an explosion coming from Red Mountain Pass: Pete Smith, June 22, 2013.

81 A mile north: "Man Killed In Explosion On US 550," *Ouray County Plaindealer*, April 17, 1986.

82 Small pieces of a car: Otto Scheidegger, March 17, 2013.

82 "A friend who had talked": "Victim of auto blast identified," *Montrose Daily Press*, April 17, 1986.

83 CBI asked OMRT: "Man Killed In Explosion On US 550," *Ouray County Plaindealer*, April 17, 1986.

83 With black humor: David Koch, June 18, 2013.

83 They found parts of the Mazda GLC: Otto Scheidegger, March 17, 2013.

83 Twisted piece: "Man Killed In Explosion On US 550," *Ouray County Plaindealer*, April 17, 1986.

83 The county loader scraped the highway: Steve Duce, March 12, 2013

84 In many places it was impossible to hike: P.D. Antonelli II, "Scott Williams killed in Uncompahgre canyon," *The Silverton Standard*, May 21, 1987.

85 Extended it and it fell: Michael Foxx, April 29, 2013.

86 "An extremely hazardous rescue operation": P.D. Antonelli II, "Scott Williams killed in Uncompahgre canyon," *The Silverton Standard*, May 21, 1987.

NO INDIVIDUAL HEROES

Chapter Nine: 1988-92 – Out of the gorge "on an icicle"
Page

87 Out of the gorge "on an icicle": Bill MacTiernan, November 26, 2013.

87 "Quicker than you can blink": "Denver Couple Given Risky Ride By Mother Cline," *Ouray County Plaindealer*, April 14, 1988.

87 OMRT carved steps in the snow: Mike Hockersmith, April 17, 2013.

87 "We just walked them right up": "Denver Couple Given Risky Ride By Mother Cline," *Ouray County Plaindealer*, April 14, 1988.

88 A twenty-two-year-old Texas driver: "OMRT Mission Report," July 11, 1988.

88 "Those backpackers hadn't found her": "Hiker Lucks Out After Losing Trail Over Bridge Of Heaven Sunday Night," *Ouray County Plaindealer*, July 7, 1988.

88 Flannel shirt: Thad Spaulding, "Mtn. Rescue Team Report," *Ouray County Plaindealer*, August 11, 1988.

89 A 300 man-hour technical retrieval: "OMRT MISSION REPORT," August 17, 1988.

89 Fell off the Bear Creek Trail: Mike McPeek, "Injured Hiker Brought Off Bear Creek Trail," *Ouray County Plaindealer*, September 1, 1988.

89 Soaked in the icy creek: Greg Genuit, July 1, 2000.

89 She lay in a ravine: Bill MacTiernan, November 30, 2013.

90 "The litter and handlers did slide down": Mike McPeek, "Injured Hiker Brought Off Bear Creek Trail," *Ouray County Plaindealer*, September 1, 1988.

90 $581.43 worth of equipment: "Ouray Police Report," *Ouray County Plaindealer*, March 23, 1989.

90 "Wet and muddy": "Ouray Mountain Rescue Equipment Recovered," *Ouray County Plaindealer*, April 20, 1989.

91 "This breakfast could save your life": "Mtn. Rescue Team Community Breakfast Fundraiser Sunday," *Ouray County Plaindealer*, June 29, 1989.

91 "A gift for climbing": Sara Seloheim, "Rescue Team Member Helps Recover Body," *Ouray County Plaindealer*, August 13, 1992.

91 Driving from their winter home: "Couple Killed When Car Plunges Into Canyon From 550," *Ouray County Plaindealer*, May 4, 1989.

92 Two hours later and 2,000 feet higher: "Hiker Rescued," *Ouray County Plaindealer*, June 22, 1989.

92 Fifteen men: "Ouray Mtn. Rescue Coordinates Helicopter Rescue of Hikers," *Ouray County Plaindealer*, August 10, 1989.

93 Thirty-eight: Amy Malick, "Search on for missing man," *Durango Herald* (CO), September 4, 1990.

93 "Tent, backpack, and personal items": Amy Malick, "Storm hampers search for Climbers," *Durango Herald*, September 5, 1990.

93 Severe weather: Rachelle A. Jacobson, "Wilderness Search Leaves No Trace," *San Juan National Forest Newsletter*, December 1990.

93 Searchers aboard a Chinook: Theresa Myers, "Search crew finds body of missing hiker," *Durango Herald*, September 6, 1990.

94 "It's all rotten rock": Craig Leland Childs, "Hiker Rescued Above Cascade Falls," *Ouray County Plaindealer*, September 27, 1990.

94 "Very small, tight-knit, highly skilled group": Craig Leland Childs, "Ouray Team Wows State Rescuers," *Ouray County Plaindealer*, December 6, 1990.

94 On a dry, sunny road: "Red Mountain Pass Claims Life," *Ouray County Plaindealer*, January 31, 1991.

94 "A cloud of white smoke": Craig Leland Childs, "Accident Claims Man's Life In Ouray," *Ouray County Plaindealer*, January 2, 1992.

94 "A cloud of white smoke": Craig Leland Childs, "Accident Claims Man's Life In Ouray," *Ouray County Plaindealer*, January 2, 1992.

95 A $7,500 medical wish list: Ken Miller, "OMR Minutes," January 8, 1992.

95 "Gorilla to carry it around": Gerald Bremseth, "OMR Minutes," April 8, 1992.

96 "The best": "Mountain Rescue Takes To The Ice," *Ouray County Plaindealer*, February 6, 1992.

96 "Not paying a whole lot of attention": Jan Studebaker, "Iceman Falleth," *Rescue 911*, narrator William Shattner, CBS, May 11, 1993.

97 To save weight: Randy Gerke, "Iceman Falleth," *Rescue 911*, narrator William Shattner, CBS, May 11, 1993.

97 "Very, very difficult to stabilize the litter": Ibid.

97 200-foot: Bill Whitt, "Iceman Falleth," *Rescue 911*, narrator William Shattner, CBS, May 11, 1993.

97 "His eyes were open": Craig Leland Childs, "Dramatic Rescue Saves Ice Climber Near Ouray," *Ouray County Plaindealer*, February 20, 1992.

97 Had never seen: "Showing skill and expertise...," *Ouray County Plaindealer*, February 27, 1992.

97 "I'm very, profoundly grateful": John Meier, "Iceman Falleth," *Rescue 911*, narrator William Shattner, CBS, May 11, 1993.

97 "It wasn't a slam-dunk": "Quotable...," *Ouray County Plaindealer*, February 20, 1992.

98 At 4:30 p.m.: Electa Draper, "Team struggles to bring down climber's body," *Durango Herald*, July 30, 1992.

99 Sixty to ninety degree gorge: "Crew recovers Climber's body," *Durango Herald*, July 31, 1992.

99 "Renowned alpinist": Electa Draper, "Team struggles to bring down climber's body," *Durango Herald*, July 30, 1992.

99 "Extremely hazardous": Sara Seloheim, "Rescue Team Member Helps Recover Body," *Ouray County Plaindealer*, August 13, 1992.

99 Assisting in the recovery: Ibid.

99 "The most dangerous extrication": Electa Draper, "Team struggles to bring down climber's body," *Durango Herald*, July 30, 1992.

99 "For Eidelloth to reach the summit of Windom and Sunlight": Electa Draper, "Searchers comb Needles for climber," *Durango Herald*, July 28, 1992.

100 "Fell into the canyon, hit the wall": Sara Seloheim, "Hiker Rescued At Bear Creek Falls," *Ouray County Plaindealer*, October 1, 1992.

100 "Turning the natural environment into a festival": Cameron M. Burns, "the ice men cometh," *Aspen Times (CO)*, December 19 and 20, 1992.

Chapter Ten: "The Good Lord Has Blessed Me"
Page

102 "The good Lord has blessed me": Earl Ellis, "Letter to Ouray Mountain Rescue," December 1988.

103 weighed it down with rocks: "OMRT Mission Account," August 1988.

103 "Men have crawled off of mountains like this": Earl Ellis, January 8, 2014.

104 Total weight on the system: "OMRT Mission Account," August 1988.

104 A very unstable refrigerator-sized rock: Ibid.

106 Did not expect to be off Sneffels: Ibid.

106 A fist sized pulverized mass of bone: Earl Ellis, January 8, 2014.

Chapter Eleven: The Blue Room
Page

107 The Blue Room: Jerry Roberts, "Powder Shock–The Anatomy of a Death, Avalanche Lessons," *The Avalanche Review*, April 1990.

107 "Instead of looking at a situation": John Marshall and Jerry Roberts, *Living (and dying) In Avalanche Country: Stories from the San Juans of Southwestern Colorado*, 1992.

108 "The low density powder was rapidly densifying": Jerry Roberts, "Powder Shock–The Anatomy of a Death," *The Avalanche Review*, April 1990.

109 "Several broad gullies, cliffs, large rock outcrops": Betsy R. Armstrong and Richard L. Armstrong, "Avalanche Summary Sheet," *Avalanche Atlas, Ouray County, Colorado.*

110 "Two large class-4 avalanches had released": Jerry Roberts, "Powder Shock–The Anatomy of a Death, Avalanche Lessons," *The Avalanche Review*, April 1990.

110 "Knew what had happened": Ibid.

110 Skier buried: Greg Leithauser, "AVALANCHE VICTIM" *Supplementary Investigation Report 90-145*, March 7, 1990.

111 George Pastor from Silverton: Walt Rule, "Field Notes."

111 "You need to get up to Red Mountain": Chris George, July 28, 2016.

113 Nineteen searchers were sure: Walt Rule, "Field Notes."

113 Under moonlight: "Montrose Man Killed In Avalanche," *Ouray County Plaindealer*, March 15, 1990.

115 At 1:15, San Juan searcher #1: Walt Rule, "Field Notes."

115 "Under nine feet of snow:" Jerry Roberts, "Powder Shock–The Anatomy of a Death, Avalanche Lessons," *The Avalanche Review*, April 1990.

115 "Loaded onto a sled": Greg Leithauser, "AVALANCHE VICTIM" *Supplementary Investigation Report 90-145*, March 9, 1990.

115 "An unnecessary accident": Jerry Roberts, "Powder Shock–The Anatomy of a Death, Avalanche Lessons," *The Avalanche Review*, April 1990.

115 A good friend of Hollis: Jim Pilkington, November 27, 2017.

Chapter Twelve: "It was my life I was working on"
Page

117 "It was my life I was working on": Betty Leavengood, "My Hiking Misadventure," *Ouray County Plaindealer*, October 1, 1992.

117 "Five ground teams": Sara Seloheim, "Lost Hiker Found Alive After Two Days," *Ouray County Plaindealer*, August 27, 1992.

118 "Two liters": Betty Leavengood, "My Hiking Misadventure," *Ouray County Plaindealer*, October 1, 1992.

118 Reviewed the maps: Dan Bender, "La Plata County Sheriff's Department Report," August 23, 1992.

118 "If they could not find her where she was supposed to be": Dan Bender, "The Search," OMRT files.

119 "I thought I could scramble around any falls and make it:" Betty Leavengood, "My Hiking Misadventure," *Ouray County Plaindealer*, October 1, 1992.

119 "Number one priority": Sara Seloheim, "Lost Hiker Found Alive After Two Days," *Ouray County Plaindealer*, August 27, 1992.

119 "Overhead, carried by winds": Dan Bender, "The Search," OMRT files.

119 "Found tracks": Dan Bender, "La Plata County Sheriff's Department Report," August 23, 1992.

120 "CP told me": Dan Bender, "The Search," OMRT files.

120 He lost her tracks: Dan Bender, "La Plata County Sheriff's Department Report," August 23, 1992.

120 "That Betty had nowhere to go but down": Dan Bender, "The Search," OMRT files.

120 Zahn alerted: Dan Bender, "La Plata County Sheriff's Department Report," August 23, 1992.

Notes

120 "I was beat by now so sat down:" Dan Bender, "The Search," OMRT files.
120 I could see in the distance the mountain: Betty Leavengood, "My Hiking Misadventure," *Ouray County Plaindealer*, October 1, 1992.
121 "Happy to see us": Dan Bender, "The Search," OMRT files.
121 "All the adrenalin and energy": Betty Leavengood, "My Hiking Misadventure," *Ouray County Plaindealer*, October 1, 1992.
122 "A demon from Dog Hell": Dan Bender, "The Search," OMRT files.
122 "Pivot to the edge": Dan Bender, "La Plata County Sheriff's Department Report," August 23, 1992.
122 It didn't turn out that way: Dan Bender, "The Search," OMRT files.
122 "Live one": Sara Seloheim, "Lost Hiker Found Alive After Two Days," *Ouray County Plaindealer*, August 27, 1992.
123 "I moved from fire to fire": Dan Bender, "The Search," OMRT files.
124 "Using both hands to press the key": Ibid.
124 "To go on a forced": Dan Bender, "La Plata County Sheriff's Department Report," August 23, 1992.
124 "The Search...." In fourteen hours, I had walked: Dan Bender, "The Search," OMRT files.

Chapter Thirteen: 1993-1998: "Let's not forget why we're here"
Page
126 "Let's not forget why": Nancy Chilton, "OMR BUSINESS MEETING," December 14, 1994.
126 Katy Film Productions: Sara Seloheim, "TV Show Films Local Rescue," *Ouray County Plaindealer*, February 4, 1993.
127 "Box Cañon": Bill MacTiernan, March 2, 2007.
128 "Prima donna" stunt man: Randy Gerke, April 23, 2016.
129 "Iceman Falleth": "List of *Rescue 911* Episodes, Episode 4.26, (May 11, 1993), Production Number: 425, *Wikipedia: The Free Encyclopedia.*
129 "Who has time": Walt Rule, "OMRT Minutes," March 10, 1993.
129 "On safety and systems": Bill MacTiernan, March 1, 2007.
130 Fourth of July breakfast: Jane Wakefield, "Treasurer's Report," July 14, 1993.
130 "WADAO (weak and dizzy all over)": Barb Sever, "OMR Minutes," September 14, 1994.
130 100 yards north of the tunnel: Walt Rule, "MISSION REPORT," February 2, 1993.
130 "It got my head": "Youth Survives Plunge Over Side," *Ouray County Plaindealer*, February 4, 1993.
130 Youth was stuck on a rock: Lawrence Sanderson, "MISSION REPORT," March 14, 1993.
130 "Within a whisper": "Rappelling Stunt Injures Montrose Youth," *Ouray County Plaindealer*, March 18, 1993.
130 When three anchors pulled loose: Walt Rule, "MISSION REPORT," August 1, 1993.
130 "Without that early notice": Laurie Shaffer, "Lucky Sneffels Climber Survives Forty-Foot Fall," *Ouray County Plaindealer*, August 5, 1993.
131 "Backcountry ambulance": Sam Rushing, "WE HAVE TO BE PREPARED," March 9, 1994.
131 "A whole lot easier": Ed Thompson, "Ouray County Emergency Services Seeing Busy Summer," *Ouray County Plaindealer*, July 21, 1994.
131 The Sheriff's Posse: Jackie Hattan, "OMR BUSINESS MEETING," November 9, 1994.

131 1969 Piper PA-28 Cherokee: Lane Mills, "2 are injured in light plane crash southwest of Montrose," *Montrose Daily Press*, March 17, 1994.

132 "In time for breakfast": Matt Milios, "Plane Crash Brings Out Mountain Rescue Team," *Ouray County Plaindealer*, March 24, 1994.

132 "Only inches from the raging Bear Creek": Ed Thompson, "Iowa Boy Rescued At Bear Creek Falls," *Ouray County Plaindealer*, June 16, 1994.

132 "We got down there, told him that he was in a pretty unique situation": Ed Thompson, "Iowa Boy Rescued At Bear Creek Falls," *Ouray County Plaindealer*, June 16, 1994.

132 "Large rock dislodged by a fellow hiker": Marti Ottinger, "Rescue Team Brings Injured Hiker Down," *Ouray County Plaindealer*, July 7, 1994.

132 After two pages and a callout: "OMR Minutes," July 13, 1994.

132 "Through the rocks and talus slopes": Marti Ottinger, "Rescue Team Brings Injured Hiker Down," *Ouray County Plaindealer*, July 7, 1994.

133 A twenty-eight-year-old Texan slipped descending: "OMRT Accident Report."

133 Managed a 200-foot descent: Ed Thompson, "Mountain Rescue Makes Three Trips In One Week," *Ouray County Plaindealer*, July 21, 1994.

134 A one-eyed horse: Sandy East, June 1, 2016.

134 Light blue tent: "OMRT Accident Report," July 15, 1994.

134 Just as a monsoon thunderstorm appeared: "OMRT Accident Report," July 15, 1994.

134 She had not followed the trail: "OMR REPORT," August 25, 1994.

135 "Often a valued technical": Jackie Hattan, "OMR BUSINESS MEETING," November 9, 1994.

135 "Spectacular and utterly unique winter attraction": Samantha Tisdel, "Ice Advocate Explains Birth Of An Ice Park," *Ouray County Plaindealer*, March 9, 1995.

135 Hoped to take jurisdiction: Samantha Tisdel, "The Birth Of Ouray's Ice Park, Part II," *Ouray County Plaindealer*, March 16, 1995.

135 Had commercialized the experience: Sandy East, "The Ouray Ice Experience..." *Ouray County Plaindealer*, April 6, 1995.

135 "Please consider": Gary Wild, 'Consider becoming part of a positive process...' "In Our Mailbox," *Ouray County Plaindealer*, April 20, 1995.

135 "Ultimate rig": Nancy Chilton, Secretary; "OMR BUSINESS MEETING," MAY 10, 1995.

135 "Very grueling": Sam Rushing, "OMR Training Exercise Report," February 10, 1995.

136 "To save time in the search effort": Samantha Tisdel, "Rescuers expect a busy '95 season," *Ouray County Plaindealer*, June 29, 1995.

136 "He was surprised we were out looking": Samantha Tisdel, "Rescuers expect a busy '95 season," *Ouray County Plaindealer*, June 29, 1995.

136 "Separated from his mother": Sara Seloheim, "Rescue team finds lost Telluride boy; hunts for man," *Ouray County Plaindealer*, August 17, 1995.

136 "Beyond our wildest expectations": Sara Seloheim, "Vini, vidi, vici: Ice Climbing fest roaring success," *Ouray County Plaindealer*, January 18, 1996.

136 A lasagna dinner that brought in $819: "TREASURER'S REPORT," February 15, 1996.

137 "Major winter attraction": David Mullings, "Ice climbing event fit city's big plan," *Ouray County Plaindealer*, January 18, 1996.

137 Thees proposed a command center: Karyn Carr, "OMR MINUTES," May 8, 1996.

137 "Teams do not have individual heroes": Karyn Carr, "OMR MINUTES," May 8, 1996.

Notes

139 "It was almost like he had something to prove": Samantha Tisdel and David Mullings, "Hiker warned before fatal lightning hit," *Ouray County Plaindealer*, June 20, 1996.

139 DA's office said the man had been fighting with his buddies: Nancy Chilton, "OMR BUSINESS MEETING," July 10, 1996.

139 Slipped and slid 1,500 feet: "Rescue for June 25, 1996," OMRT.

139 "Gave him a flashlight, water, food and blankets": Beverly Corbell, "Hiker falls 1,000 feet off Sneffels," *Ouray County Plaindealer*, June 27, 1996.

140 Was pretty banged up and his wrist was swollen: "Rescue for June 25, 1996," OMRT.

140 "An anonymous rich dude": Ibid.

140 OMRT sent a thank you: "OMR BUSINESS MEETING," July 10, 1996.

140 "Tied up six to eight people": Fred and Donna Clarke, "OMR Letter," August 22, 1996.

140 "Almost a superhuman feat": Beverly Corbell, "Anatomy of a rescue: Ouray crew reaches fallen man," *Ouray County Plaindealer*, September 19, 1996.

141 "Probably hit icy slush and lost control and went over the edge": Beverly Corbell, "Plunge down Red Mountain kills couple," *Ouray County Plaindealer*, October 10, 1996.

141 Nearly doubled: Beverly Corbell, "Ice Park doubles in size for season," *Ouray County Plaindealer*, October 10, 1996.

141 $25,104: "TREASURER'S REPORT, OMRT," December 1996 to January 8, 1997.

141 They had $9,098: "TREASURER'S REPORT, OMRT," January 14, 1998.

141 "A three-quarter ton, 454 cubic inch, 5-speed, 4-wheel drive truck": Beverly Corbell, "Mountain Rescue digs shiny new truck," *Ouray County Plaindealer*, January 22, 1998.

142 "We always find our man": Beverly Corbell, "Team rescues 'dead presidents' from trash," *Ouray County Plaindealer*, January 22, 1998.

142 Camped under a full moon: Kay Stenehjem-Hyle, "'Lean on me when you're not strong . . .'" *Montrose Morning Sun (CO)*, September 18, 1997.

142 On soup: Marija B. Vader, "The lost were found," *Montrose Morning Sun*, August 20, 1997.

142 Hiking in different directions: Kay Stenehjem-Hyle, "'Lean on me when you're not strong...'" *Montrose Morning Sun*, September 18, 1997.

142 "Mountain Rescue guys on my four-wheeler": Amy Collier, "Lost hiker found," *Montrose Daily Press*, August 20, 1997.

142 "Slam dunk": Beverly Corbell, "Slam dunk: Rescue team quickly finds lost Arkansas hunter," *Ouray County Plaindealer*, October 23, 1997.

143 "Went downhill fast and was in extreme intensive care": Beverly Corbell, "Cyclist dies mysteriously after pass fall," *Ouray County Plaindealer*, September 18, 1997.

144 "The fact that he bounced on the way down": "Climber alive after 10-story fall down ice," *Ouray County Plaindealer*, December 25, 1997.

144 "Just incredible": Amy Collier, "Ice climber falls 100 feet at Ouray park," *Montrose Daily Press*, December 22, 1997.

144 "A massive search and rescue operation": Beverly Corbell, "Airplane crash mystery ends as 'model' of folly," *Ouray County Plaindealer*, July 30, 1998.

144 Jeeps, trucks, four-wheelers and a helicopter: Beverly Corbell, "Hunt stalls; plane didn't, apparently," *Ouray County Plaindealer*, July 23, 1998.

144 "Remote control model plane": Lauri Friedman, "Remote control plane, peacocks provide confusion," *Montrose Morning Sun*, July 24, 1998.

319

144 "It probably ran out of gas": "Airplane crash mystery ends as 'model' of folly," *Ouray County Plaindealer,* July 30, 1998.

144 "Spent the night standing up on a ledge": Beverly Corbell, "Copter used in rescues of two hikers," *Ouray County Plaindealer,* August 20, 1998.

145 A corporate client: Joanie Gibbs, November 21, 2016.

146 "Suffered head and ankle injuries": Beverly Corbell, "Copter used in rescues of two hikers," *Ouray County Plaindealer,* August 20, 1998.

146 "Expressed his confidence in the team": Karen Risch, "Minutes," December 9, 1998.

Chapter Fourteen: Calling a Rescue
Page
147 Wrote in the register: Sam Rushing, January 23, 2013.

147 On a loose rock: "Woman dies on Mt. Sneffels," *Telluride (CO) Times-Journal,* September 2, 1993.

148 "I would appreciate it if you guys could rush up there": Bill MacTiernan, March 2, 2007.

148 "Fractured skull, ribs": "Woman dies on Mt. Sneffels," *Telluride Times-Journal,* September 2, 1993.

148 "Look, the mountain just killed": Bill MacTiernan, "We're sorry. We have a mission and have to go," *The Ouray Mountain Rescue Team: The Early Years,* Western Hotel, March 15, 2007.

148 "And got a few clouds and things": Ibid.

Chapter Fifteen: "A Short Haul"
Page
150 "A Short Haul": Bill Whitt, March 30, 2014.

150 Didn't feel much like climbing: Steve House, February 4, 2014.

150 "The growl of the falling stone": Steve House, *Beyond the Mountain,*" (Patagonia Books, 2009).

151 "Take care of the survivors": Ibid.

152 Forty-five to fifty degrees: Bill Whitt, "Falling Rock, Poor Position, Colorado, Ouray, Dexter Creek Slabs," *American Alpine Journal,* 1996.

153 A fixed line: Bill Whitt, May 26, 2016.

153 "Was going to be sketchy": Karyn Carr, June 25, 2016.

153 Full of sheetrock pieces: Jim Kendrick, April 25, 2014.

154 "I know he loved climbing": Steve House, *Beyond the Mountain,*" (Patagonia Books, 2009).

154 "Phenomenal job": Marcia Wood, "'A Phenomenal Job,'" *Ouray County Plaindealer,* March 3, 1995.

154 They postholed back: Bill Whitt, March 30, 2014.

Chapter Sixteen: Rule No. 1: Take Care of Yourself
Page
155 Rule No. 1: Take Care of Yourself: Bill Whitt, "Don't worry, I've got it handled," *The Ouray Mountain Rescue Team: The Early Years,* Western Hotel, March 15, 2007.

156 Tested equipment: David Mullings, "Fall kills ice climber," *Ouray County Plaindealer,* March 19, 1998.

157 "Did you untie him?": Bill Whitt, "Don't worry, I've got it handled," *The Ouray Mountain Rescue Team: The Early Years,* Western Hotel, March 15, 2007.

Notes

158 An account of the incident: Bill Whitt, "Fall on Ice, Inadequate Knot, Colorado, Ouray Ice Park," "Accident Reports," *American Alpine Journal*, 1999.

158 "Newbie ice climber": Bill Whitt, "Don't worry, I've got it handled," *The Ouray Mountain Rescue Team: The Early Years*, Western Hotel, March 15, 2007.

Chapter Seventeen: 1999-2002 – "It's pretty dark down here"
Page

159 "It's pretty dark down here": Karen Risch, "Uncompahgre Gorge Rescue," September 25, 2000.

159 Ice climber with a history of shoulder problems: Karen Risch, "Ice Park Rescue," January 1, 1999.

159 "A pretty significant pelvic fracture": Beverly Corbell, "'Jeff' survives fall into gorge," *Ouray County Plaindealer*, January 21, 1999.

161 Rushing told O'Donnell: Karen Risch, "Ice Park Rescue," January 18, 1999.

162 "After it started coming over the bank": Beverly Corbell, "Flooding creek forces dramatic rescue of 7," *Ouray County Plaindealer*, August 5, 1999.

163 "One at a time across the water": Ibid.

164 "Smooth as silk": Sam Rushing, "OMRT Minutes," August 11, 1999.

164 "It could have been": Beverly Corbell, "Flooding creek forces dramatic rescue of 7," *Ouray County Plaindealer*, August 5, 1999.

164 Sidestepped some manure: "Hiker breaks ankle," *Ouray County Plaindealer*, September 2, 1999.

164 Felt and heard it break: Karen Risch, "Oak Creek Rescue," August 31, 1999.

164 "Wondered how they'd get me down:" Penny Loerke, "Lessons learned from hiking mishap," "Letters to the Editor," *Ouray County Plaindealer*, October 7, 1999.

164 "Dry, slender and stable": Karen Risch, "Oak Creek Rescue," August 31, 1999.

164 "12 unbelievably fit men and women": Cynthia Boxenhorn, "Search and Rescue demonstrated 'heroic efforts'," "Letters to the Editor," *The Ridgway (CO) Sun*, September 23, 1999.

164 1990 1-ton Chevrolet skidded 127 feet: Elizabeth Pierson, "N.M. man plunges off Red Mountain Pass," *Durango Herald*, October 26, 1999.

164 The 450-foot drop: "Fatal Plunge," *Ouray County Plaindealer*, October 28, 1999.

164 Trooper Chris Sandoval estimated the truck was going forty-eight MPH: Elizabeth Pierson, "N.M. man plunges off Red Mountain Pass," *Durango Herald*, October 26, 1999.

165 "Under his tenure, the team raised enough": Karen Risch, "OMRT Minutes," September 8, 1999.

165 "Arrested on suspicion": Nancy Lofholm, "Ouray's sheriff has vivid history," *denverpost.com*, January 31, 2000.

165 Dominic (Junior) Mattivi was elected sheriff: Scott Schwebke, "Mattivi will be Ouray County's next sheriff," *Montrose Daily Press*, August 9, 2000.

165 A $15,000 in Tier III Rescue Fund grant: Karen Risch, "OMRT Minutes," August 9, 2000.

165 A March inspection: Adrienne McConnell and David Mullings, "More specific alcohol law gets final OK," *Ouray County Plaindealer*, June 22, 2000.

166 I thought having our Big Brother: Charlie Ricker, "Citizens can depend on rescue volunteers," "Letter to the Editor," *Ouray County Plaindealer*, April 13, 2000.

166 Asked his belayer to give him slack: Karen Risch, "Ice Park Rescue," January 13, 2000.

167 Chesapeake Bay retrievers: Karen Risch, "Uncompahgre Gorge Rescue," June 25, 2000.

167 Lance got there: Karen Risch, "Sneffels Rescue," August 5, 2000.

167 A motorist: Karen Risch, "Red Mtn. Pass Car Over Edge Near Engineer Cutoff," August 24, 2000.

168 "Her head looked like it had bounced on the rocks:" Nancy Lofholm, "'Miracle' crash survivor is ready to resume her life," *The Denver Post*, September 30, 2000.

168 Lance told: Karen Risch, "Red Mtn. Pass Car Over Edge Near Engineer Cutoff," August 24, 2000.

168 She lay: "'Miracle' crash survivor is ready to resume her life," *The Denver Post*, September 30, 2000.

169 "For this tiny landing spot": Ibid.

169 Recovering exercise physiologist: Nancy Lofholm, "After cheating death in plunge, crash survivor is ready for life," Denver Post Western Slope Bureau, *The Denver Post*, September 30, 2000.

169 OURAY MOUNTAIN RESCUE: Nancy Shippy, "Letter," October 21, 2000.

170 "When we looked at the site": Nancy Lofholm, "After cheating death in plunge, crash survivor is ready for life," Denver Post Western Slope Bureau, *The Denver Post*, September 30, 2000.

170 Jeff Schlundt of Durango reported: Karen Risch, "Cascade Cliffs Rescue," September 23, 2000.

170 He had turned around in heavy rain at 4 p.m.: Mavis Bennett, "Fall victims plucked from gorge bottom," *Ouray County Plaindealer*, September 28, 2000.

170 Capt. Rushing sent a hasty team: Karen Risch, "Cascade Cliffs Rescue," September 23, 2000.

170 Descend the gully: Ibid.

170 Belayed them: Mavis Bennett, "Fall victims plucked from gorge bottom," *Ouray County Plaindealer*, September 28, 2000.

171 Barbara Uhles reported a man: Karen Risch, "Uncompahgre Gorge Rescue," September 25, 2000.

171 Lowered the line: Mavis Bennett, "Fall victims plucked from gorge bottom," *Ouray County Plaindealer*, September 28, 2000.

171 Two Drunk Overlook: Tim Eihausen, February 3, 2017.

171 "Rolled near the start of the corner": David Mullings, "The Look Out Truck Wreck," *Ouray County Plaindealer*, October 5, 2000.

172 The tension on the rope was extreme: Karen Risch, "Gap Rescue," September 30, 2000.

172 "The most popular place in town": David Mullings, "Mulling it Over: Who gets the papers?" *Ouray County Plaindealer*, October 5, 2000.

172 A thirty-five-year-old: "Ice Park suffers second fatal," *Ouray County Plaindealer*, January 19, 2001.

172 "Public affairs manager for the American Chamber of Commerce": Bruce Barcott, "Risk," *Outside*, January 7, 2002.

172 The last of the group: Hope Tyler, "Climber error likely cause in fatal plunge," *Ouray County Plaindealer*, January 26, 2001.

172 "As twilight filled the shadowy gorge": Bruce Barcott, "Risk," *Outside*, January 7, 2002.

172 "All discussed and agreed that Pete would climb": Jeff Lowe, "OURAY POLICE DEPARTMENT STATEMENT FORM," January 17, 2001.

173 "A point where he could see both": Bruce Barcott, "Risk," *Outside*, January 7, 2002.

173 He did not hear them: Tony Schmidt, "SUPPLEMENTAL REPORT, CLIMBING ACCIDENT, CASE#01010," OURAY POLICE DEPARTMENT, 01-17-01.

173 Hoarse with bronchitis: Bruce Barcott, "Risk," *Outside*, January 7, 2002.

173 "Hearing the command, his belayer went off belay": Marc Beverly, *Accidents in North American Mountaineering*, 2002.

173 "Looked up and saw a man falling": Dana Berry, "OURAY POLICE DEPART-MENT STATEMENT FORM, CASE#01010," January 19, 2001.

173 Glasby ran down the canyon road: Bill Whitt, "Accident Report, Ice climbing fatality in Uncompahgre Gorge," January 17, 2001.

173 Coroner Gary Miller pronounced Ro dead: Tony Schmidt #303, OURAY PO-LICE DEPARTMENT, "SUPPLEMENTAL REPORT, CLIMBING ACCIDENT, CASE#01010," January 17, 2001.

173 "lowered to the position on La Ventana": Hope Tyler, "Climber error likely cause in fatal plunge," *Ouray County Plaindealer*, January 26, 2001.

173 "All of the witnesses described the same events": Richard B. Zortman, Chief of Police, "SUPPLEMENTAL REPORT, CASE#: 01010," January 17, 2001.

174 "I've even come close to losing a client": Hope Tyler, "Climber error likely cause in fatal plunge," *Ouray County Plaindealer*, January 26, 2001.

174 "Was pretty miraculous": Hope Tyler, "Two survive plunge in car near Ruby Wall," *Ouray County Plaindealer*, April 27, 2001.

174 Rocks and a mudslide hit three people: David Mullings, "Raining Rocks: Major injury averted in alpine flooding," *Ouray County Plaindealer*, August 10, 2001.

174 A concussion, a hole in her back and a broken hand: Patrick Davarn, "Falling rocks give survivors stories to tell," *Ouray County Plaindealer*, August 17, 2001.

174 A two-vehicle accident on Dallas Divide: David Mullings, "... Helicopter wrecked in Imogene Basin," *Ouray County Plaindealer*, August 10, 2001.

174 "In a steep scree-littered couloir" below Mt. Sneffels' southwest ridge: David Mull-ings, "Injured hiker plucked from peak," *Ouray County Plaindealer*, August 31, 2001.

175 The crux of the climb, a steep notch: Mike Gibbs, August 13, 2015.

175 Called for both litters: Karen Risch, "Mt. Sneffels Rescue," August 25, 2001.

175 Falling rocks as big as basketballs: Bob Risch, March 14, 2017.

176 A very lucky Spinney: "Thank You," *Ouray County Plaindealer*, September 7, 2001.

176 "Everybody drops": "Opponents unite to help rescue," *Ouray County Plaindealer*, August 31, 2001.

177 Offered *A Wistful Visitor's Sketches:* Nicole Skoloda, "OMRT Meeting Minutes," October 9, 2002.

177 Ice had become gold: Nancy Lofholm, "Ouray winters pick up with ice park," *The Denver Post*, August 19, 2001.

177 "The growing popularity of the unique facility": David Mullings, "Ice Park heads toward guide allocation plan," *Ouray County Plaindealer*, August 24, 2001.

177 "A single entity to regulate commercial guiding": Patrick Davarn, "Ice Park sys-tem one step nearer," *Ouray County Plaindealer*, August 31, 2001.

177 "Demonstrated track record": Patrick Davarn, "Local guides get Ice Park job," *Ouray County Plaindealer*, October 19, 2001.

177 South Park opened thirteen climbs: Patrick Davarn, "Expansion makes Ice Park bigger, better," *Ouray County Plaindealer*, January 18, 2002.

177 The City allowed the park: "Ice Park to seek new tap," *Ouray County Plaindealer*, April 13, 2001.

177 Who moved to Ouray with his wife Colette in 2000: Hope Tyler, "Ice Park just super for climber Mark Miller," *Ouray County Plaindealer*, January 18, 2001.

177 A sixty-one-year-old man fell forty feet: Karen Risch, "Ice Park Rescue," January 18, 2002.

192 $1,000 to revamp: "Memo to Stephen Lance, Captain, Ouray Mountain Rescue," July 17, 2003.

192 An eighty-year lease: Patrick Davarn, "Rescue Team gains permit for new barn," *Ouray County Plaindealer*, April 16, 2004.

192 Sewer: "Mt. Rescue lands parcel for new barn," *Ouray County Plaindealer*, December 19, 2003.

193 A late June rescue of a sixty-two-year-old: Karen Risch, "Sneffels Rescue," June 26, 2003.

193 Marauding marmots: "Marauding Marmots!" *Ouray County Plaindealer*, July 3, 2003.

193 105 feet: "Motorcycle victim was Georgia man," *Ouray County Plaindealer*, August 29, 2003.

194 The cyclist's father was on another road: Karen Risch, "Drinking Cup Rescue," August 20, 2003.

194 "In spite of good conditions": Karen Risch, "Ground Search – Little Gypsum Valley – San Miguel County: Sheriff's Report – K-9 Handler's Summary," November 4, 2003.

194 The young man's remains: "Letter, San Miguel County Sheriff's Office," November 27, 2007.

194 $12,500 in the building fund: "Ouray Mountain Rescue Team Inc., Balance Sheet," February 9, 2004.

194 Four-dozen bricks had been sold: Patrick Davarn, "Rescue barn permit awaits action by planning board," *Ouray County Plaindealer*, February 27, 2004.

194 "Approved the special use permit": Patrick Davarn, "Rescue Team gains permit for new barn," *Ouray County Plaindealer*, April 16, 2004.

195 The Building and Expansion Fund contained $18,000: "OMRT Inc. Balance Sheet," April 12, 2004.

195 The lowest was $135,000: David Mullings, "OMRT Meeting," April 14, 2004.

195 They had $25,000: David Mullings, "OMRT Meeting," July 14, 2004.

195 "Had early stage": Karen Risch, "Extended Search,"June 11, 2004.

197 "Was unlikely to wander": Erin Quinn, *"What happened to Cynthia Gottschalk?"*: Mysteries abound in search for lost woman, *Ouray County Plaindealer*, June 18, 2004.

197 "We've been all over": "Woman, dog still missing," *Ouray County Plaindealer*, May 28, 2004.

197 10 pounds lighter: Erin Quinn, *"What happened to Cynthia Gottschalk?"*: Mysteries abound in search for lost woman, *Ouray County Plaindealer*, June 18, 2004.

198 No response: Karen Risch, "Ground Search," June 11, 2004.

199 Died of hypothermia and exposure: Dr. Michael Benzinger, "Autopsy Report," June 14, 2004.

199 Two weeks: "Climber remains in serious condition," *Ouray County Plaindealer*, January 28, 2005.

199 In mid-February: "Climber released from hospital," *Ouray County Plaindealer*, February 18, 2005.

199 "A six-person OMRT": "Youth rescued below Sneffels," *Ouray County Plaindealer*, July 8, 2005.

199 The household: "Dog leads team to man's body," *Ouray County Plaindealer*, July 29, 2005.

200 "Amazing.": David Mullings, "So, how about a guardrail?" MULLING IT OVER, *Ouray County Plaindealer*, December 30, 2005.

200 The barn's footprint was poured: Mel Rajkowski, "February 2006 Meeting Minutes," February 8, 2006.

200 Schalla, Rich Wojciechowski: Mel Rajkowski, "OMR Team Meeting Minutes," May 10, 2006.

200 That evening, travelers reported cries for help to the west: Bob Risch, May 27, 2017.

200 Screamed bloody murder –"Someone help me!": Karen Risch, "Mission Report," June 18, 2006.

201 For a saddle: Thomas Munro, "Man falls to death on Mt. Gilpin," *Durango Herald,* June 20, 2006.

201 They initially said the fall occurred on Mt. Sneffels: Dominic Mattivi, Jr., May 31, 2017.

201 Arranged their backpacks: Karen Risch, "Mission Report," June 18, 2006.

201 "Everything": Thomas Munro, "Man falls to death on Mt. Gilpin," *Durango Herald,* June 20, 2006.

201 "He lived for climbing": "David Lauer," "Obituaries," *Fort Collins (CO) Coloradoan,* June 22, 2006.

201 "Longtime": Pat Ferrier, "Local activist killed on hike," *Fort Collins Coloradoan,* June 20, 2006.

201 "On the trail that morning": "David Lauer," "Obituaries," *Fort Collins Coloradoan,* June 22, 2006.

201 "Killing him instantly": "Camp Bird Road rockfall kills man," *Ridgway Sun,* August 2, 2006.

202 "This truly was a freak accident": Robb Magley, "Jeeper killed by falling rock," *Ouray County Plaindealer,* August 4, 2006.

202 "An experienced free climber": Patrick Swonger, "SAN JUAN COUNTY SAR TRACKER MISSION REPORT," July 24, 2006.

202 Higgins had participated: "Rescuers find hiker's body," *Ouray County Plaindealer,* July 28, 2006.

202 "To walk down Molas Trail:" Patrick Swonger, "SAN JUAN COUNTY SAR TRACKER MISSION REPORT," July 24, 2006.

202 Aided by helicopters: D. Dion, "Body of missing Utah hiker recovered after long search," *Silverton STANDARD & the MINER,* July 27, 2006.

202 Kite Lake: Tim Eihausen, February 3, 2017.

202 "The search ended:" Patrick Swonger, "San Juan County SAR TRACKER SAR MISSION REPORT," July 24, 2006.

203 Green with lichen: D. Dion, "Body of missing Utah hiker recovered after long search," *Silverton STANDARD & the MINER,* July 27, 2006.

203 "Sustained in a long fall": "Rescuers find hiker's body," *Ouray County Plaindealer,* July 28, 2006.

Chapter Twenty-One: Imogene

Page

204 "Onto a steep": "Two die at Imogene crash," *Ouray County Plaindealer,* August 13, 2004.

204 The window glass fell out perfectly shaped: Colette Miller, February 7, 2017.

204 "Lining up a photograph of Telluride Peak": "Two die at Imogene crash," *Ouray County Plaindealer,* August 13, 2004.

205 Held his head together: Jeff Skoloda, April 7, 2016.

205 She found half of one of the people": Jeff Skoloda, April 7, 2016.

205 She was lighter than the paramedic: Colette Miller, February 7, 2017.

207 Was also needed to drug Glucklich: Kim Mitchell, February 27, 2017.

207 Nordstrom's eyes focused, he spoke in complete sentences: Colette Miller, February 7, 2017.

207 Had been a day care provider: Ibid.

207 OMRT found a catered meal: Karen Risch, "Minutes," August 11, 2004.

208 "Their family suddenly": Julie Edgar, "West Bloomfield residents take in a shattered family; Woman's brother, sister-in-law were killed in Utah crash," *Detroit (MI) Free Press*, December 10, 2004.

Chapter Twenty-Two: Sullivan's Gully
Page

209 Into a dark curve where the sun never shines: Father Nathaniel Fosage, November 17, 2015.

209 "I'm sorry, we're going": John Cash, narrator, "Helping Hands," *On Star CD*, General Motors.

209 "Looking right over that edge": Joe Sullivan, September 28, 2015.

210 "Glanced down and noticed tire tracks": "Belted Passengers survive plunge 400 feet down Colorado mountain," *THE ASSOCIATED PRESS*, February 16, 2005.

210 "Yelled down the gully": John Cash, narrator, "Helping Hands," *On Star CD*, General Motors.

210 "On Star Emergency": Ibid.

211 "They all had me sit down": Julie Chen, The Early Show, "6 In Van Survive Cliff Plunge," *cbsnews.com*, February 15, 2005.

211 "Way ugly": John Cash, narrator, "Helping Hands," *On Star CD*, General Motors.

211 "Soft chute and a snow bank at river's edge": "Lady luck smiled on van occupants, officials say," *Ouray County Plaindealer*, February 18, 2005.

211 "Expecting the worst": "6 In Van Survive Cliff Plunge," *cbsnews.com*, February 15, 2005.

212 With a C-collar and spineboard: John Cash, narrator, "Helping Hands," *On Star CD*, General Motors.

212 "The other five": John Ingold, "Uplifting turn to mountain plunge," *Denver Post*, February 14, 2005.

213 "We did not want": John Cash, narrator, "Helping Hands," *On Star CD*, General Motors.

213 "I knew it was one of us": Gail Yerbec, "Auto accident strengthens Catholic family's faith," *Chronicle of Catholic Life*, May 4, 2005.

213 "Miracle on the mountain": "6 In Van Survive Cliff Plunge," *cbsnews.com*, February 15, 2005.

213 Wearing OMRT T-shirts: Kathy Couric, "Today Show," *NBC*, February 15, 2005,

213 "A quick response time": John Cash, narrator, "Helping Hands," *On Star CD*, General Motors.

Chapter Twenty-Three: "No Place To Run"
Page

215 "No place to run": Jeff Skoloda, April 7, 2016.

215 "Every instrument in the world": Bianca Prieto, "Plane crash kills 4 near Ouray," *DENVERPOST.com*, May 15, 2005.

215 Telluride Airport (KTEX), at 9,078 feet: "NSTB Narrative Summary Released at Completion of Accident," *Aircraft Accident/Incident Report, Ouray, Colorado 81427, Wednesday, May 11, 2005 12:56 MDT*: June 16, 2006.

216 "A debris trail": Jannise Johnson, "Chino family loses four in crash," "News," *dailybulletin.com*, May 14, 2005.

216 A tracking device: Ibid.

216 "Jagged, steep": "Four Killed in Plane Crash in Colorado," *The Associated Press*, May 16, 2005.

216 CAP and the National Guard: Dominic Mattivi, Jr., May 31, 2017.

216 "To weigh the dangers": Electa Draper, "Recovery unit will try copter to reach bodies on mountain," *The Denver Post*, May 17, 2005.

216 Conditions prevented safe access: Felix Doligosa, Jr., "Family mourns four killed in plane crash," *RockyMountainNews.com*, May 16, 2005.

216 "The crash site": Electa Draper, "Recovery unit will try copter to reach bodies on mountain," *The Denver Post*, May 17, 2005.

217 "Every time (the copter) set down": "Conditions delay efforts to recover air-crash victims," "BRIEFING," *The Denver Post*, May 19, 2005.

219 An absolute altitude record: "Aérospatiale SA315B Lama": *Wikipedia: The Free Encyclopedia*.

220 "Was up there, he would've moved": Katharhynn Heidelberg, "Dog helps find final victim of plane crash," *Montrose Daily Press*, June 22, 2005.

Chapter Twenty-Four: 2007-2010 – "Our Voices of Hope"
Page
222 "Our Voices of Hope": Susan and Doug Martels, "Letter to OMRT," September 4, 2008.

222 Two non- profits: Christopher Pike, "Ouray Mountain Rescue Team: Saving Lives, Saving History," *Ouray County Watch*, April 17, 2007.

222 Assisted a twenty-four-year-old Ohio woman: "HEY! I CAN SEE MY HOUSE FROM HERE! *Ouray County Plaindealer*, April 27, 2007.

222 "Tumbled": "Hiker woes bring 3 OMRT calls," *Ouray County Plaindealer*, August 31, 2007.

223 "Enough force": "2 injured by falling ice at park," *Ouray County Plaindealer*, January 19, 2007.

224 Two liters: "Hiker woes bring 3 OMRT calls," *Ouray County Plaindealer*, August 31, 2007.

224 $139,000 ($55,000 in grants): Beverly Corbell, "OURAY," *Daily Sentinel*, January 28, 2007.

224 "Community support for the project": "Mountain Rescue barn raising lands 2 grants," *Ouray County Plaindealer*, January 12, 2007.

224 Grants: Garry Schalla, "Letter to The Gates Family Foundation, Denver, CO," August 1, 2007.

226 Seventy-two clinics: "Ice Fest another 'huge success,'" *Ouray County Plaindealer*, January 19, 2007.

226 "30 different media outlets": "City bustles as 12th event fills Ice Park," *Ouray County Plaindealer*, January 12, 2007.

226 "A perfect microclimate": Helen Olsson, "American Journeys /Ouray, Colo.: Winter Revels in Ice and Steam," *New York Times*, February 23, 2007.

226 "We had an incredible year": "Warm conditions force early closing of Ice Park," *Ouray County Plaindealer*, March 23, 2007.

226 A new six-climb area with ninety feet of "dead vertical": Samantha Tisdel Wright, "Ice Park gets 'Stump Wall,'" *Ouray County Plaindealer*, October 24, 2008.

226 Twenty volunteers wearing moulage: "Responders ready for bus accident exercise," *Ouray County Plaindealer*, May 16, 2008.

226 "Fake, yet realistic-looking, wounds and injuries": Patrick Davarn, "Miller mastering 'moulage' rouge," *Ouray County Plaindealer*, May 23, 2008.

226 "Triaged by severity of injury": "Responders ready for bus accident exercise," *Ouray County Plaindealer*, May 16, 2008.

227 Were warned: "Rescue squad seeks practice 'victims,'" *Ouray County Plaindealer*, May 2, 2008.

227 "To minimize any environmental impact": "Responders ready for bus accident exercise," *Ouray County Plaindealer*, May 16, 2008.

227 "A little dazed and confused": Sam Rushing, "White (brown) Water Rescue," August 9, 2008.

227 "When dispatch called": "3 boys rescued from red cliffs," *Ouray County Plaindealer*, April 4, 2008.

227 "Ascended through steep rock": Christina Callicott, "Three Teenagers Rescued From Cliffs Above Ouray: Rescuers Endured Snow, Rockfall, Technical Terrain," *Ouray County Watch*, April 4, 2008.

228 "That face is pretty prone": Christina Callicott, "Three Teenagers Rescued From Cliffs Above Ouray: Rescuers Endured Snow, Rockfall, Technical Terrain," *Ouray County Watch*, April 4, 2008.

228 Left their BMW at Dexter Creek: "OMRT Search – Difficulty Creek Area," September 1, 2008.

229 "A helpless and fearful time": Susan and Doug Martels, "Letter to OMRT," September 4, 2008.

230 "A closer look down into the canyon": Jack Brauer, "IMPROMPTU RESCUE ON RED MOUNTAIN PASS," *mountainphotographer.com*, January 6, 2009.

231 "The Snake appeared totally within our grasp": Mike Reddy, "The Long Way Back," *THE CLIMBING ZINE*, climbingzine.com, March 6, 2017.

232 Mike MacLeod and Mark Miller arrived: Mike MacLeod, July 8, 2016.

233 "A fractured right ankle and a diagnosis that he would never climb again": Luke Mehall, "Gimps on Ice," *Prosthetic Center of Excellence News*, March 17, 2011.

233 "Extreme pain: Mike Reddy, "The Long Way Back," *THE CLIMBING ZINE*, climbingzine.com, March 6, 2017.

233 Climbed ice in New Hampshire: chadb, "Paradox Sports invades the North East, *paradoxsports.org*, February 14, 2011.

233 He completed doctoral studies: David Mullings, "MULLING IT OVER," *Ouray County Plaindealer*, December 11, 2009.

234 Belayer Randy Murphy lowered him: "Local climber on the mend after fall in Ouray ice Park," *Montrose Daily Press*, December 20, 2009.

235 A record twenty-two rescues, including four fatalities: Jenny Hart, "2010 Callouts."

235 "A climber was accidentally dropped on the 'Pic of the Vic'": Samantha Tisdel Wright, "'Good work' by team responding to Ice Park call," *Ouray County Plaindealer*, February12, 2010.

235 Had to wait a while for proper gear: Deb Folsom, "OMRT Meeting Agenda," February 11, 2010.

235 "It was a great spot to take photos": Samantha Tisdel Wright, "'Good work' by team responding to Ice Park call," *Ouray County Plaindealer*, February 12, 2010.

235 A forty-three-year-old male: Deb Folsom, "OMRT Agenda," July 14, 2010.

235 The sheriff received a third call for a fall victim at the Drinking Cup: "Family plans service Sunday for fall victim," *Ouray County Plaindealer*, July 9, 2010.

236 "Was celebrating the Fourth of July:" Ibid.

236 A hiker with a knee injury: Deb Folsom, "OMRT Meeting Minutes," August 13, 2010.

236 A fifty-year-old fall victim: Deb Folsom, "OMRT Monthly Meeting," September 8, 2010.

236 They landed 300 feet: Ibid.

237 "Was running the incident for OMRT": Kevin Koprek, July 9, 2017.

238 Thirteen middle and high school students: "Voyager-sponsored climbing team enjoys great season," *Ouray County Plaindealer*, February 11, 2009.

238 Sandbags, barbed wire and corrugated metal: "PAKISTAN PRESENTATION," *Ouray County Plaindealer*, November 13, 2009.

238 "Thanks to Zack Martin Breaking Barriers Award": Clint Estes, "Villagers warmly receptive to American ingenuity," *Ouray County Plaindealer*, January 10, 2010.

238 "Climbers, along with their cook, continued on to Nangma": Erik Lambert, "Kondus Access Denied, Dirty New Route in Nangma," *The Alpinist, ALPINIST. COM:* January 6, 2010.

Chapter Twenty-Five: "Blowin' in the Wind"
Page
239 *"Blowin' in the Wind"*: Bob Dylan, 1962.

239 Six to ten inches of fresh powder: Ann Mellick, "Avalanche Accident Report," *Colorado Avalanche Information Center*, February 26, 2010.

239 Settled heavy and lay over a layer of mush: Chris Haaland, September 25, 2017.

239 "Decided that this was safer than all being in the same spot": Ann Mellick, "Avalanche Accident Report," *Colorado Avalanche Information Center*, February 26, 2010.

240 "Initial reports indicated that two backcountry": Joel Burk, "PRESS RELEASE," February 12, 2010.

240 Ouray school bus ... "rehab-station": Deb Folsom, "Avalanche Call Out," February 11, 2010.

240 "Snow machines and skis would be required to reach the site": "Fatal avalanche human triggered," *Ouray County Plaindealer*, February 19, 2010.

241 By 5 three choppers had landed: Deb Folsom, "Avalanche Call Out," February 11, 2010.

241 "Was not buried": Ann Mellick, "Avalanche Accident Report," *Colorado Avalanche Information Center*, February 26, 2010.

241 Dominic Franz Muth: Kati O'Hare, "Ridgway avalanche kills one," *Montrose Daily Press*, February 13, 2010.

241 "Honed in on...": Ann Mellick, "Avalanche Accident Report," *Colorado Avalanche Information Center*, February 26, 2010.

242 Olathe #1 headed home: Deb Folsom, "Avalanche Call Out," February 11, 2010.

242 Intermittent snow: Dominic Mattivi, Jr., "Ridgway Hut Avalanche Rescue," February 11, 2010.

244 By 6:01 they, too, were back: Deb Folsom, "Avalanche Call Out," February 11, 2010.

244 Shortly after 10 he met them at the road: Deb Folsom, "Avalanche Call Out," February 11, 2010.

245 "Revered climber and mountain guide": Dale Strode, "Climbing world celebrates spirit of Heidi Kloos," *Durango Herald*, April 16, 2010.

245 "Lead guides up Denali": Matt Lindberg, "Ridgway woman's body found after avalanche," *Montrose Daily Press*, April 3, 2010.

245 "She received more positive reviews": Matt Lindberg, "Ridgway woman's body found after avalanche," *Montrose Daily Press*, April 3, 2010.

245 "Nepal, Russia, Argentina, Alaska": Dale Strode, "Climbing world celebrates spirit of Heidi Kloos," *Durango Herald*, April 16, 2010.

247 "High winds prevented deployment": "SEARCH PLANS FOR MISSING CLIMBER," *Ouray County Plaindealer*, April 2, 2010.

Chapter Twenty-Six: 2011-2014 – "God's own army gathered around us"
Page

249 "God's own army gathered around us": Samantha Wright, "Climbers Recount Daring Mt. Sneffels Rescue Mission," *The Watch*, September 18, 2014.

249 "Had a hankering": Samantha Wright, "Fall victim 'remembers everything,'" *Ouray County Plaindealer*, March 18, 2011.

251 Ropes were lowered: Samantha Wright, "Ice Park rescue: an 'uplifting' experience," *Ouray County Plaindealer*, March 11, 2011.

251 They dangled in mid-air: Ibid.

251 "The most painful part was the transfer from the ground": Samantha Wright, "Fall victim 'remembers everything,'" *Ouray County Plaindealer*, March 18, 2011.

251 A car plunged 300 feet: Peter Shelton, "Fiery Car Crash on Red Mountain Pass," *The Watch* (Telluride, CO), April 6, 2011.

252 "Grabbing onto a nearby tree branch": Samantha Wright, "'Good Samaritan' identified as Montrose man," *Ouray County Plaindealer*, April 1, 2011.

252 "Twenty feet": Peter Shelton, "Fiery Car Crash on Red Mountain Pass," *The Watch*, April 6, 2011.

252 "The vehicle was fully engulfed": Samantha Wright, "'Good Samaritan' identified as Montrose man," *Ouray County Plaindealer*, April 1, 2011.

252 "Used every bit of a 90-meter rope": Peter Shelton, "Fiery Car Crash on Red Mountain Pass," *The Watch*, April 6, 2011.

252 "I didn't think": Ibid.

252 "It was a big, long patient lower": Samantha Wright, "Mountain rescuer's ninja 'rock block' deemed heroic," *Ouray County Plaindealer*, July 29, 2011.

253 "Lifted his pack": Ibid.

253 "Bumped along": Samantha Wright, "BEAR CREEK BRIDGE: Car plunges down mountain," *Ouray County Plaindealer*, August 26, 2011.

253 "On a 30-plus degree slope…": Ibid.

253 A "Socata TB21": "NTSB Identification: CEN12FA098," National Transportation Safety Board.

253 "All over the place": Samantha Wright, "Four Bodies Recovered From Crash Site Near Silverton," *The Watch*, December 8, 2011.

253 January through November 2012: Jenny Hart, "2012 Rescues."

253 Injuring an ankle: Kim Mitchell, August 4, 2017.

254 Climbed a mixed (ice and rock) rap line: Clint Estes, "OMRT Meeting Minutes," January 11, 2012.

254 "difficult and complex": Samantha Wright, "ICE CLIMB RESCUE," *The Watch*, January 12, 2012.

254 A miraculous recovery: Samantha Wright, "Woman Survives Crash on Red Mountain Pass," *The Watch*, June 14, 2012.

254 "The ground dropped": Caleb Stento, "Motorist drives off road on Red Mountain," *Ouray County Plaindealer*, June 7, 2012.

255 Baril had leg pain: Ibid.

255 "Exposed, technical route": Samantha Wright, "Climber Survives Rockfall Accident on Coxcomb Peak," *The Watch*, June 28, 2012.

255 The saddle between Redcliff and Coxcomb: Tim Pasek, January 3, 2017.

255 "Saved a lot of time": Samantha Wright, "Climber Survives Rockfall Accident on Coxcomb Peak," *The Watch*, June 28, 2012.

256 "Etched his name": Caleb Stento, "Two injured, one dead in backcountry: Separate incidents require Ouray Mountain Rescue response," *Ouray County Plaindealer*, July 5, 2012.

256 "It was one of the worst slopes": Ibid.

257 "The patriarch": Samantha Wright, "Heart Attacks Kill Two; Rockfall Leads to Evac From Backcountry," *The Watch*, July 19, 2012.

257 "A chance to be with Dad": Molly Nightingale, LETTER TO THE PLAINDEALER: Family thankful for OMRT effort," *Ouray County Plaindealer*, July 5, 2012.

257 In borderline weather: "OMRT Meeting Minutes," July 2012.

257 Had climbed fifty: Kristina A. Felbeck, July 12, 2012.

257 "A doctor at the scene recognized": Samantha Wright, "Heart Attacks Kill Two; Rockfall Leads to Evac From Backcountry," *The Watch*, July 19, 2012.

258 "Taken their toll:" Ibid.

258 Fifty to sixty feet into Oak Creek Canyon: Tim Pasek, "RESCUE CALLOUT Number 12-xx.

258 Aficionado Greg Foy: Matt Minich, "Ouray home to burgeoning canyoneering scene," *denverpost.com*, September 18, 2012.

258 "Its kissing cousin, canyoneering": Samantha Wright, "Canyon Festival deepens participants' adventure," *Ouray County Plaindealer*, August 12, 2011.

258 Both the length of the fall: Caleb Stento, "Man suffers severe fall while canyoneering," *Ouray County Plaindealer*, September 20, 2012.

259 "To request helo": Tim Pasek, "RESCUE CALLOUT Number 12-xx.

259 "Just as dusk was sliding into darkness": Samantha Wright, "Daring Helicopter Rescue Saves Climber's Life," *The Watch*, September 20, 2012.

259 "Wait at the trail. Do not try to follow us": Tim Pasek, January 3, 2017.

259 "In high alpine terrain": Samantha Wright, "Daring Helicopter Rescue Saves Climber's Life," *The Watch*, September 20, 2012.

259 "Was in good enough shape": Caleb Stento, "Man suffers severe fall while canyoneering," *Ouray County Plaindealer*, September 20, 2012.

259 They had determined: Tim Pasek, "RESCUE CALLOUT Number 12-xx.

259 Twin-engine bird: Samantha Wright, "Daring Helicopter Rescue Saves Climber's Life," *The Watch*, September 20, 2012.

259 18,000-pound helicopter: Tim Pasek, "RESCUE CALLOUT Number 12-xx.

260 The litter and backcountry tech gear: Ibid.

260 Carried out the "VERY HIGH RISK" mission: Ibid.

260 "Nighttime hoist using night vision": Samantha Wright, "Daring Helicopter Rescue Saves Climber's Life," *The Watch*, September 20, 2012.

261 "Ready to turn in his clipboard": Caleb Stento, "OMRT elects a new skipper," *Ouray County Plaindealer*, December 20, 2012.

261 "Passionate ice climbers": Samantha Wright, "Ouray Ice Park Celebrates Another Successful Season," *The Watch*, March 28, 2013.

261 The first Jeff Lowe Award: Samantha Wright, "Ice Fest Founder Jeff Lowe Faces Final 'Unimaginable Climb,'" *The Watch*, January 23, 2013.

261 Fighting a progressive neurogenerative disorder: Shawna Henderson, "Ouray: Ice-climbing legend Jeff Lowe and the Switzerland of America," *SUMMIT DAILY NEWS E-EDITION*: March 17, 2016.

Notes

261 A skier with a broken ankle: Tim Pasek, "RESCUE CALLOUT Number 13-02," February 26, 2013.

261 "Backcountry touring ski hit": Mary Pat Haddock, "Backcountry rescue goes through the night," *Ouray County Plaindealer*, February 21, 2013.

262 They met Leizinger: Tim Pasek, "RESCUE CALLOUT Number 13-02," February 26, 2013.

262 Held her harness: Ibid.

262 "People who are working full time": Mary Pat Haddock, "Backcountry rescue goes through the night," *Ouray County Plaindealer*, February 21, 2013.

262 Was for a rental car on its roof: Sheridan Block, "Car falls into Red Mountain Creek," *Ouray County Plaindealer*, June 13, 2013.

263 "His back wheels went off the road": Sheridan Block and Bill Tiedje, "Dangerous rollover on Camp Bird," *Ouray County Plaindealer*, July 4, 2013.

263 400 feet below: Sheridan Block, "Rescue on Sneffels," *Ouray County Plaindealer*, July 18, 2013.

263 Pasek and Kavanaugh: RESCUE CALLOUT SUMMARY, July 10, 2013.

263 She initially lost consciousness: Ibid.

263 "We had CareFlight launch from Montrose": Tim Pasek, "OMR Updates: Revenue Mine and Avalanche," *OMRT email*: November 18, 2013.

263 Cleared out the barn for corpse / coroner work: Ibid.

264 She was her grandmother Pat Lahr's caretaker: Sheridan Block, "Lahr remembered for her creativity and love," *Ouray County Plaindealer*, November 28, 2013.

264 "Create a whimsical, life-sized pink and purple dinosaur": Samantha Wright, "Ouray Mourns the Loss of a 'Beautiful Soul,'" *The Watch*, November 28, 2013.

264 Officer Justin Crandall searched with them: Sheridan Block, "Lahr remembered for her creativity and love," *Ouray County Plaindealer*, November 28, 2013.

264 "From a considerable height": Nicholas D. Radovitch, M.D., "FINAL AUTOPSY REPORT: LAHR, ZENA NICOLE," November 21, 2013.

264 Brilliant, spiritual, and exceptionally creative: Samantha Wright, "Ouray Mourns the Loss of a 'Beautiful Soul,'" *The Watch*, November 28, 2013.

265 "To make a full recovery": Tim Pasek, "Perimeter Trail Hiker Update," February 28, 2014.

265 On a wet road: Dolgio Nergui, September 13, 2017.

265 "A family parked at an overlook": Samantha Wright, "Authorities Seek Answers In Fatal Motorcycle Crash On Red Mountain Pass," *The Watch*, July 24, 2014.

266 "Plunged about 200 feet": Samantha Wright, "Man Survives Single-Vehicle Accident on Red Mountain Pass," *The Watch*, September 10, 2014.

266 A July 17 rescue: Sam Rushing, "Lou Creek Nate Creek Rescue," July 18, 2014.

266 A GPS reading: Samantha Wright, "Team Retrieves Injured Rider From Lou Creek Pass," *The Watch*, July 24, 2014.

266 "3.5 miles to the patient:" Sam Rushing, "Nate Creek Rescue," July 18, 2014.

266 "It was a long rescue": Samantha Wright, "Team Retrieves Injured Rider From Lou Creek Pass," *The Watch*, July 24, 2014.

266 While the cell ping was relatively close: Tim Pasek, "RESCUE CALLOUT SUMMARY: Lost Hiker Twin Peaks /Silvershield Area," August 7, 2014.

267 Triangulation: Jayson Grieve, "Cell phone pinging is also known as triangulation," *Quora*, March 9, 2017.

267 "900m northwest of the cellphone ping": Tim Pasek, "RESCUE CALLOUT SUMMARY: Lost Hiker Twin Peaks /Silvershield Area," August 7, 2014.

267 The Buck Creek drainage: Don Moden, "CBSAR Agency Assist – Report," August 18, 2014.

267 Sherri Ahlbrandt's remains: Paul "Woody" Woodward, "Thank you letter for search near Crested Butte," December 3, 2014.
267 Simpkins fell, tumbling 250 feet: Sheridan Block, "Black Hawk responds in rescue at Sneffels," *Ouray County Plaindealer*, September 18, 2014.
267 "Dug in and held onto held onto Simpkins": Samantha Wright, "Climbers Recount Daring Mt. Sneffels Rescue Mission," *The Watch*, September 18, 2014.
267 "Trying to keep each other's spirits up": Ibid.
270 "The stars, oh the stars …. the Milky Way": Ibid.
270 Early hikers watched: Sheridan Block, "Black Hawk responds in rescue at Sneffels," *Ouray County Plaindealer*, September 18, 2014.
270 "Learning how to do the land side": Samantha Wright, "Climbers Recount Daring Mt. Sneffels Rescue Mission," *The Watch*, September 18, 2014.

Chapter Twenty-Seven: The End of a Fantastic Season
272 A lifelong skier and competitive racer: Seth Beers, April 6, 2017.
273 "Need help. Broke my leg": Matt Wade, "Account of Gary Ryan Rescue," June 2, 2015.
274 "Was safe at the moment": Ibid.
275 "Dire" patient report: Tim Pasek, "OMR CALLOUT SUMMARY, 2 June 2015: Rescue of Two Skiers on Snake Couloir, Mount Sneffels."
276 "Conditions were terrible": Sheridan Block, "OURAY COUNTY: Military helicopter used in Sneffels rescue," *Ouray County Plaindealer*, June 4, 2015.
276 "100 feet downslope": Wade, "Account of Gary Ryan Rescue," June 2, 2015.
277 A TALON 12: Tim Pasek, "OMR CALLOUT SUMMARY, 2 June 2015: Rescue of Two Skiers on Snake Couloir, Mount Sneffels."
277 "As the magnitude of the avalanche conditions": Ibid.
278 "Big enough to bury, injure or kill": "Blackcomb Class 2 Avalanche," *backcountryskiingcanada.com*

Chapter Twenty-Eight: "Uncommon by definition"
281 "Uncommon by definition": David Mullings, "Always on the job: Rescuers, EMTs," *Ouray County Plaindealer*, August 20, 1998.
281 Had fallen from a sixty-foot cliff: David Mullings, "Girl off a cliff: Anatomy of a rescue," *OMRT Newsletter*, November 2015.
281 Rushing took a body bag: Jenny Hart, August 24, 2017.
281 "For the Harts": David Mullings, "Girl off a cliff: Anatomy of a rescue," *OMRT Newsletter*, November 2015.
282 "To help gauge the severity": "All about brain injury and PTSD," *Brainline*, October 19, 2010.
282 "Ninety hot, difficult, downhill minutes": David Mullings, "Girl off a cliff: Anatomy of a rescue," *OMRT Newsletter*, November 2015.
282 "On November 9 Abby and her family attended an open house": Ibid.
283 Where 357 summits rise above 13,000 feet: Jennifer and Gerry Roach, "Colorado's San Juan Summits —Sorted by Elevation," *Summit Sight*, SummitSight.com
284 Born May 2, 1918: Kurt Kircher, December 2, 1998.
285 *Ouray Ice: The Beta Edition*: Bill MacTiernan, 1997.
287 "Responded to 26 callouts": *OMRT Newsletter*, December 2017.
287 Literally turned the lights out: Deb Folsom, "Avalanche Call Out," February 11, 2010.
288 "We have the respect": Sam Rushing, "May 1999 Cover Letter for the April Team Minutes," May 1999.

288 "Half the way up the trail": Cory Jackson, OMRT Minutes, June 10, 2015.

288 "Three fractured cervical vertebrae": Patricia Eischied, OMRT Minutes, June 10, 2015.

289 "Snow showers and fog prevailed": Tim Pasek, "OMRT Callout Summary: 23 May 2015: Rescue of Hiker on Blue Lakes Trail," June 8, 2015.

289 Three hours and 15 minutes: Kevin Koprek, OMRT Minutes, June 10, 2015.

289 On a training exercise: "Mark Salesse funeral service today in Comox, B.C." *CBC News/Canada*: February 28, 2015.

289 "Free-soloing alongside one of the clients": Dougald MacDonald, "Fallen Guide Mark Miller: Remembering a Legend," *Climbing.com*, February 4, 2015.

289 "Constantly monitored risks": Sheridan Block, "Miller's legacy of knowledge and service lives on," *Ouray County Plaindealer*, February 5, 2015.

292 "There is nothing like the feeling": Jeff Skoloda, *The Ouray Mountain Rescue Team: The Early Years*, Western Hotel, March 15, 2007.

293 "They are the greatest people": Christopher Pike, "Ouray Mountain Rescue Team: Saving Lives, Saving History," *Ouray County Watch*, April 17, 2007.

Bibliography

American Alpine Journal, (1996).

Colorado Department of Transportation Region Five Avalanche Atlas, (1995).

Rev. J.J. Gibbons, *In the San Juan,* (Lake City, CO: Western Reflections Publishing Company, 2008)

John Marshall and Jerry Roberts, *Living and Dying in Avalanche Country,* (Silverton, CO: A Simpler Way Book Company, 1993)

William G. May, *Mountain Search and Rescue Techniques* (RockReef D.B., 1973).

Robert Ormes with the Colorado Mountain Club, *Guide to the Colorado Mountains: Sixth Edition* (The Swallow Press INC., 1970).

Franklin Rhoda, *SUMMITS TO REACH: Report on the Typography of the San Juan Country,* 1876, ed. Mike Foster (Boulder, CO: Pruett Publishing Company, 1984).

THE SNOWY TORRENTS: AVALANCHE ACCIDENTS IN THE UNITED STATES 1910-1966, ed. Dale Gallagher ((Alta Avalanche Study Center, 1984).

Index of People, Places & Things

CPSIA information can be obtained
at www.ICGtesting.com
Printed in the USA
FFHW011331041119
55887579-61767FF